C++ and Object-Oriented Programming Paradigm

Debasish Jana
General Manager (Projects)
Techna Digital Services Pvt. Ltd.
Kolkata

Prentice-Hall of India Private Limited
New Delhi-110001
2003

Rs. 325.00

C++ AND OBJECT-ORIENTED PROGRAMMING PARADIGM
Debasish Jana

ISBN-81-203-2321-1

The export rights of this book are vested solely with the publisher.

Published by Asoke K. Ghosh, Prentice-Hall of India Private Limited, M-97, Connaught Circus, New Delhi-110001 and Printed by Jay Print Pack Private Limited, New Delhi-110015.

To

the memory of My Father

SATYA RANJAN JANA

who did not live to see

this book take shape

Contents

Preface

In many Computer Science curricula, at least two programming languages are taught. The first programming language chosen is that which has simple semantics for ease of learning of the basic constructs like datatypes, functions, control statements, loops, iterations, recursions, etc. Earlier, it used to be BASIC. Now, some people start with Pascal, while some with C either as a separate subject or with data structures. Fundamentally, data structures constitute the foundation of all programs, and any programming language is a media with which we express the steps to solve a particular problem. Later, when concepts of programming crystalize in general, people tend to learn other programming paradigms like logic programming through Prolog, Functional programming through Lisp, Standard ML, and Object-Oriented (OO) programming through Simula, Smalltalk, Eiffel, Java, or C++. A programming paradigm is the pattern or model of programming that drives the process of programming.

Object-Orientation has become the predominant paradigm for virtually all modern software development. This book explores C++ in the light of OO paradigm, distinguishing it from other procedural paradigms, especially C, and demonstrating the semantic differences between the two languages, with ample worked-out examples and program source codes. No prior knowledge of C or C++ is necessary to grasp the ideas explicated in the book. However, familiarity with the high-level procedural programming paradigm of Fortran, Pascal, and C, and the basic concepts of algorithmic approach, is an added advantage that aids the understanding of concepts. The book is primarily targeted to students and programmers interested in knowing the procedural framework through C and then shifting the paradigm to OO programming using C++.

The book begins with a programming overview with reference to different programming paradigms, focusing on C as a procedural paradigm. Chapter 2 explains the fundamental datatypes available with variables, constants, operators, and expressions. The need for statements, concepts of various statements, and different kinds of loops and control statements are explained in Chapter 3. Chapter 4 introduces arrays, pointers, and structures as the basic building blocks and constructs—the heart of C as well as C++.

Chapter 5 explains functions, command line arguments and parameter passing techniques. One of the features that makes C++ strikingly different from C is the passing of parameters. While there are two different ways of parameter passing in C++ (namely call-by-value and call-by-reference), C supports only one mechanism—call-by-value. A good understanding of the difference between parameter passing and returning by value and by reference is a must here before proceeding further.

Chapter 6 concentrates on preprocessor directives and preprocessor phases, including explanations of #define, #include, conditional compilation, and # and ## operators. Chapter 7 discusses standard C library functions and standard header files like string handling functions, basic input and output functions, and mathematical functions.

Chapter 8 onwards, the topics become more C++ specific, dealing with the OO paradigm of C++, and data abstractions through C++ classes. A Class is a way to bind the data and its associated behaviour together. An object is a runtime instance of a Class. These are discussed in detail in Chapter 8 which also defines typedefs, constructor and destructor, and scope of variables in dynamic memory management. Chapter 9 makes a holistic coverage of operator overloading, which is not an object-oriented feature, but rather a C++ language specific feature that provides ease in programming semantics. A solid understanding of the relationships of classes is an essential prerequisite for a good OO design. Thus Chapter 10 throws light on topics such as class relationships, inheritance, friends, and also defines constructor and destructor calling sequence, and static and dynamic binding.

With Chapter 11, we move on to advanced concepts like templates, namespaces, exception handling, and advanced casting operators introduced late in the language. Chapter 12 analyzes standard input and output classes and standard template library usually provided by different C++ compiler vendors.

Chapter 13 deals with data structures and its application issues. A systematic software development process is important for quality work. Therefore, in Chapter 14 , we revisit some OO terms against the backdrop of design patterns. Chapter 15 is all about structural, behavioural, packaging, and deployment modelling through Unified Modelling Language (UML), an open standard for specifying, constructing, visualizing, and documenting the architecture of a software-intensive system.

Last but not the least, choosing an IDE is the first and foremost requirement to start practising. Usual IDE environments include an editor, a compiler, libraries, a linker, a build utility, and a visual debugger. The exact layout of an editor, the compiler and linking options, the available libraries, etc. do vary between different environments. With the right accessories in place, one can compile, link, run and debug. Without an IDE, one has to look for separate command and line utilities for editing, compiling, linking, and also for build (or make) utility with its list of includable files and library files.

C++ is a very powerful, flexible, and thought-provoking language. It is very useful when blended with the object-oriented flavour. C++ is of course an easy language to learn, but it is certainly not so easy to master its intricacies. Practise, design first, then code, and follow best practices—that's the secret; once you have learnt the basics, you are better prepared to learn the intricacies.

Have fun!

DEBASISH JANA

Acknowledgements

A list of all those who have extended their support in realizing my dream would itself form a book. Let me take this opportunity to mention (the names of) at least a few of them.

I express my deep-felt thanks to Dr. Alo Ghosh, CEO, Techna Digital Services Pvt. Ltd., for providing an excellent work atmosphere and facilitating a lively exchange of ideas when I started my first exploration in C++ in the 1990s. Down the memory lane, I have very fond rememberances of brainstorming sessions with my seniors, old colleagues and friends, Mr. Prabir Ghosh, Mr. Rajsekhar Bhattacharya, Ms. Anindita Sengupta, Mr. Purnendu Sinha, and above all, Mr. Dipu Bose and Robert J. Falk. My sincere thanks are due to Mr. R.T. Goswami of BIT Mesra Kolkata Extension Centre who instilled in me a special interest in C++ and object-oriented paradigm. I am deeply indebted to Prof. Gordon Cormack of University of Waterloo and Prof. Mohit Roy and Prof. D. Ghosh Dastidar of Jadavpur University who helped me in learning the data structures and principles of programming languages. Above all, I express my gratitude to Bjarne Stroustrup, for his wonderful work which inspired me to explore C++.

Dr. Sukumar Roychowdhury, Mr. Diptendu Dutta, Prof. (Late) Ranjan Roy of St. Xavier's College, and Subrata Chatterjee and Raja Roy of St. Xavier's College, Kolkata, deserve special thanks for the motivation they provided as also for their unstinted needful guidance and support. My special thanks are due to Somak Ray and Amitava Neogi, my old students, for their active assistance in writing this book and also to my cousin Suman Das who provided me with valuable materials that helped me immensely in developing my ideas. I am obliged much to my colleagues at Techna for creating a congenial working environment that sustained my interest in writing this book.

I am beholden much to Dr. Pinaki Mitra of NIMC, Kolkata and Mr. Piyal Sarkar whose valuable friendship and support helped me in all my endeavours. I owe a special word of thanks to Debasish Jana of ERTL (East), my namesake and a close friend of mine, for providing me with lots of supporting material on the subject from time to time.

My heartfelt thanks go to all my beloved ones—my parents Bhabani Jana and (late) Satya Ranjan Jana, my sister Debasri, my beloved wife Rita and my son Prithwish—who all stood by me during adversities and encouraged me write this book.

Finally, I will be failing in my duty if I do not profusely thank the entire team of Prentice-Hall of India for their praiseworthy efforts in publishing this book.

1 Overview

Software is the fuel on which modern businesses are run, governments rule, and societies become better connected.

—Grady Booch

LEARNING OBJECTIVES

The objective of this chapter is to acquaint you with:

- Programming in general
- Programming Paradigms—Procedural, Functional, Logic and Object-Oriented
- Basics of Object-Oriented Programming
- Available Object-Oriented Languages
- Structure of a C++ program—Tokens, Comments, Identifiers, Keywords, Literals
- Program Compilation
- Object-Oriented Programming Terms—Class, Object, Encapsulation, Abstraction, Polymorphism, Inheritance, Static and Dynamic Binding

INTRODUCTION

There are essentially two parts of a computer: hardware and software. Hardware is the bare machine, and software is the set of instructions that makes the hardware work. It helps us store and retrieve information in the hardware. Development of software essentially requires the knowledge of computer programming to direct the computer in the required manner. That means, no matter how many times we execute a computer program, the same result should be received for the same set of data provided. An algorithm is a sequence of steps to solve any logical problem. The underlying control of the program thus evolves out of the algorithm which drives the execution sequence. In fact, it can be said that a programming language is an expression of the algorithm.

Basics of Programming

Irrespective of the application for which the program is meant, certain steps need to be followed while developing it. These steps are shown in Figure 1.1.

First and foremost step of any program development is the problem identification step. Once the problem is identified, i.e. what the problem is and

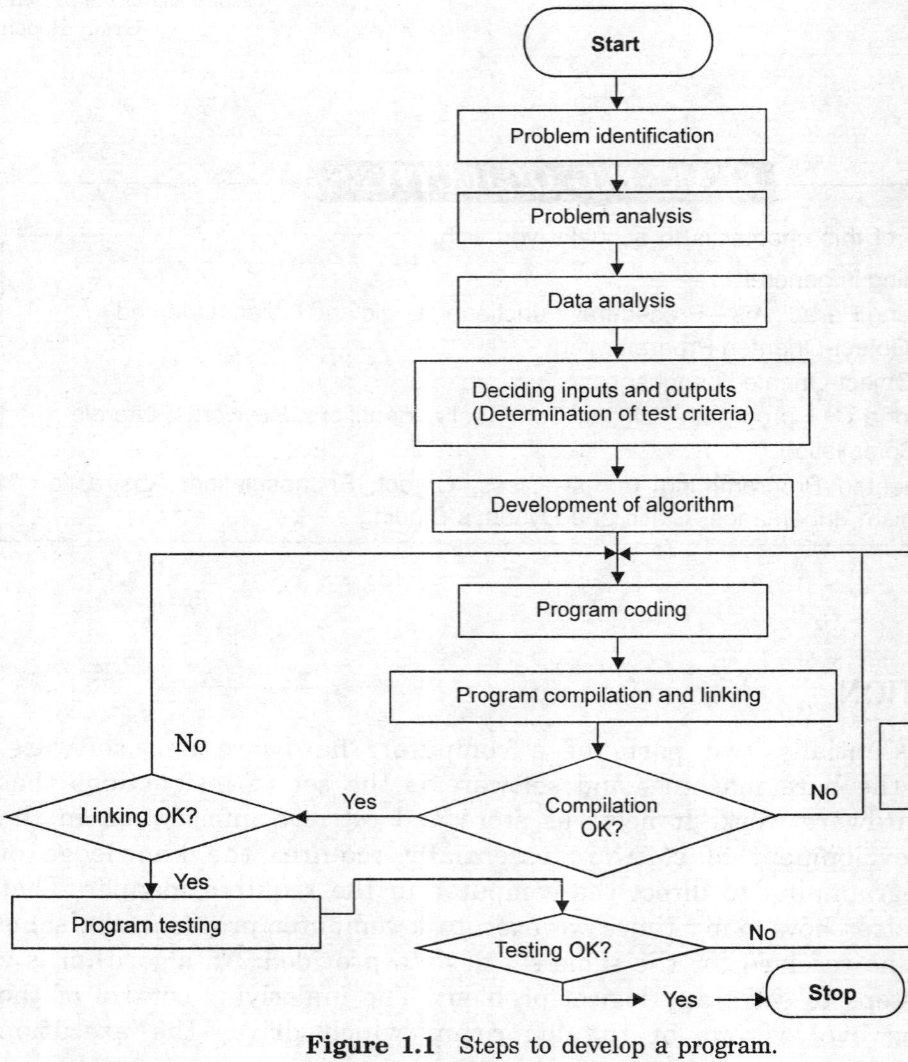

Figure 1.1 Steps to develop a program.

what result should be obtained through a program, a program analysis step is to be performed. This requires a thorough understanding of the requirements of the program, followed by an analysis of data step in which we identify the essential data that drives the program. Some data could be internally generated and some, externally fed in as input. This follows the decision of input as well as output of the entire program. The choice of input and output essentially drives the test criteria of the program, that is whether the program is able to provide desired and intended results. Once all these are identified, we have to choose suitable algorithmic approach in the form of steps that drive the execution sequence to achieve desired results.

The actual program coding which is a translation of the algorithm to a target programming language follows the step thus discussed. The programming language we are referring to here is some high-level program coding. Once the program coding has been done, it requires to be compiled to generate to corresponding machine language code in the target machine. If there are some compilation errors in terms of syntax of the programming language, the program coding has to be redone so that it correctly follows the syntax of the underlying high-level language. Once the compilation is done successfully, the corresponding object code, which is in a machine language format, is generated with some unresolved symbols. The next step is linking of the compiled object code (output of a compiler) to resolve all the symbols used. Unsuccessful linking requires reworking of the program coding to resolve the problems identified by the linker. Once linking is done successfully, the executable file is generated and this program is ready to run. Now is the time to test the program in terms of its behaviour as desired, i.e. whether the program is generating correct set of output data from the input data source set in the test criteria in earlier step. If the program does not generate desired results, then it has to be debugged to find out the actual problem (we call it a bug), which may require program recoding, provided the algorithm is designed correctly. This may require a revision of the algorithm or the steps of the program initially formulated. Once the program is tested through correctly, we say the program is done. Later, if requirements change, then we can go back to the steps and rework if necessary. Changes are always possible with the new additions of hardware and software technology. As such, our ultimate goal is to follow some flexible approach so that the reworking areas are isolated and in narrowed down parts in such a manner that rest of the program remains unaffected by changes in one part of the program.

Language Translators

Computer understands only one programming language, which is the machine language. Machine language is in strict binary form, i.e. a series of zeros and ones with all instructions and data. Machine languages are faster in execution since the computer directly starts executing it. However, they are difficult to read, write or modify by a human. Thus, human understandable high-level programming languages have been invented to express algorithms so that they become easy to read, write and modify.

There are varieties of human understandable high-level programming languages to express algorithms. Each language is capable of expressing the same algorithm. However, expression in one language may not be convenient in the other. This is because different programming languages have different expressive power. New programming languages are being invented to make it convenient for us to express our algorithms in a better way. Thus, we can choose any language for writing a program according to the need, but a computer can execute programs only after they are represented internally in machine language form in sequences of 1's and 0's.

Programs written in any high-level programming language must be translated to the machine language as representation of instructions for the computer to execute them. This process is called *compilation* and the program performing the compilation job is called the *compiler*. Special programs accept the user programs written in high-level languages, check each statement if they are grammatically (syntactically and semantically) correct, and produce a corresponding set of understandable machine language instructions.

Language processors are also known as language translators. There are two types of translators—*Interpreters* and *Compilers*. A *compiler* checks the entire user-written program (known as source program or source code), and if error-free, produces a complete program in machine language (known as object program). The object program(s) is/are *linked* together with other precompiled object codes or libraries (also in machine language form) to produce an executable file which when loaded into computer memory starts execution. The *interpreter*, on the other hand, translates one statement at a time, and if error-free executes the instruction. That is, it translates and executes the first instruction before the second, while a compiler translates the whole program before execution can begin (see Figure 1.2).

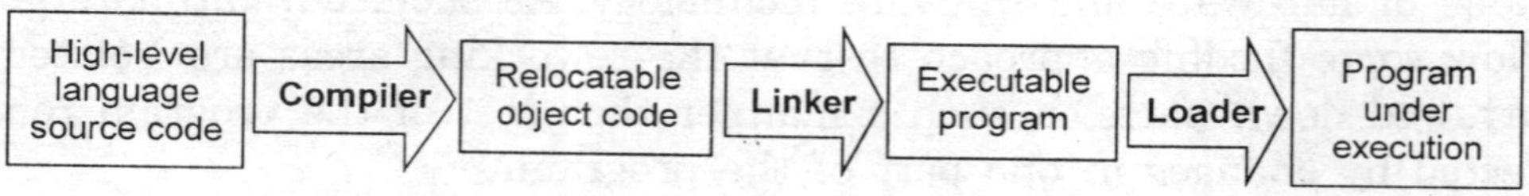

Figure 1.2 Program translation process.

The compiler varies from machine to machine and is different for every underlying operating system on which it runs. It takes high-level language source code as input and produces machine level instructions with many addresses of symbols (identifiers, function names) unresolved in a symbol table. It also produces static data (static variable) and locally defined procedure entries. It then does syntax and semantics checking based on the grammar rules of high-level programming language. The output of a compiler is a relocatable object code, which is in machine language format. This code is not ready for execution. The *linker* resolves cross-references among object files in machine language format as generated by the compiler. While doing so, it may complain about unresolved symbols or the multiplicity of defined symbols. On successful linking, the linker generates an executable machine language format code assuming that the entire executable program starts from memory location 'zero'. To run a program, the underlying operating system must load the executable file from the disk into main memory. This executable program, as generated by the linker, is loaded in computer memory by another systems program called *loader*, that obtains a portion of available physical memory for executing the program from the memory manager of the underlying operating system. The loader also translates (binds) relocatable absolute addresses of the program to actual executable addresses on the physical memory. It then copies the executable program into memory and initiates execution of instructions. The execution of a high-level language program is summarized in Figure 1.3.

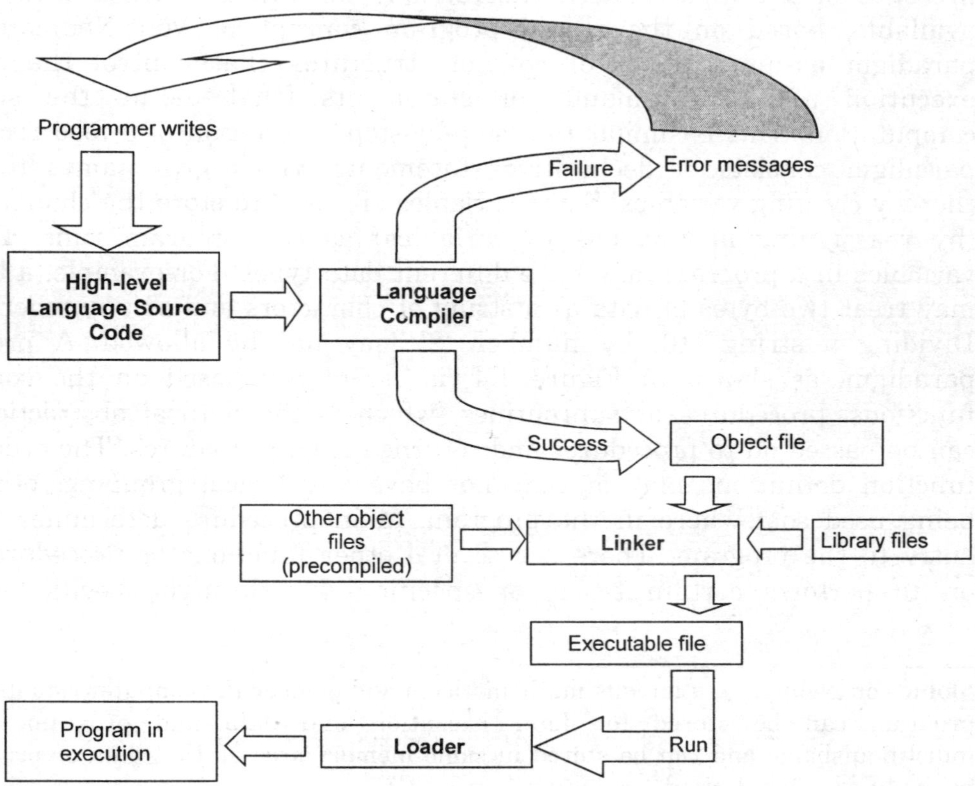

Figure 1.3 Steps to execute a high-level language program.

Programming Paradigms

A programming paradigm is the pattern or model of programming that drives the process of programming. Every high-level programming language has a paradigm that guides in problem solving within a framework and gives solutions. Every programming paradigm is a collection of conceptual patterns that control human thinking process to formulate a solution to a problem. Different programming paradigms lead to different programming techniques. Once a solution is arrived at or assimilated via a particular programming paradigm, a programming language is needed to express that thought process. As such, language of a particular paradigm must adequately reflect the conceptual patterns of the programming paradigm. There are four main programming paradigms—*imperative, functional, logic* and *object-oriented*. Each of these main paradigms evolves with an idea within some basic framework of discipline that has relevance in performing computations.

Imperative or Procedural Paradigm

Imperative or procedural programming paradigm is based on the idea "First do this and next do that", i.e. a step-by-step execution model. It assumes the presence of a computer with theoretically infinite amount of memory area available, based on the stored program concept of Von Neumann[1]. The paradigm assumes a set of control structures that control the order of execution of the commands or statements (that define the steps) in computation. This is similar to a step-by-step description of a food recipe. The paradigm consists of declarative statements which give names to values, thereby creating variables. Same variables are used to store the changing value (by reassigning new values to variables) as the program runs. Different variables in a program may have different data types. For example, a language may treat two bytes of data as a string of characters and as a number as well. Dividing a string '10' by number '2' may not be allowed. A procedural paradigm, as shown in Figure 1.4, is essentially based on the concept of functions, procedures or subroutines, which is the natural abstraction. Data can be passed on to procedures and returned from procedures. The order of the function definitions may or may not have any logical grouping, other than being used somewhere in the program. Main procedure determines the first entry to the program. There are several other functions or procedures called on to perform certain tasks, or specific logic through specific execution

[1]John Von Neumann, a famous mathematician and pioneer in Computer established that program can be stored for later execution and data and program code are indistinguishable and can be stored in same memory area so that data or program can be modified when desired.

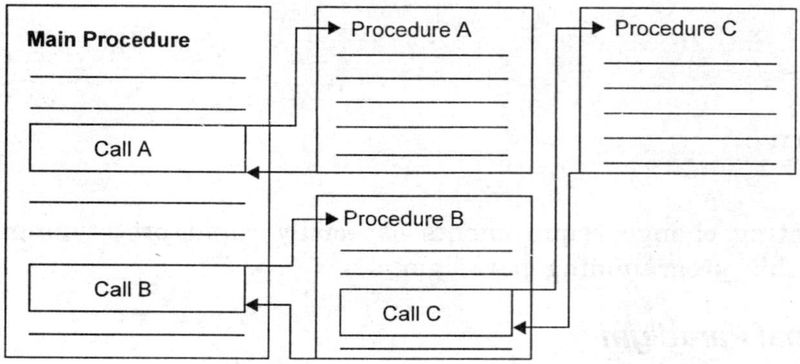

Figure 1.4 Procedural programming model.

sequences. This makes a hierarchy of tasks to be done in a sequence. The program source code is compiled and linked with any additional executable portions to make the final executable program.

Typical statement types of procedural programming paradigms include assignment and control statements with support for procedure calls and parameters passing through procedures. The representative programming languages following this paradigm are C, Pascal, Algol, Basic, Cobol and Fortran.

An example of procedural paradigm is illustrated in Example 1.1. Here we are trying to find the value of a factorial of a positive number.

EXAMPLE 1.1: Procedural algorithm for finding a factorial of a number n (n > 0).

```
procedure factorial(n)
begin
   define variable x with initial value of 1
   while the variable n is greater than 0 do
   begin
      multiply x by n to store result in x
      decrement n
   end while
   return value of variable x
end
```

Equivalent program in C

```
int factorial(int n)
{
   int x = 1;
   while (n > 0)
```

```
    {
        x = x * n;
        n = n - 1;
    }
    return x;
}
```

Implementing change requirements especially rapid prototyping is the weak point of this programming paradigm.

Functional Paradigm

Functional programming paradigm evolves from the idea of evaluating an expression and then using the resulting value for something else. This is based on mathematical model of function composition, such as Lambda Calculus. A lambda expression is like "$\lambda(x)(+\ x\ 1)$", which can be interpreted as 'the function that adds one to its parameter'. An equivalent conventional expression is "$f(x) = x + 1$". All computations are done by applying or calling functions. This implies that pure functional programming paradigm does not allow step-by-step execution model as in procedural paradigm. Result of one computation is the input to the next and so on, until some computation yields the desired result. There are intermediate values, which are passed from function to function. Functions are treated as first class values, that is they are very much similar to data, which can be created at runtime, can be passed as parameters through other functions, and can be returned as results from other functions. An example of functional paradigm is illustrated in Example 1.2. Here we are trying to find the value of a factorial of a positive number through recursive computation calling same function again and again till we get the desired result. Thus, factorial (3) results in 3∗factorial (2), which results in 3∗2∗factorial (1), which finally results in 3∗2∗1.

EXAMPLE 1.2: Functional algorithm of finding a factorial of a number n (n > 0).

```
factorial n = 1 (if n = 1)
              n * factorial(n - 1) (otherwise)
```

Equivalent program in LISP

```
(defun factorial (n)
    (cond ((eq n 0) 1)
        (t (* n (fact (- n 1))))
))
```

A procedural program may proceed by changing some globally-accessible variables. In contrast, a functional program proceeds by function calling, passing parameter values and return of values. This alleviates chances of errors associated with maintaining global variables. Functional programs do not use variables to store intermediate values. Indeed, they cannot use assignment statements. There is no strict sequence of commands, i.e. no step-by-step execution model. Instead of sequencing and looping, functional languages use recursive functions—those that are defined in terms of themselves. Functional programs correspond more directly to mathematical objects and suitable in symbolic computation and artificial intelligence areas where the computation is based on a strong mathematical model. Functional languages are used for general purpose programming also, but procedural-minded people find psychological hindrance to functional paradigm approach.

The representative programming languages following this paradigm are ML, Miranda, and Pure Lisp.

Logic Paradigm

Logic programming paradigm is based on the idea of answering a question through search for solution from a knowledge base. This is based on axioms, inferences, rules, and queries. Program execution becomes a systematic search in a set of facts, making use of a set of inference rules. A set of known facts and a set of rules result in deduction of other facts. Computation is modelled by evaluation. Evaluation starts with a goal and attempts to prove it with a known fact or by deducing it from some rule. Programmer states only the logic of the program; it is the system that drives the control. The representative programming language following this paradigm is Prolog. An example of logic paradigm is illustrated in Example 1.3.

EXAMPLE 1.3: Logic programming example in Prolog.

```
father(dasarath, ram).
father(ram, lav).
mother(kaushalya, ram).
mother(sita, lav).
grandfather(X, Y) :- father(X, Z), father(Z, Y).
grandfather(X, Y) :- father(X, Z), mother(Z, Y).
?father(X, ram).
X = dasarath.
?grandfather(X, lav).
X = dasarath.
?father(dasarath, X).
X = ram.
```

Here we are defining four different facts, two for father relationship, two for mother relationship which state facts such as dasarath is the father of ram, ram is the father of lav, kaushalya is the mother of ram and sita is the mother of lav. And then, the rule is defined that any person X, is the grandfather of another person Y, if X is the father of some other person Z, who is either the father or the mother of Y. Thus, the query "who is the father of ram?" given as father (X, ram) gives the answer dasarath. The query "who is the grandfather of lav?" gives the answer dasarath. And the query, "dasarath is the father of whom?" gives the answer ram. Here, fact, rule and constant (a particular thing) must be in small letters, and variables, in capital letters. Thus, dasarath, kaushalya and ram are constants and therefore written in small letters whereas, X and Y and are variables, and so written in capital letters.

Object-Oriented Paradigm

In contrast to procedural paradigm which has a large single store where all procedures work, in object-oriented (OO) paradigm, procedures operate on abstract values called *objects* which can be created and destroyed dynamically. This programming paradigm is based on the idea of communicating between objects to simulate the temporal evolution of a set of real world phenomena. Data as well as operations are encapsulated in objects. Objects interact by means of message passing and create the functionality of a larger program. They take in certain data, process it, and pass it to another object. The set of functions through which they interact is called the interface. Information hiding is used to protect the internal properties of an object. The state of an object may, of course, change in response to some interaction requested from some other object.

In OO paradigm, objects are grouped into classes. Objects in classes are similar enough to allow programming of the classes, as they are opposed to programming of individual objects. Classes are organized into inheritance hierarchies. This provides for class extension or specialization. Inheritance allows new objects to be defined in terms of other existing objects. To make an OO design, we need to decide which classes are needed, then provide a full set of operations for each class. Commonality of the classes can be made explicit by using inheritance. The programming languages following this paradigm are Simula, Smalltalk, Eiffel, C++, Java and many others.

NEED FOR OBJECT-ORIENTED PROGRAMMING

Object-Oriented Programming (OOP) was developed because of limitations discovered in other programming paradigms, especially its close predecessor, procedural paradigm. Pascal, C, FORTRAN, COBOL are examples of procedural programming paradigms. A program in procedural paradigm is a collection of instructions. When program becomes larger, a single list of instructions becomes unwieldy. So, the program is divided into functions or procedures, and each function or procedure has a clearly defined purpose and a clearly defined interface to other functions or procedures in the program.

Structured programming is an established technique. Grouping a number of functions together into a larger entity is called a *module*. Dividing a program into functions and modules is one of the major concerns of structured programming. Structured programming tries to cater to different blocks or modules as separate entities, with well-defined interfaces among them. No matter how well the structured programming approach is implemented, large programs tend to become excessively complex. As such, there is a necessity to eliminate concentrations on smaller modules with well-defined input and output interfaces.

OO methodologies help to build structured models of the problem domain at hand and devise well-structured solutions. Moreover, it has been proven that these OO methods lead to more stable architectures and more easily understood than those based solely on function and data flow as in procedural approach. In OOP, the fundamental construct is an object, which combines both structural (data) and behavioural (functions) aspects in a single entity. This is in contrast to conventional procedural programming paradigm where program is built through procedures that represent behavioural aspects with the use of data. Data and procedures or functions are loosely coupled in a procedural paradigm whereas in an OO paradigm, data and functions are tightly coupled to constitute objects.

BASICS OF OOP

OOP involves concepts that are new to programmers of traditional procedural languages such as Pascal, C, FORTRAN, COBOL etc. These new ideas such as data hiding, encapsulation and polymorphism, lie at the heart of OOP.

The OO paradigm has two important philosophies: *data hiding* and *data abstraction*. Data hiding philosophy emphasizes partitioning the program so that data is hidden in modules such that users of the service don't know the underlying implementation. Internal representation can be accessed from internal implementation and not by the users of the modules. *Data abstraction* philosophy clarifies on which types are needed to provide full set of operations for each type so that a new type of data, if defined, can be used similar to built-in type with all sort of permissible operations. Data abstraction involves concentrating on properties shared by many objects or situations in the real world, ignoring the differences between them.

OO LANGUAGES

Figure 1.5 shows the classification of OOPs as a collection of objects + classes + inheritance and the representative programming languages supporting different features of object-orientedness.

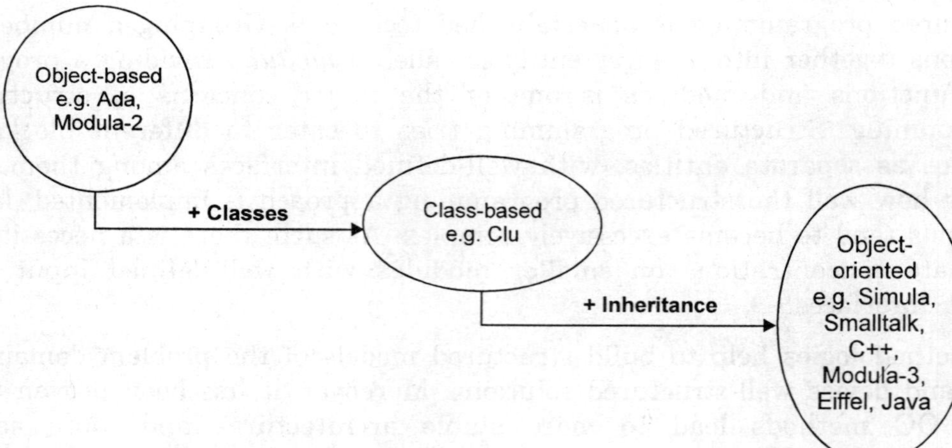

Figure 1.5 Objects + Classes + Inheritance = OO Programs.

The terminologies used in OOP are defined as follows:

Objects. These are runtime states (instances of a class) of a conceptual framework encapsulating typed data and typed operations that correspond to a real-world entity or thing for the purpose of computational modelling.

Classes. These are static (compile-time) definitions of a new type of a collection of data and associated operations (procedures or functions) from which runtime instances called objects can be created.

Inheritance. The ability to declare and define new classes as specialization from existing classes is called inheritance. Specialization is defined in terms of added data and/or procedures or methods.

Functions within an object are called *member functions* in C++. These functions are supposed to provide the only way to access data which is encapsulated among the object definition or the class. If you want to read a data item or assign a value to a data item in an object, you call a member function of the object. There should not be a direct access to the data items of an object. The data should be hidden, so that it remains safe from accidental manipulations. Data and the associated functions are thus said to be encapsulated in a single entity called an object.

Figure 1.6 shows an example of a Fraction object where there is an encapsulated data comprising of numerator and denominator. The member functions like Add, Subtract and SetValue give external interface to the other objects to interact with the Fraction object, without directly manipulating the data stored inside a *Fraction object*.

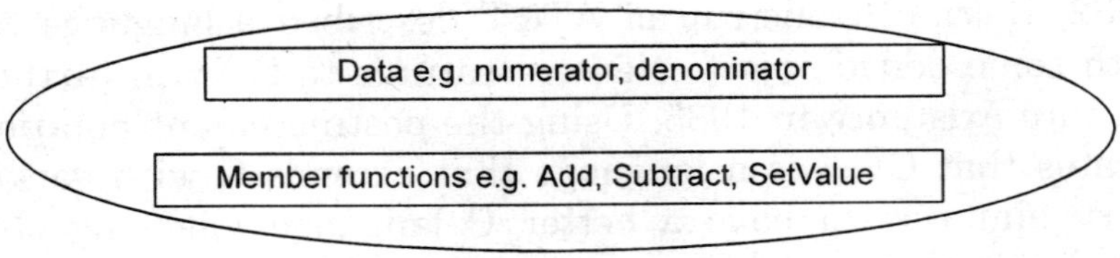

Figure 1.6 Example of a Fraction object.

Alan Kay had stated five basic characteristics of Smalltalk, the first successful object-oriented language (C++ is a successor). These characteristics represent a purist approach to OOP. The characteristics are:

1. *Everything is an object.* An object stores data. One can "make requests" to that object, as well, asking it to perform operations on itself.

2. *A program is a bunch of objects telling each other what to do by sending messages.* To make a request to an object, you "send a message" (i.e. call an appropriate function) to that object.

3. *Each object has its own memory made up of other objects.* Existing objects can be composed together to create new objects (bottom-up approach). Thus, complexity of objects can be built step-by-step by proper abstractions and compositions. Small objects clubbed together constitute bigger objects.

4. *Every object has a type.* Objects have runtime instances of conceptual pattern or type called class, and in fact, every object has an associated type.

5. *All objects of a particular type can receive the same messages.* In the true sense, this means objects of a particular class which may be specialized from another class, respond to same messages to behave similarly. This will lead to polymorphism which will send the same interface to a couple of objects belonging to a family of classes so that proper method is called in the appropriate class. This is a very powerful concept in C++.

EVOLUTION OF C++

C is a general purpose programming language following procedural paradigm. Dennis M. Ritchie originally created it in the year 1971 for specific purpose of rewriting much of the Unix operating system. C became spectacularly popular among systems programmers and also later among applications programmers with its rich variety of operators and control structures. OO paradigm was defined later, although objects and operations were not new programming concepts. Way back in 1967, Simula came into existence as the first OO language. Many other OO languages came after that.

Around 1982, Bjarne Stroustrup of AT&T described a language called *C with Classes* with some added object-oriented features to C. With further iterations, C++ came into existence in 1985. Using the postincrement notation, the name C++ indicates that C++ is a language that extends C with various facilities. The primary aim was to have a better C language following object-oriented paradigm as a top feature of C as in procedural paradigm. In the OOP world, C++ became a popular OO language with as strong a foothold as was for C in systems programming in the seventies and eighties.

OO languages have several advantages over procedure-oriented languages such as C, Pascal, FORTRAN etc. In OOP, extremely large pieces of program code (which is very common in contemporary applications) become easier to maintain, and are made more reliable and conveniently reusable if they're written with "object" orientation rather than with "procedure" orientation.

C++ is a superset of C. Almost every correct statement in C is also a correct statement in C++, although the reverse is not true. The most important elements added to C to create C++ are concerned with classes, objects, inheritance and features of OOP. Some non-object-oriented features have also been added in C++ like friends, operator overloading and so on. Figure 1.7 shows a set relationship of features available in C and C++.

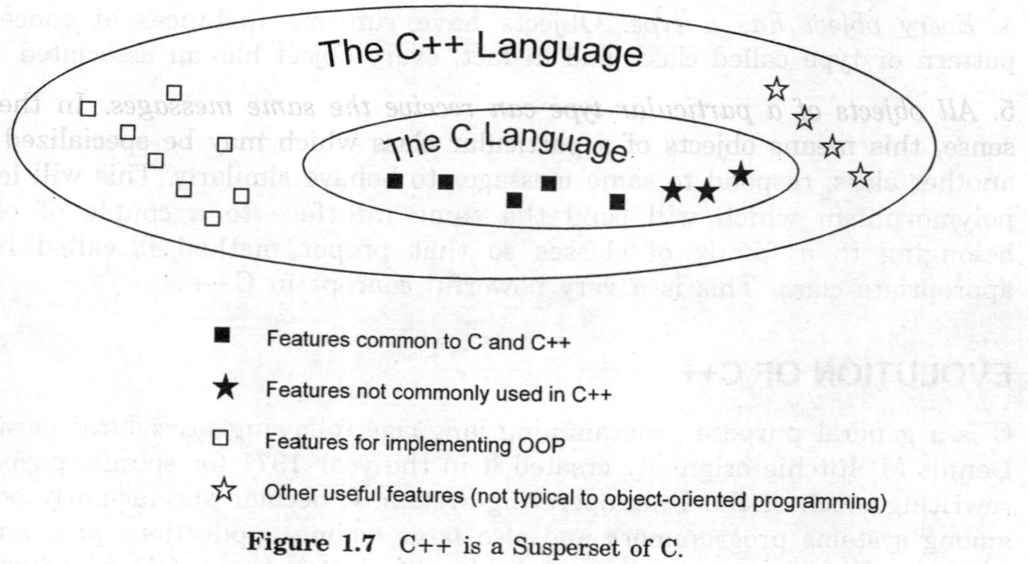

Figure 1.7 C++ is a Susperset of C.

Structure of a C++ Program

A C++ program is a collection of one or more *files*. A program file consists of a sequence of declarations which include function definitions, which are a series of executable statements, with appropriate definition of variables and initializing statements. A declaration introduces one or more names into a program. That name could be the name of a variable, constant or a function and the like. A program file can have comments, functions and preprocessor directives. Let's see a sample program in Example 1.4.

EXAMPLE 1.4:

```
#include <iostream.h> /* Dated 01-10-2001 */
int main ()
{
   cout << "Hi There";
   return 0;
}
```

Here `#include <iostream.h>` statement is the preprocessor directive. /* begins a comment and */ ends a comment. `int main()` is the prototype of a function definition, and the two braces { and } signify the respectively beginning and closing of the main function.

Functions

Functions are one of the fundamental building blocks of C++. The first program consists almost entirely of a single function called `main()`. The parentheses following the word main are the distinguishing features of a function. Without them, the compiler would think that the `main` refers to a variable, which could mean data or function name itself, or some other program element. The `int` preceding the function name indicates that this particular function returns a value at the end of the function. The body of the function is surrounded by braces ({ }). They surround or delimit a block of program statements. Every function must use a pair of braces.

When you first execute or run a C++ program, the first statement executed will be the `main` function. If there is no such function called `main` in your program, the linker will signal an error, and executable file wouldn't be generated.

Preprocessor Directives

Before the actual compilation process starts in C and C++ languages, a preprocessor is run on the source code. The preprocessor is a simple program that replaces patterns given in the source code with some other patterns as defined, using preprocessor directives. Preprocessor directives are used to save and increase the readability of the code. The preprocessor directive in a line begins with a hash (#) sign. A preprocessor `#include <iostream.h>`

directive causes the preprocessor to replace the directive with the whole contents of the specified file named iostream.h which is treated as a header file.

Some Terminologies

Before we go into our first C++ program, let's introduce some basic terminologies of a programming language in the following subsections.

Comments

Comments are portions of declarations discarded by the compiler to perform the translation process from high-level language C++ to a corresponding machine language. With comments, notes or descriptions on portions of a program can be added. C++ supports two ways to mark comments. The characters /* start a block comment, which ends with the characters */. These block comments cannot be nested with one another. The characters // start a line comment, which ends at the end of the line in which they occur. The characters /*, // and */ do not have any special meaning within a line comment that starts with //. Similarly, the characters // do not have any special meaning within a block comment.

Tokens

Tokens are textual elements in a data. There are five kinds of tokens: identifiers, keywords, literals, operators, and other separators. Blanks or spaces, horizontal and vertical tabs, newlines, formfeeds, and comments (collectively known as whitespaces) are ignored by the compiler unless they are meant to separate adjacent tokens. Symbols # and ## are treated as tokens.

Identifiers. A valid identifier is an arbitrarily long sequence of letters, digits or underline symbols (_). There are few compilers that can take only the first 32 characters of an identifier as significant, ignoring the rest. Neither spaces nor marked letters can be a part of an identifier. In addition, variable identifiers would always have to begin with a letter or an underline character (_), and not a digit. Identifiers starting with the underline character is usually reserved for setting external linkages. Identifiers containing a double underscore (_ _) are reserved for use by C++ implementations and, as such, should be avoided. The C++ language is case sensitive, i.e. upper and lower case letters are recognized. For example, the variable MYVAR is not the same as that of myvar or variable Myvar.

Keywords. The following identifiers (Table 1.1) are reserved for use as keywords, and cannot be used otherwise. Reserved words must not be used as names of objects, types, functions or anything else.

Table 1.1

Keyword	*Purpose*
asm	Assembly language specifier has strong dependence on the underlying system
auto	Optional local declaration
bad_cast	Error specifier for bad type casting
bad_typeid	Error specifier for bad typeid specifier
bool	Datatype declaration of type Boolean comprising of TRUE or FALSE
break	Used to exit block of statements like loop, switch
case	Choice in a switch
catch	Catch block that handles a thrown exception
char	Datatype declaration of a type character
class	Beginning of a class definition
const	Implies that variable cannot be changed
const_cast	Adds or removes constness of data
continue	Continues to go to the bottom of block statements like loops
default	Optional last case specifier of a switch statement
delete	Deallocate space created by new (free cannot be used in this case)
do	Executable statement as in do-while loop
double	Datatype declaration for double precision floating point numbers
dynamic_cast	Allow casting a pointer type if legal, else return null
else	Executable statement, part of conditional statement "if"
enum	Datatype declaration for enumeration type
except	Except block that handles a thrown exception
explicit	Disallows constructors to do implicit conversions e.g. Xa = 7;
export	If precedes by something, implies that that can be used by other files
extern	If precedes by something, implies that variable is defined externally
false	Particular value of type bool
finally	Part of exception handler
float	Datatype declaration of floating point
for	Executable statement used in **for** loop
friend	Who can see private members of a class
goto	Jump within function to a designated label statement
if	Executable statement
inline	Expand the code rather than call it
int	Datatype declaration of integer
long	Prefix declaration applicable to many types
long int	Example of a type that is a long integer

(*contd.*)

Table 1.1 (*contd.*)

Keyword	*Purpose*
long unsigned	Example of sequence of reserved words
mutable	Override const member functions in classes
namespace	A scope for declarations and function prototypes
new	Allocate storage and call the constructor, if applicable, deallocate storage later with 'delete' (do not use malloc for allocation+ initialization purpose for objects)
operator	Followed by an operator symbol
private	The items after this keyword is not visible outside the class
protected	The items after this keyword is visible to classes that inherit this class
public	The items after this keyword is visible outside the class
register	Prefix declaration meaning keep variable in register
reinterpret_cast	Converts a type into any different type (e.g. int to pointer)
return	Executable statement with or without a value
short	Prefix declaration applied to many types
signed	Prefix declaration applied to some types
sizeof	Operator applied to variables and types, gives size in bytes
static	Prefix declaration to make local variable static
static_cast	A normal cast with no run time checking
struct	Declaration of a structure, like a record
switch	Executable statement for cases
template	Defines template class or function
this	Pointer to current object available within member function implementations
throw	Throws an exception which is caught by the exception handler later
true	Value of type bool
try	Part of the exception handler as a try block that precedes a catch block
type_info	Provides information about a type
typedef	Creates a new type name for an existing type
typeid	Function for getting the type of a typename, can be used to check identity comparison
typename	Specifies the following name as a type
union	Declaration of variables that are in the same memory locations
unsigned	Prefix declaration applied to some types
using	Makes an entity in a namespace directly visible

(*contd.*)

Table 1.1 (*contd.*)

Keyword	*Purpose*
virtual	This type of function is hidden if defined by an inheritor
void	Declaration of a typeless variable or no formal parameters
volatile	Prefix declaration meaning the variable can be changed at any time
wchar_t	Datatype declaration for type wide character (for internationalization)
while	Executable statement, while loop or do-while loop
xalloc	Memory allocation

Some compiler may also include some more specific reserved keywords. For example, many compilers which generate 16 bits code (like some compilers for DOS) include also ***far, huge*** and ***near*** as keywords.

Operators. Characters and character combinations are used as operators. Each operator is considered as a single token. Usage of operators is summarized in Table 1.2.

Table 1.2

Operator	*Usage*
!	logical negation
%	remainder or modulus
^	bitwise exclusive OR
&	bitwise exclusive AND
*	multiplication (binary) or dereference (unary)
(	left parenthesis (start of an argument list)
)	right parenthesis (end of an argument list)
–	subtraction (binary) or negative sign (unary)
+	addition (binary) or positive sign (unary)
=	assignment
{	left brace, start of a block of statements
}	right brace, end of a block of statements
		bitwise logical OR operation
~	bitwise negation operation
[	left square bracket, beginning of an index operator
]	right square bracket, ending of an index operator

(*contd.*)

Table 1.2 (*contd.*)

<table>
<tr><th>Operator</th><th>Usage</th></tr>
<tr><td>\</td><td>backslash (line continuation)</td></tr>
<tr><td>;</td><td>semicolon, statement end marker</td></tr>
<tr><td>'</td><td>single quote, enclose single character</td></tr>
<tr><td>:</td><td>colon (used as separator)</td></tr>
<tr><td>"</td><td>double quote, enclose a string literal</td></tr>
<tr><td><</td><td>less than or as a beginning angular bracket enclosing filename in preprocessor directive</td></tr>
<tr><td>></td><td>greater than or as an ending angular bracket enclosing filename in preprocessor directive</td></tr>
<tr><td>?</td><td>conditional operator</td></tr>
<tr><td>,</td><td>comma, separates arguments</td></tr>
<tr><td>.</td><td>dot operator to extract elements/functions from structures/objects</td></tr>
<tr><td>/</td><td>division operator</td></tr>
<tr><td>–></td><td>member-of operator</td></tr>
<tr><td>++</td><td>increment (post or pre)</td></tr>
<tr><td>––</td><td>decrement (post or pre)</td></tr>
<tr><td>–>*</td><td>dereferenced member-of</td></tr>
<tr><td><<</td><td>bitwise left shift or insertion operator</td></tr>
<tr><td>>></td><td>bitwise right shift or extraction operator</td></tr>
<tr><td><=</td><td>less than or equal to</td></tr>
<tr><td>>=</td><td>greater than or equal to</td></tr>
<tr><td>==</td><td>equal to</td></tr>
<tr><td>!=</td><td>not equal to</td></tr>
<tr><td>&&</td><td>logical AND</td></tr>
<tr><td>||</td><td>logical OR</td></tr>
<tr><td>*=</td><td>a *= b => a = a * b</td></tr>
<tr><td>/=</td><td>a /= b => a= a/b</td></tr>
<tr><td>%=</td><td>a %= b => a= a% b</td></tr>
<tr><td>+=</td><td>a += b => a= a+ b</td></tr>
<tr><td>–=</td><td>a –= b => a= a– b</td></tr>
<tr><td><<=</td><td>a <<= b => a= a<< b</td></tr>
<tr><td>>>=</td><td>a >>= b => a= a>> b</td></tr>
<tr><td>&=</td><td>a &= b => a= a & b</td></tr>
<tr><td>^=</td><td>a ^= b => a= a ^ b</td></tr>
<tr><td>|=</td><td>a |= b => a= a | b</td></tr>
<tr><td>::</td><td>scope resolution operator</td></tr>
</table>

Literals. There are many kinds of literals (also called as constants) like integer constants, character constants, floating point constants and string literals.

An integer constant has a fixed value like 2345, 467, –34 and so on. Decimal integer constants are not preceded by any special character. Octal (Base 8) integer constants are preceded by a 0 (zero) character and hexadecimal (Base 16) integer constants are preceded by the characters 0x. For example, the literal constants 75 (decimal), 0113 (octal) and 0x4b (hexadecimal) are all equivalent to each other. The suffixes l and L specify ***long int***.

A floating point constant consists of an integer part, a decimal point, a fraction part, an e or E character (that expresses "by ten high to..") with optional signed integer exponent and an optional type suffix. The suffixes f and F specifies ***float***, the suffixes l and L specify ***long double***. Unless specified otherwise, a floating point constant is a ***float***. For example, 3.14159, 6.02e23 (i.e. 6.02×10^{23}), $1.9e^{-19}$ (i.e. 1.9×10^{-19}), 4.0 and so forth.

A character constant is one or more characters enclosed within a single quote, e.g. 'z', 'X' etc. to represent a single character. The value of the single character constant is a numeric value of the character as given in the character set. These are special characters that cannot be expressed by a single character like newline (\n) or tab (\t). All of these are preceded by an inverted slash (\) representing the escape sequences. An escape sequence specifies a single character. A list of such escape sequences is as follows:

`\n` newline
`\v` vertical tab
`\"` double quotes
`\r` carriage return
`\b` backspace
`\?` question mark
`\f` form feed
`\a` alert (beep)
`\\` inverted slash
`\t` horizontal tab
`\'` simple quotes

In addition, an ASCII code can be numerically expressed with an inverted slash bar (\), is followed by an ASCII code expressed in octal (base 8) or hexadecimal (base 16). In case of octal, the number follows immediately the backslash (for example, \23 or \40), and in case of hexadecimal, an x character is put before the number (for example, \x20 or \x4A). Adjacent string literals are concatenated. For example, `"Hello"` `"World"` implies string literal `"Hello`

`World"`. Escape sequences can be a part of a string literal, e.g. `"First \t Second"`, `"First\nSecond\nThird"`.

FIRST C++ PROGRAM

The best way to learn any programming language is to begin writing programs in it. So, here we go to our first C++ program:

Program Source Code 1.1

```
// my first program in C++
#include <iostream.h>
int main ()
{
 cout << "Hi There";
 return 0;
}
```

Output 1.1

```
Hi There
```

Let's say we assign some filename, for example, **first.cpp** to our program. The program can be written in a text editor and then it can be compiled, and if successfully compiled, subsequently linked to generate an executable file, which can be run. The output is the result of the program once compiled and executed. Our source code prints as output, the phrase `"Hi There"` on the screen. The way to compile a program is given in a later subsection. Let's make a step-by-step analysis of our first program.

First Line – Comment Line – `// my first program in C++`
This is a comment line. In this case, the comment line gives a brief description on what our first program is intended for. This can also be replaced by a block comment like /* my first program in C++*/ to have the same effect.

Second Line – Preprocessor Directive – `#include <iostream.h>`
Sentences beginning with a hash sign (#) are meant for preprocessor directives. Preprocessing is a phase of compilation that is performed prior to the analysis of program text. In this case, `#include <iostream.h>` tells the compiler preprocessor to include the iostream.h header file. This is the basic standard input-output library in C++, and it has to be included because it is used later in the program. Preprocessing directives must begin in the first column, with no spaces between the # and the 'include' keyword, and also, they must not be terminated by a semicolon.

Third Line – Function Declarator – `int main ()`

This line corresponds to the beginning of the main function declaration. All C++ programs begin their execution through the main function. Wherever it is in the program—beginning, middle or end—main function is always the first to be executed when a program starts. Every C++ program must have a main function. 'int' refers to the return type. This means that the main function, on completion, will return an integer value. The return type can be void also, in which case, the main function cannot return any value to the caller of the program. If we don't mention `int` or anything else as the return type, then integer return type is considered by default. The main function declaration is followed by a pair of parenthesis () because it is a function. In C++, all functions are followed by a pair of parenthesis () that, optionally, may include arguments. The content of the main function follows immediately its formal declaration enclosed between key-bracket signs ({}).

Fourth Line – Function Begin – {

The opening brace { marks the beginning of a function.

Fifth Line – Function Body – `cout << "Hi There";`

This instruction displays `"Hi There"` string literal on the screen. `cout` is the standard output stream in C++ (the screen) as defined in the `iostream.h` header file. The sentence ends with a semicolon character (;). This character indicates the end of an instruction and must be included after every instruction in any C++ program.

Sixth Line – Returning from Function – `return 0;`

The return instruction makes the `main()` function to end and return the code that the instruction is followed by, in this case, 0. This is the normal termination of a program that has not found any errors during its execution.

Seventh Line – Function End – }

The closing brace } marks the end of a function.

Thus, with all these functions we have displayed a string literal. The program has been structured in different lines to make it more readable, but it can be written in a fewer lines obeying the statement terminators like

```
int main () { cout << "Hi There"; return 0; }
```

with exactly the same meaning.

Let us write another program with more instructions and some more comments:

Program Source Code 1.2

```
// my second program in C++
#include <iostream.h>
int main ()
{
   cout << "Hi There"; // says Hi There
   cout << "I am Here"; /* says I am Here */
   return 0;
}
```

Output 1.2

```
Hi ThereI am Here
```

In this case we used the `cout <<` method twice in two different instructions. And though line comments and block comments have been used, the effect of the instructions are unaffected by these as those are ignored by the compiler. The output of the program is the concatenation of two string literals `"Hi There"` and `"I am Here"` without a space or line feed in between.

Input and Output

The standard input device is the keyboard and standard output device is the console or screen. In the ***iostream*** C++ library, ***cin*** is the standard input stream taking input from the keyboard and ***cout*** is the standard output stream giving output to the console. Additionally, there are two more output streams: ***cerr*** and ***clog*** specially designed to show error messages that can be directed to the standard output (generally the screen) or to a log file.

Input (cin)

Input streams use the extraction (>>) operator for standard types. The ***cin*** input stream can be used with the extraction operator >> (a pair of "greater than" signs). Extraction operator (>>) extracts the values of the identifiers from the input stream ***cin***.

For example:

```
int count;
cin >> count;
```

declares the identifier count as an integer and then waits for an input from ***cin*** input stream (keyboard) in order to store it in this integer identifier. ***cin*** can only process any input from the keyboard once the newline or return key has been pressed. Let us write a program as follows:

Program Source Code 1.3

```
/* I/O example */
#include <iostream.h>
int main ()
{
    int num;
    cout << "Please enter an integer number: ";
    cin >> num;
    cout << "The value you entered is " << num;
    cout << " and its square is " << num * num << endl;
    return 0;
}
```

Output 1.3

```
Please enter an integer value: 25
The value you entered is 25 and its square is 625
```

The user of the program should supply correct form of data when it is taken as input from the keyboard. If datatype is adhered to, that is, if the desired input and the actual input differ in types, then there is a possibility of erroneous results and erratic behaviour of the program.

More than one data input can be taken from ***cin***.

```
cin >> x >> y;
```

is equivalent to:

```
cin >> x;
cin >> y;
```

In both cases, the user must supply two data, one for variable x and another for variable y that may be separated by any valid blank separator—a space, a tab character or a newline.

Output (cout)

Output streams use the insertion (<<) operator for standard types. The ***cout*** stream can be used with the insertion operator << (a pair of "less than" signs). Insertion operator (<<) inserts the identifiers following the insertion operator to the output stream ***cout***.

```
cout << "Hi There";  // prints Hi There on screen
cout << x;           // prints the content of variable x on
                        screen
cout << "x";         // prints string literal x on screen
cout << 100;         // prints number 100 on screen
```

The insertion operator (<<) may be used more than once on a same sentence like:

```
cout << "Hi " << "There, " << "I am learning C++";
```

This would print the message `Hi There, I am learning C++` on the screen. The insertion operator (<<) can be used multiple times for different types of data.

```
cout << "Hi There, I have started learning C++ "

<< x << "days back";
```

If we suppose that variable x contains the value 2, then this would print:

```
Hi There, I have started learning C++ 2 days back
```

To have line feeds in the output, corresponding escape sequences need to be used. For example,

```
cout << "Hi There, ";
cout << "I am learning C++";
```

will show "Hi There, I am learning C++" in a single line on the screen. Whereas,

```
cout << "Hi There,\n";
cout << "I am learning C++";
```

will show two lines on the screen, as follows:

```
Hi There,
I am learning C++
```

Now, the statements

```
cout << "Hi There, " << endl;
cout << "I am learning C++";
```

will have the same effect with the use of 'endl' manipulator instead of the newline character to print in two lines as follows:

```
Hi There,
I am learning C++
```

Compilation

A compiler is a software or program that reads the source code of a program written in a high-level language (e.g. C++) and translates it into an equivalent program in machine language (shown in Figure 1.8). The important aspect of compilation is to perform translation to the target language in case the source program is correctly translatable. Otherwise, the compiler has to produce error messages caused by wrong usage of the source language in the source program. These error messages are mainly due to the grammatical mistakes done by a programmer.

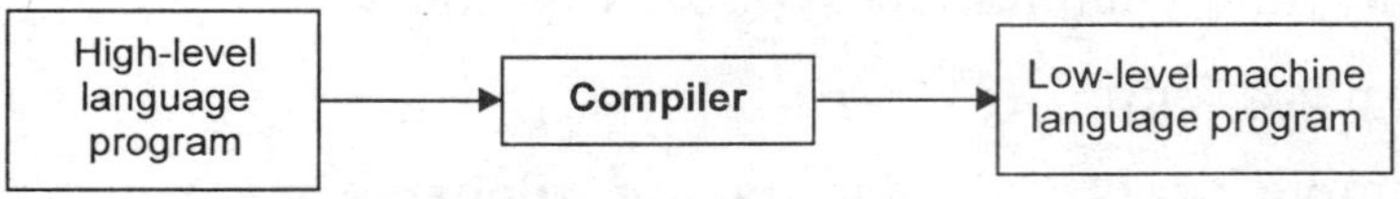

Figure 1.8 Role of a compiler.

The tasks of a compiler can be divided very broadly into two sub-tasks: analysis of the source program, and the generation of the object code (machine language). The analysis task consists lexical analysis, syntax analysis, and semantic analysis. The object code generation phase also includes code optimization part. Lexical analysis scans a source program from left to right character by character and after removing the whitespaces and comments, finds out the tokens. These tokens are taken together to the next subphases to do the syntax and semantic analysis to check if there is any error in usage. If so, the compiler generates errors and not the object code. If syntax and semantic analysis are acceptable, then the code generation part does the actual translation to object code with necessary code optimizations.

Compiling Console Programs

A console program is a program that communicates with the user mainly through the console, that is, through input taken from the keyboard and output showing on console or screen. This type of application is supported by most of the existing operating systems. The compilation method varies depending on the development environment of the compiler, as well as on the underlying operating system and the supplier of the program.

All C++ compilers support compilation of the console programs. There are many C++ compilers available in the market for varied hardware and operating system platforms. Most of these have an integrated development environment that supports the editing, compilation and execution of the programs from within the development environment. However, they also support compilation through command line. All the required arguments are passed from the command line.

To start C++ in a Turbo environment, move to the directory in which you plan to do your C++ program development. From this directory, enter TC at the DOS prompt. Select "New" from the "File" menu. An Edit window will appear, with the filename NONAME00.CPP. To change the name, you can use "Save As" from the "File" menu. The new name appears at the top of the Edit window.

The program that you typed into the edit window constitutes the source file, which when saved to disk, is an ASCII file similar to that generated by a word processor. It has the .CPP extension. The source file is not an executable program. It comprises only of instructions on how to create a program. Turbo C++ command line compilation syntax is as follows:

```
tcc filename.cpp
```

This will compile and link and create filename.exe which is ready for execution.

Transforming your source file into an executable program requires two steps: First, you must compile the source file into an object file (which has a .obj extension). This contains machine language instruction that can be executed by the computer. The programmer may have divided the program into several source files. Each of these source files is then compiled into separate object file and then these object files must be linked together. The linking step is necessary, because it combines the object files into a single executable program. Figure 1.9 shows the screenshot of a compilation done on a C++ source code named DJIOTEST.CPP using Turbo C++ compiler.

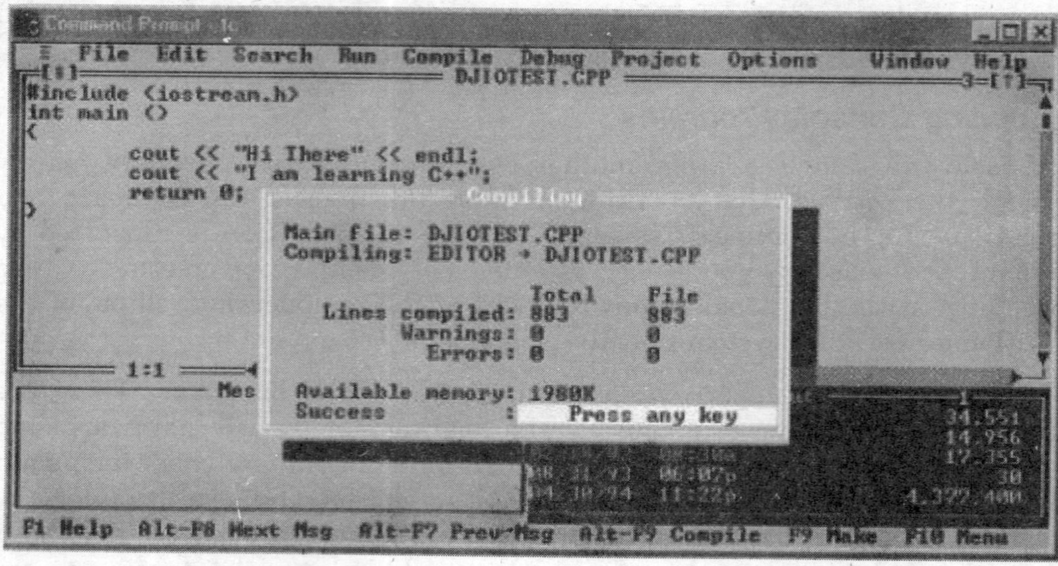

Figure 1.9 Successful compilation using Turbo C++.

The output of the program (after successful execution) is shown in Figure 1.10.

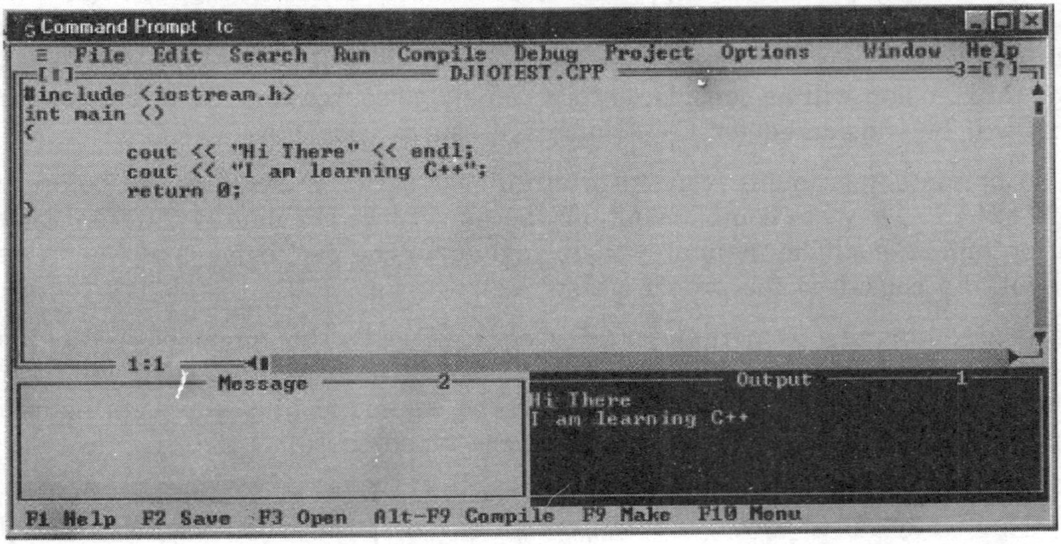

Figure 1.10 Output of the program in Turbo C++.

Next, let's study an example of a compilation from command line using Microsoft Visual C++.

Compiling from Command Line with Microsoft Visual C++

Visual C++ has an integrated development environment. It also supports the compilation of programs without the use of the integrated development environment, rather simply from the command line. First of all, we need that some system environment variables such as %INCLUDE% and %LIB% be suitably defined. These define the directories where the include and library files are. It is also recommended to add the directories where the executable file that we need to compile are, to the path.

During the initial installation of Visual C++ a BAT file called VCVARS32.BAT would have been automatically created defining all these environment variables. This BAT file is located at the subdirectory BIN that remains in the directory where Visual C++ has been installed. If the environment variables are not set automatically, VCVARS32.BAT may have to be executed manually.

The Command Line (CL) Compiler

There is a utility called CL.EXE to compile programs from the command line. It's usage is as follows:

```
CL option(s) file(s) @command_file /link link_options
```

Here, the only parameter file which is compulsory is the one which has a list of source code files and libraries that we want to compile together. The different file types will be distinguished according to its extension, e.g. usually for C extension will be considered for C language source code files, and cpp and cxx will be considered for C++ language source code files.

The option(s) parameter can go intermingled between the files, or before or after them. They are compiler options, because there are mainly different types of optimizations. The manual or help related to the particular compiler in use should be consulted for proper usage.

The @command_file parameter is used to specify the name of a file that contains other command line options preceded by an at sign (@). CL will insert the contents of that file at the point of the command line where its name is specified as if the contents of the file were typed there.

Finally /link link options is used to specify options to the linker that are automatically called by CL if the /c option is not specified. It specifies the type of executable file that we want to create, the location of libraries and include files and other linker options like the debugging level. After the source file is successfully compiled and linked, an executable file with some default or desired extension (e.g. .EXE in Windows 95/98/NT, other extensions in other operating systems) is created. The executable file so generated, can now be run or executed to see the desired output displayed on the console or screen.

The first step in the process of building a program is creating source code files with the code statements in header and/or source files. When you invoke the compiler, the preprocessor runs first to create the compiler input. The compiler creates an object file that contains machine code, linker directives, sections, external references, and function and data names generated from the source files. Finally, the linker combines all of the object codes from statically-linked libraries and other object files, resolves the named resources, and creates an executable file. Typically, a makefile coordinates the combination of these elements and tools in creating the executable file.

An example of a typical build process can be seen in Figure 1.11.

GETTING FAMILIAR WITH THE OOP TERMS

Due to the youth of the paradigm, the terminology has not yet been standardized. However, we need to have an understanding of some of the commonly used terminology used in this field.

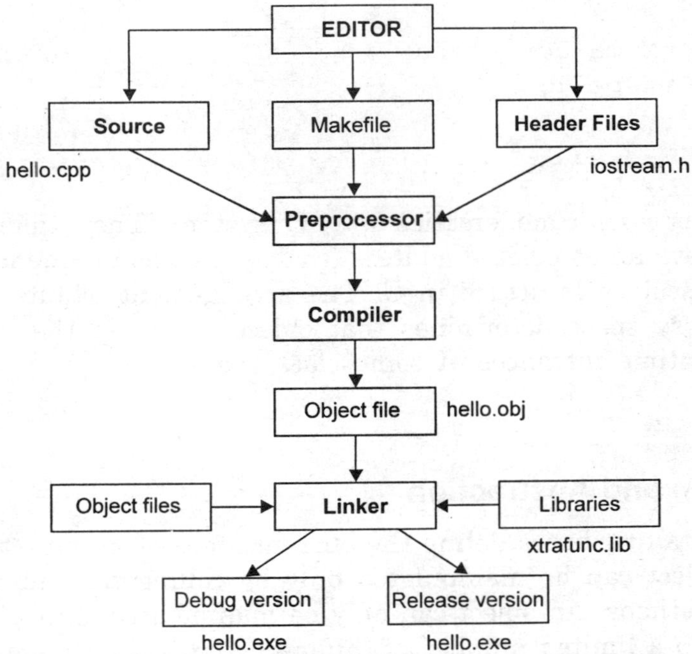

Figure 1.11 An example of a typical build process.

Class and Object

A class is a generalization of a C structure. It is a construct for implementing a user-defined type. Once defined, such types may be conveniently used as the languages primitive types. The instances of a class are called objects. A class specifies the representation of objects and a set of operations that are applicable to such objects. We have already discussed two important philosophies of OOP—data hiding and data abstraction. Ideally, a class is an implementation of an abstract data type. This implies that the implementation details of the class are private to the class. The public interface of a class comprises of two categories of operations. The first category consists of accessor functions that return meaningful abstractions about the object's state. The second category consists of transformer functions that move an object from one valid state to another. Now, for an example:

Example 1.5:

```
class Person
{
   private:
      char * name;
      short age;
```

```
   public:
      void SetName(const char *);
      short GetAge();
      .........
};
```

Objects are basic runtime entities in OO system. They take up space in memory and have an associated address (that is used as unique identifiers) like a record in Pascal or structure in C. The arrangement of bits in an object's allocated memory space determines that object's state at the given moment. Objects are runtime instances of some class, e.g.

```
   Person  p1, p2;
```

Encapsulation and Abstraction

The object's data attributes define the current state of an object. The current state of the object can be manipulated only by calling the publicly accessible interfaces or methods. An object can only be manipulated through an interface that responds to a limited number of different kinds of messages or calling of methods. The internal structure of objects is hidden from the client. There remain some methods, which provide an interface between the service provider object and other service taker objects. The way of packaging an object's data members within the protective custody of its function members or methods is called *data encapsulation*. With encapsulated data, the components of an object should not be accessible using the dot notation as is possible in C structs. For example, in C, if `Person` is declared as a structure type, and `p1, p2` are instances of the structure type, we can access the members of the structure through dot notation like `p1.name`, `p1.age` or `p2.name` and `p2.age`, such as in Example 1.6.

EXAMPLE 1.6:

```
typedef struct
{
   char * name;
   short age;
} Person;
Person p1, p2;
```

Encapsulation of data within objects offer several advantages, two of which are as follows:

Modularity. If data is encapsulated within objects and objects can be manipulated only by a few public interfaces available, then keeping the same interface, if one changes the implementation of a class of objects, then the users or clients of the objects remain unaffected. As such, the client programs do not need to be changed because of change in implementation of the objects they use. This helps to create modular programs.

Information hiding. Objects communicate with each other through available public interfaces. An object can maintain private information and methods that can be changed at any time without affecting the other objects that depend on it. One doesn't need to understand the working of a TV circuitry while viewing a particular program on his/her TV set.

Data abstraction is a way of representation of abstract data types to expose the interface, not the implementation, where data is hidden inside the type by exposing the operations applicable.

Polymorphism

It means the ability to take more than one form. In OOP, this means being able to invoke different kinds of functionalities using the same interface. Traditionally, parametric polymorphism has been achieved either through loopholes in type checking or by the use of macro processors. C allows the definition of polymorphic functions simply by not checking that types match the function calls; it is upto the programmer to ensure he or she is doing something sensible.

The function ***printf*** accepts one or more arguments of one type, with types encoded as a string which is passed as the first argument. In OO paradigm, a polymorphic reference is the one that can refer to more than one class of object over time. The static type of a reference remains the same (as determined from the declaration at compile time), but it's dynamic type may change during the program execution. The sending of same message (a function call with a fixed interface) results in the execution of different bodies of code depending on the dynamic type of the reference (receiving object). Thus, polymorphism allows generic code to be reused, since it performs the same task on different types of objects.

Inheritance

A natural organization of classes form a class hierarchy in terms of either tree or network. There is always a top node in a hierarchy. The organization has a tremendous effect on how the classes may be used by clients. Inheritance gives a relation between classes that allows for the definition and implementation of one class to be based on that of other existing classes. The derived class inherits attributes from the base classes. Both the internal structure as well as the interface may be inherited.

Figure 1.12 shows that class Y is inherited from class X. Class X is called the base or super class and class Y is called sub or derived class. It is because of its inheritance property, that class Y derives the properties, attributes and behaviours of that of class X, and, in addition, class Y may have incremental part in terms of properties, attributes and behaviours. We say that, Y IS_A X, i.e. Y is a specialization of X. The mapping from the members of X to the derived members of Y is defined by the rules of the language in conjunction with the code written for class Y. The mapping may be much richer than identity. In general, an attribute of class X may be renamed, re-implemented, replicated, nullified, have its visibility changed, or undergo other kinds of transformation as it is mapped from class X to class Y. A disciplined use of the transformation is a key towards engineering robust software. If inheritance is to be used as the IS-A relation then the transformation must be severely restricted.

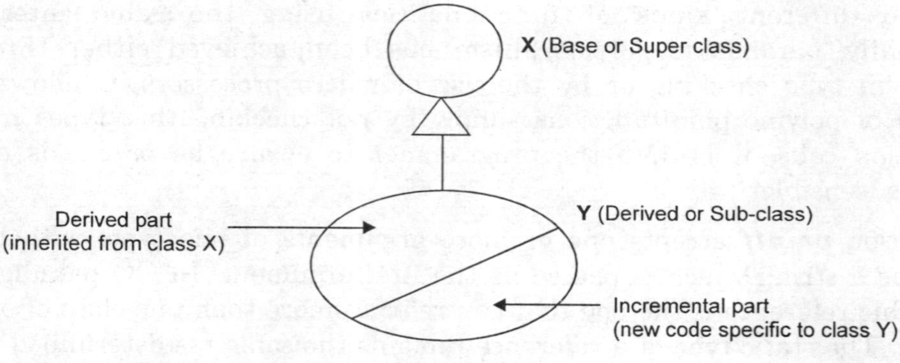

Figure 1.12 Inheritance.

Static and Dynamic Binding

The binding of a function call with the code to be executed is fixed at compile time in programming languages with static binding (e.g. C). Dynamic binding means that the code associated with a given function call is not known until the moment of the call at runtime. Figure 1.13 shows that class Y is inherited from class X and both the classes have member functions named f() and when an instance of X class called x is assigned to an instance of class Y (which is inherited from class X), the function call f() for the object x dynamically binds to the current dynamic type of the object. Thus, the function call x.f() behaves differently at runtime, depending on the type for which it is applicable.

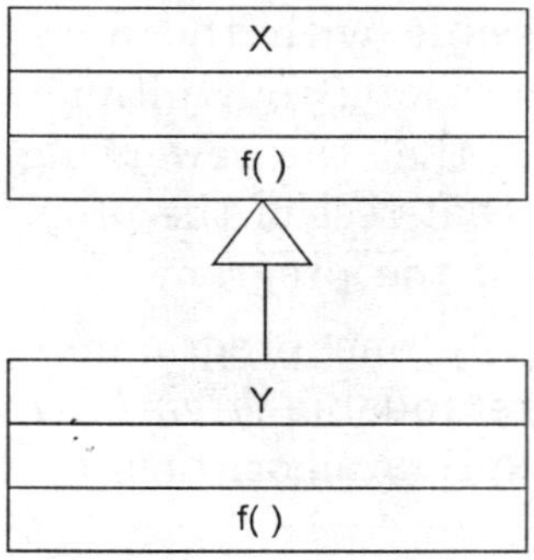

Y is inherited from X, both classes have member function named f( )

```
X x;
Y y;
x . f( );        // calls X's f
x = y;
x . f( );        // calls Y's f
```

Figure 1.13 Static and dynamic binding.

Polymorphism does not allow objects to change their types during the lifetime of a program (dynamic typing), but rather it allows a variable to refer to objects of various types (dynamic binding). Figure 1.14 shows static and dynamic binding as well as static and dynamic typing as supported in different programming languages. Thus, C supports static typing as well as static binding, whereas C++ supports dynamic binding but static typing. Smalltalk supports both dynamic typing as well as dynamic binding.

	BINDING	
Typing	**Static**	**Dynamic**
Static	C, Pascal	C++, Java
Dynamic	?	Smalltalk

Figure 1.14 Static and dynamic binding/typing in programming languages.

SUMMARY

The key concepts introduced in this chapter are as follows:

- Development of software essentially requires knowledge of computer programming. The underlying control of program comes from algorithm, which drives the execution sequence.

- Changes are always possible with the advent of new hardware and software technologies. Therefore, our ultimate goal should be to devise some flexible strategies so that the reworking areas are isolated and in narrowed down parts, so that rest of the program remains unaffected by the changes in one part of the program.
- Computer understands only one programming language—the *machine language*. Human understandable *high-level programming languages* have been invented to express algorithms so that they become easy to read, write and modify.
- The translation process from high-level language to machine language is called compilation and the program performing the compilation job is called the *compiler*. It checks the entire user-written program (known as source program or source code) and if error-free, produces a complete program in machine language (known as object program). The *interpreter* on the other hand translates one statement at a time and, if error-free, executes the instruction.
- On successful linking, the linker generates an executable machine language format code. To run a program, the underlying operating system must load the executable file from the disk into main memory.
- Every high-level programming language has a paradigm that guides in problem-solving within a framework to derive solutions. Imperative or procedural programming paradigm is based on the idea of "First do this and next do that", i.e. a step-by-step execution model. Functional programming paradigm is based on the idea of evaluating an expression and then using the resulting value for something else. This is based on mathematical model of function composition. Logic programming paradigm is based on the idea of answering a question through search for solution from a knowledgebase. This is based on axioms, inference rules, and queries. In procedural paradigm we have a large single store where all procedures work, whereas in Object-Oriented (OO) paradigm, procedures operate on abstract values called objects rather than on stored representations.
- Data and procedures or functions are loosely coupled in procedural paradigm whereas in OO paradigm, data and functions are tightly coupled to constitute objects.
- OO paradigm has two important philosophies: *data hiding* and *data abstraction*. Data hiding philosophy involves partitioning of the program so that data is hidden in modules such that users of the service do not know the underlying implementation. Data abstraction is a way of representation of abstract data types to expose the interface, not the implementation, where data is hidden inside the type and the operations

applicable are exposed. Data abstraction philosophy requires deciding the types needed to provide full set of operations for each type so that a new type of data, if defined, can be used similar to built-in type of data, with all sorts of permissible operations.

- A C++ program is a collection of one or more *files*. A program file consists of a sequence of declarations. Declarations include function definitions, which are a series of executable statements with appropriate definition of variables and initialiser statements. A program file can have comments, functions and preprocessor directives.
- A class is an implementation of an abstract data type. Once defined, such types may be conveniently used similar to the languages of primitive types. Objects are runtime instances of some class.
- The way of packaging an object's data members within the protective custody of its function members or methods is called *data encapsulation*.
- Polymorphism means the ability to take more than one form. In OOP, this means being able to invoke different kinds of functionalities using the same interface.
- Inheritance gives a relation between classes that allow for the definition and implementation of one class to be based on that of other existing classes.
- The binding of a function call with the code to be executed is fixed at compile time in programming languages with static binding (e.g. C). Dynamic binding means the code associated with a given function call is not known until the moment of the call at runtime. C supports static typing as well as static binding, whereas C++ supports static typing but dynamic binding.

REVIEW QUESTIONS

1. What is the difference between a compiler and an interpreter?
2. What are the different programming paradigms?
3. What is the difference between procedural programming paradigm and OOP paradigm?
4. What are tokens? Cite examples.
5. What do you mean by whitespaces? Is comment considered to be a whitespace?
6. Can comments be nested, i.e. can you have a comment within a comment? Write a program with a nested comment and see if you can compile it. Try with line comments as well as block comments.

7. What do you mean by compilation and linking?

8. Write a C++ program to read two integers as input and print their sum as output with proper messages before reading and during printing to aid the user.

9. What do you mean by preprocessor and preprocessor directive?

10. Write a program to print any message on screen.

11. If the escape sequence \n is not used, then will the output be different?

12. What will be the output of the following program:

```
// test program in C++
#include <iostream.h>
int main ()
{
    cout << " This is the first line ";
    cout << "\n This is the second line ";
    return 0;
}
```

13. In the context of OOP, define the following terms:

- Encapsulation and Abstraction
- Class and Object
- Polymorphism
- Base and Derived class
- Static and Dynamic binding

2 Declarations and Expressions

When I use a word it means just what I choose it mean—neither more nor less.
—Humpty Dumpty

LEARNING OBJECTIVES

The objective of this chapter is to acquaint you with:

- Concept of data type associated with a data
- Fundamental data types and their qualifiers
- Declaring variables, constants and enumerated constants
- Several variables, constants and enumerated constants
- Several types of operators used in expressions
- Operator precedence and associativity

INTRODUCTION

Every data is associated with a data type. Data type helps data to work with related types. Depending on data type, required space is allocated for the data to occupy memory. A data must be associated with a type to tell the computer how much space is required to store that data in memory. The exact size of data corresponding to a data type varies from machine to machine. In C, data can be converted easily from one type to any other type. As such, C is called a weakly typed language. The ability to convert from one type to another easily makes C a very flexible language. Many programmers use these flexible features of C to write powerful programs. C++, which is built on the basis of C, has attempted to be strongly typed. This means type checking in C++ is relatively strict. Type conversions can be done within a permissible range. However, since C++ supports all the features of C, type checking in it is not very strong.

Data types are of two kinds: (i) fundamental or built-in and (ii) derived.

Fundamental Data Types

There are many basic or fundamental data types built-ins in C language. C++ being a superset of C, has also these basic data types available. The data types can be classified as *integer* data types and *floating-point* data types. The basic data types available are as follows:

- Five integer data types : ***char***, ***int***, ***short***, ***long*** and ***bool***.
- Three floating point data types: ***float***, ***double*** and ***long double***.

In a 16-bit environment, ***short*** is identical to ***int***, whereas, in 32-bit environment, ***long*** is identical to ***int***. Thus, it varies from machine to machine and implementation to implementation.

Every identifier in C must be explicitly declared and associated with a data type in order to give a cue to the computer that how much space should be reserved in memory to store that identifier. The ***char*** data type is meant for storing single character, e.g. 'a', 'A'. Each character has a corresponding ASCII[1] value, which usually can be stored in single byte of memory. You can just specify an identifier as ***char***, as in the following statement:

```
char c;
```

This statement declares c as a signed character. This means that the programmer intends to store a signed character value, i.e. c may be either a positive or a negative numeric value corresponding to a character. For example, the ASCII value of A is 65, thus, if we initialize

```
c = 65;
```

or

```
c = 'A'
```

both mean the same thing. In fact, c = 'A' is more meaningful to express the programmer's intention.

---

[1] ASCII stands for American Standard Code for Information Interchange. Computers use ASCII code to represent letters with 0s and 1s. For example, in ASCII code the capital letter A is always represented by the number 65, i.e. 1000001, in binary. The standard ASCII code defines $128(=2^7)$ character codes (from 0 to 127), of which, the first 32 are control codes (non-printable), and the other 96 are representable characters.

However, internally, c = 'A' is translated to store the ASCII value of the character 'A' in c, i.e. 65. If we assume that a character occupies a single byte of memory, then a single byte can store -2^7 to $+(2^7 - 1)$, i.e. -128 to $+ 127$(2^8 or 256 distinct values), if it stores signed values. If unsigned values are stored, then this can have one of 2^8 or 256 distinct values ranging from 0 to $(2^8 - 1)$, i.e. 0 to +255. Single byte storage for characters can be expected for languages like English, French and so on, where a number of distinct alphabets (lower and upper cases) and other symbols like comma (,), semicolon (;) etc. are within the permissible range of a single byte storage. However, languages like Japanese and Chinese have much more character sets for which single byte storage is not sufficient. For these two byte storage is required to store a single character. As such, while programming with data corresponding to a data type, the program should not assume the storage criteria of the data type. This is because, the storage of a character varies from language to language (English character requires single byte storage, Japanese character requires double byte storage). And also, since the size of data varies from machine to machine, in order to write portable programs, i.e. the ability to run the program on different machines and in different human languages (like English, French etc.), the programmer should prefer to write code using some high-level abstraction in mind without being bogged down by the actual storage needed.

Other basic data types available are:

int This refers to Integer. Its storage size depends on the wordsize of the machine. For signed integers on 16-bit machine, this can store -2^{15} to $+(2^{15} - 1)$, i.e. -32768 to $+32767$ (2^{16} or 65536 distinct values), and on a 32-bit machine, this can store -2^{31} to $+(2^{31} - 1)$, i.e. -2147483648 to $+2147483647$ (2^{32} or 4294967296 distinct values). For unsigned integers, the range will be between 16-bit machine, 0 to $(2^{16} - 1)$, i.e. 0 to $+65535$ (2^{16} or 65536 distinct values).

float This means floating point number. This usually requires 4 bytes of storage. The actual size varies from machine to machine.

double This is also called double precision floating point number. This usually requires 8 bytes of storage. The actual size varies from machine to machine.

bool This is the short form for boolean value. This is a recently added data type in the ANSI-C++ standards. As such, every compiler doesn't support this. Its value can be either *true* or *false*.

In addition to these fundamental data types, there also exist the pointers and the ***void*** parameter type specification.

Table 2.1 shows a summarized range of values usually permitted for a set of fundamental data types on a 32-bit machine. However, the range of values permitted is actual system or implementation dependent. The standard header file <limits.h> specifies the largest and smallest values for each of the fundamental types for a particular implementation.

Table 2.1

Basic C++ Variable Types

Type	*Other Name*	*Numerical Range of Values*		*Bytes of*
		Low	High	*Memory*
char	signed char	–128(–255 for double byte character)	+127(+255 for double byte character)	usually 1 (or 2)
int	signed int	–2,147,483,648	+2,147,483,647	4
enum	—	same as int	same as int	same as int
float	—	-3.4×10^{-38} (7 digits).	$+3.4 \times 10^{+38}$ (7 digits)	4
double	—	-1.7×10^{-308} (15 digits)	$+1.7 \times 10^{+308}$ (15 digits)	8
long double	—	-1.2×10^{-4932} (19 digits)	$+1.2 \times 10^{+4932}$ (19 digits)	10

Qualifiers to Data Types

In addition to type specifiers for data, there are some further qualifications available in C++ language. They are: ***unsigned***, ***signed***, ***short*** and ***long***.

In some cases, the programmer may decide to declare an identifier to be unsigned. This means on a 16-bit machine, an unsigned integer can take up 0 to $(2^{16} - 1)$, i.e. 0 to +65535 (2^{16} or 65536 distinct values). Unless otherwise specified, by default, any identifier would be represented as signed. Thus, the statement

```
char c;
```

declares c as a signed character. This means that the programmer intends to store a signed character value, i.e. c may be either a positive or a negative numeric value corresponding to a character.

And the statement

```
unsigned char c;
```

declares c as an unsigned character. This means that the programmer intends to store an unsigned character value, c, may be either 0 or a positive numeric value corresponding to a character.

The qualifiers ***short*** and ***long*** apply for integer types. The type specifier ***int*** is optional here. For example the following statement:

```
short int count;
```

or simply

```
short count;
```

This specifies that count is a signed short integer. The short ***int*** declaration is used in situations where space utilization is known to be small. For a 32-bit machine, the length of a short integer would be 16-bits, integer would be 32-bits and long would be 32-bits. This means that on a 32-bit machine, a signed short integer can store -2^{15} to $+(2^{15} - 1)$, i.e. −32768 to +32767 (2^{16} or 65536 distinct values), an integer as well as a long integer can store -2^{31} to $+(2^{31} - 1)$, i.e. −2147483648 to +2147483647 (2^{32} or 4294967296 distinct values). For a 32-bit machine, integer and long integer occupy same space. However, for older 16-bit systems, the length of a short integer would be 16-bits, and long would be 32-bits. In the present days, when main memory is no longer an expensive resource, the need to optimize memory utilization has probably lost its significance to some extent.

The example of unsigned ***short int*** type specifier is as follows:

```
unsigned short int count;
```

or simply

```
unsigned short count;
```

On a 32-bit machine, the unsigned short integer can store 0 to $+(2^{16} - 1)$, i.e. 0 to +65535 (2^{16} or 65536 distinct values), and an integer as well as a long integer can store 0 to + $(2^{32} - 1)$, i.e. 0 to +4294967295 (2^{32} or 4294967296 distinct values). The example of signed long ***int*** type specifier is as follows:

```
long int count;
```

or simply

```
long count;
```

The example of unsigned long int type specifier is as follows:

```
unsigned long int count;
```

or simply

```
unsigned long count;
```

When a long integer is assigned a value, the letter L must be written immediately after the rightmost digit. For example,

```
long int count = 34567L;
```

Table 2.2 shows a summarized range of additional qualifiers for a set of fundamental data types on a 32-bit machine.

Table 2.2

Basic C++ Variable Types

Type	*Other Name*	*Numerical Range of Values*		*Bytes of*
		Low	*High*	*Memory*
unsigned char	—	0	255 (+511 for double byte character)	usually 1 (or 2)
unsigned int	—	0	+4,294,967,295	4
enum	—	same as int	same as int	same as int
short	signed short int	–32,768	+32,767	2
unsigned short	—	0	+65,535	2
long	signed long int	–2,147,483,648	+2,147,483,647	4
unsigned long	—	0	+4,294,967,295	4

Remember that integer type ***int*** extracts a performance penalty compared with type ***start***. It is slower in arithmetic operations, and occupies more memory space making your program size longer. Similarly, the floating point types double and long double are slower and longer than type float. You should always try to use the smallest variable type that stores the values you are using in your program.

Variables

All variables must be declared before they are used or accessed. Declarations provide sizes and data types to the compiler, so that it can generate appropriate code. Variables are identifiers, which need to be stored in some part of memory. More precisely, variables need storage locations. A variable can be defined with an associated data type to store a determined value in some portion of the memory. Variables must be used in a manner consistent with their associated data type. Each variable needs an identifier that distinguishes it from the others. The data type specifier (like int, short, float, ...) need to be followed by a valid variable identifier name optionally, with initialization declarations. For example,

```
int i = 3;
```

declares an integer variable called i and initializes the variable i with a value of 3. Since it is a variable, the value of i can be changed later. If we simply declare a variable without the initialization like the following:

```
int i;
```

it simply declares an integer variable called i without any initial value assigned to it, i.e. its value is undetermined by default at the time of defining the variable.

In addition you can initialize a variable at the time of defining the variable as:

```
type identifier = initial_value;
int i = 3;
```

C++ has another way (not available in C) of initializing variables by enclosing the initial value between parenthesis () as:

```
type identifier (initial_value);
int i(3);
```

Once declared, variables can be used within the rest of their scope in the program.

Several variables can be declared of the same type by declaring all of them in the same line, separating the identifiers with commas. For example:

```
int i, j;
```

This declares two variables of type integer (i and j), and is equivalent to defining them separately as:

```
int i;

int j;
```

To change an integer type (by default signed) to an unsigned integer type, precede the data type keyword with the keyword unsigned. For example, an unsigned variable of type ***char*** would be defined as:

```
unsigned char uchr;
```

Let us create a Program (Code 2.1).

Program Source Code 2.1

```
// Program 2.1
#include<iostream.h>
int main()
{
   /* Range of values on a 32-bit Windows NT based
      machine usually, for signed integer: range
      -2,147,483,648 to +2,147,483,647,
      unsigned integer : range 0 to +4,294,967,295 */
 int SignedInt = 2000000000;
 unsigned int UnsignedInt = 2000000000;

 int SignedResult;
 unsigned int UnsignedResult;

 // calculation result exceeds range of
 // permitted values
 SignedResult = (SignedInt * 2 ) / 3;

 // calculation result is within
 // permissible range
 UnsignedResult = (UnsignedInt * 2 ) / 3;

 cout << "Demonstrates wrong result caused by "
      << "exceeding range \n";
 cout << "Signed Integer Calculation giving "
      << "result as : \n(";
 cout << SignedInt << " * 2) / 3 = "
      << SignedResult << endl << endl;
 cout << "Demonstrates correct result caused by "
      << "permissible range \n";
 cout << "Unsigned Integer Calculation giving "
      << "result as : \n(";
 cout << UnsignedInt << " * 2 ) / 3 = "
      << UnsignedResult << endl;

 return 0;
}
```

Output 2.1

```
Demonstrates wrong result caused by exceeding range
Signed Integer Calculation giving result as :
(2000000000 * 2) / 3 = -98322432

Demonstrates correct result caused by permissible range
Unsigned Integer Calculation giving result as :
(2000000000 * 2 ) / 3 = 1333333333
```

Here, a numerical calculation exceeds the range of permissible values resulting in wrong result, at the same time, keeping result within permissible range of values gives correct result.

Constants

We can define some name for a constant that can be used in programs without declaring variables. This can be done simply by using the #define *preprocessor directive*[2]. The format is as follows:

```
#define identifier value
```

This defines a value for the identifier and is not associated to any data type, say,

```
#define PI 3.14159
#define NEWLINE '\n'
#define MAX 100
```

These define three new constants without data type associations. After their declarations they can be used, for example, as

```
area = 2 * PI * radius;  // implies area = 2 * 3.14159 * radius;
cout << NEWLINE;  // implies cout << '\n';
```

The preprocessor replaces all occurrences of the defined constants (defined through preprocessor directive #define), textually, by the constants to which they have been defined. For this reason, #define constants are considered macro constants. #define directive causes preprocessors to replace subsequent instances of the identifier with the given sequence of tokens. White space surrounding the replacement token sequence is discarded. While defining preprocessor directive through #define, it assumes the whole line as the directive and does not require a semicolon (;) or comment at the end of it. If one includes a semicolon character (;) or a comment at the end, it will also be added when the preprocessor will substitute any occurrence of the defined constant in the body of the program. For example, if one defines as:

```
#define PI 3.14159;
```

then the statement

```
area = 2 * PI * radius;
```

translates to:

```
area = 2 * 3.14159; * radius;
```

---

[2]A preprocessor directive starts with # in line as the first character other than white space. The result of preprocessing is a series of tokens which goes as input to the compilation phase.

breaking a single statement into two, which may not be intended. Similarly, if one puts a comment after, like,

```
#define PI 3.14159 ; // value of PI
```

then the statement

```
area = 2 * PI * radius;
```

translates to :

```
area = 2 * 3.14159 ; // value of PI * radius;
```

making it have an unintended interpretation of the statement as area = 2 * 3.14159 and nothing else. Also, since there is no data type association with a #defined constant, and the value of the #defined constant is textually replaced in program, unintended data type associations may crop in.

Declared Constants

Constants can be declared with ***const*** prefix with a specific data type associated with a variable. A ***const*** variable can only be initialized; it cannot be assigned a new value thereafter. That means the compiler will not allow to intentionally or unintentionally change the value of the ***const*** variable as it has been declared as a constant. The declaration looks like:

```
const data type variable-name = initialization-value;
```

For example,

```
const float PI = 3.14159;
const char NEWLINE = '\n';
const int MAX = 100;
```

These define three new constants with proper data type associations. After their definitions, they can be used, for example, as

```
area = 2 * PI * radius; // implies area = 2 * 3.14159 * radius;
cout << NEWLINE;        // implies cout << '\n';
```

Unlike #defined constant, if one includes a semicolon character (;) or a comment at the end of constant variable declaration, it will not be added, since this is not a textual substitution. For example, say, we declare the following:

```
const float PI = 3.14159; // value of PI
```

then the statement

```
area = 2 * PI * radius;
```

translates to:

```
area = 2 * 3.14159 * radius;
```

making it to have an intended interpretation of the statement.

In case the data type is not specified with a constant variable, the compiler assumes that it is type ***int***. For example,

```
const MAX = 100;
```

declares MAX as a constant integer with a value of 100.

Enumerated Constants

An enumeration data type represents a set of values that can be declared. C++ allows user-defined variable types, called ***enum*** (from enumerated) types. For example,

```
enum Boolean {FALSE, TRUE};
```

declares Boolean as an enumerated type which can take values from FALSE(=0) or TRUE(=1). The usage can be as follows:

```
enum Boolean flag;
```

The variables flag can only be assigned, one of the values FALSE or TRUE and no others. The two enumerators have the consecutive integer values 0 (for FALSE), through 1 (for TRUE), so that if one assigns the value TRUE to flag, it will be set to be 1. Although enumerated values are stored as integer constants, enum variables are of distinct type to define integer constants.

In an enumerated list, any enumerator may be specified to an integer value, different from the constant associated with it by default. The enumerator to its right gets value 1 greater, and further down the list, each enumerator becomes 1 more than the preceding. For example,

```
enum
{
        north, east = 3, south, west
}       direction;
```

In this declaration, north has the value 0, while east, south and west are 3, 4 and 5, respectively.

Operators and Expressions

Expressions are sequences of operators, operands in the form of constants and variables, and punctuators, which specify a computation as per the rules of the underlying language. Expressions are evaluated based on the operators they contain and the context in which they are used. Operators are reserved words and signs forming a basis for C++ language. Different categories of operators are discussed in the following subsections. In general, there are three categories of operators: arithmetic operators, comparison or relational operators and logical operators.

Relational Operators

The relational operators compare two operands and determine the validity of a relationship. If the relationship, which is to be validated by the operator, is true, the value of the result is 1 and 0 otherwise. The result is not an *lvalue*. By *lvalue* we mean an expression that represents a data object that can be both examined and altered. Both operands of the relational operator must have arithmetic types or be pointers to the same type. The result has type ***int***. Relational operators are as follows:

```
> < >= <= == !=
```

Table 2.3 lists the relational operators stating their usage.

Table 2.3

Operator	*Usage*
<	Checks whether the value of the first operand is less than the value of the second operand.
>	Checks whether the value of the first operand is greater than the value of the second operand.
<=	Checks whether the value of the first operand is less than or equal to the value of the second operand.
>=	Checks whether the value of the first operand is greater than or equal to the value of the second operand.
==	Checks whether the value of the first operand is equal to the value of the second operand.
!=	Checks whether the value of the first operand is not equal to the value of the second operand.

The equality operators (== and !=) have a lower precedence than the other relational operators (<, >, <= and >=). All the relational operators of same precedence have left-to-right associativity. For example, the expression a > b > c is interpreted as the expression (a > b) > c, i.e. if the value of a is greater than the value of b, the first relationship is true and yields the value 1. This value is then compared with the value of c.

Assignation Operator

The assignation operator (= or equality sign) assigns a value to a variable, e.g.

```
a = 10;
```

assigns the integer value 10 to integer variable a. The part at the left of the = operator is termed as *lvalue* (left value) and the right one as *rvalue* (right value). *lvalue* should usually be a variable, whereas right side value can be any constant, variable, result of operation or any combination of such. The left operand in all assignment expressions must be a modifiable *lvalue*. That means the *lvalue* must not be a constant, e.g. a = b, cannot be done if a is declared as ***const int***. In an assignation operation evaluation always takes place from right (*rvalue*) to left (*lvalue*), i.e. right-to-left associativity. The statement `a = b;` assigns to the variable a value (*lvalue*) that the variable b (*rvalue*) contains, irrespective of any previous value which was stored in it.

The result of an assignment expression is an *lvalue* in C++ (unlike C, where it is not). For example, the following expression

```
a = 20 + (b = 10);
```

is equivalent to

```
b = 10;
```

and then

```
a = 20 + b;
```

This implies that the first 10 is assigned to b and then a is assigned the value of 20 plus the result of the previous assignation of b (i.e. 10), thus a gets the value of 30. Thus, we can also write statements like

```
a = b = c = 10;
```

This assigns integer value 10 to each of the three variables a, b and c.

Assignment differs from initialization of a variable. When we declare a variable first time (not yet used) with its associated data type and one initialization value like `int a = 10;` then the variable a is declared as an integer variable with an initial value of 10. Here, although, we have used the = (equality) sign, this is not an assignment for the variable a, rather, this is an initialization of the variable a. After a variable is defined and initialized like this, then subsequent use of = (equality) sign for the variable is termed as assignment, like `a = 10;`

It should also be noted that if we assign `b` to `a` (by writing a = b), then at the time of assignment, a takes the current value of b, and subsequent changes in value of b will have no effect on the value of a. For example, let us create a Program Code as follows (2.2):

Program Source Code 2.2

```
// Program 2.2
#include <iostream.h>
int main ()
{
   int a = 10;
   int b = 5;
   cout << "a = " << a <<", b = " << b << endl;
   a = b;
   cout << "a = " << a << ", b = " << b << endl;
   b = 7;
   cout << "a = " << a << ", b = " << b << endl;
   return 0;
}
```

Output 2.2

```
a = 10, b = 5
a = 5, b = 5
a = 5, b = 7
```

Arithmetic Operators

The five arithmetical operations supported by the C++ language are:

- \+ addition
- – subtraction
- * multiplication
- / division
- % modulus

Addition (+), subtraction (–), multiplication (*) and division (/) operations are as expected as conventional mathematical operators. +, – and * can be used as unary as well as binary operators. The unary plus operator (+) and minus operator (–) maintain the positive or negative value of the operand, which can have any arithmetic type. The result is not an *lvalue*.

Addition (+), subtraction (–), multiplication (*) and division (/) operations can be used as binary mathematical operators which operate on two operands. For example, the multiplication operator (*) yields the product of its two operands. The operands must have an arithmetic type (integer, float, double, etc.). The result is not an *lvalue*. That means the result cannot be used on left hand side of an assignment operator. In an arithmetic expression, if all data correspond to same data type, then there will be no type conversions taking place. If mixed data types are used, then the resultant expression type depends on the first operand or *lvalue* of an expression. For example, if one uses assignment operator to assign a floating point number to an integer like:

```
int a;
a = 3.24;
```

will store the integer value 3 in a after type conversion from floating point value 3.24 to integer value 3.

The division operator (/) yields the quotient of its operands. The two operands must have an arithmetic type. The result is not an *lvalue*. For integer divisions if both operands are positive integers and the division operation produces a remainder, then the integer quotient is stored in the result. For example,

```
int a;
a = 7/2;
```

will store the integer value 3 (integer quotient when 7 is divided by 2) whereas,

```
float a;
a = 7.0/2.0;
```

will store the floating point value 3.5 (floating point quotient when 7 is divided by 2).

All these operators are binary operators, that means they require two operands. For example, 2 * 3 implies the product of 2 and 3, where 2 and 3 are the two operands.

The modulus operator (%) yields the remainder from the division of the first operand by the second operand. For example, the expression 7 % 2 yields 1 . The result is not an *lvalue*. Both operands must have an integral type. If the second operand evaluates to 0 , the result is undefined. The sign of the remainder is the same as the sign of the quotient. If either operand has a negative value, and a, b are integers, the result is such that the following expression always yields back the value of a provided b is not 0 and a/b is representable:

```
(a/b)* b + a % b
```

will yield a back, to be precise, if before the expression a had the value of 7 and b had the value of 2, then (a/b) will yield 3 which when multiplied with b or 2 will yield 6, which when added to (a % b) or (7 % 2) or 1 will yield 7 which was the original value of a.

Increment and Decrement Operator

The unary increment operator (++) adds 1 to the value of the operand. The operand receives the result of the increment operation. The operand must be a modifiable *lvalue* of arithmetic or pointer type. The increment operator ++ can be put before or after the operand. If it appears before the operand (pre-increment mode), the operand is incremented first, and then the incremented value is used in the expression. If ++ appears after the operand (post-increment mode), then the value of the operand is used in the expression first and then the operand is incremented. Following is a Program (Code 2.3):

Program Source Code 2.3

```
// Program 2.3
#include <iostream.h>
int main ()
{
    int a = 10;
    int b = 5;
    int c = 15;
    cout << "a =" << a << ", b =" << b << ", c =" << c << endl;
    c = (++a) + (b++);
    cout << "a =" << a << ", b =" << b << ", c=" << c << endl;
    return 0;
}
```

Output 2.3

```
a = 10, b = 5, c = 15
a = 11, b = 6, c = 16
```

Here, c = (++a) + (b++); is equivalent to the following three expressions:

`a = a + 1;` // in pre-increment mode, a is incremented before use, thus a // becomes 10 + 1 = 11

`c = a + b;` // in post-increment mode, b is incremented after use, thus c // becomes a + b, i.e. 16

`b = b + 1;` // b is now incremented, thus b becomes 6

There is a difference between prefix and postfix forms of the increment operator: The result of a C++ post- or pre-increment operator has the same data type as the operand, but pre-increment operator results in a *lvalue* whereas post-increment operator as in Program 2.4 does not. In C language, both are not *lvalue*.

Now, let's see another example:

Program Source Code 2.4

```
// Program 2.4
#include <iostream.h>
int main ()
{
   int a = 10;
   int b = 5;
   int c = 15;
   cout << "a =" << a << ", b =" << b << ", c =" << c << endl;
   ++c = (a++) + (b++);
   cout << "a =" << a << ", b =" << b << ", c =" << c << endl;
  return 0;
}
```

Output 2.4

```
a = 10, b = 5, c = 15
a = 11, b = 6, c = 15
```

Here we have modified Program 2.3 by adding a pre-increment operator for c in line 9 and changing pre-increment of a by post-increment. Thus, both a and b will be incremented, but after they are used in line no. 9. ++c is a *lvalue*, which is allowed to appear on the left hand side of an assignment expression. This expression will increment the value of c first making c = 16, and then c will be used to take the assignment from a + b which is 10 + 5, i.e. 15. If we make use of post-increment of c in line no. 9 as follows:

```
c++ = (a++) + (b++);
```

The compiler does not allow this, since c++ is not an *lvalue*.

As alternates, we may use equivalently, either of the following for incrementing a variable:

```
a ++;
a += 1;
a = a+1;
```

In stand-alone mode, ++a and a++ are same, as they are not used elsewhere.

Similar to increment (++) operator, decrement(––) operator can be used in post as well as pre decrement mode.

Compound Assignment Operators

The compound assignment operators consist of a binary operator and the simple assignment operator (=). They perform the operation of the binary operator on both operands and yield the result of that operation to the left operand. This is how these operators allow to modify the value of a variable with one of the basic operators. Compound assignation operators are as follows:

```
+= -= *= /= %= >>= <<= &= ^= |=
```

For example, `a += b;` is equivalent to the statement: `a = a + b`; and thus, `a += b * c`; is equivalent to `a = a + (b * c)`. These can now be summarized in a tabulated form (Table 2.4).

Table 2.4

Operator	*Example*	*Equivalent Expression*
+=	a += b	a = a + b
–=	a –= b	a = a – b
*=	a *= b	a = a * b
/=	a /= b	a = a / b
%=	a %= b	a = a % b
>>=	a >>= b	a = a >> b
<<=	a <<= b	a = a << b
&=	a &= b	a = a & b
^=	a ^= b	a = a ^ b
|=	a |= b	a = a | b

Bitwise Operators

Bitwise operators (binary) yield a result by applying boolean operation with each bit of its first operand to the corresponding bit of the second operand. A bit is the minimum amount of information storing either value 1 or 0. The result is not an *lvalue*. In case of Bitwise AND (&) operator, if both of the bits are 1, the corresponding bit of the result is 1; otherwise, the result is 0. In case of Bitwise Inclusive OR (|) operator, if both of the bits are 0, the corresponding bit of the result is 0; otherwise, the result is 1. In case of Bitwise Exclusive OR (^) operator, if both bits are 1's or both bits are 0's, the corresponding bit of the result is 0. Otherwise, it sets the corresponding result bit to 1. The bitwise negation operator (~) yields the bitwise complement of the operand. In the binary representation of the result, every bit has the opposite value (i.e. 1 if 0, and 0 if 1) of the same bit in the binary representation of the operand. Other bitwise operators are as follows:

& | ^ << >>

Table 2.5 shows the result of applying a particular bitwise operator on two bits.

Table 2.5

a	*b*	*a&b*	*a|b*	*a^b*	*~a*	*a<<*	*a&b*	*a&b*
0	0	0	0	0	1	0	0	0
0	1	0	1	1	1	0	0	0
1	0	0	1	1	0	0	0	0
1	1	1	1	0	0	1	1	1

The following example shows the values of a, b, and the result of a & b represented as 16-bit binary numbers:

bit pattern of a : 0000000001011100
bit pattern of b : 0000000000101110
bit pattern of a & b : 0000000000001100
bit pattern of a | b : 0000000001111110
bit pattern of a ^ b : 0000000001110010

The bitwise shift operators (<< >>) move the bit values of an integral operand. The left operand specifies the value to shift. The right operand specifies the number of positions that the bits in the value are shifted. The result is not an *lvalue*. Both operands have the same precedence and are left-to-right associative. Left shift operator << indicates the bits are to be shifted to the left and the right shift operator >> indicates the bits are to be shifted to the right. The << or >> operator fills vacated bits with zeros. For example, if variable a has the value 4019, the bit pattern (in 16-bit format) of a is: 0000111110110011, then the expression a <<3 yields: 0111110110011000

Logic Operators

Logic operators are as follows:

! && ||

The logical negation operator (!) yields the value 1 (true) if the operand evaluates to false i.e. 0, and yields the value 0 (false) in case the operand evaluates to true, i.e. a nonzero value. The operand must be of scalar type, but the result of the operation has always type ***int*** and is not an *lvalue*.

The expressions !a and (a == 0) are equivalent.

The expression !(6 <= 4) yields 1 (true) because (6 <= 4) would be 0 (false).

Logic operators && and || correspond with boolean logic operations **AND** and **OR** respectively. The result of them depends on the relation between its two operands. Here's an overview (see Table 2.6).

Table 2.6

First Operand Value (a)	*Second Operand Value (b)*	*Result of a && b*	*Result of a || b*
true	true	true	true
true	false	false	true
false	true	false	true
false	false	false	false

The logical AND operator (&&) yields the value 1 (true) if both operands evaluates to a nonzero value and yields 0 (false) otherwise. The logical OR operator (||) yields the value 1 (true) if either of the operands evaluates to a nonzero value and yields 0 (false) otherwise. Both operands must have a scalar type. The && and || operator evaluates left-to-right of the operands. In case of && operator, If the left operand evaluates to 0, the right operand is not evaluated. In case of || operator, if the left operand evaluates to 1, the right operand is not evaluated. The logical operator (&& or ||) is very different from bitwise operator (& or |). For example, (1 && 2) evaluates to 1, while (1 & 2) evaluates to 0.

Another example follows:

`((7 == 7)&&(2 > 4))` returns false `(`*`true && false`*`)`

`((7 == 7)|| (2 > 4))` returns true `(`*`true || false`*`)`

The usual arithmetic conversions on each operand are performed. The result has type ***int*** and is not an *lvalue*.

Conditional Operator

The conditional operator (?) evaluates a conditional expression that contains a condition (operand 1), an expression to be evaluated if the condition has a nonzero value (operand 2), and an expression to be evaluated if the condition has the value 0 (operand 3). Conditional expressions take the following form:

```
condition? result1 : result2
```

If ***condition*** evaluates to ***true*** the expression yields ***result1***, otherwise, it yields ***result2***. For example, `a > b ? a : b` returns a if a is greater than b, and returns b otherwise. `7 == 6 ? 5 : 6` returns 5 since 7 is not equal to 6.

The following expression determines which variable has the greater value, b or c, and assigns the greater value to the variable a:

```
a = (b > c) ? b : c;
```

Cast Operators

Many operators cause implicit type conversions, called cast operators, which change the data type of a value. If we add values having different data types, both values are converted to the same type. For example, if we add an ***int*** value and a float value together, the compiler converts the int value to the float type, e.g. 3 + 4.5 will yield 7.5. Type casting operators allows converting a data of a given data type to another data type. Most C++ operators perform type conversions to bring the operands of an expression to a common type. The conversions depend on the specific operator and the type of the operand(s). Explicit type conversions can be used by preceding the expression to be converted by the new type enclosed between parenthesis (), for example:

```
int a;
float b = 4.5;
a = (int) b;
```

The code converts the floating point number 4.5 to an integer value (4). Here, the type casting the operator has used is (***int***). Another way to do the same thing in C++ is by preceding the expression to be converted by the type and enclosing the expression between parenthesis, e.g.

```
i = int (f);
```

Both ways of type casting are valid in C++, however, the second type of casting is not available in C.

Every expression is divided into sub-expressions consisting of one operand and one or two associated operands. For binary operators, if the operands differ in their data type, then implicit data conversions take place by converting the data type that requires smaller storage to the data type that requires larger storage. For example, in an expression, 3 + 4.5, for the binary + operator, the first operand is an integer and second one is a floating point number; since float is of higher width than ***int***, the entire expression is considered to be a floating point expression. Therefore, the first operand is converted to a floating point number 3.0 before applying the binary + operator on the operands 3.0(converted) and 4.5(as given). The implicit data conversions available for the built-in types are as follows:

short->int	char ->int	int->unsigned int
unsigned int->long	long->unsigned long	unsigned long->float
float->double	double->long double	

Following this implicit type conversions from narrower type to wider type, we can implicitly convert from, for example, a short to a long or a unsigned ***int*** to a double and so on. If we forcibly convert from a wider type to a narrower type, for example a double to an ***int***, that causes data loss as we are converting a data requiring larger storage to a data requiring smaller storage.

A sample program follows, to illustrate permissible range of values enjoyed on type casting.

Program Source Code 2.5

```
// Program 2.5
#include<iostream.h>
int main()
{
   /* on 32-bit machine usually
      Signed short : range -32,768 to +32,767
      Signed long : range -2,147,483,648 to +2,147,483,647 */

   short SignedShort;
   long  SignedLong;

   SignedShort = 30000;
   // result too large, exceeds maximum limit
   SignedShort = SignedShort * 10;
   // should get 30000 back, but we don't
   SignedShort =  SignedShort / 10;
   // and we get wrong answer
   cout << "SignedShort = " << SignedShort << endl;

   SignedShort = 30000;
   // now, result within limits
   SignedLong = ( long ) (SignedShort * 10 );
   // should get 30000 back, and we do
   SignedShort =  SignedLong / 10;
   // and we get right answer
   cout << "SignedShort = " << SignedShort << endl;

   return 0;
}
```

Output 2.5
SignedShort = -2768 SignedShort = 30000

sizeof() Operator

This operator accepts one parameter that can be either a data type of a variable or a variable itself and returns the size in bytes of that type or object. For example, `a = sizeof (char);` will return 1 or 2 depending of character storage is single byte or double byte. The value returned by ***sizeof*** is a constant, so it is always determined before program execution. While writing programs in C++, even if we know the target operating system and the target machine on which the program will run, it is strongly recommended that we should not assume usage of bytes depending on a particular data type. Instead, we should use ***sizeof()*** operator. This increases portability of the program across varied operating system and hardware platforms.

Operator Precedence and Associativity

In complex expressions with several operands, one operator takes precedence over the other. For example, in the expression: a = 10 + 7 % 2, % operator takes over precedence + operator. Thus, 7 % 2 is evaluated first, yielding 1 and the resulting statement becomes a = 10 + 1 yielding 11. Precedence states the priority of applying one operator over the other in the same expression. Associativity is the left-to-right or right-to-left order for grouping operands to operators that have the same precedence. That determines in the case where there are several operators of the same priority level, which one must be evaluated before—the rightmost one or the leftmost one. For example, in the following statements, the value of 15 is assigned to both a and b because of the right-to-left associativity of the = operator. The value of c is assigned to b first, and then the value of b is assigned to a.

```
b = 10;
c = 15;
a = b = c;
```

From greatest to the least, the priority order is shown in Table 2.7.

Table 2.7

<table>
<tr><th>Priority</th><th>Operator</th><th>Description</th><th>Associativity</th></tr>
<tr><td>1</td><td>::</td><td>scope</td><td>Left to Right</td></tr>
<tr><td>2</td><td>() [ ] –> . sizeof</td><td></td><td>Left to Right</td></tr>
<tr><td></td><td>++ ––</td><td>post and pre increment/decrement (post has higher precedence than pre)</td><td></td></tr>
<tr><td></td><td>~</td><td>Complement to one (bitwise)</td><td></td></tr>
<tr><td>3</td><td>!</td><td>unary NOT relational operator</td><td>Right to Left</td></tr>
<tr><td></td><td>& *</td><td>Reference and Dereference (pointers)</td><td></td></tr>
<tr><td></td><td>(type)</td><td>Cast operator</td><td></td></tr>
<tr><td></td><td>+ –</td><td>Unary sign</td><td></td></tr>
<tr><td>4</td><td>* / %</td><td>arithmetical operators</td><td>Left to Right</td></tr>
<tr><td>5</td><td>+ –</td><td>arithmetical operators</td><td>Left to Right</td></tr>
<tr><td>6</td><td><< >></td><td>bit shift (bitwise) operators</td><td>Left to Right</td></tr>
<tr><td>7</td><td>< < = > >=</td><td>Relational operators</td><td>Left to Right</td></tr>
<tr><td>8</td><td>== !=</td><td>Relational operators</td><td>Left to Right</td></tr>
<tr><td>9</td><td>& ^ |</td><td>Bitwise operators</td><td>Left to Right</td></tr>
<tr><td>10</td><td>&& ||</td><td>Logic operators</td><td>Left to Right</td></tr>
<tr><td>11</td><td>?:</td><td>Conditional operator</td><td>Right to Left</td></tr>
<tr><td></td><td>= += –= *= /= %=</td><td>Simple and Compound assignment operator</td><td>Right to Left</td></tr>
<tr><td>12</td><td>>>= <<= &= ^= |=</td><td></td><td></td></tr>
<tr><td>13</td><td>,</td><td>Comma, Separator</td><td>Left to Right</td></tr>
</table>

Associativity defines in the case where there are several operators of the same priority level, which one must be evaluated before—the rightmost one or the leftmost one.

SUMMARY

The key concepts introduced in this chapter are as follows:

- A data must be associated with a type to tell the computer how much space is required to store that data in memory. The exact size of data corresponding to a data type varies from machine to machine.
- The basic or fundamental data types available are five integer data types (***char***, ***int***, ***short***, ***long*** and ***bool***) and three floating point data types (***float***, ***double*** and ***long double***).

- In addition to type specifiers for data, there are some further qualifications available in C++ language. They are, ***unsigned***, ***signed***, ***short*** and ***long***.
- All variables must be declared before they are used or accessed.
- We can define some name for a constant that can be used in programs without declaring variables. This can be done simply by using the #define preprocessor directive.
- Constants can also be declared with ***const*** prefix with a specific data type associated with a variable. A ***const*** variable can only be initialized; it cannot be assigned a new value thereafter.
- An enumeration data type represents a set of values that can be declared. C++ allows user-defined variable types, called ***enum*** (from enumerated) types.
- Expressions are sequences of operators, operands in the form of constants and variables, and punctuators which specify a computation as per the rules of the underlying language.
- In general, there are three categories of operators—arithmetic, comparison or relational, and logical operators. Some operators result in an *lvalue*. By *lvalue* we mean an expression that represents a data object that can be both examined and altered.
- The relational operators (>, <, >=, <=, ==, !=) compare two operands and determine the validity of a relationship. The assignation operator(= or equality sign) assigns a value to a variable. Bitwise operators (binary) yield a result by applying boolean operation with each bit of the first operand to the corresponding bit of second operand. Logic operators correspond to boolean logic operations.
- There is a difference between prefix and postfix forms of the increment operator: The result of a C++ post- or pre-increment operator has the same data type as the operand, but pre-increment operator result is an *lvalue* whereas post-increment operator result is not. In C language, both cases are not *lvalue*. Similarly for prefix and postfix forms of the decrement operator.
- Typecasting operators allows converting a data of a given data type to another data type. Most C++ operators perform type conversions to bring the operands of an expression to a common type.
- sizeof() operator accepts one parameter, that can be either a data type of a variable or a variable itself and returns the size in bytes that type or object takes when stored in memory.

- In complex expressions with several operands, one operator takes precedence over the other. Precedence states the priority of applying one operator over other in the same expression.
- Associativity is the left-to-right or right-to-left order for grouping operands to operators that have the same precedence. Associativity defines in the case where there are several operators of the same priority level, which one must be evaluated before, the rightmost one or the leftmost one.

REVIEW QUESTIONS

1. What is the significance of data types? Is it mandatory to associate a type with any data in C++?
2. What are the built-in data types available in C++? Cite examples.
3. What is the difference between a variable and a constant?
4. A constant can be defined using preprocessor directive #define or a ***const*** qualifier—which one is preferred and why?
5. Explain the usage of enumeration, citing suitable examples.
6. What do you mean by *lvalue*? Provide a list of basic operators and state whether they can be *lvalue* or not.
7. What is the difference between a = b and a == b? Can they be used interchangeably?
8. What is the difference between a & b and a && b? Can they be used interchangeably?
9. Illustrate the usage of ***cast*** operator by citing suitable examples.
10. What is the difference between writing (int) a and int (a)? If we use either one, what should be the data type of a?
11. What is the advantage of using sizeof() operator?
12. Have four integer variables a, b, c and d. Initialize a to 1 + 1, b to three times a, c to b divided by 4, d to difference of c and a, e to –d. Print the values of a, b, c, d and e.

    Now, have four floating point variables a, b, c and d. Initialize a to 1+1, b to three times a, c to b divided by 4, d to difference of c and a, e to –d. Print the values of a, b, c, d and e.

    Examine the differences of integer and floating point operations.

13. Have seven boolean variables a, b, c, d, e, f and g. Initialize a, b to true. Assign c to a or b, d to a and b, e to xor b, f to (not a and b) or (a and not b)(what does that mean?) and g to not of a.

    Print the values of a, b, c, d, e, f and g.

14. Write a program to assign two numeric values to two variables N1 and N2, perform arithmetic operations (addition, subtraction, multiplication and division) and display the results.

15. Given that light speed is 30,00,00,000 m/s, calculate how much distance (in km) is traversed by light in a span of one year.

16. Write a program to calculate Compound Interest for given period of time and rate of interest on given amount. Assume variables as necessary.

17. Write a program to print the truth table for Boolean expression AB + BC. The table will have only entries 0 or 1.

3 Statements

Computers are good at following instructions, but not at reading your mind.

—D. Knuth

LEARNING OBJECTIVES

The objective of this chapter is to acquaint you with:

- Need for statements
- Concept of labeled expression, null and compound statements
- Different kinds of control statements—if, switch and conditional operators
- Different kinds of loop—for, while, do-while
- Jump statements

INTRODUCTION

Statements specify the action(s) that the program or program segment performs. Expressions are sequences of operators, operands, and punctuators that specify a computation which can be executed. An expression ending with a ;(semicolon) is called a statement. It is the smallest independent computational unit. Every statement appears inside the definition of a function constituting the function. C++ statements or instructions are usually executed sequentially unless the underlying statement specifically modifies that sequence. During its execution process, the statement may branch off into or repeat portions of the statements. Several control structures like conditional or looping statements are used to make decisions and repeat actions. A statement that forms a component of another statement is called the "body" of the enclosing statement. A block of instructions is defined as a group of instructions enclosed within curly braces {and}, and separated by semicolons (;). Declarations and statements can be nested within other declarations and statements, but neither can be nested inside an expression.

A statement can be one of the following categories: labeled statement, expression statement, compound statement, control statement, jump-statement, declaration statement and try-throw-catch statements.

The C++ statement syntax is mostly identical to that of ANSI C. The main difference of variable declarations is that, in C, variable declarations are allowed only at the beginning of a block whereas in C++, variables can be declared anywhere within a block. Declaring variables inside a block enables us to have more precise control over the scope of the variables so declared.

Labeled Statement

A label is an identifier followed by a colon (:) character. Label allows transferring program flow of control to other statements within the same function. This is the only type of identifier that has function scope. Control is transferred to the statement marked by the label through the ***goto*** or ***switch*** statements.

A labeled statement has the following form:

```
identifier: statement
```

This is illustrated in Example 3.1.

The case and default labels can only appear within the body of a switch statement.

EXAMPLE 3.1:

```
initialize:  i = 0; /* initialization statement for i */
```

Expression Statement

An expression statement contains one or more expressions. It evaluates the given expression or expressions in a specified order. This order is defined by a specific implementation, except when the language demands a particular order of evaluation. The precedence and associativity of operators, as discussed earlier, affect the grouping and evaluation of operands in expressions. An operator's precedence is meaningful only if other operators with higher or lower precedence are present. Expressions with higher-precedence operators are evaluated first. The most common expression statements are *assignments* and *function calls*.

An expression statement has the following form:

```
expression;
```

Let us understand this with the help of Example 3.2.

EXAMPLE 3.2:

```
cout << "Hi There"; /* prints Hi There on screen */
a = b * c;          /* assigning the product of b and c to a */
(a <0)?++b :++c;    /* conditional increment of b or c depending
                       on a < 0 condition */
a = b |0x0001;      /* assignment to a, the bitwise-OR operation
                       of b and hexadecimal 0001*/
```

All the outcomes from the expression evaluation are realized before the next statement is executed. No transfer of control or iteration takes place as a result of an expression statement. An empty expression statement is called a *null statement*.

Null Statement

The simplest statement is the null statement which performs no operation. It takes the form of just a semicolon (;). A null statement can have a label as in a labeled statement or it may signify null statement as body of an iterative statement (Example 3.3).

The statement given in Example 3.3 increments the variable i upto 3. Because the initializations occur within the ***for*** expressions, a statement is only needed to finish the ***for*** syntax; no operation is required.

EXAMPLE 3.3:

```
for(i = 0; i < 3; i++);
```

One can use a null statement when one requires a label before the end of a block statement, as you find in Example 3.4.

EXAMPLE 3.4:

```
void func(void)
{
  if (error_detected)
     goto depart;
  /* further processing */
  depart: ;  /* null statement required */
}
```

Compound Statement

A compound statement, commonly known as *blocks*, consists of zero or more statements enclosed in curly braces ({}). A compound statement allows grouping any number of data definitions, declarations, and statements into one statement. The compiler treats a compound statement as a single statement. As such, a block can be used wherever a single statement is allowed.

A block statement has the form:

{}

In C, any definitions and declarations must come before the statements. Redefining a data object inside a nested block hides the outer object while the inner block runs. If a data object is usable within a block and your program does not redefine its identifier, all nested blocks can use that data object.

The following code (Example 3.5) fragment checks if the value of the variable price is greater than 100; if so, it prints a message on screen that price is too large, followed by newline. After printing the message, the enumerated variable flag is set to TRUE. The variable flag is set to FALSE otherwise, when the value of the variable price is less than or equal to 100.

EXAMPLE 3.5:

```
/* Boolean enumerated datatype is defined */
enum Boolean { FALSE, TRUE };
/* flag is a Boolean variable */
enum Boolean flag; // may be FALSE or TRUE
if ( price > 100 )
{
   /* prints the message on screen that Price
      is too large followed by newline */
   cout << "Price is too large\n";
   flag = TRUE; // sets flag to TRUE
}
else
   flag = FALSE;
```

Here, the expression statement that sets flag = FALSE is a simple statement, and the statements which get executed when price is greater than 100 constitute a compound statement.

Control Statement

Not many programs execute all their statements in a strict order, from beginning to end. The flow of control jumps from one part of the program to another, depending on the computations performed in the program. Program statements that cause such jumps are called control statements. The statement is of two categories: decisions (conditional-statement) and loops (looping-statement). In a loop, a statement or a block of statements undergoes repeated execution. In a conditional statement, depending on the result of evaluation of a condition a statement or a block of statements is executed. How many times a loop is executed, or whether a decision results in execution of a section of code, depends on whether certain expressions evaluate to true or false. These expressions typically involve a kind of operator called a *relational operator*. The relational operator compares two values. Let us build a program (Code 3.1).

Program Source Code 3.1

```
#include <iostream.h>
int main()
{
    int number;
    cout << "Please Enter a number: ";
    cin >> number;
    cout << "number < 10 is " << (number < 10) << endl;
    cout << "number > 10 is " << (number > 10) << endl;
    cout << "number == 10 is " << (number == 10) << endl;
    return 0;
}
```

Output 3.1

```
Please Enter a number: 20
number < 10 is 0
number > 10 is 1
number == 10 is 0
```

From the output, it is evident that C++ compiler considers that a true expression has the value 1 and a false expression has the value 0. In fact, a non-zero value is interpreted to be true and zero value is interpreted to be false.

Decisions

Programs also need to make one-time decisions. In a program, a decision causes a one-time jump (thereby skipping executing a portion of the program) to a different part of the program, depending on the value of an expression.

Decisions can be made in C++ in several ways. The most important is with the ***if...else*** statement, which chooses between two alternatives. This statement can be used without the ***else***. Another decision statement, ***switch***, creates branches for multiple alternative sections of code, depending on the value of a single variable or evaluation of an expression. Finally the conditional operator is used in specialized situations.

if-statement. An ***if*** statement conditionally processes a statement when the specified test expression evaluates to a nonzero value. The expression must evaluate to a scalar type. The syntax of the ***if*** statement is shown in Figure 3.1.

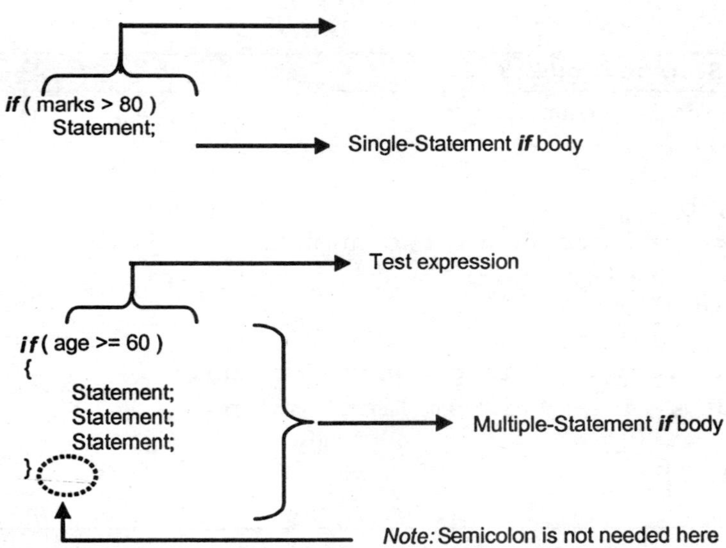

Figure 3.1 Syntax of ***if*** statement.

The following Example (3.6) causes the character variable grade to be assigned to the value A, if the value of integer variable marks is greater than or equal to 80.

EXAMPLE 3.6:

```
....... // some code is here
if (marks >= 80)
    grade = 'A';
```

Example 3.7 displays `a is greater than b` if the value of a is greater than b. If the value of a is less than or equal to b (i.e. the else condition) the message `a is not greater than b` is displayed.

EXAMPLE 3.7:

```
if (a > b)
   cout << "a is greater than b\n";
else
   cout << "a is not greater than b\n";
```

The usage of a compound-statement constituting multiple statements in the if-body can be illustrated with a program (Code 3.2). Two numbers are taken as input. If the first number is greater than the second, two messages are printed stating first one is greater and second one is smaller. If the first number is not greater than the second, no message is printed.

Program Source Code 3.2

```
#include <iostream.h>
int main()
{
   int a, b;
   cout << "Please Enter two numbers : ";
   cin >> a >> b;
   if (a > b)
   {
      cout << a << " is greater" << endl;
      cout << b << " is smaller" << endl;
   }
   return 0;
}
```

Output 3.2

```
Please Enter two numbers: 30 20
30 is greater
20 is smaller
```

The ***if***-body can consist of a single statement. In that case, the single statement is not enclosed within braces (however, it's no harm in putting single statement also in braces). When ***if***-body consists of multiple statements or compound-statement, all the statements or block of statements are enclosed within braces.

if...else statement. The if-statement lets you do something if a condition evaluates to true. If it doesn't, nothing happens. Suppose we would like to do certain thing if a condition evaluates to true, and do something else if it evaluates to false. That makes us use ***if...else*** statement. The syntax of such a statement is shown in Figure 3.2.

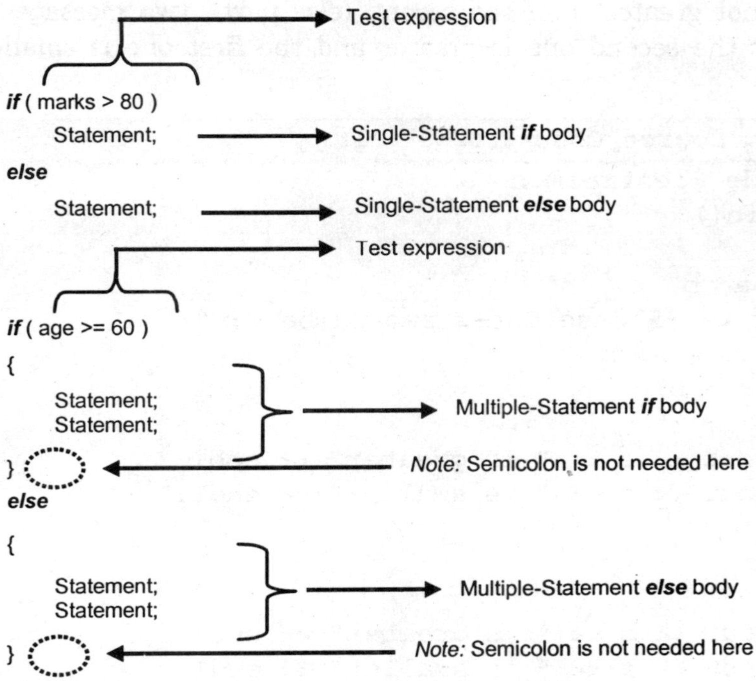

Figure 3.2 Syntax of ***if...else*** statement.

You can *optionally* specify an ***else*** clause on the ***if*** statement. If the test expression evaluates to a nonzero value, the statement following the expression executes and the ***else*** clause is ignored. If the test expression evaluates to 0 and an ***else*** clause exists, the statement associated with the else clause executes.

Thus, in ***if*** syntax, if the expression given in the statement evaluates to a nonzero value (true), the statement dependent on the evaluation is executed; otherwise, it is skipped. In the ***if...else*** syntax, the second statement is executed if the result of evaluating the expression is zero.

An ***if*** statement thus takes the following form:

```
if (expression)
    statement or block of statements
else
    statement or block of statements
```

The code fragment (Program Source Code 3.3) shows a modification of Program Source Code 3.2 with the usage of else. Two numbers are taken as input; if the first number is greater than the second, two messages are printed, stating that the first one is greater and the second one is smaller. If the first number is not greater than the second (else part), two messages are printed, stating that the second one is greater and the first one is smaller.

Program Source Code 3.3

```
#include <iostream.h>
int main()
{
    int a, b;
    cout << "Please Enter two numbers: ";
    cin >> a >> b;
    if (a > b)
    {
        cout << a << " is greater" << endl;
        cout << b << " is smaller" << endl;
    }
    else
    {
        cout << b << " is greater" << endl;
        cout << a << " is smaller" << endl;
    }
    return 0;
}
```

Output 3.3

```
Please Enter two numbers: 20 30
30 is greater
20 is smaller
```

Matching the 'else'. Example 3.8 shows a nested ***if*** statement, where it displays `a is greater than b` if the value of a is greater than b. The else condition, as stated earlier, signifies that the value of a is less than or equal to b. If we put another ***if*** statement in else clause to check if a is equal to b, then it displays `a is greater than b`. The else clause of the second ***if*** statement thus signifies that a is less than b where the message `a is less than b` is displayed.

EXAMPLE 3.8:

```
if (a>b)
    cout << "a is greater than b\n";
```

```
else if ( a == b )
   cout << "a is equal to b\n";
else // a must be less than b
   cout << "a is less than b\n";
```

Another example of nested ***if*** is given in Example 3.9. An else clause always associates with the closest ***if*** statement. If you follow the nested block of statements, you compare the values of three variables a, b and c and you can have six different scenarios of relative ordering of a, b and c. They are:

EXAMPLE 3.9:

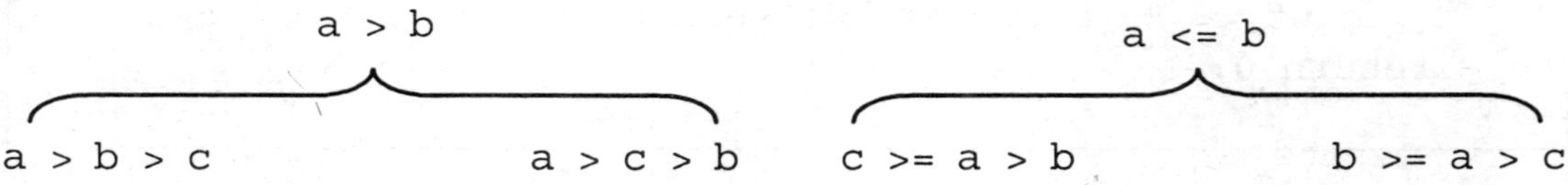


```
if (a > b)
    if (b > c)
        cout << "a > b > c\n";
    else if (a > c)
        cout << "a > c > b\n";
        else
            cout << "c >= a > b\n";
else // a <= b
      if (a > c)
          cout << "b >= a > c\n";
      else if (b >= c)
          cout << " b >= c >= a\n";
          else
             cout << "c > b >= a\n";
```

There is a potential problem in nested ***if...else*** statements: you can inadvertently match an ***else*** with the wrong if. When ***if*** statements are nested and else clauses are present, a given else is associated with the closest preceding ***if*** statement within the same block. The following example provides an explanation.

In Program Source Code 3.4, omitting the braces causes the ***else*** clause to associate with the nearest nested ***if*** statement.

Program Source Code 3.4

```
#include <iostream.h>
int main()
{
   int a, b, c;
   cout << "please input three numbers a, b and c: ";
   cin >> a >> b >> c;
   if(a == b)
      if(b == c)
      cout << "a, b, c are equal\n";
   else
      cout << "a and b are different\n";
   return 0;
}
```

Output 3.4.1

```
please input three numbers a, b and c: 20 30 30
```

Output 3.4.2

```
please input three numbers a, b and c: 10 10 30
a and b are different
```

Output 3.4.3

```
please input three numbers a, b and c: 10 10 10
a,b,c are equal
```

When a = 20, b = 30, c = 30, a and b are different, so the first conditional, expression, i.e. (a == b) evaluates to false, and you will expect that the else part is invoked, printing "a and b are different". But, as a matter of fact, nothing is printed. Why? Because the else is matched with wrong if. When a = 10, b = 10, c = 30, it is printed that a and b are different, which is not. The rule of matching the else clause is:

*An **else** is matched with the last if that doesn't have its own **else.***

A correct version of the undesired matching of else is given in Program Code 3.4a. It shows a nested ***if*** statement that does not have an else clause. Since an else clause always associates with the closest ***if*** statement, braces may have to be used. The braces force a particular else clause to associate with the correct ***if*** statement.

Program Source Code 3.4a

```
#include <iostream.h>
int main()
{
   int a, b, c;
   cout << "please input three numbers a, b and c: ";
   cin >> a >> b >> c;
   if(a == b)
   {
      if (b == c)
      cout << "a, b, c are equal\n";
   }
   else
      cout << "a and b are different\n";
   return 0;
}
```

Output 3.4a.1

```
please input three numbers a, b and c: 20 30 30
a and b are different
```

Output 3.4a.2

```
please input three numbers a, b and c: 10 10 30
```

Output 3.4a.3

```
please input three numbers a, b and c: 10 10 10
a, b, c are equal
```

As you can perceive, the omitting of braces causes the else clause to associate with the nearest nested ***if*** statement.

```
if(a == b)
   if(b == c)
      cout << "a, b, c are equal \n";
else
    cout << "b, c are not equal \n";
```

Use of second brace or curly brace ({ }) is recommended to explicitly clarify the pairing of complicated if and else clauses, such as in the following example:

EXAMPLE 3.10:

```
if(a == b)
{
   if(b == c)
      cout << "a, b, c are equal \n";
   else
      cout << "a, b are equal but b, c are not equal \n";
}
else
   cout << "a, b are not equal\n";
```

Although the braces are not strictly necessary, they clarify the pairing between ***if*** and ***else*** statements.

Switch statement. The ***switch*** statement allows selection among multiple sections of code, depending on the value of an expression. The objective is to check several possible constant values for an expression. This takes the following form:

```
switch (expression)
{
   case constant1:
      block of instructions 1
      break;
   case constant2:
      block of instructions 2
      break;
   .
   .
   .
   default:
      default block of instructions
}
```

It works in the following way: switch evaluates expression and checks whether the evaluated value is equal to constant1, if so, it executes block of instructions 1 until it finds the break statement, where the program will transfer its control to the end of the entire switch block. If the evaluated expression is not equal to constant1, then it checks if it is equal to constant2. If so, it will execute block of instructions 2 until it finds the break statement. Finally, if the value of expression has not matched any of the previously specified constants (many case sentences can be specified), the program executes the instructions included in the ***default:*** section, if exists. The default section is optional, though however, is recommended to be used for tracking accidental unintentional errors.

The break statement. There is a break statement at the end of each case section. The ***break*** keyword causes the entire switch statement to exit from the switch block. That is, the break statement transfers control to the statement immediately following the switch statement. Don't forget the break; without it, control passes down to the statement for the next case, which is usually not what you wanted (unless you want to fall through the code). Here, break is used to terminate sections of code usually before a case label.

The default keyword. The ***default*** keyword gives the switch construction a way to take action if the value of the loop variable doesn't match any of the case constants. The usage of the switch statement is given in Figure 3.3.

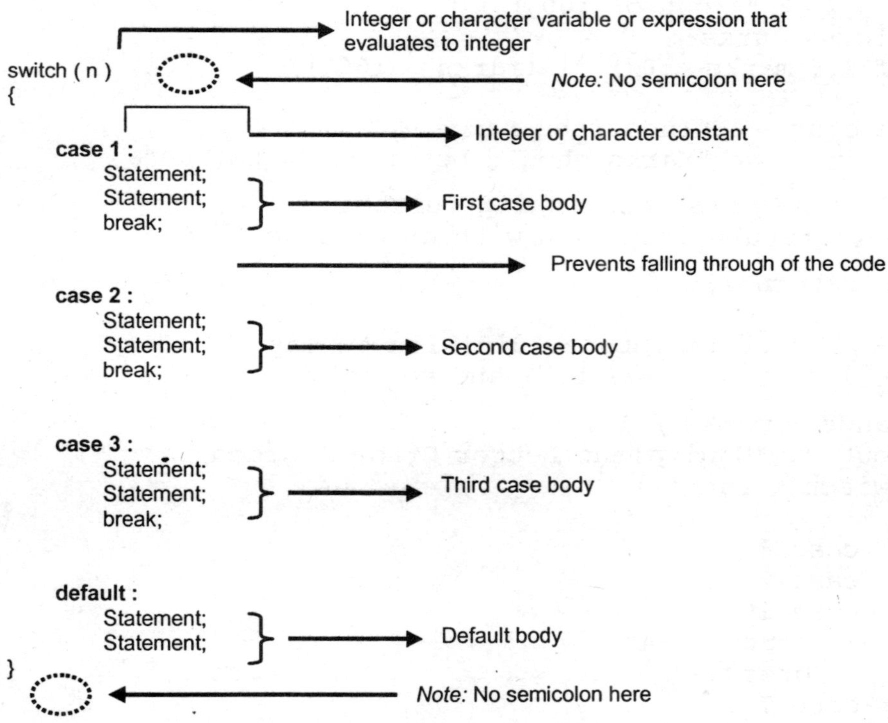

Figure 2.3 Syntax of a ***switch*** statement.

If you have a large decision tree, and all the decisions depend on the value of the same variable, you will probably want to consider a switch statement instead of a series of ***if...else*** or ***else if*** constructions.

An example program follows (Program Source Code 3.5).

Program Source Code 3.5

```
#include <iostream.h>
int main()
{
   /* print letter grade from marks according
      to the following rule :
      80 and above : A, 70 and above : B,
      60 and above : C, rest : D */
   int marks, range;
   cout << "Please input the marks obtained"
        << " (out of 100 ) : ";
   cin >> marks;
   if ( ( marks < 0 ) || (marks > 100 ))
   {
      cout << "Incorrect range : "
           << "Marks should be within 0 to 100";

      /* no point continuing further,
         return from main with error code 1 */
      return 1;
   }
   /* we perform integer division to map
      0-9 to 0, 10-19 to 1 and so on */

   range = marks / 10;
   cout << "Equivalent Letter Grade Awarded is : ";
   switch ( range )
   {
      case 8 :
      case 9 :
      case 10 :
         cout << "A" ;
         break;
      case 7 :
         cout << "B" ;
         break;
      case 6 :
         cout << "C" ;
         break;
      default :
         cout <<"D" ;
         break;
      }
      return 0;
   }
```

Output 3.5.1

```
Please input the marks obtained (out of 100): 105
Incorrect range: Marks should be within 0 to 100
```

Output 3.5.2

```
Please input the marks obtained (out of 100): 55
Equivalent Letter Grade Awarded is: D
```

Output 3.5.3

```
Please input the marks obtained (out of 100): 76
Equivalent Letter Grade Awarded is: B
```

Output 3.5.4

```
Please input the marks obtained (out of 100): 100
Equivalent Letter Grade Awarded is: A
```

In this program, we take marks (falling within range 0 to 100) as input, and print the equivalent letter grade according to the following rule:

080–100	:	A
070–079	:	B
060–069	:	C
000–059	:	D

We take the marks as input and first check whether it falls within valid range 0 to 100; if not, we print an appropriate message and come out of program without continuing further. If the marks falls within the acceptable range, we find a range as follows:

100–100	:	10
090–099	:	9
080–089	:	8

and so on.

This can be done by dividing the number by 10 and taking the quotient. This is in fact an integer division. The keyword switch is followed by a switch variable enclosed within parentheses, since braces delimit a number of case statements. Each case keyword is followed by a constant, which is followed by a colon (:) like, case 10: .

Let us now write a program using two code fragments—***switch*** and ***if-then-else***.

<table>
<tr><th>switch example</th><th>equivalent if-then-else example</th></tr>
<tr><td>switch (x)
{
  case 1:
    cout << "x=1";
    break;
  case 2:
    cout << "x=2";
  break;
    default:
    cout << "x is not equal"
        << "to 1 or 2";

}</td><td>if (x == 1)
{
    cout << "x =1";
}
else if (x == 2)
{
    cout << "x=2";
}
    else
{
    cout << "x is not equal"
        << "to 1 or 2";
}</td></tr>
</table>

The inclusion of the break instructions at the end of each case block prevents code control to jump or fall through next block of codes applicable for next case. This may be intended or not intented. For example, ***switch*** can only be used to compare an expression with different constants. Thus we cannot put variables like n*2 or ranges like (1..4) in case statements, as these are not valid constants. Here's how it goes:

<table>
<tr><th>switch example</th><th>equivalent if-then-else example</th></tr>
<tr><td>switch (x)
{
  case 1:
  case 2:
    cout << "x is equal"
        << "to 1 or 2";
    break;
  default:
    cout << "x is not equal"
        << "1 or 2";
}</td><td>if ((x == 1) || (x == 2))
{
    cout << "x is equal"
        << "to 1 or 2";
}
else
  {
    cout << "x is not equal"
        << "to 1 or 2";

}</td></tr>
</table>

The conditional operator. The conditional operator (?) evaluates a conditional expression that contains a condition (operand 1), an expression to be evaluated if the condition has a nonzero value (operand 2), and an expression to be evaluated if the condition has the value 0 (operand 3). Conditional expressions take the following form:

```
condition ? result1 : result2
```

if ***condition*** evaluates to ***true*** the expression yields ***result1***, otherwise, it yields ***result2***. An example is shown in Figure 3.4.

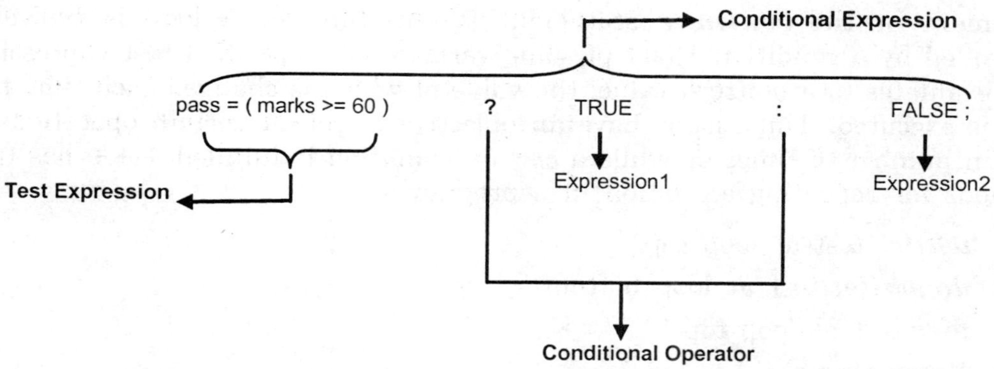

Figure 3.4 Example of a conditional operator.

The conditional operator : exists because of a common programming situation such as, when a variable is given one value if something is true and another value if it is false. Here (Example 3.11) is an ***if...else*** statement that gives the variable named min the value of alpha or the value of beta, depending on which is smaller.

EXAMPLE 3.11:

```
if (alpha < beta)
      min = alpha;
else
      min = beta;
```

This sort of construction is so common that the designers of C++ have invented a compressed way to express it : the conditional operator. Here's the equivalent of the same program fragment, using a conditional operator.

```
min = (alpha < beta) ? alpha : beta;
```

If the test expression is true, then the entire conditional expression takes on the value of the operand following the question mark (?), alpha in this example. If the test expression is false, the conditional expression takes on the value of the operand following the colon (:), beta in this example.

Loops

There are several ways to execute a statement or block of statements repeatedly. Loops cause a portion of your program to be repeated a certain number of times. The repetition continues while a condition is true. When the condition becomes false, the loop ends and the control passes to the statements following the loop. In general, repetitive execution of a statement or a block of statements (i.e. compound statement) is called *looping*. In compound statements, the statements are executed in order, except when either the ***break*** statement or the ***continue*** statement is encountered. A loop is typically controlled by a conditional test of some variable or a specified test expression that evaluates to a nonzero value, the value of which is changed each time the loop is executed. Thus, loops have an objective to repeat certain operations a certain number of times or while a certain condition is fulfilled. C++ has five methods for repeating an action in a program.

1. ***while:*** test at loop top
2. ***do/while:*** test at loop bottom
3. ***for:*** test at loop top
4. ***Recursion***
5. ***Unconditional Branch:*** local (goto) and non-local (setjmp and longjmp)

The first three constitute the loop.

while statement. The while statement executes a statement repeatedly until the test expression specified evaluates to zero. The test of the expression takes place before each execution of the loop. A while loop executes its associated statement or block of statements (given as a compound statement) zero or more times, depending on the value of the evaluated test expression. The while statement has the following form:

```
while (expression)
    statement
```

Program code 3.6 takes from input the value of an integer variable called *count*. Then depending on the value if the variable count so inputted, it prints the number of lines showing the value of the variable count until the value of count becomes 0. The program segment starts with inputting the variable count. The test condition count > 0 is evaluated at the top of the loop, and the loop statement is executed until the test condition count > 0 evaluates to zero. Each time the loop statement is executed, a line is printed as count = <value of count > and then the variable count is decremented. If before the start of the loop the count is inputted to zero or negative value, the loop never executes.

Program Source Code 3.6

```
#include <iostream.h>
int main ()
{
   int count;
   cout << "Enter the value of count: ";
   cin >> count;
   while (count > 0)
   {
      cout << "count = " << count << endl;
      count--;
   }
   cout << "done\n";
   return 0;
}
```

Output 3.6.1

```
Enter the value of count: 5
count = 5
count = 4
count = 3
count = 2
count = 1
done
```

Output 3.6.2

```
Enter the value of count : 0
done
```

Output 3.6.3

```
Enter the value of count : -2
done
```

do-while statement. The ***do-while*** statement lets you repeat a statement or compound statement until a specified test expression evaluates to zero. Unlike while loop, the test of the expression takes place *after* each execution of the loop. A ***do-while*** loop executes its associated statement or block of statements (given as a compound statement) one or more times, depending on the value of the evaluated test expression. The ***do-while*** statement has the following form:

```
do
   statement
while (condition);
```

Now let's see the code fragment example in another program (Code 3.7) similar to that given in the ***while*** loop before. It takes from input the value of an integer variable called count. Then, depending on the value the variable count so inputted, it prints number of lines showing the value of the variable count until the value of count becomes 0. The test condition count > 0 is evaluated at the bottom of the loop, and the loop statement is executed until the test condition count > 0 evaluates to zero while checked at the bottom of the loop. Since the test condition is checked at the bottom of the loop, irrespective of the value of count inputted, the loop executes at least once.

Program Source Code 3.7

```
#include <iostream.h>
int main ()
{
   int count;
   cout << "Enter the value of count: ";
   cin >> count;
   do
   {
      cout << "count = " << count << endl;
      count--;
   } while (count > 0)
      cout << "done\n";
      return 0;
   }
```

Output 3.7.1

```
Enter the value of count: 5
count = 5
count = 4
count = 3
count = 2
count = 1
done
```

Output 3.7.2

```
Enter the value of count: 0
count = 0
done
```

Output 3.7.3

```
Enter the value of count: -2
count = -2
done
```

for* statement.** The ***for statement repeats a statement or a compound statement a specified number of times. The body of a ***for*** statement is executed zero or more times until an optional condition evaluates to zero. One can use optional expressions within the ***for*** statement to initialize and change values of variables during the ***for*** statement's execution. The syntax of ***for*** statement is illustrated in Figure 3.5.

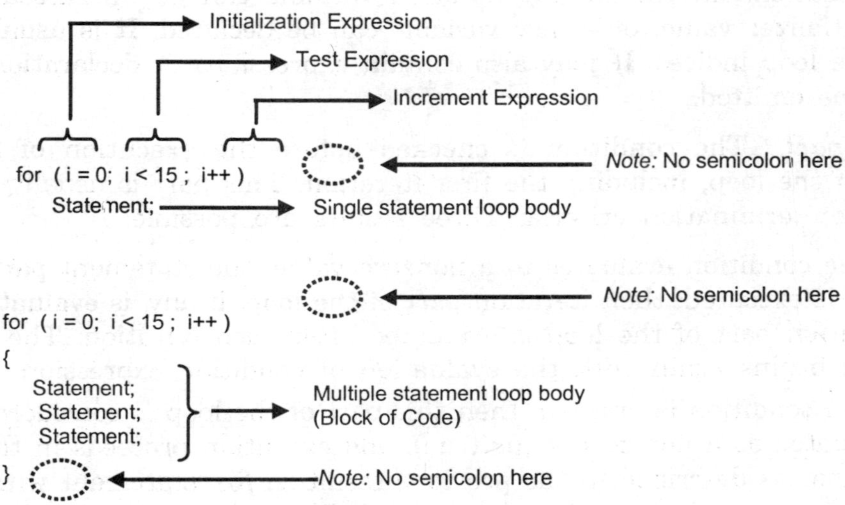

Figure 3.5 Syntax of ***for*** loop.

Program Source Code 3.8 displays the squares of the numbers from 0 to 14.

Program Source Code 3.8

```
#include <iostream.h>
int main()
{
   int i;
   for (i = 0; i < 15; i++)
     cout << i * i << " ";
   return 0;
}
```

Output 3.8

```
0 1 4 9 16 25 36 49 64 81 100 121 144 169 196
```

The ***for*** statement thus takes the following form:

```
for (initialization; condition; iteration)
    statement;
```

for statement can be divided into three separate parts.

Initialization-part. This occurs before any other element of the ***for*** statement or the substatement. An already declared variable can be initialized to any desired initializer value, or a new variable can be declared. It is usually used to initialize loop indices. It may also contain expressions or declarations. This part may be omitted.

Condition-part. The condition is checked before the execution of a given iteration of the loop, including the first iteration. This part is usually used to test for loop-termination criteria. Three results are possible:

- If the condition evaluates to a nonzero value, the statement part of the loop is executed; then iteration part of the loop, if any, is evaluated. The iteration part of the loop is evaluated after each iteration. The process then begins again with the evaluation of condition expression.
- If the condition is omitted, then this part of the loop is considered to be evaluated as a non-zero value(true), and execution proceeds in the same manner as described in the previous result. A ***for*** statement without an explicit condition part executes for infinite number of times unless forced to terminate when a break or return statement within the statement body is executed, or when a ***goto*** (to a labeled statement outside the for statement body) is executed.
- If the condition evaluates to a zero value (0), execution of the for statement terminates and control passes to the next statement in the program.

Iteration-part. At the end of each iteration of the loop; condition is tested after iteration part is evaluated. It is usually used to increment loop indices. This part also can be omitted.

The ***for*** statement executes the statement repeatedly until condition part evaluates to zero. The initialization-part, condition-part, and iteration-part fields are all optional.

An example of loop is as follows:

EXAMPLE 3.12:

```
for (initialization-part; condition-part; iteration-part)
{
    // statements
}
```

is equivalent to the following ***while*** loop:

```
initialization-part;;
while(condition-part)
{
   // statements
   iteration-part;
}
```

A convenient way to specify an infinite loop using the ***for*** statement can be illustrated as follows:

EXAMPLE 3.13:

```
for(; ;)
{
   // statements to be executed.
}
```

which is equivalent to

```
while(1)
{
   // statements to be executed.
}
```

The initialization-part of the for loop can be a declaration statement or an expression statement, including the null statement. The initializations can include any sequence of expressions and declarations, separated by commas. A variable declared inside an initialization part has local scope within the outer block, as if it had been declared immediately prior to the ***for*** statement block. Although the name of a variable can be used in more than one for loop in the same scope, the declaration can appear only once.

Variables defined in for statements. In the following ***for***-loop,

```
for (int i = 10; i > 0; i --)
```

the loop variable i is defined inside the for statement. This is a common construction in C++. It defines the variable as close as possible to its point of use in the listing. Variables defined in the loop statement this way are visible from the point of definition onward in the listing (unlike variables defined within a block, which are visible only within the block).

Multiple initialization and test expressions. You can put more than one expression in the initialization part of the ***for*** statement, separating the different expressions by commas. You can have more than one increment expression, although you can have only one test expression (compound test expression is allowed). An example follows:

EXAMPLE 3.14:

```
for (i = 10, k = 0; (( i > 0 ) && ( k < 10 )); i --, k++)
{
   // body of loop
}
```

Program Source Code 3.9 counts down from the value of the variable count to zero. The initial value of the variable is taken from input.

Program Source Code 3.9

```
#include <iostream.h>
int main ()
{
   int count;
   cout << "Enter the value of count: ";
   for (cin >> count;count > 0; count--)
   {
      cout << "count = " << count << endl;
   }
   cout << "done\n";
   return 0;
}
```

Output 3.9.1

```
Enter the value of count: 5
count = 5
count = 4
count = 3
count = 2
count = 1
done
```

Output 3.9.2

```
Enter the value of count: 0
Done
```

Output 3.9.3

```
Enter the value of count: -2
Done
```

Another example given as Source Code 3.10 has two ***for***-loops. Before the first ***for*** loop runs, "count up" is printed. In the first ***for*** loop, we declare variable i as integer in the initialization part. The condition part (loop terminator condition) checks whether i is less than 5 or not. Then statement `cout << i << "\n"` is executed to print the value 0 which is the current value of the variable i. Next, the iteration part is evaluated, i.e. ++i is evaluated so i becomes 1. The condition i < 5 is checked again. Since 1 < 5, the statement cout `<< i << "\n"` is executed again to print the current value of i, which is 1. This process continues until i becomes 5. Then "count down" is printed before starting the next for loop. This loop does not redeclare the variable i, as it is in the same scope. Also we omit the initialization part. Thus, it starts with the last assigned value to i, i.e. i=5. The loop continues to print the value of i until i reaches 0, while decrementing i at each iteration part of the ***for*** loop. Finally, "done" is printed.

Program Source Code 3.10

```
#include <iostream.h>
int main ()
{
        cout << "count up\n";
        for( int i = 0; i < 5; ++i )
                cout << i << "\n";

        cout << "count down\n";

        /* The loop index, i, cannot be declared
            in the initialisation part again because
            it is still in scope */
        for(; i >= 0; --i )
            cout << i << "\n";
    cout << "done\n";
    return 0;
}
```

Output 3.10

```
count up
0
1
2
3
4
count down
5
4
3
2
1
0
done
```

Although the three fields of the ***for*** statement are normally used for initialization, condition checking for loop termination, and incrementing at each iteration, they are not restricted to these uses. For example, the Program Source Code 3.11 prints the numbers 1 to 5. The loop statement is a null statement here.

Program Source Code 3.11

```
#include <iostream.h>
int main()
{
   for(int i = 0; i < 5; cout << i++ << endl)
      ;
   return 0;
}
```

Output 3.11

```
0
1
2
3
4
```

Jump Statement

Jump statements perform an immediate local transfer of control. They are of four types:

- goto
- break
- continue
- return

goto

The ***goto*** statement performs an unconditional transfer of control to the named label as given in a labeled statement. The label must be in the current function body. This is not a recommended way of use, as it affects the structuredness of a program.

break

The ***break*** statement is used to exit a looping or switch statement. It transfers control to the statement immediately following the looping statement or switch statement. The break statement terminates only the innermost loop or switch statement. In loops, break is used to terminate before the termination criteria evaluates to a zero value. In the switch statement, break is used to terminate sections of code usually before a case label. The example Program Source Code 3.12 illustrates the use of the break statement in a ***for*** loop.

Program Source Code 3.12

```
#include <iostream.h>
int main ()
{
   int count;
   cout << "Enter the value of count : ";
   cin >> count;
   for (;;) // no termination condition
   {
      if (count <= 0) break;
           cout << "count = " << count << endl;
      count--;
   }
   cout << "done\n";
   return 0;
}
```

Output 3.12.1

```
Enter the value of count: 5
count = 5
count = 4
count = 3
count = 2
count = 1
done
```

Output 3.12.2

```
Enter the value of count: 0
Done
```

Output 3.12.3

```
Enter the value of count: -2
Done
```

Here, we have used a ***for*** statement with no initialization part, no condition part, no iteration part. That means we have defined an infinite loop. In the statement body, we check if the value of the variable count is less than or equal to zero, then we terminate the loop by putting a break. This works in the same manner as the example given in Program Code 3.9. As count becomes zero, the loop terminates.

continue

The ***continue*** statement forces immediate transfer of control to the loop-continuation statement of the smallest enclosing loop. The "loop-continuation" is the statement that contains the controlling expression for the loop. As such, the statement may appear only in the statement body part of a loop statement (it may be the sole statement in that statement block). In a for loop, execution of a ***continue*** statement causes evaluation of iteration-part and then condition-part. The statement thus causes the program to skip the rest of the loop in the present iteration as if the end of the statement block had been reached, and causes it to jump to the iteration that follows it.

Program Source Code 3.13 shows how the ***continue*** statement can be used to bypass sections of code and skip to the next iteration of a loop. Here, it counts down from the value of the variable count to zero. While counting, it skips the value 3.

Program Source Code 3.13

```
#include <iostream.h>
int main ()
{
   int count;
   cout << "Enter the value of count: ";
   for (cin >> count; count > 0; count--)
   {
      if (count == 3) continue;
      cout << "count = " << count << endl;
   }
   cout << "done\n";
   return 0;
}
```

Output 3.13.1

```
Enter the value of count: 5
count = 5
count = 4
count = 3
count = 2
count = 1
done
```

Output 3.13.2

```
Enter the value of count: 0
done
```

Output 3.13.3

```
Enter the value of count: -2
done
```

return

The ***return*** statement allows a function to immediately transfer control back to the calling function (or, in the case of the main function, transfer control back to the operating system).

exit

The function ***exit*** is defined in *stdlib* library. The purpose of exit is to terminate the program in course with a specific exit code. Its syntax of calling is:

```
exit (exit_code);
```

The exit code is used by some operating systems and may be used by calling programs. By convention, an exit code of 0 means that the program finished normally and any other value means error.

Declaration Statement

Declaration statements introduce new names into the current scope. These names can be:

- Type names (class, struct, union, enum, typedef, and pointer-to-member)
- Object names
- Function names

Try-Throw-Catch Statements

Exception handling in C++ uses the ***try***, ***catch***, and ***throw*** statements, through which our program can communicate unexpected events to a higher execution context that is better able to recover from such abnormal events. These exceptions are handled by code that is outside the normal flow of control.

SUMMARY

The key concepts introduced in this chapter are as follows:

- A statement is the smallest independent computational unit. Statements specify the action(s) that the program or program segment performs.
- A statement is one of the following categories: labeled, expression, compound, conditional, looping, jump, declaration and try-throw-catch statements.
- In C, variable declarations are allowed only at the beginning of a block whereas in C++, variables can be declared anywhere within a block. Declaring variables inside a block enables us to have more precise control over the scope of the variables so declared.
- Label allows transferring program flow of control to other statements within the same function.
- An expression statement contains one or more expressions. It evaluates the given expression or expressions in a specified order.
- The control statement is of two categories: decisions (conditional-statement) and loops (looping-statement). In a loop, a statement or a block of statements undergoes repeated execution. In a conditional statement, depending on the result of evaluation of a condition, a statement or a block of statements is executed.
- Decision statement ***if...else*** chooses between two alternatives. This statement can also be used without the else. Another decision statement, ***switch***, creates branches for multiple alternative sections of code, depending on the value of a single variable or evaluation of an expression.
- C++ has five methods for repeating an action in a program: (i) while: test at loop top (ii) do/while: test at loop bottom (iii) for: test at loop top (iv) recursion and (v) unconditional branch: local (goto) and non-local (setjmp and longjmp).
- The jump statements perform an immediate local transfer of control. They are of four types: goto, break, continue and return.

REVIEW QUESTIONS

1. What is an expression?
2. What is the difference between the two expressions, a = 4 and a == 4?
3. What is the output of the following code if value of count is 4? What about, if the value is –1?

Program Source Code

```
#include <iostream.h>
int main ()
{
    int count;
    cout << "Enter the value of count: ";
    cin >> count;
    do
    {
       cout << "count = " << count << endl;
       count--;
    } while (count > 0)
    cout << "done\n";
    return 0;
}
```

4. Will the output in Q. 3 be different if count is declared to be unsigned int variable? State reasons.
5. Will the output in Q. 3 be different if count is declared to be unsigned int variable and ***do-while*** is replaced by an equivalent ***while*** loop? State reasons.
6. Replace the ***do-while*** by an equivalent ***for*** loop keeping the same program structure in Q. 3.
7. Write a small program that accepts number as input and prints a grade depending on the number range, (80 and above) Grade 'A', (60 to 79) Grade 'B', (40 to 59) Grade 'C' and (Below 40) Grade 'F'. You should take the number as input and print the corresponding letter grade. Use ***if-then-else*** structure and switch-case for your program.

8. Print the following pattern using ***for*** loops:

```
**********

*********

********

*******

******

*****

****

***

**

*
```

9. Have an integer variable called month. Initialize it to 4, have a string variable season. Use switch-case block to assign season to Winter, Spring, Summer, Monsoon, Autumn, Late Autumn depending on the value of month as 12-1, 2-3, 4-5, 6-7, 8-9, 10-11. Print a message stating under which season the month of April falls.

10. Write a program to create the following output.

```
          *

         * *

        * * *

       * * * *

     *  * * * *

       * * * *

        * * *

         * *

          *
```

11. Write programs to print the following:

(a) N natural numbers in ascending/descending order.

(b) Sum of first N even/odd numbers in ascending/descending order.

(c) N prime numbers.

(d) Composite numbers between 1 and N integers.

(e) All perfect numbers less than 160. A perfect number is one whose sum of factors (excluding the number itself) is same as the number. For example, 6 is a perfect number as 6 = 1 + 2 + 3.

12. Write a program to check whether given number is Armstrong or not.

13. Write a program to sum up the following series for a given value of X:

$1 + X + X^2 + X^3 + \cdots + X^N$, N is given

$1 - X/1! + X^2/2! + X^3/3! + X^4/4! \cdots$ upto an approximation of 10^{-5}.

4 Array, Pointer and Structure

To iterate is human, to recurse divine.
—L. Peter Deutsch

LEARNING OBJECTIVES

The objective of this chapter is to acquaint you with:

- Defining arrays and accessing array elements
- Array initialization and assigning values to array elements
- Multidimensional arrays
- Character array and character strings
- Addresses and pointers
- Void pointer, address-of and indirection operator
- Pointer-to-pointers
- Difference of pointer and array
- Pointer arithmetic
- Defining structures

INTRODUCTION

You will now learn some basic concepts and building blocks of data structures. Designing and using data structures is an important programming skill. As we have already told that every data is associated with a data type, which helps data to work with related types. Depending on data type, required space is allocated for the data to occupy memory. In order to enable programs to make use of related types of data, data values must be in an organized form. The organized collection of data is called a *data structure*. The programs have to follow certain rules to access and process the structured data. Similarly there are standard data structures of basic built-in data types, which are often used in their own form and they can form the basis for complex data structures. Examples of such data structures are array and structure. Data structures may be classified as linear and non-linear type. In linear data structure the data items are arranged in a linear sequence like in an array. In a non-linear data structure, the data items are not in sequence like in a tree. Data structures may also be classified as homogenous and non-homogenous types. Homogenous data structures contain same type of data like an array whereas non-homogenous data structures contain different types of data like a record. Another way of classifying data structures is as static or dynamic data structures. In static structures, size required is fixed at compile time, whereas, dynamic structures grow or shrink in size as required at run time, i.e. during the program execution.

Array

In everyday life, we commonly group similar objects into units. We buy peas in cans and eggs in cartons. In computer programming languages also, we need to group together data items of the same type. The mechanism that accomplishes this in C++ is the array. Arrays can hold a few data items, or tens or thousands or more. The data items grouped in an array can be simple types like int, float, or they can be user-defined types like structures and objects. Arrays exist in almost every computer language, including Pascal, BASIC and many others. Arrays in C++ are similar to those in other languages, and identical to those in C.

Defining Arrays

Arrays are basic building blocks for more complex data structures. An Array is a homogenous collection of a series of data elements (or variables) in which all elements are of same type and are stored consecutively in the memory. Like other variables in C++, an array must be defined, before it can be used to store information. And like other definitions, an array definition specifies a variable type and a name. Additionally, it specifies the size, which again specifies how many data items the array will contain. The specification of size immediately follows the name of the array and is surrounded by square brackets. Figure 4.1 shows an array definition.

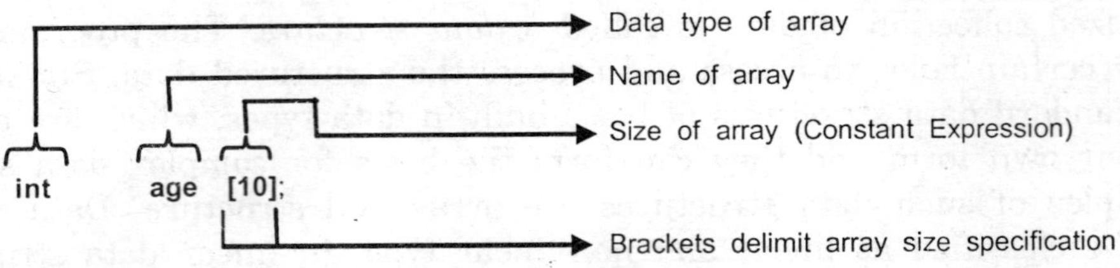

Figure 4.1 Example of an array definition.

Like any other variable, an array must be declared before it is used. A typical declaration for an array in C++ is:

```
datatype array_name [no_of_elements];
```

where data type is a valid type of data (***int, float***...), array_name is a valid variable identifier representing the array and the no_of_elements field that goes enclosed within square brackets [ ] specifies how many of these elements does the array contain. The `no_of_elements` field may contain a constant expression that evaluates to a constant value which is of an integer type and has a value greater than 0. For example, `int age[10];` declares the array named *age* with ***int*** as the data type of each of the elements in the array and number of elements in the array is 10. Here 10 is a constant. The `no_of_elements` field can be made a constant expression as follows:

```
int age[3 + 7];
```

Here, the constant expression 3 + 7 evaluates to a constant value 10.

However, the compiler does not allow a declaration like the following:

```
int a = 3;
int age[a + 7];
```

Here, a is a variable, and `a+7` not being a constant expression, doesn't evaluate to a constant value.

Instead, the following declaration is allowed;

```
const int a = 3;
int age[a + 7];
```

Here, a is a declared constant with an initial value of 3. And, the expression `a + 7` being a constant expression evaluates to a constant value. Hence, this is allowed.

Arrays are blocks of static memory of a given size and the compiler must be able to determine exactly how much memory is needed for the array so that it can occupy predetermined space in memory before any instruction could be executed. As such, while declaring an array as

```
data type    array_name [no_of_elements];
e.g.         int age[10];
```

the no_of_elements field given within square brackets [ ] must be a constant expression which evaluates to a constant positive integer.

Array Elements

The items in an array are elements (in contrast to the items in a structure, which are called *members*). As stated earlier, all the elements in an array are of the same type, only the values vary. Since each element in the array named age is an integer, it occupies four bytes each in a 32-bit machine (may vary from machine to machine). As specified in the definition, the array named age has exactly ten elements. An index value to the array name can individually refer each array element. For example,

```
int a;
```

defines a single integer variable called a; whereas,

```
int age[10];
```

defines a series of 10 (ten) integer data elements stored consecutively collectively known or referred to as an array variable of type integer named *age*. The subscript value 10 used within square brackets defines number of data elements in the array named *age*. Each of the individual integer data elements is accessed by referring to an offset from the array name *age*.

Array elements are indexed starting with zero and ending with one less the number of elements in the array, i.e. 9 in the given example. Thus, the first array element is age[0] and the last is age[9]. You might think that the last element is indexed 10 in an 10-element array, but it's one less, i.e. 9, not 10(since the index value starts from zero). Between 0 and 9, both ends inclusive, the array *age* has 10 (ten) elements. Thus, instead of declaring ten different integer variables, each one with a unique identifier, we can use an array with a unique identifier named *age* to store 10 different integer values (Figure 4.2).

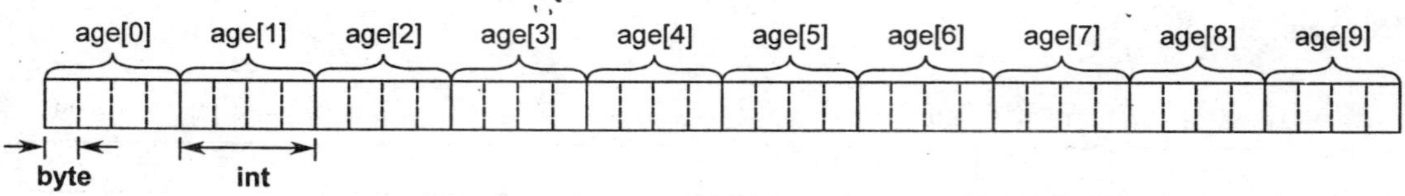

Figure 4.2 Byte allocations for an array of 10 integers.

In the given figure, for the array named *age*, each blank compartment represents an array element of declared type, ***int***, in this case. For any declared array, the index value or subscript starts from 0 (zero) irrespective of the size of the array.

Accessing Array Elements

The expression used in accessing the array element is:

```
age[i];
```

where, `i` can be any value between 0–9.

This consists the name of the array, followed by brackets delimiting a variable i. Which of the ten array elements is specified by this expression depends on the value of i, `age[0]` refers to the first element, `age[1]` to the second, `age[2]` to the third and so on, `age[9]` refers to the tenth element. The variable or constant in bracket is called the *array index*.

Initialization of an Array

When declaring an array without any initialization statements, it is not usually initialized, so its content is undetermined until we store some values in it. The initializer for an array contains the equality (=) symbol that is followed by a comma-separated list of constant expressions enclosed within braces ({ }). For example,

```
int age[10] = {5, 2, 3, 6, 8, 1, 5, 7, 3, 2};
```

This would have declared an array like the following one:

The number of elements in the array initialized within braces { } should match the length in elements that we declared for the array enclosed within brackets [ ]. As you can find in the example, the array named age is declared to have 10 elements having its 10 different initial values given within braces { }, one for each element in the array. C++ allows empty square brackets [ ], by omitting the number of elements when the size of the array is defined by the number of values given between braces { } as in:

```
int age[ ] = {5, 2, 3, 6, 8, 1, 5, 7, 3, 2};
```

In both the declarations, the individual array elements are initialized as follows:

age[0]	age[1]	age[2]	age[3]	age[4]	age[5]	age[6]	age[7]	age[8]	age[9]
5	2	3	6	8	1	5	7	3	2

In the above examples, the array shows a completely initialized one-dimensional array named age. However, one may opt to partially initialized an array as follows:

```
int age[10] = {5, 2, 3, 6, 8, 1};
```

This initializes the array elements as follows:

age[0]	age[1]	age[2]	age[3]	age[4]	age[5]	age[6]	age[7]	age[8]	age[9]
5	2	3	6	8	1	?	?	?	?

In this case, the array elements age[6], age[7], age[8] and age[9] are not usually initialized, by default, as such, their content is undetermined until we store some values in it.

If we omit the number of elements while declaring the array by providing empty square bracket [ ], as in

```
int age[ ] = {5, 2, 3, 6, 8, 1};
```

then, the array age is declared to have 6 elements with its initial values defined within braces. This is because the size of the array is defined by the number of values given between braces { }. The array elements are thus initialized as follows:

	age[0]	age[1]	age[2]	age[3]	age[4]	age[5]
age	5	2	3	6	8	1

Assigning Values to Array Elements

An alternate way of initializing the array elements is by explicitly assigning specific values to specific array element. Individual elements of arrays are accessed using the array subscript operator ([ ]). The index value given within square brackets ([ ]) indicates a particular element in the array. Since this value starts from 0, index 0 refers to the 1st element in an array, and index value 4 refers to 5th element in the array. For example, we may initialize using the array subscript operator as follows:

```
int age[10];
age[0] = 5;
age[1] = 2;
age[2] = 3;
age[3] = 6;
age[4] = 8;
age[5] = 1;
age[6] = 5;
age[7] = 7;
age[8] = 3;
age[9] = 2;
```

which does the equivalent job as done by the following initializer statement, although not same (previous statements perform assignment on existing array elements, whereas following statements perform initializations of array elements at the same time as defining the array):

```
int age[ ] = {5, 2, 3, 6, 8, 1, 5, 7, 3, 2};
   or,
int age[10] = {5, 2, 3, 6, 8, 1, 5, 7, 3, 2};
```

It should be noted that the *lvalue* of an assignation can only be an element of an array and not the entire array and once declared, we cannot assign an entire array as follows:

```
int age[10];
age = {5, 2, 3, 6, 8, 1, 5, 7, 3, 2};  // is not allowed
```

Thus, individual array elements has to be initialized using the subscript operator ([ ]) described thus.

Here's another example of an array at work (Program Source Code 4.1). This one, sales, invites the user to enter a series of six values, representing sales of apple for each day of the week (excluding Sunday) and then calculates the average of these values. We use the array of float so that fractional monetary values can be entered.

Program Source Code 4.1

```
#include <iostream.h>
const int SIZE = 6;
int main()
{
   float sales[SIZE]; // array declared, not initialized
   cout << "Please input sales figure for "
         << SIZE << " days" << endl;
   for ( int i = 0; i < SIZE; i++)
         cin >> sales[i]; // array elements getting
                          // assigned to values
   cout << endl << i;
   float total = 0;
   for (int j = 0; j < SIZE; j++ )
         total += sales[j];
   float average = total / SIZE;
   cout << "Average Sales = " << average << endl;
   return 0;
}
```

Output 4.1

```
Please input sales figure for 6 days
352.44
867.70
781.32
867.35
746.21
189.45
Average Sales = 634.078
```

Defining Multidimensional Arrays

One can declare an array of arrays (more commonly known as a "multidimensional" array) by following the array declarator with a list of square bracketed constant expressions as given in the following form:

```
type-specifier declarator [constant-expression]
            [constant-expression] ...
```

Each constant-expression in brackets defines the number of elements in a given dimension: Two-dimensional arrays have two bracketed expressions, three-dimensional arrays have three, and so on.

A two-dimensional array is defined with two size-specifiers, each enclosed in brackets, e.g.

```
float Sales[DISTRICTS][MONTHS];
```

where, `DISTRICTS` signify number of districts, `MONTHS` signify number of months, and both have constant values.

One way to interpret this statement is that `Sales` is an array of arrays. It is an array of DISTRICTS elements, each of which is an array of MONTHS elements. Let's assume, DISTRICTS = 4, MONTHS = 3. Then, the two-dimensional array *Sales* will contain twelve (12) elements. This is illustrated in Figure 4.3. `Sales[0]` signifies sales for district index 0, comprising of three months' sales i.e. `Sales[0][0]`, `Sales[0][1]`, `Sales[0][2]`, and `Sales[0][0]` signify sales figure of district index 0 and month index 0.

Another two-dimensional array follows:

```
int age[5][10].
```

declares a two-dimensional array with first index or subscript ranging from 0 to 4 and second index or subscript ranging from 0 to 9.

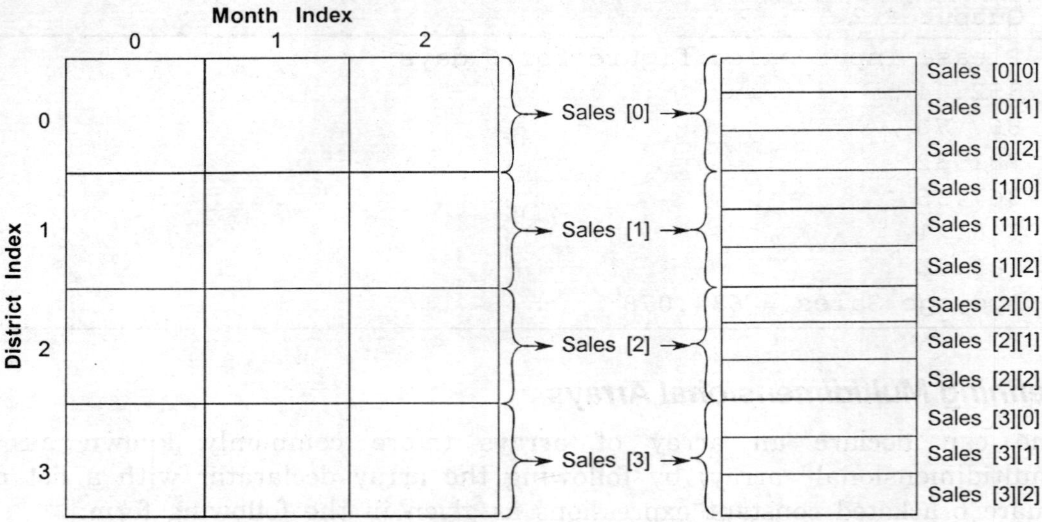

Figure 4.3 A two-dimensional array illustration.

A two-dimensional matrix named, say `mat` can be defined as follows:

```
int mat[3][4];
```

In order to initialize the individual elements of a matrix (a two-dimensional array) to say a common initial value, say, 0, we may write as:

```
int mat[3][4] = {0,0,0,0,0,0,0,0,0,0,0,0};
```

Here, the matrix mat has 3 rows and 4 columns, all initialized to the value 0 and the initializers are given as a flat list. Or, it may be grouped as follows:

```
int mat[3][4] = {{0,0,0,0}, {0,0,0,0},{0,0,0,0}};
```

Here, the initializer values are given in groups of row elements (3 subgroups => 3 rows)

Alternately, using two nested for-loops, we could have assigned 0 to the array elements as follows:

```
int i, j, mat[3][4];
for (i = 0; i < 3; i++)
{
    for(j = 0; j < 4; j++)
    {
        mat[i][j] = 0;
    }
}
```

A multidimensional array can be initialized by the following methods:

1. Initializing the element values in the order of value assignment performed by the compiler: usually, the last dimension is increased first. Thus, the initialization given by

   ```
   int mat[3][4] = {1, 2, 3, 4, 5, 6, 7, 8, 9, 10, 11, 12};
   ```

   initializes the first row of the matrix as {1,2,3,4}, second row as {5,6,7,8} and so on, considering row as the first dimension and column as the second dimension. Here, we cannot write

   ```
   int mat[ ][ ] = {1, 2, 3, 4, 5, 6, 7, 8, 9, 10, 11, 12};
   ```

   Instead, we may write as:

   ```
   int mat[ ][4] = {1, 2, 3, 4, 5, 6, 7, 8, 9, 10, 11, 12};
   ```

   with explicit second dimension value and implicit first dimension value to have the same effect of initializations. This is because, the last dimension is increased first. The last dimension cannot be implicit, unless it is the only dimension as in a single-dimensional array.

2. Braces can be used to group the values of the array elements required to be initialized. Braces can be put around each element, or around any nesting level of elements. The definition of the matrix mat[3][4] contains three elements in the first dimension(i.e. 3 rows), the initializations can contain braces around each of the row elements as in:

   ```
   int mat[3][4] = {{1, 2, 3, 4}, {5, 6, 7, 8},{9, 10, 11, 12}};
   ```

3. Nested braces can be used to initialize elements in a dimension selectively. For example, the following definition explicitly initializes six elements in a 12-element two-dimensional array or matrix having 3 rows(first dimension), and 4 columns(second dimension):

   ```
   int mat[3][4] = {{1, 2}, {5, 6, 7}, {9}};
   ```

   This will selectively initialize the array elements as follows:

   ```
   age[0][0] = 1   age[0][1] = 2   age[0][2] = ?  age[0][3] = ?
   age[1][0] = 5   age[1][1] = 6   age[1][2] = 7  age[1][3] = ?
   age[2][0] = 9   age[2][1] = ?   age[2][2] = ?  age[2][3] = ?
   ```

   the values shown as ? are uninitialized unless it is initialized by the compiler as 0 value. The matrix with its initial cell element values filled in looks like the one shown in Figure 4.4.

Mat — **Column Numbers**; **Row Nos.**

	0	1	2	3
0	1	2	?	?
1	5	6	7	?
2	9	?	?	?

Figure 4.4 Illustration of filling (initializing) partial array elements.

An example program is provided in Program Source Code 4.2.

Program Source Code 4.2

```
#include <iostream.h>
int main ()
{
   int i, j;
   int b[3][4] = {1, 2, 3, 4, 5, 6, 7, 8, 9, 10, 11, 12};
   for (i = 0; i < 3; i++)
   {
      for (j = 0; j < 4; j++)
      {
         cout << "b[" << i<< "]"
              << "[" << j << "]="
              << b[i][j] << endl;
      }
   }
   return 0;
}
```

Output 4.2

```
b[0][0] = 1
b[0][1] = 2
b[0][2] = 3
b[0][3] = 4
b[1][0] = 5
b[1][1] = 6
b[1][2] = 7
b[1][3] = 8
b[2][0] = 9
b[2][1] = 10
b[2][2] = 11
b[2][3] = 12
```

Here, the array called b is initialized with the values 1,2,3,..... You may try with different variations of array initializations with explicit and implicit array dimensions specified.

One should never attempt to write data beyond the last element of the array. For example, if one attempts to write to the 11th element in a single-dimensional array having 10 elements, the result could be that the data will be assigned to an undesired location. Also, there may be unintended damages. The compiler cannot detect this as in Example 4.1.

EXAMPLE 4.1:

```
int i, j, mat[3][4];
for (i = 0; i < 3; i++)
{
   for (j = 0; j < 4; j++)
   {
      mat[i][j] = 0;
   }
}
```

This is the example of assigning 0 to each of the 12 elements in a 3x4 matrix. If we write the for-loop for j as: for `(j = 0; j <= 4; j++)` instead of for `(j = 0; j < 4; j++)` then the loop variable j runs from 0 to 4(instead of 3) and will try to assign value to locations mat[0][4], mat[1][4] and mat[2][4] which are illegal locations as these elements are not part of the 3x4 matrix, and this leads to unintended runtime errors. This type of situation should be avoided.

Accessing Multidimensional Array Elements

Array elements in two-dimensional array require two indices

```
sales [d][m]
```

Note that each index has its own set of brackets. Don't write sales[d,m]; this works in some languages but not in C++. An example of a multidimensional array is given in Program Source Code 4.3.

Program Source Code 4.3

```
#include <iostream.h>
const int DISTRICTS = 4;
const int MONTHS = 3;
int main()
```

(contd.)

Program Source Code 4.3 *(contd.)*

```
{
   int d, m;
   float sales[DISTRICTS][MONTHS];  // array declared, not
                                    // initialized
   // read data for sales figures
   //(districtwise, monthwise)
   for ( d = 0; d < DISTRICTS; d++)
   {
      for ( m = 0; m < MONTHS; m++)
      {
         cout << "Enter sales for district " << d+1;
         cout << ", month " << m+1 << " : ";
         cin >> sales[d][m];
      }
   }
   cout << endl << endl << "\t\t\tMonth" << endl;
   cout << "\t\t1\t\t2\t\t3"<< endl;

   for ( d = 0; d < DISTRICTS; d++)
   {
      cout << endl << "District " << d + 1 << "\t";
      for ( m = 0; m < MONTHS; m++)
      {
         cout << sales[d][m] << "\t\t";
      }
   }
   cout << endl;
   return 0;
}
```

Output 4.3

```
Enter sales for district 1, month 1: 3964.23
Enter sales for district 1, month 2: 4135.87
Enter sales for district 1, month 3: 4397.98
Enter sales for district 2, month 1: 867.75
Enter sales for district 2, month 2: 923.59
Enter sales for district 2, month 3: 1037.01
Enter sales for district 3, month 1: 12.77
Enter sales for district 3, month 2: 378.32
Enter sales for district 3, month 3: 798.22
```

(contd.)

Output 4.3 *(contd.)*

```
Enter sales for district 4, month 1: 2983.53
Enter sales for district 4, month 2: 3903.73
Enter sales for district 4, month 3: 9494.98

                  Month
                  1              2              3

District 1        3964.23        4135.87        4397.98
District 2        867.75         923.59         1037.01
District 3        12.77          378.32         798.22
District 4        2983.53        3903.73        9494.98
```

Character Array

Character arrays can be initialized in one of the following two ways:

1. By initializing entire character array with a string literal as follows:

   `char chStr[5] = "abcd";`

   Here, the character array is initialized with a string literal, and the compiler appends a trailing character '\0' (end-of-string or null character). As such, the size of the character array must be at least one more than the number of characters in the string literal.

2. By initializing the individual array elements as follows:

   `char chArr[4] = { 'a', 'b', 'c', 'd' };`

   This creates an unterminated string (that is, one without a 0 or null value to mark its end) and cannot be used in cases where null-terminated string is expected.

A string is an array of characters ending with a null character('\0'). Since most string handling relies on the presence of the trailing string-terminator character, we use unbounded character array declarations initialized with strings as follows:

`char chStr[ ] = "abcd";`

Here, the implicit size of the chStr is taken as 5, with the following character initializations done:

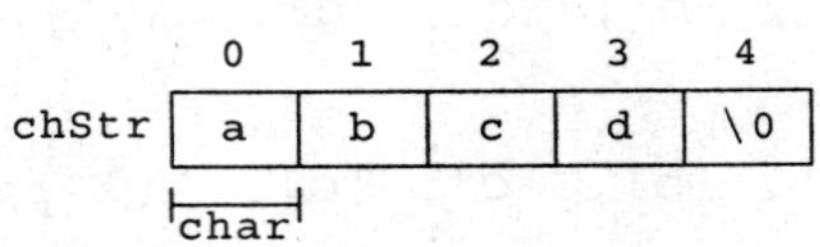

The fifth element, i.e. `chStr[4]` is the null character, which terminates the string literal.

The declaration

```
char chStr[ ] = "abcd";
```

is equivalent to:

```
char chStr[ ]  = {'a', 'b', 'c', 'd', '\0'};
```

or

```
char chStr[5]  = {'a', 'b', 'c', 'd', '\0'};
```

but not equivalent to:

```
char chStr[4]  = {'a', 'b', 'c', 'd'};
```

where, `chStr` will be created as an unterminated string.

Generally, the compiler does not allow the string length to be longer than the specified array size. If the string length is shorter than the specified array size, the remaining elements of the array may remain uninitialized or maybe initialized to 0, depending on compiler. However, if the string is null terminated, then the character array can be safely used in cases where null-terminated strings are expected.

As stated earlier, the *lvalue* of an assignation can only be an element of an array and not the entire array. A string of characters can be assigned to an already declared array of char using individual assignation to the elements in the array as:

```
char chStr[5];
chStr[0] = 'a';
chStr[1] = 'b';
chStr[2] = 'c';
chStr[3] = 'd';
chStr[4] = '\0';
```

which is equivalent to single statement initialization (not assignment) where assignment is joined together with the declaration of the array as in:

```
char chStr[ ] = "abcd";
```

or

```
char chStr[ ]  = {'a', 'b', 'c', 'd', '\0'};
```

or

```
char chStr[5]  = {'a', 'b', 'c', 'd', '\0'};
```

Assigning values to a character array or string can be handled by a list of built-in string functions.

Passing Arrays to Functions

Function declaration with array argument. In a function declaration, array arguments are represented by the data type and sizes of the array:

```
void display( float[ ][ MONTHS ] );
```

Why doesn't the function need the size of the first dimension? Again, remember that a two-dimensional array is an array of arrays. The function thinks argument as an array of districts. It doesn't need to know how many districts there are, but it does need to know how big each district (by multiplying the bytes per element times the index is). So, we must call it the size of each element, which is MONTHS, but how many there are which is DISTRICTS. It follows that if we were declaring a function that used a one-dimensional array as an argument, we would not need to use the array size:

```
void somefunc(int elem[ ]);
```

Function call with array argument. When the function is called, only the name of the array is used as an argument:

```
display(sales);
```

This name (sales, in this case) actually represents the memory address of the array.

Function definition with array argument. In the function definition, the declarator looks like this:

```
void display(float funsales[DISTRICTS][MONTHS])
```

The array argument uses the data type, a name, and the sizes of the dimensions. The array name used by the function (funsales in this example) can be different from the name that defines that array (sales), but they both refer to the same array. All the array dimensions must be specified and the function needs them to properly access the array elements. An example program is given in Program Source Code 4.4.

Program Source Code 4.4

```
#include <iostream.h>
const int DISTRICTS = 4;
const int MONTHS = 3;
void display(float [DISTRICTS][MONTHS]);
int main()
{
    float sales[DISTRICTS][MONTHS]={{1432.07, 234.60, 654.01},
    {327.00, 13838.32, 12589.88}, {9328.34, 934.00, 4492.30},
    {12838.29, 2332.63, 32.93}};
    display(sales);
    return 0;
}
void display(float funsales[DISTRICTS][MONTHS] )
{
    int d, m;
    cout << endl << "\t\t\tMonth" << endl;
    cout << "\t\t1\t\t2\t\t3"<< endl;
    for (d = 0; d < DISTRICTS; d++)
    {
        cout << endl << "District " << d + 1 << "\t";
        for (m = 0; m < MONTHS; m++)
        {
            cout << funsales[d][m] << "\t\t";
        }
    }
    cout << endl;
}
```

Output 4.4

```
                    Month
            1           2           3
District 1  1432.07     234.6       654.01
District 2  327         13838.3     12589.9
District 3  9328.34     934         4492.3
District 4  12838.3     2332.63     32.93
```

Addresses and Pointers

The ideas behind pointers are not complicated. Here's the first key concept: Every byte in computer's memory has an address. Addresses are numbers, just as they are for houses on a street. The numbers start at 0 and go up from there 1, 2, 3 and so on. If you have a 32-bit machine, it can address upto 2^{12} MB memory i.e. 2^{32} (= 429,4967,296) bytes of memory (including virtual memory space). 1 K = 2^{10} bytes = 1024 bytes and 1 M = 2^{20} bytes. Thus, on a 32-bit machine, memory address can go upto 429,4967,295 starting from memory address zero. For 1MB of memory, the maximum memory address is 1,048,575 (since 1 MB = 2^{20} bytes = 1,048,576 bytes).

Your program, when is loaded into memory, occupies a certain range of these addresses for its code area and some other range of address for stack and heap area. Local variables are stored in stack data area and dynamic memory allocations are done using the heap area. That means every variable and every function in your program starts at a particular address.

Let us assume that when loaded into memory for execution, your program named Program1 is loaded starting from memory address 4198, 415. And within it, there are three variables Var1 of type ***int***, Var2 of type ***double*** and Var3 of type ***int***. As we specified earlier in a 32-bit machine the usual number of bytes occupied by an ***int*** and ***double*** types are four and eight bytes respectively. Let us also assume that these three variables Var1, Var2 and Var3 occupy consecutive memory address within the range of addresses occupied by your program data area of Program1. Main function has local data variables Var1, Var2, and Var3. They are stored on the stack data area. And their relative positioning will vary from one implementation to another. Say, these addresses are as follows:

- 1245, 040 for ***int*** variable Var1 which occupies four bytes, i.e. Var1 occupies memory address 1245, 040 to 1245, 043.
- 1245, 044 for ***double*** variable Var2 which occupies eight bytes, i.e. Var2 occupies memory address 1245, 044 to 1245, 051.
- 1245, 052 for ***int*** variable Var3 which occupies four bytes, i.e. Var3 occupies memory address 1245, 052 to 1245, 055.

An example memory map of program loaded in a 32-bit machine memory is shown in Figure 4.5.

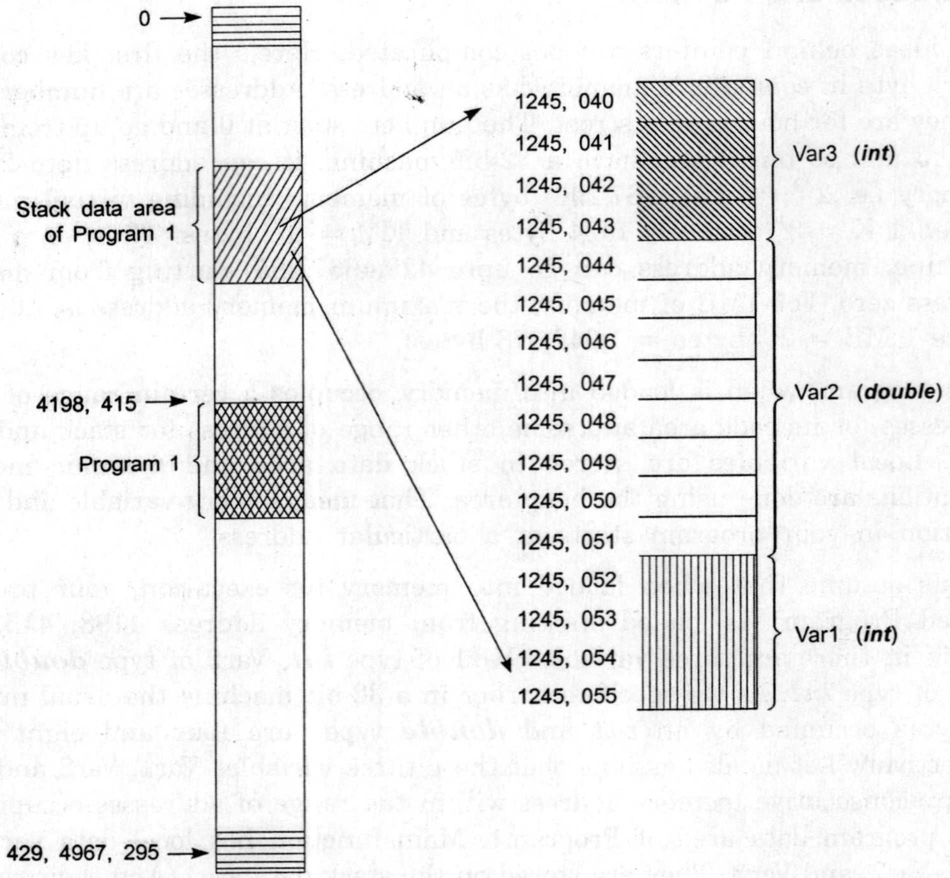

Figure 4.5 Example memory map of program loaded in a 32-bit machine.

Let's take an example program (Program Source Code 4.5).

Program Source Code 4.5

```
#include <iostream.h>
int main()
{
    int   Var1 = 11;
    double  Var2 = 22.0;
    int   Var3 = 33;

    cout << endl << "main starts at " << (long) main;

    cout << endl << "Var1 of type int is located at "
                 << (long) & Var1;
```

(*contd.*)

Program Source Code 4.5 *(contd.)*

```
    cout << " having value = " << Var1;
    cout << endl << "Var2 of type double is located at "
        << (long) &Var2;
    cout << " having value = " << Var2;
    cout << endl << "Var3 of type int is located at "
        << (long) &Var3;
    cout << " having value = " << Var3;
    return 0;
}
```

Output 4.5

```
main starts at 4198415
Var1 of type int is located  at 1245052 having value = 11
Var2 of type double is located  at 1245044 having value = 22
Var3 of type int is located  at 1245040 having value = 33
```

We have stated earlier that variables are identifiers, which need to be stored in some part of memory. For our purpose, we will assume availability of a sequential memory locations for use of our program. This means that memory is a succession of locations with a size of single byte, each having a unique address. If a data is located at memory location 2004 in the memory, we presume that this is a unique location in memory and memory locations being consecutive, 2004 location lies in between 2003 and 2005. A pointer value 0 is also referred as a NULL *pointer.* It does not point to any item. It is recommended to use a NULL pointer instead of uninitialized pointer value. And also, a pointer should be set to NULL in case it is no longer in use or doesn't point to an active location.

A pointer type variable holds the address of a data element or a function. A variable declared as a pointer also occupies a memory address. A pointer occupies a full word, i.e. on a 32-bit machine, a pointer itself occupies 32-bit or 4-bytes of memory space (may vary from machine to machine). A pointer declaration names a pointer variable and specifies the type of the data to which the variable points. As such, it is not the same to point to a ***char*** than an ***int*** or a ***float*** type. If a pointer is declared to point to integer type, the compiler will issue a type mismatch message if one tries to load it with a floating point number. A declaration of pointer follows the form:

```
type * pointer_name;
```

where type is the type of item pointed, not the type of the pointer itself. For example:

```
int * num;
char * char;
float * flnum;
```

These are three pointer declarations. Each one of them points to a different data type, but being a pointer, each of them occupy the same memory space (the size of a pointer depends on the operating system). Although the data to which they point do not occupy the same, nor are they of the same type, one is ***int***, another one ***char*** and the other one ***float***.

The following example declares `ptri` as a pointer to an integer data:

```
int * ptri;
```

If the keyword ***const*** appears before the *, the declarator describes a pointer to a constant data. If the keyword ***const*** appears between the * and the identifier, the declarator describes a constant pointer. In the following example, `cptri` is a constant pointer to a variable integer data:

```
int * const cptri;
```

And, in the declaration, `const int * ptrci;` it declares a variable pointer to constant integer data.

In the declaration, `const int * const cptrci;` it declares a constant pointer to constant integer data.

```
int *ptri, *ptrj;
```

Here again `ptri` and `ptrj` are declared as two pointers to integer data declared in the same line.

It should be noted that you would have to put an asterisk (*) before each pointer you declare.

Void Pointer

The void data type always represents an empty set of values. One cannot declare a variable of type void. The only item that can be declared with the type specifier void is a pointer. If a pointer's type is void *, the pointer can indicate any variable that is not declared with the ***const*** keyword. A void pointer cannot be dereferenced. It can be converted into any other type of data pointer (explicit casting is required in C++, optional in C) and vice versa (see Example 4.2).

EXAMPLE 4.2:

```
void a;         // incorrect
void *ptrv;     // correct
int  *pint;
int i;
int main()
{
   ptrv = &i;
   // Casting is optional in C, required in C++
   pint = (int *)pv;
   return 0;
}
```

Type casting or assignations are needed to turn void pointer to a pointer of a concrete data type that can be referred.

Address-of Operator

Whenever a variable is declared, it occupies space in memory. The compiler decides where in memory the variable will be placed. The unary address-of operator (&) gives the address-of its operand. The result of the address-of operation is a pointer to the operand with its type as pointer to the data type associated with the operand. The address-of operator can only be applied to variables with fundamental, structure, or union types or to array elements.

Here's an example:

EXAMPLE 4.3:

```
int * ptri;
int i = 6;
ptri = &i;
```

This would assign to **ptri** the address-of variable **i**, which occupies a unique space in memory by virtue of declaring it as an integer variable. Let us assume that, the variable **ptri** (pointer to integer type) is stored in a memory location 1022 and occupies 4 bytes of memory (may vary depending on machine and operating system). The variable **i** (integer type) is stored in a memory location 1026 and occupies 4 bytes of memory. Then, the content of location 1026 is the value of **i** i.e. 6 (since **i** is initialized to 6). The address-of the variable **i** is 1026. As such, ptri gets the value of 1026, and thus, the pointer variable **ptri** points to the variable **i**. This situation is pictorially represented in Figure 4.6.

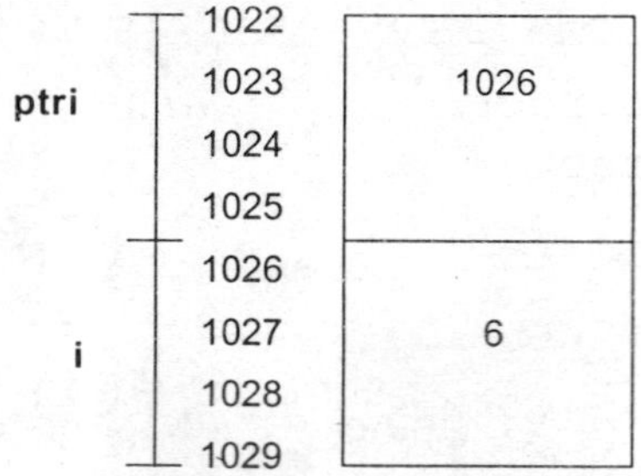

Figure 4.6 Pointer memory map illustration.

Indirection Operator

We know about binary * operator which stands for multiplication operation using two operands. Using the unary indirection operator (*), we can access the value of the data a pointer refers to. The indirection operator (or more commonly known as value pointed by) dereferences a pointer; i.e. it converts a pointer value to an *l-value*. The operand of the indirection operator must be a pointer to a data type. The result is the type from which the pointer type is derived. Thus, if the pointer points to a memory location, the result of applying the indirection operator is an *l-value* having the contents of the memory location, provided the memory location is a valid one, otherwise, the result will be undefined. It is important to remember that pointers must have a value.

An address 0x8f4ffff4 can be thought of as a pointer constant. A pointer like **ptr** can be thought of as a pointer variable. The pointer variable can be assigned to the constant value 0x84ffff4. When we define a variable of type ***int***, which is uninitialized, it contains unpredictable value or simply no value. It may hold a garbage value, but this has no meaning. In case of pointers, a garbage value is the address of something in the memory but probably not of something that we want. So, before a pointer is used, a specific address must be placed in the value.

Invalidate a pointer. There are some most common conditions that invalidate a pointer value or memory location of a valid item, such as, the pointer

1. is a null pointer.
2. specifies the address of some item, which no longer exists.
3. specifies an address that is inappropriately aligned for the type of the item pointed to.
4. specifies an address not used by the executing program.

Let's refer to Example 4.3 again

```
int * ptri;
int i = 6;
ptri = &i;
```

Here, the pointer variable **ptri** is stored at location 1022, integer variable **i** is stored at location 1026 having the value 6, and by virtue of assigning address-of the variable **i** to **ptri**, that contains the value 1026, which is the memory location or address of the variable **i**. Now, if we write the following after the above three statements:

```
i = *ptri;
```

it means, we would like to assign the indirection or dereferencing of the pointer **ptri**, i.e. the integer variable **i** is assigned the value of the item the pointer **ptri** refers to, i.e. the contents of the memory location 1026 (value of the variable **ptri**), i.e. 6. This can be made clear by visualizing the memory map as given in the previous subsection in Figure 4.6.

The following example situation shows **ptri** cannot be properly dereferenced because it is a null pointer.

EXAMPLE 4.4:

```
int * ptri = NULL;
int i = 6;
i = *ptri;
```

An example is given as Program Source Code 4.6.

Program Source Code 4.6

```
#include <iostream.h>
int main()
{
    int i = 6;
    int j = 7;
    int * ptr;
    ptr = &i;
    *ptr = 10;
    ptr = &j;
    *ptr = 20;
    cout << "i = " << i << ", j = " << j << endl;
    return 0;
}
```

Output 4.6

```
i = 10, j = 20
```

In order to explain the program given thus and to understand the effects, let's use a memory map (Figure 4.7). Let's assume, the integer variables **i** and **j** are stored in a memory locations 1022 and 1026 respectively and occupies 4 bytes of memory each. The pointer variable **ptr** is stored in a memory location 1030 and occupies 4 bytes of memory. The steps of execution of the above program is explained in the following diagram. This shows, how the use of the address-of and the indirection operator changes the values of the variables **i** and **j** which were initialized to 6 and 7 respectively.

Situation after executing line number

	Memory Address	06	07	08	09	10
i	1022 1023 1024 1025	6	6	10	10	10
j	1026 1027 1028 1029	7	7	7	7	20
ptr	1030 1031 1032 1033	?	1022	1022	1026	1026

Figure 4.7 Memory map for Program Source Code 4.6.

A variation of Program Source Code 4.6 follows in Source Code 4.6a:

Program Source Code 4.6a

```
include <iostream.h>
int main()
{
   int i = 6;
   int j = 7;
   int *ptri, *ptrj;
```

(*contd.*)

Program Source Code 4.6a *(contd.)*

```
07.     ptri = &i;
08.     ptrj = &j;
09.     *ptri = 10;
10.     *ptrj = *ptri;
11.     ptrj = ptri;
12.     *ptrj = 20;
13.     cout << "i = " << i << ", j = " << j << endl;
14.     return 0;
15. }
```

Output 4.6a

```
i = 20, j = 10
```

The memory map shown in Figure 4.8 will help to understand the changing of values of variables **i** and **j** step-by-step. We assume that, **i, j, ptri** and **ptrj** are at locations 1022, 1026, 1030, 1034, respectively.

	Memory address	Situation after executing line number 06	07	08	09	10	11	12
i	1022 1023 1024 1025	6	6	6	10	10	10	20
j	1026 1027 1028 1029	7	7	7	7	10	10	10
ptr	1030 1031 1032 1033	?	1022	1022	1022	1022	1022	1022
ptrj	1034 1035 1036 1037	?	?	1026	1026	1026	1022	1022

Figure 4.8 Memory map for Program Source Code 4.6a.

The following rules should be noted for using indirection operator (*) and address-of operator (&):

1. An asterisk before a variable in a declaration tells the compiler that this is a pointer, for example, `int * pi;` declares a pointer to integer.

2. An asterisk before a pointer variable in the code means that we are referring to the variable the pointer is addressing; e.g. `*pi = 4;` means we like to assign 4 to the memory location which is addressed by the pointer **pi**.

3. An ampersand before a variable means that we are referring to the address of the variable, not its contents, e.g. `int * pi; int j;` and `pi = &j;` mean that the pointer **pi** is assigned the address of the variable **j**;

Pointers to Pointers

Pointers can be used to point to other pointers as well. In order to do that, an asterisk (*) is needed to add for each level of reference. For example, refer to Program Source Code 4.7.

Program Source Code 4.7

```
#include <iostream.h>
int main()
{
    int i;
    int * ptri;
    int ** pptri;
    i = 6;
    ptri = &i;
    pptri = &ptri;
   cout << "i = " << i << endl
       << "*ptri = " << *ptri << endl
       << "**pptri = " << **pptri << endl;
   return 0;
}
```

Output 4.7

```
i = 6
*ptri = 6
**pptri = 6
```

Here, **pptri** is of type ***int** ***, ***pptri** or **ptri** is of type ***int** **, and ****pptri** or ***ptri** or **i** is of type ***int***. The memory map is shown in Figure 4.9, assuming variable **i** is at location 1022, **ptri** is at 1026 and **pptri** is at location 1030.

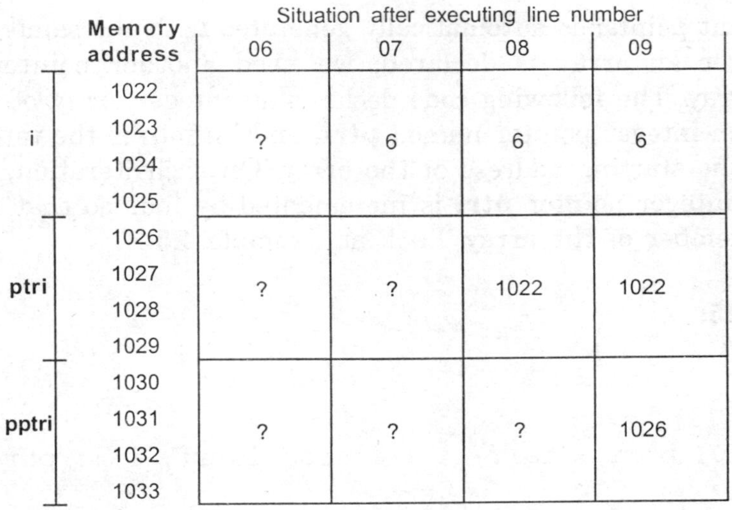

Figure 4.9 Memory map for Program Source Code 4.7.

Pointers and Arrays

When an array is declared, a pointer is automatically generated whose name is that of the array. This array pointer is a constant (its value cannot be changed thereafter), and contains the address of the zeroth or the first element of the array. In the following example, we assign a pointer to integer variable called **ptr** to point to the first element of the array **intarr** by assigning the pointer **ptr** to the array name **intarr**.

```
int intarr [20];
int * ptr;
p = intarr; // valid
intarr = p; // invalid
```

We cannot, however, assign a pointer to an array, because array once defined has a fixed or constant starting address as given by the compiler and that address cannot be changed thereafter by assigning to any other pointer. As such, **intarr = p** assignment is invalid.

The array index of an array is known as offset operators and they are equivalent to add the offset value to the value of the starting address of the array. For example, the following expressions are equivalent and valid either if **age** is a pointer or if it is an array.

```
age[2] = 1;          // age [offset of 2] = 1
*(age + 2) = 1;      // pointed by (age + 2) = 1
```

Since a constant pointer is automatically generated with the same name of the array whenever an array is declared, we need another pointer to iterate through an array. The following code declares an integer array of 10 elements named **iarr**, an integer pointer named **ptri**, and initializes the integer pointer by assigning the starting address of the array. On each iteration, the address stored in the integer pointer **ptri** is incremented by four so that it will point to the next member of the array. Look at Example 4.5.

EXAMPLE 4.5:

```
int main()
{
   int iarr[12], *ptri;
   for (i = 0, ptri = iarr; i < sizeof(iarr); i++, ptri++)
   {
      *ptri = 0;
   }
      return 0;
}
```

Here, we have used an operator named *sizeof* which gives the amount of storage, in bytes, required to store an item of the type of the operand. This operator allows to avoid specifying machine-dependent data sizes in programs. In the above example, sizeof(iarr) will yield a value of 12 * **sizeof(int)**, i.e. 48 considering an integer occupies 4 bytes of memory in a 32-bit machine(varies from machine to machine). The function **sizeof**(**ptri**) would have yielded just 4, as the pointer **ptri** occupies 4 bytes of memory in a 32-bit machine(varies from machine to machine).

Consider the statement:

```
int   intarr[5] = {31, 43, 77, 52, 93};
```

Memory map illustration of this statement is given in Figure 4.10.

If we have two pointers pointing to different locations in the same array, one pointer can be subtracted from the other. This operation yields the number of elements in the array in between the two addresses to which the pointers refer.

Pointer Constants and Pointer Variables

Suppose that, instead of adding **j** to **intarr** to step through the array addresses, you wanted to use the increment operator. Could you write *(intarr++)? The answer is no, and the reason is that you can't increment a

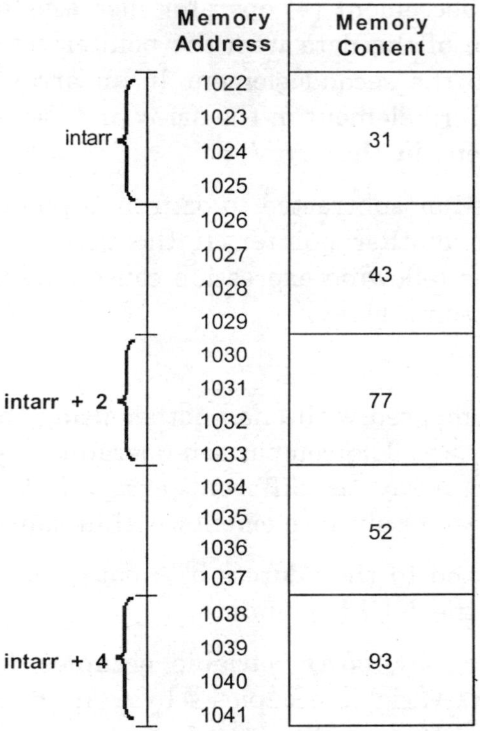

Figure 4.10 Memory map.

constant. The expression **intarr** is the address where the system has chosen to place your array, and it will stay at this address until the program terminates. **intarr** is a constant. You cannot say intarr++.

Pointer Arithmetic

The following arithmetic operations are supported on pointers:

- Increment and decrement
- Addition and subtraction
- Comparison
- Assignment

A pointer declaration must include a type of the variable pointed to. The compiler needs to know whether a pointer is a pointer to ***int*** or a pointer to ***double*** so that it can perform the correct arithmetic to access the elements of the array. It multiplies the index value by 4 in case of an ***int***(on a 32-bit machine), by 8 in case of a ***double*** (on a 32-bit machine).

The increment (+) or decrement (–) operator increases or decreases the value of a pointer by the size of the data item the pointer refers to. For example, if the pointer **p** refers to the second element in an array, the **++p** makes the pointer **p** refer to the third element in the array and the **--p** makes the pointer refer to the first element in the array.

An integer can be added or subtracted to or from a pointer, however, a pointer cannot be added with another pointer. If the pointer **p** points to the first element in an array, the following expression causes the pointer to point to the fourth element in the same array:

```
p = p + 3;
```

Two pointers can be compared with one another using the following operators: ==, !=, <, >, <= and >=. The comparison operators == and != can compare elements within same array or different array. However, the comparison operators <, >, <=, >= apply to elements within same array.

A pointer can be assigned to the address of a data item, the value of another compatible pointer or the NULL pointer.

Let's take an example, say, ***char*** variable occupies 1 byte, short variable occupies 2 bytes and ***int*** variable occupies 4 bytes in memory (Program Source Code 4.8). Let's suppose that we have 3 pointers:

```
int * ptri;       // pointer to integer
char *  ptrc;     // pointer to character
short * ptrs;     // pointer to short
```

And we have an integer array declared and initialized as:

```
int   iarr[4] = {65, 66, 67, 68};
```

and say, the starting location of the array named **iarr** is 1022, to which all the three pointers point to at the beginning. Thus, we have the memory map shown in Figure 4.11, and we know that **ptri**, **ptrc**, and **ptrs** all point to memory locations 1022 initially.

So if we add 1 to each of these pointers:

ptri + 1 will contain 1026 (size of integer i.e. 4 added)

ptrc + 1 will contain 1023 (size of character i.e. 1 added)

ptrs + 1 will contain 1024 (size of short i.e. 2 added)

	Memory Address	ptri Index	Value	ptrc Index	Value (ASCII Code)	ptrs Index	Value
iarr[0]	1022	0	65	0	'A'	0	65
	1023			1	0		
	1024			2	0	1	0
	1025			3	0		
iarr[1]	1026	1	66	4	'B' = 66	2	66
	1027			5	0		
	1028			6	0	3	0
	1029			7	0		
iarr[2]	1030	2	67	8	'C' = 67	4	67
	1031			9	0		
	1032			10	0	5	0
	1033			11	0		
iarr[3]	1034	3	68	12	'D' = 68	6	68
	1035			13	0		
	1036			14	0	7	0
	1037			15	0		

Figure 4.11 Memory map with three pointers.

The reason behind is that when adding one to a pointer it means that this will point to the following element of the type with which it has been defined, and therefore the size in bytes of the type pointed to is added to the pointer.

Program Source Code 4.8

```
#include <iostream.h>
int main()
{
   int  i;
   int  iarr[4] = {65, 66, 67, 68};
   int  *ptri;  char *ptrc;  short *ptrs;
   ptri = iarr;
   ptrc = (char *) iarr;
   ptrs = (short *) iarr;
   for ( i = 0; i < 4; i++)
      cout << "ptri[" << i << "]=" << *(ptri+i) << endl;
```

(*contd.*)

Program Source Code 4.8 *(contd.)*

```
    for (i = 0; i < 16; i++)
        cout << "ptrc[" << i << "]=" << *(ptrc+i) << endl;
    for (i = 0; i < 8; i++)
        cout << "ptrs[" << i << "]=" << *(ptrs+i) << endl;
    return 0;
}
```

Output 4.8

```
ptri[0] = 65   ptrc[0] = A   ptrc[5] =     ptrc[10] =     ptrc[15] =     ptrs[4] = 67
ptri[1] = 66   ptrc[1] =     ptrc[6] =     ptrc[11] =     ptrs[0] = 65   ptrs[5] = 0
ptri[2] = 67   ptrc[2] =     ptrc[7] =     ptrc[12] = D   ptrs[1] = 0    ptrs[6] = 68
ptri[3] = 68   ptrc[3] =     ptrc[8] = C   ptrc[13] =     ptrs[2] = 66   ptrs[7] = 0
               ptrc[4] = B   ptrc[9] =     ptrc[14] =     ptrs[3] = 0
```

It should be noted that increment (++) and decrement (--) operators have a greater priority than the indirection operator (*), therefore the following expression may lead to ambiguities:

`*p++; // equivalent to *(p++),` i.e. contents of the incremented p.

The expression `*p++ = *q++;` first assigns `*q to *p` and then both q and p are incremented. Thus, the above expression is equivalent to:

```
*p = *q; p++; q++;
```

Use of parenthesis () is strongly recommended in order to avoid surprises in results.

Pointers and Functions

If the function is intended to modify variables in the calling program, then the variables cannot be passed by value, since the function obtains one copy of the variable. However, either a reference argument or a pointer can be used in this situation.

Structure

A structure in C (C++ structure will be covered later) contains an ordered set of data items of different sizes grouped together. The ***struct*** keyword defines a structure type and/or a variable of a structure type. It is like the following:

```
struct type_name {
type1 item1;
type2 item2;
```

```
type3 item3;
....
} var_name;
```

where type_name is the name for a structure type(optional) with the set of data items defined, and the optional parameter var_name is a valid identifier for the structure type defined. Within the braces { } the types and the names corresponding to the items that compose the structure are defined.

For example, let's say we declare the following structure of DATE as a structure type and DateOfBirth, DateOfAnniversary as names of structure variables.

```
struct DATE
{
   short day;
   short month;
   short year;
} DateOfBirth, DateOfAnniversary;
```

We have first defined the structure type DATE with three fields: day, month and year each of short type. We have then used the name of the structure type (DATE) to declare two variables of that type: DateOfBirth and DateOfAnniversary. Here, we are directly declaring the variables DateOfBirth and DateOfAnniversary of structure type alongwith the declaration of the DATE structure. Once declared, DATE has become a new valid type name like the fundamental types like ***int***, ***char*** or ***short***. We may now declare a new variable called DateOfJoining as follows:

```
struct DATE DateOfJoining;
```

or simply,

```
DATE DateOfJoining;
```

The latter declaration is allowed in C++, not in C. The first one is allowed both in C and C++.

We may also define the DateOfJoining variable as a direct structure without mentioning the structure type. In that case, we cannot reuse the structure type, every time we would like to define a similar structure variable, we have to redefine the structure. It is defined as follows:

```
struct
{
   short day;
   short month;
   short year;
} DateOfJoining;
```

Fields in a structure can be referenced by following the name of the structure by a dot and before the name of the field. For example, DateOfBirth.day, DateOfJoining.year, etc.

Let's see example Program Source Code 4.9 that assigns values to the members of the structures.

Program Source Code 4.9

```
#include <iostream.h>
int main()
{
    struct DATE
    {
        short day;
        short month;
        short year;
    } DateOfBirth, DateOfAnniversary;
    DateOfBirth.day = 07;
    DateOfBirth.month = 12;
    DateOfBirth.year = 1966;
    DateOfAnniversary.day = 11;
    DateOfAnniversary.month = 07;
    DateOfAnniversary.year = 1993;
    cout << "Date of Birth: "
         << DateOfBirth.day << "/"
         << DateOfBirth.month << "/"
         << DateOfBirth.year
         << endl;
    cout << "Date of Anniversary: "
         << DateOfAnniversary.day << "/"
         << DateOfAnniversary.month << "/"
         << DateOfAnniversary.year
         << endl;
    return 0;
}
```

Output 4.9

```
Date of Birth: 7/12/1966
Date of Anniversary: 11/7/1993
```

Another example in Program Source Code 4.10 defines an array of structures that is named Dates. Each element of Dates contains three members: the short variable day, short variable month and short variable year. Dates[0] contains date of birth, and Dates[1] contains date of anniversary. We also define an array of strings named DateLabel, which is of dimension 2x30. This means DateLabel is an array of strings with an accommodation of two strings, DateLabel[0] defines the first string "Date of Birth" and DateLabel[1] defines the second string "Date of Anniversary". Each string is defined to have a capacity of 30 characters maximum to hold null terminated strings. We have defined implicit size in first dimension value and explicit size in second dimension of array DateLabel. The program output is the same as the output of the previous program.

Program Source Code 4.10

```
#include <iostream.h>
int main()
{
   int i;
   char DateLabel[][30] = {"Date of Birth",
                           "Date of Anniversary"};
   struct DATE
   {
      short day;
      short month;
      short year;
   } Dates[2];

   Dates[0].day = 07;
   Dates[0].month = 12;
   Dates[0].year = 1966;

   Dates[1].day = 11;
   Dates[1].month = 07;
   Dates[1].year = 1993;

   for (i = 0; i < 2; i++)
   {
      cout << DateLabel[i] << " : "
           << Dates[i].day << "/"
           << Dates[i].month << "/"
           << Dates[i].year
           << endl;
   }
   return 0;
}
```

```
Output 4.10
Date of Birth: 7/12/1966
Date of Anniversary: 11/7/1993
```

Like any other type, structures can be pointed by pointers. The rules are the same as applied for fundamental data types. The pointer must be declared as pointer to the structure. Fields in a pointer to structure can be referenced by following the name of the pointer to structure by an arrow (->) and the before name of the field. For example, `pDateOfBirth->day`, `pDateOfBirth->year` where `pDateOfBirth` is defined as Date `*pDateOfBirth`.

`pDateOfBirth->year`

and

`(*pDateOfBirth).year` are equivalent.

We now modify the above program example to use an array of pointers to structures. The array Dates is now replaced by an array of two pointers called pDates. `pDates[0]` points to the address of a structure variable named DateOfBirth, and `pdates[1]` points to the address of a structure variable named DateOfAnniversary. It is dangerous to keep any pointer declared but pointing to garbage. This can happen in case of uninitialized pointer variable. Thus, it is strongly recommended to assign pointers to valid addresses of data, before the use of pointers in programs. Let's see this modified example in Program Source Code 4.11 using pointers to structures instead of array of structures.

Program Source Code 4.11

```
#include <iostream.h>
int main()
{
    int i;
    char DateLabel[][30] = {"Date of Birth",
                           "Date of Anniversary"};
    struct DATE
    {
        short day;
        short month;
        short year;
    };
    DATE DateOfBirth;
    DATE DateOfAnniversary;
    DATE *pDates[2];
```

(*contd.*)

Program Source Code 4.11 *(contd.)*

```
    pDates[0] = &DateOfBirth;
    pDates[1] = &DateOfAnniversary;

    pDates[0]->day = 07;
    pDates[0]->month = 12;
    pDates[0]->year = 1966;

    pDates[1]->day = 11;
    pDates[1]->month = 07;
    pDates[1]->year = 1993;

    for (i = 0; i < 2; i++)
    {
       cout << DateLabel[i] << " : "
            << pDates[i]->day  << "/"
            << pDates[i]->month << "/"
            << pDates[i]->year
            << endl;
    }
    return 0;
}
```

Output 4.11

```
Date of Birth: 7/12/1966
Date of Anniversary: 11/7/1993
```

Nesting Structures

Structures can also be nested so that a valid element of a structure can also be another structure. For example,

```
struct PERSON
{
   char name[60];
   DATE DateOfBirth;
};
```

defines a structure type named PERSON with two elements: name as a character string of size 60, and a DateOfBirth field which is another structure of structure type DATE. We define a variable named aPerson of type PERSON to hold the data for the person. We read the data from input and output the data read. This will be like the Program Source Code 4.12.

Program Source Code 4.12

```
#include <iostream.h>
int main()
{
    struct DATE
    {
        short day;
        short month;
        short year;
    };
    struct PERSON
    {
        char  name[60];
        DATE  DateOfBirth;
    };

    PERSON aPerson;

    cout  << "Please input the name of the person: ";
    cin   >> aPerson.name;
    cout  << "Please input the date of birth of the person : ";
    cin   >> aPerson.DateOfBirth.day
          >> aPerson.DateOfBirth.month
          >> aPerson.DateOfBirth.year;

    cout  << "We have got one person whose : "<< endl
          << "Name is : " << aPerson.name << endl
          << "Date of Birth is : "
          << aPerson.DateOfBirth.day << "/"
          << aPerson.DateOfBirth.month << "/"
          << aPerson.DateOfBirth.year << endl;
    return 0;
}
```

Output 4.12

```
Please input the name of the person: Soumen
Please input the date of birth of the person: 5 6 1991
We have got one person whose:
Name is: Soumen
Date of Birth is: 5/6/1991
```

When the ***sizeof*** operator is applied to a class, struct, or union type, the result is the number of bytes in the variable of that class, struct, or union type, plus any padding added to align members on word boundaries. For example, the sizeof(DATE) would yield 6 considering sizeof(short) would yield 2 in 32-bit machine. If a structure is defined in a way the total of the size of the elements is odd number, then the size of the structure will be taken as nearest even number greater than or equal to (ceiling) the total size of the elements of the structure. Thus, the size of the following structure will be taken as 4, although the total of the sizes of the individual elements is 3.

```
struct ASTRUCTURE
{
    char aChar;
    short aShort;
};
```

on 32-bit machine and unibyte character,

`sizeof(char) = 1, sizeof(short) = 2, but sizeof(ASTRUCTURE) = 4` (not 1 + 2, i.e. 3).

SUMMARY

The key concepts introduced in this chapter are as follows:

- The organized collection of data is called a *data structure*. The programs have to follow certain rules to access and process the structured data.
- Arrays are basic building blocks for more complex data structures. An array is a homogenous collection of a series of data elements (or variables) in which all elements are of same type and are stored consecutively in the memory.
- When declaring an array without any initialization statement, it is not usually initialized, so its content is undetermined until we store some values in it. The initializer for an array contains the equality (=) symbol that is followed by a comma-separated list of constant expressions enclosed within braces ({ }).
- One can declare an array of arrays (more commonly known as a "multidimensional" array).
- A string is an array of characters ending with a null character('\0'). Most string handling relies on the presence of the trailing string-terminator character.
- Local variables are stored in stack data area, and dynamic memory allocations are done using the heap area.

- Every variable and every function in a program starts at a particular address. A pointer type variable holds the address of a data element or a function. A variable declared as a pointer also occupies a memory address.
- A pointer value 0 is also referred as a NULL pointer. It does not point to any item. It is recommended to use a NULL pointer instead of uninitialized pointer value. Also, a pointer should be set to NULL in case it is no longer in use or doesn't point to an active location.
- The void data type always represents an empty set of values. One cannot declare a variable of type void. The only item that can be declared with the type specifier void is a pointer.
- The unary address-of operator (&) gives the address of its operand. The result of the address-of operation is a pointer to the operand with its type as pointer to the data type associated with the operand. Using unary indirection operator (∗), we can access the value of the data a pointer refers to.
- Pointers can be used to point to other pointers as well. In order to do that, an asterisk (∗) is needed to add for each level of reference.
- When an array is declared, a pointer is automatically generated, whose name is that of the array. This array pointer is a constant (its value cannot be changed thereafter), and contains the address of the zeroth or the first element of the array.
- We cannot assign a pointer to an array, because array once defined has a fixed or constant starting address as given by the compiler and that address cannot be changed thereafter by assigning to any other pointer.
- An integer can be added or subtracted to or from a pointer. However, a pointer cannot be added with another pointer. Pointers can also be compared.
- A structure in C contains an ordered set of data items of different sizes grouped together. Structures can also be nested so that a valid element of a structure can also be another structure.

REVIEW QUESTIONS

1. A program segment such as

```
int y = 10;
int *x = &y;
```

Find out which of the following expressions are equivalent? Which do not change y?

```
x++, (x++),  *++x, *(++x)
```

2. How do the following statements differ?
   - `char * const p;`
   - `const char *p;`
   - `const char * const p;`
3. What is the relationship between an array and a pointer? What is the difference?
4. What are the first and last elements in OneArray[30]?
5. Illustrate with examples the declaration of multidimensional arrays.
6. What is the total number of elements in OneArray[20][3][4]?
7. What is the last character in the string "`Hello  World`"? What is the last but one?
8. What is the size of a structure?
9. Can a structure contain arrays? Can an array contain structures? Illustrate with examples.
10. How do you extract members from a pointer to structure? Illustrate with examples.
11. Given a date in the format dd/mm/yy. Write a program to accept a valid date and display appropriate message for invalid dates as shown in sample output:

```
Input Date: 32 12 01
<Invalid Day Enter Again>
Input Date: 02 13 01
<Invalid Month Enter Again>
Input Date: 02 12 01
<Valid Date>
```

12. Modify the above program to store the valid dates entered in an array of structures of date record and print them in the order of months (1 first, 12 last).
13. Given an amount in rupees, write a program to output the number of notes of each denominations needed, if the total number of notes is

required to be minimum, e.g. if the amount is Rs. 1137, the output will be:

```
No. of 500 rupee notes = 2
No. of 100 rupee notes = 1
No. of  20 rupee notes = 1
No. of  10 rupee notes = 1
No. of   5 rupee notes = 1
No. of   2 rupee notes = 1
_________________________________
TOTAL               15
_________________________________
```

14. The famous saree shop Kala Niketan wishes to fund out how many sarees it is selling, each of the colors Red(R), Blue(B), Green(G), and White(W). Write a program which accepts a string of input in the form

GRYBBYGWRRBPBWPB

and produces output in the form

```
No. of Green Sarees    :   2     Red Sarees   :   3
White Sarees           :   2     Blue Sarees  :   5
Others                 :   4
```

5 Functions

If you can't hear me, it's because I'm in parentheses.
—Steven Wright

LEARNING OBJECTIVES

The objective of this chapter is to acquaint you with:

- Declaration, definition and call of a function
- Inline functions
- Main function arguments
- Reference variables
- Function overloading
- Parameter passing concepts—call by value vs. call by reference
- Concept of recursion
- Scope of variables
- Return from functions by value as well as by reference
- Pointer to functions

INTRODUCTION

You were already introduced to the concepts of the main function, which is the first to be executed when a program starts. Before going deeper into object-oriented programming concepts, we start with conventional procedural programming approach.

In procedural programming paradigm, a program is built through procedures or functions that represent behavioural aspects with the use of data. With increased growth in size and complexity, keeping track of monolithic program logic becomes difficult. As such, it is strongly felt to break a program into several separate modules with clear-cut purpose or activity defined, and of course manageable as a whole. Many a times, the same task depicted by the same lines of code is repeated several times in a program under execution. Instead of repeating the same lines of code representing the task at various places in the program, we can declare a function name representing the lines of code to be repeated and invoke the function to execute the sequences of code. Thus, we can structure our programs in a more modular way using functions.

A function groups a number of program statements into a unit and gives it a name. This named unit is then invoked from other parts of the program. Functions helps to conceptualize a better organization of a program. Dividing a program into several functions is one of the major principles of structured programming. In fact, the primary advantage of having functions is that functions make programs more modular, and modularity bestows a large number of additional advantages, such as greater maintainability, the ability to develop programs in teams and so on. Another reason to use functions is to reduce the program size. The function code is stored in its entirety in one contiguous place in memory, even though the function is executed many times during the program execution. Figure 5.1 illustrates that main function has called a function named func1( ) twice and function func2 with one integer of parameter 4 in the course of execution of the main program.

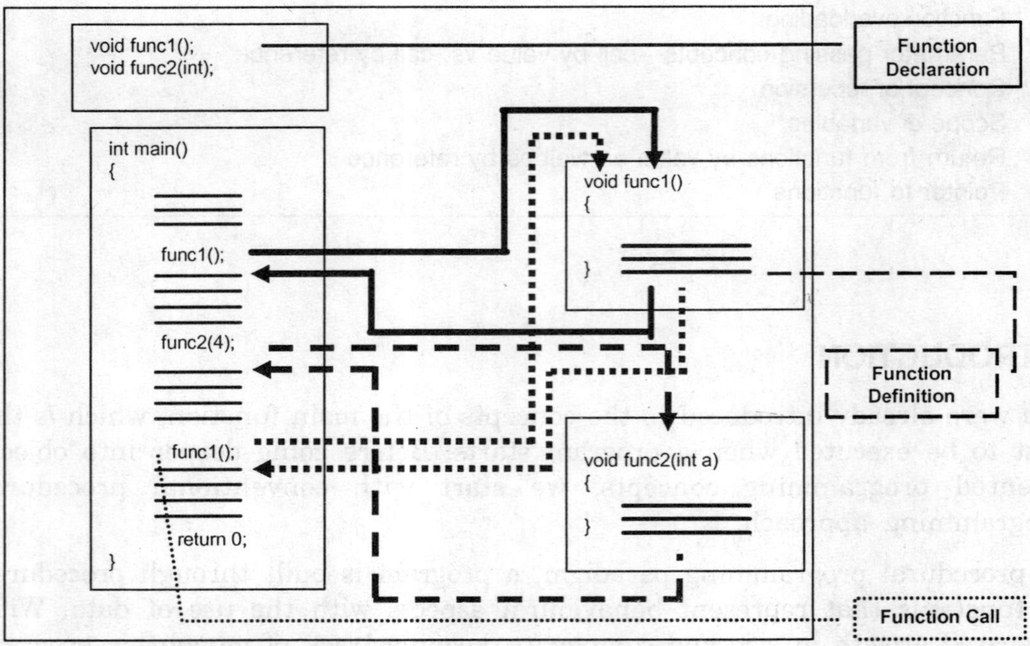

Figure 5.1 Flow of control to functions.

The flow of control to function call and return are shown using appropriate arrows. For example, when func1 is called without any argument, the program control goes to the function body of func1, and after execution of the block of statements of func1, the program control comes back to the statement immediately following the call to func1.

Declaration, Definition and Call

There is a distinction between a function declaration, a function definition and a function call. This is illustrated in Table 5.1. A *function declaration* consists of a return type, a function name, and a list of arguments as number and type of arguments. Just as you cannot use a variable without first telling the compiler what it is, you also cannot use a function without telling the compiler about it. The most common approach is to declare all the functions before the beginning of the program. The *function call* is merely calling the function with the function name passing the parameters, and optionally taking the return value to some variable. The function call must conform to the function *signature* (comprising of function name and its arguments maintaining the order, number and type of arguments) as declared. A *function definition* contains a function declaration and the body of the function with the declarations of its local variables, and the statements that determine the job of the function. If function definition precedes function call, then separate function declaration is not required.

A function can have only one definition but more than one declarations. This means a function can be defined only once, but can be declared multiple times.

Table 5.1 Function Components

Component	*Purpose*	*Example*
Declaration	Specifies function name, argument types, and return value. Alerts compiler (and programmer) that actual function definition will follow later.	void func1(int);

Definition	The function itself. Contains the lines of code that constitute the function.	void func1(int a)
		{
		   cout << a; // lines of code
		}

Call	Causes the function to be executed	func1(4);

The following is its format:

```
return_data type function_name (argument1, argument2, ...)
{
  statements
}
```

where

- return_data type is the type of data returned by the function.
- function_name is the name by which it will be possible to call the function.
- argument 1, 2.. (as many can be specified as necessary) consists of a data type followed by a particular name, called parameter to the function. It's like variable declaration (for example, int x) and acts within the function like any other variable. They serve to allow passing parameters to the function when the function is called. Commas separate the different parameters.
- statements constitute the function's body consisting of zero or more statements.

An example program follows (Program Source Code 5.1).

Program Source Code 5.1

```
#include <iostream.h>
int product(int x, int y)
{
  return x * y;
}

int main()
{
  int a, b, c;
  cout << "Please input a number: ";
  cin >> a;
  cout << "Please input another number: ";
  cin >> b;
  c = product(a, b);
  cout << "The product of " << a
       << " and " << b
       << " is " << c << endl;
  return 0;
}
```

```
Output 5.1
Please input a number: 4
Please input another number: 5
The product of 4 and 5 is 20
```

Here, product is the name of the function which takes two parameters x and y, both of integer type, and returns an integer type of data. The function body has just one statement that states to return the product of the parameters passed. Thus, whenever the product function is called with two arguments or parameters, we get the product of the arguments as the return value from the function. The main function uses the product function to calculate the product of two numbers read as input data. The output uses insertion operator (>>) to output the product of the two numbers. Here, we have made one call to function product, however, we can call several times to pass different parameters to have different results.

A function call has to match the type and number of arguments of the function as declared. The function product takes two parameters x and y. The arguments passed to the function through the function call are a and b which are passed to x and y respectively. The result of the function after processing is returned from the function product and c gets the return value. The return statement returns the control back to the caller function that has called it (main here), following the program by the same point where the function product was called. The return is also called within the function product with the value of the result of the product of x and y (return x * y;) which is returned by the function.

```
c   = product (   a,     b );
↑                 ↓      ↓
int product(int  x, int y)
```

A function declaration usually precedes the function definition and specifies the name, return type and other attributes of a function. This is called *prototypes*. A function prototype refers to the return type, name, and argument list components of a function. The compiler uses the prototype to check argument types and to convert arguments, if required. Prototypes can appear several times in a program, if the declarations are compatible. They allow the compiler to check for mismatches between the parameters of a function call and those in the function declaration. It's a good practice to place the function prototypes in header files (usual extension .hpp), and the function definitions in source files (usual extension .cpp). In case of library functions, the declarations of the functions are in the specified header files (e.g. stdio.h, string.h, iostream.h) which should be included at the beginning of the program, so that declaration can precede function call usage. The actual function definitions of the library functions are precompiled and put in the library files, which need to be linked with compiled version of your program to make the final executable file. As such, when we use a library function, we don't need to write the declaration or definition.

The next example (Program Source Code 5.2) defines the function product with the return type float. Since this is a noninteger return type, the example declares the function prototype of product prior to the function call. For integer return types, we can optionally omit the return type because return type integer is by default (in case no return type is mentioned). For example, we have defined the main function without a return type here (integer return type is assumed by default).

Program Source Code 5.2

```
#include <iostream.h>
// function prototype declaration for product
float product(float, float);
main()
{
  float a,b,c;
  cout << "Please input a floating point number: ";
  cin >> a;
  cout << "Please input another floating point number: ";
  cin >> b;
  c = product(a, b); // function call
  cout   << "The product of " << a
         << " and " << b
         << " is " << c << endl;
  return 0;
}
float product(float x, float y)
{
   // function definition
  return x * y;
}
```

Output 5.2

```
Please input a floating point number: 1.2
Please input another floating point number: 1.3
The product of 1.2 and 1.3 is 1.56
```

Specifying a return type of void on a function declaration indicates that the function does not return a value.

Program Source Code 5.3 defines the function `PrintProduct` with the return type void.

```
Program Source Code 5.3
```

```
#include <iostream.h>
void PrintProduct(int, int);
int main()
{
    int a, b;
    cout << "Please input an integer: ";
    cin >> a;
    cout << "Please input another integer: ";
    cin >> b;
    PrintProduct(a, b);
    return 0;
}
void PrintProduct(int a, int b)
{
    int c;
    c = a * b;
    cout << "The product of " << a
         << " and " << b
         << " is "<< c << endl;
    return;
}
```

```
Output 5.3
```

```
Please input an integer: 3
Please input another integer: 4
The product of 3 and 4 is 12
```

The function `PrintProduct` calculates the product of the two integer arguments and prints with suitable message as shown. The statement return followed by semicolon (;) as the last statement of a function is optional because it doesn't return anything except returning the control to the calling program and after the last statement is executed, control automatically transfers to the caller. It is meaningful if the control is conditionally returned from within a function. Here, we have passed arguments to the function `PrintProduct` as a and b (local variables of main function) and within `PrintProduct` function

they get mapped to a different set of variables named a and b. If an argument name is the same as a name outside the function, the program hides the name outside the function. A function returns a value when a return statement containing an expression is executed. The expression is evaluated, converted to the return datatype if necessary, and returned to the point at which the function was called. If a function is declared with void return type, a return statement containing an expression generates a warning and the expression is not evaluated.

Whenever a function is called, the system switches context from the calling function to the caller with a set of local variables available in the caller function and hides the context of local variables available in the calling function.

Inline Functions

Inline functions are used to reduce the overhead of a normal function call. The *inline* specifier is a suggestion to the C++ compiler that inline substitution of the function body is to be preferred to the usual function call implementation. The suggestion may be ignored at the discretion of the compiler. By inlining we mean that instead of transferring control to and from the function code segment, one may directly embed a copy of the function body whenever the function is called. That is, function call will be replaced by function code. An inline function can be declared and defined simultaneously. Inline functions are best used for small functions which are sensitive to the function call overheads. Small inline functions, may consist of one or two simple expressions and create less code than the equivalent function call because the compiler doesn't generate code to switch context, i.e. handling of arguments and of return value. In case of larger functions, the context switching overhead caused by calling/returning is proportionately less compared to the function execution and as such, benefit from inlining in larger functions is less. The *inline* keyword tells the compiler to substitute the code (at its discretion) within the function definition for every instance of a function call. For example, the compiler may not inline a function if the function is found to be too large to be inline.

The following code fragment shows an inline function definition with its declaration:

```
inline int add(int i, int j){return i + j;}
```

Any function can be inline. The use of the inline specifier does not change the meaning of the function. An inline function follows the usual function definition rules, and obeys all the usual scope and type checking rules. Instead of code generation for context switching, i.e. transferring control and passing parameters to a single copy of the function's code, a suitably modified copy of the function's code replaces the call. The inline expansion of a function may not preserve the evaluation order of the actual arguments. A program example is provided as Program Source Code 5.4.

Program Source Code 5.4

```
#include <iostream.h>
inline int product(int x, int y)
{
   return x * y;
}
int main()
{
  int a, b, c;
  cout << "Please input a number: ";
  cin >> a;
  cout << "Please input another number: ";
  cin >> b;
  c = product(a, b); // will be replaced by c = a * b;
  cout << "The product of " << a
       << " and " << b
       << " is " << c << endl;
  return 0;
}
```

Output 5.4

```
Please input a number: 4
Please input another number: 5
The product of 4 and 5 is 20
```

Main Function Arguments

It was earlier stated that all C++ programs begin their execution through the main function. Wherever it is in the program, in the beginning, middle or end, main function is always the first to be executed when a program starts. As a rule, every C++ program must have one function named main. The main function should return a value of type ***int***, which goes to the caller of the executable file, i.e. another program calling this program or the operating system. Thus it explicitly defines main( ) as:

```
int main ( );  or
int main (int argc, char * argv[ ]);
```

The main function should have a return statement to terminate the execution, for example,

```
int main ( )
{
    // do stuff...
    return (Number);
}
```

Number should be 0 to designate success, and negative value to designate failure. The higher the negative value is, the higher the severity level of the failure would be.

One can declare the main function with or without arguments. With arguments, the main function takes the following form:

```
int main (int argc, char * argv[ ]);
```

This allows convenient command-line parsing of arguments. Although any name can be given to these arguments, it's a common practice to name them as `argc` and `argv`.

`argc` An integer that contains the count of arguments that follow in argv. The argc parameter is always greater than or equal to 1. It indicates how many arguments you entered on the command line when running the program.

`argv` An array of null-terminated strings representing command-line arguments entered by the user of the program. The value of argc indicates the number of pointers in the array argv. By convention, argv[0] is the command with which the program is invoked, `argv[1]` is the first command-line argument, and so on, until `argv[argc-1]`, which is the last one.

The following example (5.1) prints the arguments entered on a command line in reverse order such that the last argument is printed first and first argument is printed last.

EXAMPLE 5.1:

```
#include <iostream.h>
int main(int argc,char *argv [])
{
  cout << "Program Name: " << argv[0] << endl;
  cout << "Arguments (in reverse order): " ;
  while(--argc >0)
       cout << argv[argc]);
  return 0;
}
```

If the program is named `testarg.exe` and is invoked with two arguments `arg1` and `arg2` as, `testarg arg1 arg2`, then it will give the following output:

```
Program Name: testarg
Arguments (in reverse order): arg2 arg1
```

The arguments `argc` and `argv` would contain the following values:

Item		Value
argc	:	3
argv[0]	:	pointer to string "testarg"
argv[1]	:	pointer to string "arg1"
argv[2]	:	pointer to string "arg2"

Reference Variables

A C++ reference is an alias or another name for an item. All operations that are applied to a reference work on the item are referred to by this. The address of a reference is same as the address of the aliased object. One can define a reference type by placing the ampersand(&) after the data type specifier. All reference items should be initialized at the time of declaration. The datatype void & is not permitted.

An example program follows as Program Source Code 5.5:

Program Source Code 5.5

```
#include <iostream.h>
int main()
{
    int i;
    int & j = i;
    int *pi = &i;
    int * & pj = pi;
    cout << "Please input an integer: ";
    cin >> i;
    cout << "Before incrementing *pi"<< endl
         << "i = " << i
         << ", j = " << j
         << ", *pi = " << *pi
         << ", *pj = " << *pj << endl;
    (*pi)++; // incrementing *pi
    cout << "After incrementing *pi" << endl
         << "i = " << i
```

(*contd.*)

Program Source Code 5.5 *(contd.)*

```
18.        << ", j = " << j
19.        << ", *pi = " << *pi
20.        << ", *pj = " << *pj << endl;
21.     return 0;
22.  }
```

Output 5.5

```
Please input an integer: 4
Before incrementing *pi
i = 4, j = 4, *pi = 4, *pj = 4
After incrementing *pi
i = 5, j = 5, *pi = 5, *pj = 5
```

Let's now take a memory map to understand the effects of this program. First, assume the integer variable **i** is stored in a memory location 1022. The integer variable **j** being a reference of **i**, doesn't occupy separate memory location; rather shares same memory address as that of **i**. Say, the pointer variable **pi** is stored in memory locations 1026 and occupies 4 bytes of memory, then the pointer variable **pj** is an alias of **pi**. The steps of execution of the given program are explained in the Figures 5.2a and 5.2b. This shows, how the aliasing of i and j (j as reference variable to i) and aliasing of **pj** and pj (**pj** acting as a reference of **pi**) are done.

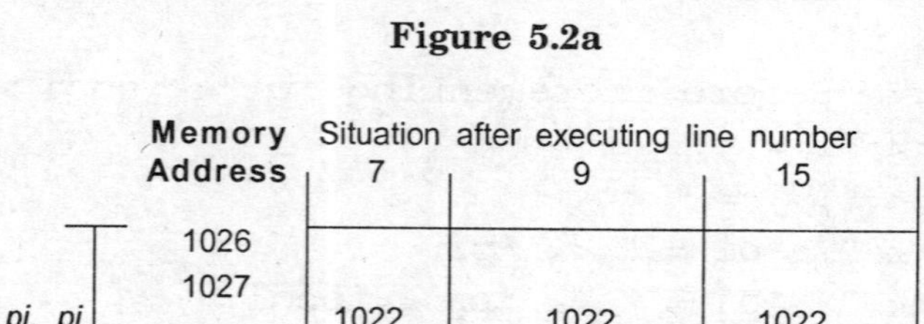

Figure 5.2a

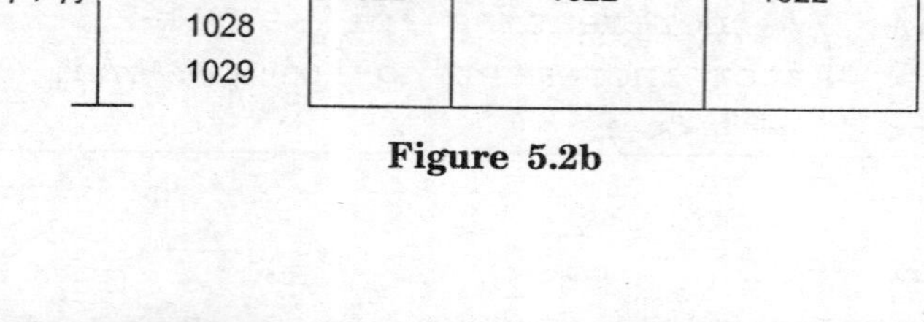

Figure 5.2b

If we change line 5 of the Figure 5.2b given program as `int j = i;` instead of `int & j = i;` then `j` occupies separate space in memory and gets the initial value from `i` (at the time of initialization).

The item name used to initialize a reference must be of the same type as the reference. Otherwise, it must be of a type that is convertible to the reference type. If one initializes a reference to a constant by using an item that requires conversion, a temporary item is created. The following example creates a temporary data of type ***int***.

```
float a = 4.5;
const int &i = a;   //reference to a constant integer
```

Attempting to initialize a nonconstant reference with an item that requires a conversion is an error. Thus, the following code will be erroneous:

```
float a = 4.5;
int &i = a;   //error
```

Function Overloading

A function can be overloaded by having multiple declarations of the same function name in the same scope. The declarations differ in the type and number of arguments in the argument list. When an overloaded function is called, the types of the actual arguments are compared with the types of the formal arguments. Thus, it selects the correct function. Overloaded functions enable programmers to supply different semantics for a function, depending on the types and number of arguments. An example program is given in Program Source Code 5.6.

Program Source Code 5.6

```
#include <iostream.h>
    int product(int x, int y)
    {
     return x * y;
    }
    float product(float x, float y)
    {
       return x * y;
    }
int main()
{
    int a, b, c;
```

(*contd.*)

Program Source Code 5.6 *(contd.)*

```
float f,g,h;
  cout << "Please input two integers: ";
  cin >> a >> b;
  c = product(a, b); // will call int product(int x, int y)
  cout << "The product of " << a
       << " and " << b
       << " is " << c << endl;
  cout << "Please input two floating point numbers: ";
  cin >> f >> g;
  h = product(f,g);    // will call float
                       // product(float x, float y)
  cout << "The product of "<< f
       << " and " << g
       << " is " << h << endl;
    return 0;
}
```

Output 5.6

```
Please input two integers: 4 5
The product of 4 and 5 is 20
Please input two floating point numbers: 1.2 2.3
The product of 1.2 and 2.3 is 2.76
```

Here, the function `product` is overloaded. We have called the function product twice with different parameters. The function matching the arguments passed will therefore be called.

Default Arguments

In C++, one can provide default values for function arguments. If an expression is specified in an argument declaration, the expression is used as a default argument. Default arguments are used in calls where trailing arguments that is, the last argument(s) are missing. Thus, the following code is illegal:

```
float fracval(int = 0, int); //illegal
```

An example program follows (Program Source Code 5.7). Here, `fracval` function is declared with two default arguments numerator (defaulted to 0) and denominator (defaulted to 1). We may call the function `fracval` with two parameters (no parameter is defaulted), one parameter (second parameter is defaulted) or no parameter (both parameters are defaulted). The function declaration, however, will have to pass two arguments for numerator and denominator. When the function is called, depending on actual parameters passed, additional parameters (if required) are passed by default.

Program Source Code 5.7

```
#include <iostream.h>
//function declaration with default parameters
float fracval(int = 0, int = 1);
int main()
{
  int a,b;
  float f;
  cout << "Please input numerator and denominator "
       << "of a fraction : ";
  cin >> a >> b;

  //calls fracval(a,b) with no default parameter
  f = fracval(a,b);
  cout << "The fraction value " << a << "/" << b
       << " = " << f << endl;

  cout << "Please input the numerator "
       << "(denominator assumed to be 1) ";
  cin >> a ;
  //calls fracval(a,1) with second parameter defaulted
  f = fracval(a);
  cout << "The fraction value " << a << "/1"
       << " = " << f << endl;

  cout << "And the default fraction value is "
       << "(num=0, denom=1) :\n";
  // calls fracval(0,1) with both parameters defaulted
  f = fracval();
  cout << "The fraction value " << "0/1"
       << " = " << f << endl;
  return 0;
}
// fracval function definition
float fracval(int numerator, int denominator)
{
   float val;
   val = ((float) numerator) / ((float) denominator);
   return val;
}
```

Output 5.7

```
Please input numerator and denominator of a fraction: 3 4
The fraction value 3/4 = 0.75
Please input the numerator(denominator assumed to be 1) 3
The fraction value 3/1 = 3
And the default fraction value is (num=0, denom=1):
The fraction value 0/1 = 0
```

While specifying an expression in an argument to be default argument, all subsequent arguments must have default arguments supplied in this or previous declarations of the function. A default argument cannot be redefined by a later declaration (not even the same value). However, a declaration may add default arguments not given in previous declarations. Study, for example, the following declarations

```
float fracval(int = 0, int = 1);  // ok
float fracval(int = 0, int = 1);  // redefinition of default
                                  // parameter, error
```

Here's another example of redefinition:

```
float fracval(int, int = 1); // ok
float fracval(int = 0, int); // ok, adding default arguments
                             // is allowed
```

Parameter Passing

By now, you should have understood the differences between declaring a function, calling a function and defining a function. If a function requires inputs, then the definition of the function will contain a number of formal parameters, and the call to the function contains actual arguments. When the function call is executed, the actual arguments in the function call have to be associated with the formal parameters in the function definition. This process is called *parameter passing* or simply passing arguments to functions. There are two different ways of parameter passing in C++, namely call-by-value and call-by-reference, whereas C language supports only one mechanism of parameter passing through call-by-value.

Call-by-value

A function call specifies a function name and a list of arguments. The calling function passes the value of each argument to the specified function. The parameters passed at the time of calling the function and the parameters in the actual function definition are stored in different memory locations and at the time of the function call, the formal gets initialized with the values of the parameters passed. We can see from the Program Source Code 5.8 that, since C passes parameters by value, the function swap as defined, does not have its desired effect of swapping the variables.

Program Source Code 5.8 (call-by-value)

```
#include <iostream.h>
void swap(int a, int b)
{
    int temp;
    temp = a;
    a = b;
    b = temp;
}
int main()
{
    int x = 3;
    int y = 4;
    cout << "Before swap: x =" << x << ", y =" << y << endl;
    swap(x, y);
    cout << "After swap: x =" << x << ", y =" << y << endl;
    return 0;
}
```

Output 5.8

```
Before swap: x = 3, y = 4
After swap: x = 3, y = 4
```

Call-by-reference

When you pass arguments of a function by value, a function call does not modify the actual values of the arguments. If a function needs to modify the actual value of an argument, you must pass the argument by reference. This is as opposed to being passed by value. By reference, we mean that the reference variable doesn't occupy separate memory; rather it is the alias of the variable for which it is a reference. Reference parameters refer to parameters in function definitions whose values are passed by reference, rather than by value. To indicate that a particular parameter is a reference parameter, one merely puts an & between the type of the parameter and the parameter name. An example is provided in Program Source Code 5.9.

Program Source Code 5.9 (call-by-reference)

```
#include <iostream.h>
void swap(int & a, int & b)
{
    int temp;
    temp = a;
    a = b;
    b = temp;
}
int main()
{
    int x = 3;
    int y = 4;
    cout << "Before swap: x =" << x << ", y =" << y << endl;
    swap(x,y);
    cout << "After swap: x =" << x << ", y =" << y << endl;
    return 0;
}
```

Output 5.9

```
Before swap: x = 3, y = 4
After swap: x = 4, y = 3
```

A similar situation may be simulated using pointers and using the side effect of dereferencing a pointer (Program Source Code 5.10). This will have the same effect as that of calling by reference. However, the pointers are also passed as value here. If we change the value of the pointer, we change the value stored in the copy and not on the master.

Program Source Code 5.10 (call-by-value) (through pointer)

```
#include <iostream.h>
void swap(int * a, int * b)
{
    int temp;
    temp = *a;
    *a = *b;
    *b = temp;
}
int main()
{
```

(*contd.*)

Program Source Code 5.10 (call-by-value) (through pointer) *(contd.)*

```
   int x = 3;
   int y = 4;
   cout << "Before swap: x =" << x << ", y =" << y << endl;
   swap(&x,&y);
   cout<< "After swap: x =" << x << ", y =" << y <<endl;
   return 0;
}
```

Output 5.10

```
Before swap: x = 3, y = 4
After swap: x = 4, y = 3
```

Another example follows (Program Source Code 5.11):

Program Source Code 5.11 (passing constants)

```
#include <iostream.h>
void PrintCharManyTimes(char, int);

int main()
{
   PrintCharManyTimes('-', 40);
   cout << "Data type Range" << endl;
   PrintCharManyTimes('=', 18);
   cout  << "char\t" <<  "-128 to 127" << endl
         << "int\t"  <<  "-32,768 to 32,767" << endl
         << "double\t" << "-2,147,483,648 to 2,147,483,647"
         << endl;
   PrintCharManyTimes('-', 40);

   return 0;
}

void PrintCharManyTimes(char chToPrint, int noOfTimes)
{
   for (int j = 0; j<noOfTimes; j++)
      cout << chToPrint;
   cout << endl;
}
```

Output 5.11

```
----------------------------------------
Data type Range
==================
char    -128 to 127
int     -32,768 to 32,767
double  -2,147,483,648 to 2,147,483,647
----------------------------------------
```

In this program we pass constants to function as arguments. As defined, constants are also passed as values. If we like to pass constants as non-constant references as in the declaration "`void PrintCharManyTimes(char&, int&);`", there would be compilation errors. However, the declaration as well as definition for the function as "`void PrintCharManyTimes(const char&, const int&);`" works, because a constant data can be passed as a constant reference or value but not as non-constant reference.

Recursion

Functions can call themselves. It is useful for some tasks like for to calculate the factorial of a number. For example, to obtain the factorial of a number (n) its mathematical formula is:

```
n! = n * (n - 1) * (n - 2) * (n – 3) ··· * 1
```

more precisely, 4! (factorial of 4) would be:

```
4! = 4 * 3 * 2 * 1 = 24
```

and a recursive function to do so could be as in Program Source Code 5.12:

Program Source Code 5.12 (Recursive version)

```
#include <iostream.h>
long fact(long a)
{
    if (a > 1)
        return (a * fact(a - 1));
    else
        return 1;
}
int main ()
{
   long n;
   cout << "Please input a number: ";
   cin >> n;
   cout << n << "!" " = " << fact(n);
   return 0;
}
```

Output 5.12

```
Please input a number: 4
4! = 24
```

An iterative version follows in the Program Source Code 5.12a. In iterative version, we use a loop to control the iteration and thereby save usage of stack, as the function call does not enter into calling itself as in recursion.

Program Source Code 5.12a (Iterative version)

```
#include <iostream.h>
long fact(long a)
{
     int result = 1;
     if (a > 1)
     {
          for (int i = 1; i <= a; i++)
          {
               result = result * i;
          }
     }
     return result;
}
int main ()
{
  long n;
  cout << "Please input a number: ";
  cin >> n;
  cout << n << "!" " = " << fact(n);
  return 0;
}
```

Output 5.12a

```
Please input a number: 4
4! = 24
```

Scope of Variables

Formal arguments (arguments specified in function definitions) to functions are considered to be in the scope of the outermost block of the function body. When a function declares local variables (called *automatic variables*), they exist temporarily on the stack area, while a function is being called. The linker does not require to persistently know about automatic variables because of their local scope, and as such, it requires no linkage.

Variables and functions may be declared with a *static* qualifier. Usually, local variables declared within a function body are destroyed when the function call is done. If the function is called again, the local variables are created again with fresh set of values (initialized or uninitialized, as the case may be) and destroyed as well when the function call is done. However, if a variable is declared as *static*, the variable gets a long life, same as that of the entire program and remains alive till the program is alive. This variable is initialized once when the function is called first time, and retains its value even if the function call is done. When the function is called again, the static variable is not reinitialized (contrast to non-static local variables, which get reinitialized when the function is called again). Thus, a static data can remember or retain values between function calls.

Instead, global variables, having global scope, i.e. lifetime as the life of the entire program, can be used. However, with static variables, the variable gets a global scope even if defined locally and is available only within the function body where it is defined and nowhere else, thus preventing the chance of getting modified by some other piece of code.

Here's an example of the use of static variables (Program Source Code 5.13).

Program Source Code 5.13

```
#include <iostream.h>
int gi = 1; // global variable
void func()
{
   int i = 1; // nonstatic local variable
   static int si = 1; // static variable

   i++; // i becomes two
   si++; // si gets incremented from last retained value
   gi++; // gi gets incremented from current value of gi

   cout << "i = " << i << ", si = "
        << si << ", gi = " << gi << endl;
}
int main ()
{
   int i;

   for (i = 0; i < 10; i++)
```

(*contd.*)

Program Source Code 5.13 *(contd.)*

```
  {
      cout << "(" << i << ") Call to func(): ";
      gi++; // global gi also incremented
      func();
  }
  return 0;
}
```

Output 5.13

```
(0) Call to func() : i = 2, si = 2, gi = 3
(1) Call to func() : i = 2, si = 3, gi = 5
(2) Call to func() : i = 2, si = 4, gi = 7
(3) Call to func() : i = 2, si = 5, gi = 9
(4) Call to func() : i = 2, si = 6, gi = 11
(5) Call to func() : i = 2, si = 7, gi = 13
(6) Call to func() : i = 2, si = 8, gi = 15
(7) Call to func() : i = 2, si = 9, gi = 17
(8) Call to func() : i = 2, si = 10, gi = 19
(9) Call to func() : i = 2, si = 11, gi = 21
```

In this code, each time func( ) is called in the for loop, it prints a different value for the static variable **si** and global variable **gi**. For variable **i** within func(), the keyword static is not used, and thus, the value printed is always equal to 2. The static variable si is incremented within the function func(), and not visible outside func() although remains alive for the entire program duration. The global variable **gi** is incremented within the function func() and main() function as well, and is visible as well as incrementable or modifiable in many places.

Other usage of *static* is to indicate unavailability outside a certain scope. If a function or variable (variable not declared inside a function, but declared outside all functions) is declared static, it indicates unavailability of this name outside of the current file. The function name or variable remains local to the file (file scope), and cannot be used from functions declared in another file.

The ***extern*** keyword sends the message to the compiler that a variable or a function definition exists in some other file (may not be in the current file), and using this variable or function can be allowed, provided that matches with the declaration are preceded by ***extern*** keyword. When the compiler encounters the declaration like '`extern int gi`' it knows that the definition for **gi** must exist somewhere (this file or some other file) as a global variable and will be resolved at the linking time. When the compiler gets the definition of **gi**, all access and usage of **gi** links to this definition. Static variables or functions declared with file scope cannot be used in other files using extern.

In an executing program, an identifier stored in some part of memory represents a variable or a function. Linker sees storage as two types: internal linkage and external linkage. Internal linkage says that storage to be created for an identifier is only for the file being compiled (file scope using static). If some other file also declares identifier with the same name in file scope (as static), it means that storage is created separately for each file being compiled without any conflict whatsoever. External linkage says that storage to be created for an identifier is to be shared by all the files being compiled. One file thus defines the storage of the identifier, other files share the same identifier through extern keyword (thereby causing external linkage).

Return-by-value and Return-by-reference

When many arguments may be sent to a function, only one may be returned from it. This is a limitation when you need to return more information. However, there are other approaches to returning multiple variables from functions. One is to pass arguments by reference and the other is to return a structure instead of a single data. You should always include a function return type in the function declaration as well as definition, even if you do not use the return value in the actual call. If nothing is to be returned, use the keyword void to indicate this fact.

A return statement specifies the return value. The following code snippets show a function definition, including the return statement:

```
int product(int i, int j)
{
    return i*j; //return statement
}
```

The function product() can be called, as shown in the following code fragment:

```
int a = 4;
b = 5;
int answer = product(a, b);  //answer is 20
```

In this example, the return statement initializes a variable of the returned type with the int value 20. The compiler checks the type of the returned expression against the returned type. It performs all standard and user-defined conversions, as necessary.

References can also be used as return types for functions. The reference returns the *lvalue* of the item to which it refers. This allows one to place function calls on the left side of assignment statements. Referenced return values should be used when overloading assignment operators and subscripting. This way, we can use the results of the overloaded operators as actual values. Returning a reference to an automatic variable (like **int i**;) gives unpredictable results.

Pointer to Functions

A pointer to a function points to the address of the function's executable code. One can use pointers to call functions and to pass functions as arguments to other functions. One cannot perform pointer arithmetic on pointers to functions. A declaration of a pointer to a function must have the pointer name in parentheses. Without them, the compiler interprets the statement as a function that returns a pointer to a specified return type. For example,

```
int *f(int a);  //function f returning an int*
int (*g)(int a);  //pointer g to a function returning an int
```

SUMMARY

The key concepts introduced in this chapter are as follows:

- Instead of repeating the same lines of code representing the task at various places in the program, we declare a function name representing the lines of code to be repeated and invoke the function to execute the sequences of code.
- A *function declaration* (also called function prototype) consists of a return type, a function name, and a list of arguments as number and type of arguments.
- The *function call* is merely calling the function with the function name passing the parameters and optionally taking the return value to some variable. A function call has to match the type and number of arguments of the function as declared.
- A *function definition* contains a function declaration and the body of the function with the declarations of its local variables, and the statements that determine the job of the function.
- A function can have only one definition, but more than one declarations.
- Whenever a function is called, the system switches context from the calling function to the caller with a set of local variables available in the

caller function and hides the context of local variables available in the calling function.

- The *inline* function tells the compiler to substitute the code (at its discretion) within the function definition for every instance of a function call. This reduces context-switching overhead caused by normal function call.
- Arguments given in command line are passed through main function arguments.
- A C++ reference is an alias or another name for an item. A reference variable doesn't occupy separate memory location rather, it shares the same memory address as that of the referenced item.
- Overloaded functions have the same name, but differ in type, order or number of arguments in the argument list.
- Default arguments are used in calls where trailing arguments are missing.
- In call-by-value, the parameters passed at the time of calling the function and the parameters in the actual function definition are stored in different memory locations and at the time of the function call, the formal gets initialized with the values of the parameters passed.
- In call-by-reference, the parameters in the calling function and called function share the same memory address. C supports call-by-value only whereas C++ supports call-by-value as well as call-by-reference.
- In recursion, functions call themselves. In iterative version, we use a loop to control the iteration and thereby save usage of stack, as the function call does not enter into calling itself as in recursion.
- There can be different scope of variables—global (within entire program scope), local (non-persistent within a function), static (global within a file scope), and persistent static variable within a function scope.
- Functions can return by value or by reference.
- Pointers to functions can be used to call functions as well as pass functions as arguments. Pointer arithmetic cannot be performed on pointer to functions.

REVIEW QUESTIONS

1. What are the advantages of function prototypes?
2. What is the difference between call-by-value and call-by-reference? Illustrate with suitable examples.

3. When is a function defined as inline and why?
4. Illustrate with suitable examples the concepts of function overloading.
5. What is the effect of default arguments? Illustrate with suitable examples.
6. Illustrate through suitable examples the concept of recursion.
7. What is the difference between function prototype and function definition?
8. Write a C++ function that takes two integer arguments and returns the result of product of the first argument by the second. If second argument is missing, a default value of 1 is taken as the second argument.
9. Compare between recursion and iteration.
10. What is the difference of static and extern keyword when used for function declaration and variable declaration?
11. Write a program to print all the prime numbers between 1 and 100.
12. The sequence for Fibonacci numbers begins with integers 1, 1, 2, 3, 5, 8, 13, 21, 34, 55, ... where each number after the first two is the sum of the two preceding numbers. Write an iterative program to calculate and display Fibonacci numbers.
13. Write a recursive version for Q. No. 12.
14. The greatest common divisor (GCD) of two positive integers is the largest integer that divides both of them. Thus the GCD of 8 and 12 is four and the GCD of 9 and 18 is 9. Write a recursive function, int gcd (int x, int y) that implements the division algorithm. If y = 0, then the GCD of x and y is x otherwise the GCD of x and y is the same as GCD of y and x mod y.
15. Write an iterative variant of GCD for Q. No. 14.
16. Using the factorial function as given in Program Source Code 5.12, print the table of values of

$$^{n}C_{r} = \frac{n(n-1)\dots(n-r+1)}{r!}$$

17. Write a recursive function to calculate the sum of the following series for a given value of n:

$$\sum_{i=1}^{n}\left(\frac{1}{n!}\right)$$

18. Write a function named Payment that calculates the wages for a given number of hours worked and hourly pay rate. The number of hours worked over 60 are to be paid at the rate of one and half times the regular pay rate. Use the above function in the main program to calculate the payment for 5 employees. Decide your own input-output format.

19. Write a program to emulate the DOS COPY system command. That is, it should copy contents of a text file to another file. Invoke the program for the command line arguments—the source file and the destination file. In the program check that the user has typed the correct number of command line arguments and that the file specified can be opened.

20. Write a program to find whether the given three numbers A, B and C passed through command line arguments form a Pythagorean triplet or not. The program should take command like arguments and through a function call check whether they form Pythagorian triplet or not and accordingly print appropriate message.

21. Write a program to read a string of maximum 255 characters and perform the following operations using appropriate function calls:

(a) Reverse and print the reversed string

(b) Find the number of words

(c) Print each word in the string on a separate line

22. Five readings have been obtained after an analysis by Mr. A. Mr. B has repeated the same analysis and obtained different set of result.

Readings of Mr. A	Readings of Mr. B
23.4	25.9
24.5	25.2
24.8	24.9
26.7	26.4
26.2	24.9

(a) Write a program to find out the mean, variance and standard deviation of readings obtained by Mr. A and Mr. B separately.

$$\text{Mean } (\bar{x}) = \frac{\sum_{i=1}^{N}(x_i)}{N}$$

$$\text{Variance} = \frac{\sum_{i=1}^{N}(x_i - \overline{x})^2}{N}$$

$$\text{Standard Deviation} = \sqrt{\text{Variance}}$$

x_i implies various readings $x_1, x_2, \ldots, x_N$

$$\text{Cov }(X, Y) = \frac{\sum_{i=1}^{N}(x_i - \overline{x})(y_i - \overline{y})}{N}$$

$$\text{Coeff. of Coreleration} = \frac{\text{Cov}(X,Y)}{\sqrt{\text{Var}(X).\ \text{Var}(Y)}}$$

(b) Find covariance and correlation of the two series of data.

6 Preprocessor Directives

There are two ways of constructing a software design. One way is to make it so simple that there are obviously no deficiencies. And the other way is to make it so complicated that there are no obvious deficiencies.

—C.A.R. Hoare

LEARNING OBJECTIVES

The objective of this chapter is to acquaint you with:

- Preprocessor directives and preprocessing phases
- Trigraph and Digraph sequences
- #define, #undef, #ifdef, #ifndef, #else, #elif directives
- # and ## operators
- #line, #error, #pragma directives
- #include directive

INTRODUCTION

Before the actual compilation process starts in C and C++ languages, a preprocessor is run on the source code. The preprocessor is a simple program that replaces patterns given in the source code with some other patterns as defined using preprocessor directives. Preprocessor directives are used to save typing and to increase the readability of the code. Preprocessing does the following tasks (we refer current file as file under compilation):

- Replace tokens in the current file with specified replacement tokens.
- Embed files within the current file.
- Conditionally compile sections of the current file.

- Generate diagnostic messages.
- Change the source line number of the next line, and change the file name of the current file.

By preprocessor directives we mean some indicators for the preprocessor given in our code which are not meant to be program instructions but meant to be instructions to the preprocessor to perform specific actions like making some prior changes in the code before the real compilation starts. These directives are different from normal C++ statements which ends with a semicolon (;).

A preprocessor directive may include a blank (space), the horizontal tab, and comments. The new-line character can also separate preprocessor tokens. The preprocessed source program file must be a valid C or C++ program.

The following are the preprocessor directives:

#define	Defines a preprocessor directive.
#undef	Removes a preprocessor macro definition.
#error	Defines text for a compile-time error message.
#include	Embed files within the current file.
#if	Conditionally suppresses portions of source code, depending on the result of a constant expression.
#ifdef	Conditionally includes source text if a macro name is defined.
#ifndef	Conditionally includes source text if a macro name is not defined.
#else	Conditionally includes source text if the previous #if, #ifdef, #ifndef, or #elif test fails.
#elif	Conditionally includes source text if the previous #if, #ifdef, #ifndef, or #elif test fails, depending on the value of a constant expression.
#endif	Ends conditional text.
#line	Supplies a line number for compiler messages.
#pragma	Specifies implementation-defined instructions to the compiler.

The # sign (number sign) must be the first nonwhite-space character on the line containing the preprocessor directive; there may be white-space characters appearing between the # sign and the first letter of the preprocessor directive. The # is not part of the directive name and can be separated from the directive name with white spaces. Some directives include arguments or values. A preprocessor directive ends at the new-line character unless the last character of the line is the \(backslash) character. Lines containing preprocessor directives can be continued by immediately preceding the new-line marker with a backslash (\) which is interpreted as a continuation marker. The preprocessor, however, removes the backslash character (\) and the following new-line character, to join the physical source lines into continuous logical lines. Preprocessor directives can appear anywhere in a source file, but they apply only to the remainder of the source file.

Phases of Preprocessing

Preprocessing appears as if it occurs in several phases.

1. New-line characters are introduced as needed to replace system-dependent end-of-line indicators, and any other system-dependent character-set translations are done. Trigraph sequences are replaced with equivalent single characters.
2. Each pair of a \(backslash) immediately followed by a new-line character is removed so that the next source line is appended to the line that contained the sequence.
3. The source text is decomposed into preprocessing tokens and sequences of white space. Each comment is replaced by a single white space. A source file cannot end with a partial token or comment.
4. Preprocessing directives are executed, and macros are expanded.
5. Escape sequences in character constants and string literals are replaced by their equivalent values.
6. Adjacent string literals are concatenated.

The rest of the compilation process operates on the preprocessor output, which is syntactically and semantically analyzed and translated. The compiler output is then linked as necessary with other programs and libraries.

Trigraph Sequences

Some characters from the C/C++ character set are not available in all environments. One can enter these characters into a C/C++ source program by using a sequence of three characters that are called a trigraph. Before preprocessing, each trigraph sequence in a string or literal is replaced by the single character that it represents.

??=	#	number sign
??(	[	left bracket
??)	]	right bracket
??<	{	left brace
??>	}	right brace

<table>
<tr><td>??/</td><td>\</td><td>backslash</td></tr>
<tr><td>??’</td><td>|</td><td>caret</td></tr>
<tr><td>??!</td><td>|</td><td>vertical bar</td></tr>
<tr><td>??-</td><td>˜</td><td>tilde</td></tr>
</table>

At compile time, the compiler translates the trigraphs found in string literals and character constants into the appropriate characters they represent.

For example, if arr is an array and i is the index variable to refer the elements of the array, then

```
arr[i] = 4;
```

can also be equivalently written as

```
arr??(i??)=4;
```

Digraph Characters

Some unavailable characters in a C/C++ source program can be represented by using a digraph character which is a combination of two keystrokes. The preprocessor reads digraphs as tokens during the preprocessor phase. Digraphs can be created by using macro concatenation.

The digraph characters are:

%: or %%	#	number sign
<:	[	left bracket
:>	]	right bracket
<%	{	left brace
%>	}	right brace
%:%: or %%%%	##	preprocessor macro concatenation operator

Digraphs in string literals or in character literals are not replaced. For example:

```
char *s = "<%%>"; // remains "<%%>"
char c = '<%';    // remains '<%'
```

#define

A preprocessor **define** directive directs the preprocessor to replace all subsequent occurrences of a macro or an identifier with specified replacement tokens. The white spaces surrounding the replacement token sequence is discarded. It is as follows:

```
#define name value
```

This defines a macro or identifier called name that is replaced by value wherever name occurs in subsequent positions in the code. For example:

```
#define MAX_SIZE 100
char str1[MAX_SIZE];
char str2[MAX_SIZE];
```

It defines two character strings to store up to 100 characters.

#define can also be used to generate macro functions. It takes the following form:

```
#define name(arg1, arg2,..., argn) tokenstring
```

No space should be there between the first identifier and the left parenthesis to define a function-like macro definition. All subsequent occurrences of the macro named name with specified number of arguments will be replaced with the tokenstring.

For example,

```
#define max(a, b) a > b ? a : b
```

defines a macro named max which takes two arguments a and b. Example 6.1 shows the use of the macro.

EXAMPLE 6.1:

```
int main()
{
   int x = 6, y;
   y = max(x, 3); // expands to y = x > 3 ? x : 3;
   cout << y;
   return 0;
}
```

This code will print 6.

Note: Semicolons in, or at the end of a token string are part of the sequence. For example,

```
#define MAX_SIZE 100;
int size = MAX_SIZE - 1;
```

expands to unintended but valid two statements instead of one intended statement as

```
int size = 100; - 1; // intention was to make int size = 100 - 1;
```

The # Operator

The #(single number sign) operator converts a parameter of a function-like macro into a character string literal. If an occurrence of a paremeter in a replacement token sequence is immediately preceeded by a # token, the parameter and the # operator will be replaced in the expansion by a string literal containing the spelling of the corresponding argument. A backslash (\) character is inserted in the string literal before each occurrence of a backslash (\) or a quote (") within or delimiting a character constant or string literal in the argument. For example,

```
#define str(x) #x
#define concat(x,y) #x #y
```

expands all subsequent invocations of the macro `str` and `concat` into a character string literal that contains the argument that is passed to `str` or `concat`. It should be noted in the expansion of `concat` that adjacent string literals are concatenated. Here are the results:

Invocation	Result of Macro Expansion
`str(1)`	`"1"`
`str(Hello World)`	`"Hello World"`
`concat(Hello,World)`	`"Hello" "World" => "HelloWorld"`

The following rules are applicable for # operator:

1. The preprocessor converts a parameter that follows the # operator in a function-like macro into a character string literal that contains the argument that is passed to the macro.
2. The preprocessor deletes white-space characters that appear before or after the argument that is passed to the macro.
3. The preprocessor uses a single space character to replace multiple white-space characters that are embedded within the argument that is passed to the macro.
4. If the argument that is passed to the macro contains a string literal, and if a \ (backslash) character appears within the literal, the preprocessor inserts a second \ character before the original one when it expands the macro.
5. If the argument passed to the macro contains a " (double quotation mark) character, a \ character is inserted before the quote mark (") when the macro is expanded.
6. If the argument passed to the macro contains a ' (single quotation mark) character, a \ character is inserted before the quote mark (') when the macro is expanded.

7. The conversion of an argument into a string literal occurs before macro expansion on that argument.
8. If more than one ## operator or # operator appears in the replacement list of a macro definition, the order of evaluation of the operators is not defined.
9. If the result of the macro expansion is not a valid character string literal, the behaviour is undefined.

The Null Directive

The null directive performs no action. It consists of a single # on a line of its own. The null directive should not be confused with the # operator or the character that starts a preprocessor directive. For example; # means no action in terms of preprocessor.

The ## Operator

The double number sign operator (##) concatenates two tokens in a macro invocation (text or arguments), that a macro definition contains. If a ## operator appears in a replacement token sequence between two tokens, first if either of the adjacent tokens is a parameter it is replaced, then the ## operator and any white space surrounding it are deleted. The result is, therefore, concatenation. For example, consider a macro, concat, which is defined using the directive, #define concat(x,y) x##y. The preprocessor concatenates the tokens x and y. For example,

Invocation	Result of Macro Expansion
`concat(1,4)`	`14`
`concat(Hello,World)`	`HelloWorld`

A sample is given in Program Source Code 6.1.

Program Source Code 6.1

```
#include <iostream.h>
#define concat(a) a##ball
#define foot F
#define football sport
#define sport "sport"
int main ()
{
  cout << concat(foot);
  return 0;
}
```

```
Output 6.1
sport
```

In this program, `concat(foot) => foot##ball => football => sport =>"sport"`. Thus, the final output is the string sport i.e. "sport".

The following rules are applicable for ## operator:

1. The ## operator cannot be the very first or very last item in the replacement list of a macro definition.
2. The preprocessor concatenates the last token of the item in front of the ## operator with the first token of the item that follows the ## operator.
3. Concatenation takes place before the preprocessor expands any macros in arguments.
4. If the result of a concatenation is a valid macro name, the result is available for further replacement. It is available even if it appears in a context in which it is not normally available.
5. If more than one ## operator or # operator appears in the replacement list of a macro definition, the order of evaluation of the operators is not defined.

#undef

#undef fulfills the inverse functionality than #define. It causes the preprocessor to end the scope of a preprocessor definition. For example,

```
#define MAX_SIZE 100
char str1[MAX_SIZE];
#undef MAX_SIZE
#define MAX_SIZE 200
char str2[MAX_SIZE];
```

It defines two character strings `str1` and `str2`. `str1` can store up to 100 characters whereas `str2` can hold upto 200 characters.

#ifdef, #ifndef, #if, #endif, #else and #elif

A preprocessor conditional compilation directive causes the preprocessor to conditionally suppress portions of the source code compilation. These directives test a constant expression or an identifier. They determine which tokens the preprocessor should pass on to the compiler and which tokens it should bypass during preprocessing. The directives are

```
#if, #ifdef, #ifndef, #else, #elif and #endif.
```

#ifdef allows a section of a program to be compiled only if the defined constant that is specified as parameter has been defined independently of its value. Its operation is:

```
#ifdef name
   // code here
#endif
```

For example:

```
#ifdef MAX_SIZE
   char str1[MAX_SIZE];
#endif
```

In this case, the statement `char str1[MAX_SIZE];` will be considered for compilation only if the MAX_SIZE has been previously defined, whatever be its value. If it has not been defined, that statement will be discarded from being compiled.

`#ifndef` does the opposite: the statements between the `#ifndef` directive and the `#endif` directive is compiled only if the constant name that is specified has not been defined previously. For example,

```
#ifndef MAX_SIZE
   #define MAX_SIZE 100
#endif
char str1[MAX_SIZE];
```

In this case, if on arriving at this piece of code the defined constant MAX_SIZE has not yet been defined it would be defined with a value of 100. Otherwise, if it is already defined, it would maintain the value that it had (the #define statement won't be executed).

The #if and #elif directives compare the value of the expression to zero. If the constant expression evaluates to a nonzero value, the preprocessor passes the tokens that immediately follow the condition to the compiler. Here's an example (6.2).

EXAMPLE 6.2:

```
#if MAX_SIZE>100
  #undef MAX_SIZE
  #define MAX_SIZE 100
```

```
#elif MAX_SIZE>50
   #undef MAX_SIZE
   #define MAX_SIZE 50
 #else
   #undef MAX_SIZE
   #define MAX_SIZE 25
#endif
char str[MAX_SIZE];
```

The above piece of preprocessor directives undefine `MAX_SIZE` if already defined and sets value 100 (if >100), 50 (if >50 and <=100) and 25 otherwise. Then, str is set as a character array of `MAX_SIZE` defined.

The preprocessor conditional compilation directive spans several lines such as the following:

1. The condition specification line.
2. Lines containing code that the preprocessor passes on to the compiler if the condition evaluates to a nonzero value (optional).
3. The #else line (optional).
4. Lines containing code that the preprocessor passes on to the compiler if the condition evaluates to zero (optional).
5. The preprocessor #endif directive.

For each #if, #ifdef, and #ifndef directive, there are zero or more #elif directives, zero or one #else directives, and one matching #endif directive. One can consider all the matching directives to be at the same nesting level.

#line

When we compile a program, and if there are compilation errors, the error is displayed preceded by the name of the file and the line within the file where the error has taken place. A preprocessor line control directive supplies line numbers for compiler messages. It causes the compiler to view the line number of the next source line as the specified number. Thus, the #line directive tells the preprocessor to change the compiler's internally stored line number and filename to a given line number and filename. It takes the following form:

```
#line number "filename"
```

Where `number` is the new line number that will be assigned to the next code statement. The line number of subsequent statements will be incremented after each statement is processed. `filename` is an optional parameter that is meant to replace the file name that is normally shown in case of error from this directive until the other one changes it again, or the end of the file is reached.

If filename is omitted, the previous filename remains unchanged. For example, see Program Source Code 6.2 and 6.2a.

Program Source Code 6.2 (filename: E:\djana\Programs\a.cpp)

```
int main ()
{
   #line 1 "file one"
   int x-;
   #line 2
   int y+;
   return 0;
}
```

Compilation Error is shown as (compiled using Microsoft Visual C++ v. 6.0)

```
file one(1): error C2059: syntax error: '-'
file one(2): error C2059: syntax error: '+'
```

Program Source Code 6.2a (filename: E:\djana\Programs\a.cpp)

```
int main ()
{
   int x-;
   int y+;
   return 0;
}
```

Compilation Error is shown as (compiled using Microsoft Visual C++ v. 6.0)

```
E:\djana\Programs\a.cpp(3): error C2059: syntax error: '-'
E:\djana\Programs\a.cpp(4): error C2059: syntax error: '+'
```

In Code 6.2, the filename is given as "file one" with line number starting from 1 (as defined in the #line directive), whereas in the second Code (6.2a), the actual filename and actual line numbers are given while showing compilation errors.

The source line number and filename can be altered by writing a #line directive. The translator uses the line number and filename to determine the values of the predefined macros __FILE__ and __LINE__. These macros can be used to insert self-descriptive error messages into the source code. A list of ANSI specified predefined macros are given in Table 6.1.

Table 6.1

Macro Name	*Description*
__DATE__	The compilation date of the current source file. The date is a string literal of the form Mmm dd ,yyyy. The month name Mmm is the same as for dates generated by the library function asctime declared in TIME.H.
__FILE__	The name of the current source file. __FILE__ expands to a string enclosed within double quotation marks.
__LINE__	The line number in the current source file. The line number is a decimal integer constant. It can be altered with a #line directive.
__TIME__	The most recent compilation time of the current source file. The time is a string literal of the form hh:mm:ss.
__TIMESTAMP__	The date and time of the last modification of the current source file, expressed as a string literal in the form Ddd Mmm Date hh:mm:ss yyyy, where Ddd is the abbreviated day of the week and Date is an integer from 1 to 31.

An example is provided in Program Source Code 6.3.

Program Source Code 6.3 (filename: E:\djana\Programs\a.cpp)

```
#include <iostream.h>
#define TRUE 1
#define FALSE 0
#define ASSERT(cond) \
if( !(cond) )\
{     cout << "assertion error line " \
           << __LINE__ \
           << ",file(" << __FILE__ << ")" << endl; \
}
int main()
{
      ASSERT(TRUE);
      int i = 0;
      ASSERT(FALSE);
      return 0;
}
```

Output 6.3

```
assertion error line 14,file(E:\djana\Programs\a.cpp)
```

In the above program, we define a macro named ASSERT which takes a parameter called cond, depending on the value of which, this will print assertion error line showing the line number and file name using __LINE__ and __FILE__ built-in macro. The main program has two ASSERT call and the second ASSERT call prints assertion error showing line number and the file name.

#error

This directive aborts the compilation process when it is found returning the error that is specified as parameter. Error directives produce compile-time error messages. When #error directives are encountered, compilation terminates, as for example,

```
#ifndef __cplusplus
   #error Sorry, C++ compiler is required to compile this program
#endif
```

This example aborts the compilation process if the defined constant __cplusplus is not defined. Normally, C++ compilers define this constant __cplusplus on their own, and as such, if any other compiler (say, C) is used instead to compile a C++ program, and the code contains the three lines mentioned above, the compilation can be stopped, showing the error string as "Sorry, C++ compiler is required to compile this program".

#include

A preprocessor **include** directive causes the preprocessor to replace the directive with the whole contents of the specified file. There are two ways to specify a file to be included:

```
#include "filename"
#include <filename>
```

The filename is optionally preceded by a directory specification. It must name an existing file.

If you enclose the file name in double quotation marks (" "), the preprocessor instructs the preprocessor to look for include files in the same directory of the file that contains the #include statement, and then in the directories of whatever files that include (#include) that file. The preprocessor then searches along the path specified by the /I compiler option, then along the paths specified by the INCLUDE environment variable.

If you enclose the file name in angular brackets < >, it instructs the preprocessor to search for include files first along the path specified by the /I compiler option, then along the path specified by the INCLUDE environment variable, for example,

#include "payroll.h" will search the file in current directory first. If not available, it will search standard or specified places for the specified file. If you enclose the file name in angular brackets, the characters < and >, the preprocessor searches only the standard or specified places for the specified file, for example, `#include <stdio.h>` The new-line and >characters cannot appear in a file name that is delimited by < and >. The new-line and "(double quotation marks) characters cannot appear in a file name that is delimited by double quotation marks. However, the > character can appear in such a file name.

Include files can be "nested", that is, an #include directive can appear in a file named by another #include directive. In order to include (open) a file only once by the compiler, we can write for a file named a.hpp like the following:

```
#ifndef A_HPP
#define A_HPP
// other C/C++ statements here .....
#endif
```

#pragma

A pragma is an implementation-defined instruction to the compiler. This directive is used to specify diverse options to the compiler. These options are specific for the platform and the compiler in use. Pragmas are machine or operating-system-specific by definition, and are usually different for every compiler. As such, the reference manual for the particular compiler in use should be consulted to know for the possible parameters that can be defined with #pragma. For example, in Microsoft Visual C++, #pragma once specifies that the file in which the pragma resides, will be included (opened) only once by the compiler in a compilation process. A common use of pragma is the following:

```
//File: header.h
#pragma once
//C or C++ code statements .....
```

SUMMARY

The key concepts introduced in this chapter are as follows:

- The preprocessor is a simple program that replaces patterns given in the source code with some other patterns as defined using preprocessor directives.
- Some unavailable characters in a C/C++ source program can be represented by using a trigraph character which is a combination of three keystrokes.
- Some unavailable characters in a C/C++ source program can be represented by using a digraph character which is a combination of two keystrokes.
- #define directive directs the preprocessor to replace all subsequent occurrences of a macro or an identifier with specified replacement tokens.
- The #(single number sign) operator followed by a parameter converts the parameter of a function-like macro into a character string literal.
- The null directive (a single #on a line of its own) performs no action.
- The double number sign operator (##) concatenates two tokens in a macro invocation (text or arguments), that a macro definition contains.
- #undef directive causes the preprocessor to end the scope of a preprocessor definition done by #define.
- A preprocessor conditional compilation directive (#if, #ifdef, #ifndef, #else, #elif, #endif) causes the preprocessor to conditionally suppress portions of the source code compilation.
- #line control directive tells the preprocessor to change the compiler's internally stored line number and filename to a given line number and filename.
- There are some ANSI specified predefined macros like __DATE__ , __FILE__, __TIME__, __TIMESTAMP__ with appropriate definitions.
- When #error directives are encountered, compilation terminates.
- #include directive causes the preprocessor to replace the directive with the whole contents of the specified file.
- #pragma directive is used to provide an implementation-defined instruction to the compiler.

REVIEW QUESTIONS

1. Briefly describe the phases of preprocessing.
2. Why is there a difference between macro and inline function? Which one is preferred and why?
3. Name four predefined macros.
4. How would you use the #error directive?
5. How can you stop including the same file more than once in a nested inclusion?
6. What is the use of #line directive? Illustrate with suitable examples.
7. What is #pragma? Illustrate with suitable examples.
8. What is the role of #error directive?
9. What is the difference of #include "filename" and #include <filename>?
10. What is the role of the INCLUDE environment variable?
11. How can conditional compilation be done using preprocessor directive?
12. When does the preprocessor directive get invoked?
13. What are digraph and trigraph? When are they used?
14. Illustrate with suitable examples the difference between # and ## operator.

7 Standard C Library Functions and Standard Header Files

Systems are not born into an empty world.
—Bertrend Meyer

LEARNING OBJECTIVES

The objective of this chapter is to acquaint you with:

- Standard C library functions and corresponding standard header files like assert.h, ctype.h, math.h, stdio.h, stdlib.h etc.

INTRODUCTION

C++ comes with a rich set of library. It's so extensive that it will be difficult to describe them in detail. However, to acquire knowledge of library functions supported, it is required to consult the library documentation provided by the particular compiler vendor. However, there are some standard libraries available in all the different compiler vendors. These are worth mentioning. In this section, we will list couple of library functions available in standard C language. C++ being a superset of C, all standard library available in C are available in C++ as well. C++ specific standard library functions will be discussed after we introduce the basic constructs of C++ specific.

Why Library?

There are many functions which are often required by most of the users of the language. However, they cannot be expressed in the core language such as input/output. Although they could be implemented in the language, they can be implemented more efficiently if the compiler knows how they are defined, such as the square root function. A library is built on a single conceptual framework, it encourages users to use that same framework in its own programs such as algorithms. The standard library functions do not include every facility that meets the requirement of every possible user. However, the main purpose of standard library is to provide a set of standard functions that can be linked into the code. The users don't need to be bothered about how these functions are implemented; they have to just call them, using the prototype of the functions, as defined in the standard header files corresponding to the standard libraries. The standard libraries (.lib files) are linked to the object codes (.obj files) generated after compilation of the source files (.c or .cpp). To use a library, the programmer typically includes a header file (.h or .hpp) in the source code. For example, you could write #include <iostream.h>, as you have seen in many previous examples. The angle brackets around the file name signal the compiler to look into the directory where the header files associated for the standard libraries are kept.

There are many libraries covering functions ranging from file manipulation to setting date and time to math functions. The C library contains functions for input and output, mathematics, exception handling, string and character manipulation, dynamic memory management, as well as date and time manipulation. Use of this library helps to maintain program portability, because the underlying implementation details for the various operations need not concern the programmer. This section reviews a few of the most popular functions in the standard C libraries.

Although the names of system calls and library functions are not reserved if appropriate headers are not included, they should not be used as identifiers. Duplication of a predefined name may lead to confusion for the maintainers of the code and can cause errors at link time or run time. If a library function call is required in a program, the function names in that library should not be used elsewhere as other names, in order to avoid name duplications. The appropriate headers should be included when using standard library functions.

Header Files

Some standard header files[1] associated with standard libraries are listed in the forthcoming sections.

---

[1]There are a number of standard header files specified in the C language standard. These standard header files are included into program source code files or other include files through the preprocessor #include mechanism. These files usually define useful constants (using the #define preprocessor.

<assert.h>

This file contains functions related to diagnostics, which use a micro like

```
void assert(int expression);
```

The most typical use of the *assert* macro is to identify program errors during development. The argument given to *assert* should be chosen so that it holds true only if the program is operating as intended. This macro returns true if its parameter, which is an expression, evaluates as true; conversely some action is taken if the parameter evaluates as false. In many compilers, if assert fails (expression evaluates to false), a message is printed on *stderr* and abort function is called to terminate execution. Name of the source file and corresponding line number in message are given through preprocessor macros __FILE__ and __LINE__. If NDEBUG is defined where <assert.h> is included, and assert macro is ignored. An example program is provided as Program Source Code 7.1.

Program Source Code 7.1

```
#include <assert.h>
#include <iostream.h>
int main()
{
    int x = 10;
    cout << "First call to assert" << endl;
    assert(x==10);
    cout << "Second call to assert" << endl;
    assert(x!=10);
    cout << "Done" << endl;
    return 0;
}
```

Output 7.1

```
First call to assert
Second call to assert
Assertion failed: x! = 10, file E:\Programs\test\a.cpp, line 9
abnormal program termination
```

Frequent use of assert() macros carries no penalty, because these macros are removed from the code when the debugging is undefined by the programmer. They provide good internal documentation as to say what the programmer believes to be true at the given line where assert is called in the program flow. assert() macros are not intended to handle runtime error conditions such as bad data, out-of-memory conditions, unable to open file, and so on. Instead, these macros are created to identify only programming errors. More precisely, if assert() fails, the programmer knows that the source has a bug.

<ctype.h>

This file contains functions related to character class tests. Each of these functions returns 0 if the argument passed does not satisfy the test condition. And each of these routines returns non-zero values depending on the particular test condition described. The functions are given in Table 7.1.

Table 7.1

Function Prototype	*Description*
int isalnum(int c);	isalnum returns a non-zero value if either isalpha or isdigit is true for c, that is, if c is within the ranges A–Z, a–z, or 0–9.
int isalpha(int c);	isalpha returns a non-zero value if c is within the ranges A–Z or a–z.
isupper(c) or islower(c)	isupper returns a non-zero value if c is an uppercase character (A–Z). islower returns a non-zero value if c is an lowercase character (a–z).
int iscntrl(int c);	iscntrl returns a non-zero value if c is a control character (0x00 –0x1F or 0x7F).
int isdigit(int c);	isdigit returns a non-zero value if c is a decimal digit, i.e. falls within the ranges 0–9.
int isgraph(int c);	isgraph returns a non-zero value if c is a printable character other than a space.
int islower(int c);	islower returns a non-zero value if c is a lowercase character (a–z).
int isprint(int c);	isprint returns a nonzero value if c is a printable character, including the space character (0x20–0x7E).
int ispunct(int c);	ispunct returns a non-zero value for any printable character that is not a space character nor a letter or digit, i.e. not a character for which isalnum is true.
int isspace(int c);	isspace returns a non-zero value if c is a white-space character (0x09–0x0D or 0x20). White space character includes space, formfeed, newline, carriage return, tab, vertical tab.
int isupper(int c);	isupper returns a non-zero value if c is an uppercase character (A–Z).
int isxdigit(int c);	isxdigit returns a non-zero value if c is a hexadecimal digit (A–F, a–f, or 0–9).
int tolower(int c);	tolower converts a copy of c, if possible, to lowercase and returns the result. There is no return value reserved to indicate an error.
int toupper(int c);	toupper converts a copy of c, if possible, to uppercase and returns the result. There is no return value reserved to indicate an error.

Notes. In ASCII (7-bit), printing characters are 0x20 (' ') to 0x7E ('~'); control characters are 0x00 (NULL) to 0x1F (US) and 0x7F (DEL).

An example program given for your understanding in Program Source Code 7.2.

Program Source Code 7.2

```
/*This program counts the number of digits in the given
strings */
#include <iostream.h>
#include <ctype.h>
#define SIZE 3
int main(void)
{
   char *str[SIZE] = {"ab12cd", "34ef56", "gh78jk"};
   int NoOfAlphabets[SIZE] = {0, 0, 0};
   int i;
   char *temp;
   for (i = 0; i < SIZE; i++)
   {
      NoOfAlphabets[i] = 0; // initialize counter
      //for each str count number of alphabets in each string
      for (temp = str[i]; *temp !='\0'; temp++)
      {
         if (isalpha(*temp)) // if alphabet
            NoOfAlphabets[i]++; // increment counter
      }
      cout << "Number of Alphabets in string "
           << str[i]
           << "is"
           << NoOfAlphabets[i]
           << endl;
   }
  return(0);
}
```

Output 7.2

```
Number of Alphabets in string ab12cd is 4
Number of Alphabets in string 34ef56 is 2
Number of Alphabets in string gh78jk is 4
```

<errno.h>

This file defines the system-wide error numbers (set by system calls). *errno* is a global variable holding error codes used by the *perror* and *strerror* functions for printing error messages. *errno* is set on an error in a system-level call. Since *errno* holds the value for the last call that set it, this value may be changed by succeeding calls. *errno* should be always checked immediately before and after a call that may set it. All possible *errno* values are defined as manifest constants in ERRNO.H.

<float.h>

This file contains implementation-defined Floating-Point Limits giving the range and other characteristics of the double and float data types. Here are some samples (see Table 7.2). The values given here, may vary from implementation to implementation.

Table 7.2

Constant	*Value*	*Description*
DBL_DIG	15	Number of decimal digits of precision
DBL_EPSILON	2.2204460492503131e-016	Smallest double floating-point number x such that 1.0 + x != 1.0
DBL_MANT_DIG	53	Number of bits in mantissa
DBL_MAX	1.7976931348623158e+308	Maximum double floating-point number
DBL_MAX_10_EXP	308	Maximum decimal exponent
DBL_MAX_EXP	1024	Maximum binary exponent
DBL_MIN	2.2250738585072014e-308	Minimum normalized double floating-point number (positive value)
DBL_MIN_10_EXP	(–307)	Minimum decimal exponent
DBL_MIN_EXP	(–1021)	Minimum binary exponent
_DBL_RADIX	2	Exponent radix
_DBL_ROUNDS	1	Addition rounding: near
FLT_DIG	6	Number of decimal digits of precision
FLT_EPSILON	1.192092896e-07F	Smallest floating-point number x such that 1.0 + x != 1.0
FLT_MANT_DIG	24	Number of bits in mantissa
FLT_MAX	3.402823466e+38F	Maximum floating-point number
FLT_MAX_10_EXP	38	Maximum decimal exponent
FLT_MAX_EXP	128	Maximum binary exponent
FLT_MIN	1.175494351e-38F	Minimum normalized floating-point number (positive value)
FLT_MIN_10_EXP	(–37)	Minimum decimal exponent
FLT_MIN_EXP	(–125)	Minimum binary exponent
FLT_RADIX	2	Exponent radix
FLT_ROUNDS	1	Addition rounding: near

<limits.h>

This file contains implementation-defined limits for integral data-types giving the range and other characteristics of the integer data types. A sample is given in Table 7.3. The values given in it may vary from implementation to implementation.

Table 7.3

Constant	*Value*	*Description*
SCHAR_MAX	127	Maximum signed char value
SCHAR_MIN	–128	Minimum signed char value
UCHAR_MAX	255(0xff)	Maximum unsigned char value
CHAR_BIT	8	Number of bits in a char
USHRT_MAX	65535(0xffff)	Maximum unsigned short value
SHRT_MAX	32767	Maximum (signed) short value
SHRT_MIN	–32768	Minimum (signed) short value
UINT_MAX	4294967295(0xffffffff)	Maximum unsigned int value
ULONG_MAX	4294967295(0xffffffff)	Maximum unsigned long value
INT_MAX	2147483647	Maximum (signed) int value
INT_MIN	–2147483647–1	Minimum (signed) int value
LONG_MAX	2147483647	Maximum (signed) long value
LONG_MIN	–2147483647–1	Minimum (signed) long value
CHAR_MAX	127(255 if default char is unsigned)	Maximum char value
CHAR_MIN	–128(0 if default char is unsigned)	Minimum char value
MB_LEN_MAX	2	Maximum number of bytes in multibyte char

<math.h>

This file contains functions related to mathematical functions. The functions are given in Table 7.4.

Table 7.4

Function Prototype	*Description*
double sin(double x);	sin returns the sine of x. Parameter x is taken in radians.
double cos(double x);	cos returns the cosine of x. Parameter x is taken in radians.
double tan(double x);	tan returns the tangent of x. Parameter x is taken in radians.

(contd.)

Table 7.4 *(contd.)*

Function Prototype	*Description*
double asin(double x);	asin returns the arcsine of x. Parameter x is taken as angle in radians.
double acos(double x);	acos returns the arccosine of x. Parameter x is taken as angle in radians.
double atan(double x);	atan returns the arctangent of x. Parameter x is taken as angle in radians.
double atan2(double y, double x);	atan2 returns the arctangent of y/x. Parameter x, y are taken as angle in radians.
double sinh(double x);	sinh returns the hyperbolic sine of x. Parameter x is taken as angle in radians.
double cosh(double x);	cosh returns the hyperbolic cosine of x. Parameter x is taken as angle in radians.
double tanh(double x);	tanh returns the hyperbolic tangent of x. Parameter x is taken as angle in radians.
double exp(double x);	The exp function returns the exponential value of the floating-point parameter, x, if successful. On overflow, the function returns INF (infinite) and on underflow, exp returns 0.
double log(double x);	The log functions return the logarithm of x if successful. If x is negative, this function returns an indefinite value. If x is 0, they return INF (infinite).
double log10(double x);	The log10 functions return the logarithm of x (base 10) if successful. If x is negative, this function returns an indefinite value. If x is 0, they return INF (infinite).
double pow(double x, double y);	The pow function computes x raised to the power of y. No error message is printed on overflow or underflow. $x \neq 0.0$ and $y = 0.0$ returns 1, $x = 0.0$ and $y = 0.0$ returns 1, $x = 0.0$ and $y < 0.0$ returns INF.
double sqrt(double x);	The sqrt function returns the square-root of x. If x is negative, sqrt returns an indefinite value.
double ceil(double x);	The ceil function returns a double value representing the smallest integer that is greater than or equal to x. There is no error return. ceil(4.5) returns 5, ceil(5.0) returns 5.
double floor(double x);	The floor function returns a double value representing the largest integer that is smaller than or equal to x. There is no error return. floor(4.5) returns 4, floor(4.0) returns 4.
double fabs(double x);	fabs returns the absolute value of its argument. There is no error return. fabs(–4) returns –4, fabs (–4.345) returns 4.345.

(contd.)

Table 7.4 *(contd.)*

Function Prototype	*Description*
double ldexp(double x, int n);	The ldexp function returns the value of $x * 2^n$ if successful. On overflow (depending on the sign of x), ldexp returns +/– HUGE_VAL; the errno variable is set to ERANGE. $ldexp(3,4)=3*2^4=48$
double frexp(double x, int* exp);	frexp returns the mantissa. If x is 0, the function returns 0 for both the mantissa and the exponent. There is no error return. The frexp function breaks down the floating-point value (x) into a mantissa (m) and an exponent (n), such that the absolute value of m is greater than or equal to 0.5 and less than 1.0, and x = m*2n. The integer exponent n is stored at the location pointed to by exp.
double modf(double x, double* ip);	The modf function breaks down the floating-point value x into fractional and integer parts, each of which has the same sign as x. The signed fractional portion of x is returned. The integer portion is stored as a floating-point value at ip. This function returns the signed fractional portion of x. There is no error return.
double fmod(double x, double y);	fmod returns the floating-point remainder of x/y. The fmod function calculates the floating-point remainder f of x/y such that x = i * y + f, where i is an integer, f has the same sign as x, and the absolute value of f is less than the absolute value of y.

An example program is provided in Program Source Code 7.3.

Program Source Code 7.3

```
#include <iostream.h>
#include <math.h>
const double PI = 3.1415926535;
int main()
{
    double x = PI/2.0;
    double y = 4.5;
    double z = 2.302585093;
    int n;
    cout << "sine of PI/2 is "
         << sin(x)
         << endl;
```

(contd.)

Program Source Code 7.3 *(contd.)*

```
    cout << "cosine of PI/2 is "
         << cos(x)
         << endl;
    cout << "exponent of " <<  z << "is "
         << exp(z)
         << endl;
   z = frexp( y, &n );
    cout << "fxrep of " <<  y << " gives n = "
         << n
         << endl;
    return 0;
}
```

Output 7.3

```
sine of PI/2 is 1
cosine of PI/2 is 4.48966e-011
exponent of 2.30259 is 10
fxrep of 4.5 gives n = 3
```

<setjmp.h>

This file contains functions related to non-local jump instructions. The functions are essentially as given in Table 7.5.

Table 7.5

Function Prototype	*Description*
int setjmp(jmp_buf env);	The setjmp function saves a stack environment, which can be subsequently restored using longjmp. When used together, setjmp and longjmp provide a way to execute a "non-local goto." They are typically used to pass execution control to error-handling or recovery code in a previously called routine without using the normal calling or return conventions. A call to setjmp saves the current stack environment in env. A subsequent call to longjmp restores the saved environment and returns control to the point just after the corresponding setjmp call. All variables (except register variables) accessible to the routine receiving control contain the values they had when longjmp was called.

(contd.)

Table 7.5 (*contd.*)

Function Prototype	*Description*
void longjmp(jmp_buf env, int val);	The longjmp function restores a stack environment and execution locale previously saved in env by setjmp. setjmp and longjmp provide a way to execute a nonlocal goto; they are typically used to pass execution control to error-handling or recovery code in a previously called routine without using the normal call and return conventions. A call to setjmp causes the current stack environment to be saved in env. A subsequent call to longjmp restores the saved environment and returns control to the point immediately following the corresponding setjmp call. Execution resumes as if value had just been returned by the setjmp call. The values of all variables (except register variables) that are accessible to the routine receiving control contain the values they had when longjmp was called. The values of register variables are unpredictable. The value returned by setjmp must be nonzero. If value is passed as 0, the value 1 is substituted in the actual return.

<signal.h>

This file contains functions related to handling of signals in exceptional conditions. Some constants (as required by sig parameter used in the functions mentioned subsequently) are defined in Table 7.6.

Table 7.6

Constant Name	*Description*
SIGABRT	Abnormal termination. The default action terminates the calling program with exit code 3.
SIGFPE	Arithmetic, more precisely, Floating-point error such as overflow, division by zero, or invalid operation. The default action terminates the calling program.
SIGILL	Illegal instruction. The default action terminates the calling program.
SIGINT	CTRL+C interrupt. The default action issues interrupt numbered INT 23H.
SIGSEGV	Illegal storage access. The default action terminates the calling program.
SIGTERM	Termination request sent to the program. The default action terminates the calling program.

The signal handling functions are given in Table 7.7.

Table 7.7

Function Prototype	*Description*
void (*signal(int sig, void (*handler)(int)))(int);	Installs handler for subsequent signal sig. If handler is SIG_DFL, implementation-defined default behaviour is used; if handler is SIG_IGN, signal is ignored; otherwise function pointed to by handler is called with argument sig. signal returns the previous handler or SIG_ERR on error. When signal sig subsequently occurs, the signal is restored to its default behaviour and the handler is called. If the handler returns, execution resumes where signal occurred. Initial state of signals is implementation-defined. The signal function allows a process to choose one of several ways to handle an interrupt signal from the operating system. The sig argument is the interrupt to which signal responds; it must be one of the constants as defined in SIGNAL.H like SIGABRT, SIGFPE, SIGILL, SIGINT, SIGSEGV, SIGTERM. *signal* returns the previous value of func associated with the given signal. For example, if the previous value of func was SIG_IGN, the return value is also SIG_IGN. A return value of SIG_ERR indicates an error, in which case errno is set to EINVAL.
int raise(int sig);	Sends signal sig to the executing program. Non-zero returned if unsuccessful. Zero returned on success. If a previous call to signal has installed a signal-handling function for sig, raise executes that function. If no handler function has been installed, the default action associated with the signal value sig is taken.

<stdarg.h>

This file contains functions related to facilities for stepping through a list of function arguments of unknown number and type. The signal handling functions are given in Table 7.8.

Table 7.8

Function Prototype	*Description*
void va_start(va_list ap, lastarg);	Initialization macro to be called once before any unnamed argument is accessed. ap must be declared as a local variable, and lastarg is the last named parameter of the function.
type va_arg(va_list ap, type);	Produces a value of the type (type) and value of the next unnamed argument. Modifies ap.
void va_end(va_list ap);	Must be called once after arguments processed and before function exit.

An example program (Program Source Code 7.4) follows:

Program Source Code 7.4

```
/*****************************************************

* The program below illustrates passing a variable    *
* number of arguments                                  *
*****************************************************/

#include <iostream.h>
#include <stdarg.h>
int sum(int first, ... );

int main()
{
   /* Call with 3 integers (-1 is used as terminator) */
   cout << "sum is: " << sum(2, 3, 4, -1) << endl;

   /* Call with 4 integers. */
   cout << "sum is: " << sum(5, 7, 9, 11, -1) << endl;

   /* Call with no integer : just -1 terminator */
   cout << "sum is: " << sum(-1) << endl;
   return 0;
}
/* Returns the sum of a variable list of integers. */
int sum(int first, ...)
{
   int s = 0, i = first;
   va_list marker;
  va_start(marker, first); /* Initialize variable
                                    arguments */
   while(i != -1)
   {
      s += i;
      i = va_arg(marker, int);
   }
   va_end(marker);   /* Reset variable arguments      */
   return s;
}
```

```
Output 7.4
sum is: 9
sum is: 32
sum is: 0
```

<stdio.h>

This file contains functions related to Input and Output. The following data types/data (Table 7.9) are defined for use with input/output functions.

Table 7.9

Name	*Description*
FILE	Type which records information necessary to control a stream.
stdin	Standard input stream. Automatically opened when a program begins execution.
stdout	Standard output stream. Automatically opened when a program begins execution.
stderr	Standard error stream. Automatically opened when a program begins execution.
FILENAME_MAX	Maximum permissible length of a file name.
FOPEN_MAX	Maximum number of files which may be opened simultaneously.
TMP_MAX	Maximum number of temporary files during program execution.

stdin, stdout, and stderr file pointers are constants, and cannot be assigned new values. The freopen function can be used to redirect the streams to disk files or to other devices. The operating system allows you to redirect a program's standard input and output at the command level.

The input/output functions are as defined in Table 7.10.

Table 7.10

Function Prototype	*Description*
FILE* fopen(const char* *filename,* const char* *mode);*	*Opens* file *filename* and returns a stream, or NULL on failure. *mode* may be (combinations of): "r" Opens for reading. If the file does not exist or cannot be found, the fopen call fails. "w" Opens an empty file for writing. If the given file exists, its contents are destroyed. "a" Opens for writing at the end of the file (appending) without removing the End-of-File(EOF) marker before writing new data to the file; creates the file first if it doesn't exist.

(*contd.*)

Table 7.10 (*contd.*)

Function Prototype	*Description*
"r+"	Opens for both reading and writing. (The file must exist.)
"w+"	Opens an empty file for both reading and writing. If the given file exists, its contents are destroyed.
"a+"	Opens for reading and appending; the appending operation includes the removal of the EOF marker before new data is written to the file and the EOF marker is restored after writing is complete; creates the file first if it doesn't exist.
FILE* freopen(const char* filename, const char* mode, FILE* stream);	Opens file filename with the specified mode and associates with it the specified stream. Returns stream or NULL on error and generally used for changing files associated with stdin, stdout, stderr.
int fflush(FILE* stream);	Flushes a stream. fflush returns 0 if the buffer is successfully flushed. The value 0 is also returned in cases in which the specified stream has no buffer or is open for reading only. A return value of EOF indicates an error. fflush(NULL) flushes all output streams.
int fclose(FILE* stream);	Closes a stream(after flushing, if output stream). Returns EOF on error, zero otherwise.
int remove(const char* filename);	Removes file filename. Returns non-zero on failure.
int rename(const char* oldname, const char* newname);	Changes name of file oldname to newname. Returns non-zero on failure.
FILE* tmpfile();	Creates temporary file (mode "wb+") which will be removed when closed or on normal program termination. Returns stream or NULL on failure.
int setvbuf(FILE* stream, char* buf, int mode, size_t size);	Controls stream buffering and buffer size. setvbuf returns 0 if successful, or a nonzero value if an illegal type or buffer size is specified. Parameters are stream(pointer to FILE structure), User-allocated buffer, mode of buffering, buffer size in bytes(allowable range: 2 < size < 32768. Internally, the value supplied for size is rounded down to the nearest multiple of 2).
void setbuf(FILE* stream, char* buf);	Controls buffering for stream. The stream argument must refer to an open file that has not been read or written. If the buffer argument is NULL, the stream is unbuffered. If not, the buffer must point to a character array of length BUFSIZ, where BUFSIZ is the buffer size as defined in STDIO.H. The user-specified buffer, instead of the default system-allocated buffer for the given stream, is used for I/O buffering. The stderr stream is unbuffered by default, but setbuf can be used to assign buffers to stderr.

(*contd.*)

Table 7.10 (*contd.*)

Function Prototype	*Description*
int fprintf(FILE* stream, const char* format, ...);	Prints formatted data to a stream. Converts (with format) and writes output to stream. Number of characters written [negative on error] is returned. Format specifications always begin with a percent sign (%) and are read left to right. When fprintf encounters the first format specification (if any), it converts the value of the first argument after format and writes it accordingly. The second format specification causes the second argument to be converted and write, and so on. If there are more arguments than there are format specifications, the extra arguments are ignored. The results are undefined if there are not enough arguments for all the format specifications.
int printf(const char* format, ...);	printf(f, ...) is equivalent to fprintf(stdout, f, ...).
int sprintf(char* s, const char* format, ...);	Like fprintf, but output written into string s, which must be large enough to hold the output, rather than to a stream. Output is NULL-terminated. Return length does not include the NULL character.
int vfprintf(FILE* stream, const char* format, va_list arg);	Equivalent to fprintf except that the variable argument list is replaced by arg, which must have been initialized by the va_start macro and may have been used in calls to va_arg. stdarg.h should be referred.
int vsprintf(char* s, const char* format, va_list arg);	Equivalent to sprintf except that the variable argument list is replaced by arg, which must have been initialized by the va_start macro and may have been used in calls to va_arg.
int fscan (FILE* stream, const char* format, ...);	Performs formatted input conversion, reading from stream according to given format. The function returns when format is fully processed. Returns EOF if end-of-file or error occurs before any conversion; otherwise, the number of items converted and assigned. Each of the arguments following the format must be a pointer. Format string may contain: • Blanks, Tabs: ignored • ordinary characters: expected to match next non-white-space • %: Conversion specification, consisting of %, optional assignment suppression character *, optional number indicating maximum field width, optional [hlL] indicating width of target, conversion character.

(*contd.*)

Table 7.10 (*contd.*)

Function Prototype	*Description*
	Conversion characters are: • d: decimal integer; int* parameter required • i: integer; int* parameter required; decimal, octal or hex • o: octal integer; int* parameter required • u: unsigned decimal integer; unsigned int* parameter required • x: hexadecimal integer; int* parameter required • c: characters; char* parameter required; up to width; no '\0' added; no skip • s: string of non-white-space; char* parameter required; '\0' added • e,f,g: floating-point number; float* parameter required • p: pointer value; void* parameter required • n: chars read so far; int* parameter required • [...]: longest non-empty string from set; char* parameter required; '\0' • [^...]: longest non-empty string not from set; char* parameter required; '\0' • %: literal %; no assignment
int scanf(const char* format, ...);	scanf(f, ...) is equivalent to fscanf(stdin, f, ...).
int sscanf(char* s, const char* format, ...);	Like fscanf, but input read from string s.
int fgetc(FILE* stream);	Returns next character from stream as an unsigned char, or EOF on end-of-file or error.
char* fgets(char* s, int n, FILE* stream);	Reads mostly the next n-1 characters from stream into s, stopping if a new line is encountered (after copying the new line to s). s is NULL-terminated. Returns s, or NULL on end-of-file or error.
int fputc(int c, FILE* stream);	Writes c, converted to unsigned char, to stream. Returns the character written, or EOF on error.
char* fputs(const char* s, FILE* stream);	Writes s, which need not contain '\n' on stream. Returns non-negative on success, EOF on error.
int getc(FILE* stream);	Equivalent to fgetc, except that it may be a macro.
int getchar();	Equivalent to getc(stdin).
char* gets(char* s);	Reads next line from stdin into s. Replaces terminating newline with '\0'. Returns s, or NULL on end-of-file or error.

(*contd.*)

Table 7.10 *(contd.)*

Function Prototype	*Description*
int putc(int c, FILE* stream);	Equivalent to fputc except that it may be a macro.
int putchar(int c);	putchar(c) is equivalent to putc(c, stdout).
int puts(const char* s);	Writes s and a newline to stdout. Returns non-negative on success, EOF on error.
int unget(int c, FILE* stream);	Pushes c (which must not be EOF) converted to unsigned char onto stream, such that it will be returned by the next read. Only one character of pushback is guaranteed for a stream. Returns c, or EOF on error.
size_t fread(void* ptr, size_t size, size_t nobj, FILE* stream);	Reads at most nobj objects of size size from stream into ptr. Returns the number of objects read. feof and ferror must be used to determine status.
size_t fwrite(const void* ptr, size_t size, size_t nobj, FILE* stream);	Writes to stream stream, nobj objects of size size from array ptr. Returns the number of objects written (which will be less than nobj on error).
int fseek(FILE* stream, long offset, int origin);	Sets file position for stream. For a binary file, position is set to offset characters from origin, which may be SEEK_SET (beginning), SEEK_CUR (current position) or SEEK_END (end-of-file); for a text stream, offset must be zero or a value returned by ftell (in which case origin must be SEEK_SET). Returns non-zero on error.
long ftell(FILE* stream);	Returns current file position for stream stream, or -1L on error.
void rewind(FILE* stream);	rewind(stream) is equivalent to fseek(stream, 0L, SEEK_SET); clearerr(stream).
int fgetpos(FILE* stream, fpos_t* ptr);	Assigns current position in stream stream to *ptr. Type fpos_t, suitable for recording such values. Returns non-zero on error.
int fsetpos(FILE* stream, const fpos_t* ptr);	Sets current position of stream to *ptr. Returns non-zero on error.
void clearerr(FILE* stream);	Clears the end-of-file and error indicators for stream.
int feof(FILE* stream);	Returns non-zero if end-of-file indicator for stream is set.
int ferror(FILE* stream);	Returns non-zero if error indicator for stream is set.
void perror(const char* s);	Prints s and implementation-defined error message corresponding to errno. fprintf(stderr, "%s: %s\n", s, "error message") :stderror should be referred.

A ***format Specification***, which consists of optional and required fields, has the following form:

```
%[flags] [width] [.precision] [{h|l|I64|L}]type
```

Each field of the format specification is a single character or a number signifying a particular format option. The simplest format specification contains only the per cent sign and a type character which is the format conversion character (for example, %d for integer data). If a per cent sign is followed by a character that has no meaning as a format field, the character is copied to stdout. For example, to print a per cent sign, %% may be used.

The type or format conversion character contains the required character that determines whether the associated argument is interpreted as a character, a string, or a number as follows:

d, i	int; signed decimal notation
o	int; unsigned octal notation
x, X	int; unsigned hexadecimal notation
u	int; unsigned decimal notation
c	int; single character
s	character string, characters are printed up to the first null character or until the precision value is reached.
f	double; Signed value having the form [–]dddd.dddd, where dddd is one or more decimal digits. The number of digits before the decimal point depends on the magnitude of the number, and the number of digits after the decimal point depends on the requested precision.
e,E	double; Signed value having the form [–]d.dddd e [sign]ddd where d is a single decimal digit, dddd is one or more decimal digits, ddd is exactly three decimal digits, and sign is + or –.
g,G	double; Signed value printed in f or e format, whichever is more compact for the given value and precision. The e format is used only when the exponent of the value is less than –4 or greater than or equal to the precision argument. Trailing zeros are truncated, and the decimal point appears only if one or more digits follow it.
p	print as pointer; Prints the address pointed to by the argument in the form xxxx:yyyy where xxxx is the segment and yyyy is the offset, and the digits x and y are uppercase hexadecimal digits.
n	Number of characters successfully written so far to the stream or buffer; this value is stored in the integer whose address is given as the argument.
%	print %

Between % and format conversion character, the optional fields that control other aspects of the formatting are as follows:

Flags. Optional character or characters that control justification of output and printing of signs, blanks, decimal points, and octal and hexadecimal prefixes. More than one flag can appear in a format specification. The following is the list of the possible flags (Table 7.11).

Table 7.11

Flag	*Meaning*	*Default*
–	Left align the result within the given field width	Right align
+	Prefix the output value with a sign (+ or –) if the output value is of a signed type	Sign appears only for negative signed values (–).
0	If width is prefixed with 0, zeros are added until the minimum width is reached. If 0 and – appear, the 0 is ignored. If 0 is specified with an integer format (i, u, x, X, o, d) the 0 is ignored	No padding.
blank (' ')	Prefix the output value with a blank if the output value is signed and positive; the blank is ignored if both the blank and + flags appear	No blank appears.
#	When used with the o, x, or X format, the # flag prefixes any nonzero output value with 0, 0x, or 0X, respectively.	No blank appears.
	When used with the e, E, or f format, the # flag forces the output value to contain a decimal point in all cases.	Decimal point appears only if digits follow it.
	When used with the g or G format, the # flag forces the output value to contain a decimal point in all cases and prevents the truncation of trailing zeros.	Decimal point appears only if digits follow it.Trailing zeros are truncated.
	Ignored when used with c, d, i, u, or s.	

Width. Optional number that specifies the minimum number of characters output.

Precision. Optional number that specifies the maximum number of characters printed for all or part of the output field, or the minimum number of digits printed for integer values.

h | l | I64 | L. Optional prefixes to type that specify the size of argument. h => short or unsigned short, l => long or unsigned long, L => long double.

<stdlib.h>

This file contains functions related to utility functions. The functions given in Table 7.12 are defined.

Table 7.12

Function Prototype	*Description*
double atof(const char* s)	Returns numerical value of s. Equivalent to strtod(s, (char**)NULL).
int atoi(const char* s)	Returns numerical value of s. Equivalent to (int)strtol(s, (char**)NULL, 10).
long atol(const char* s)	Returns numerical value of s. Equivalent to strtol(s, (char**)NULL, 10).
double strtod(const char* s, char** endp)	Converts prefix of s to double, ignoring leading white space. Stores a pointer to any unconverted suffix in *endp if endp non-NULL. If answer overflows, HUGE_VAL is returned with the appropriate sign; if underflows, zero is returned. In either case, errno is set to ERANGE.
long strtol(const char* s, char** endp, int base)	Converts prefix of s to long, ignoring leading quite space. Stores a pointer to any unconverted suffix in *endp if endp non-NULL. If base between 2 and 36, that base used; if zero, leading 0X or 0x implies hexadecimal, leading 0implies octal, otherwise decimal. Leading 0X or 0x permitted for base 16. If answer overflows, LONG_MAX or LONG_MIN returned and errno is set to ERANGE.
unsigned long strtoul(const char* s, char** endp, int base)	As for strtol except result is unsigned long and error value is ULONG_MAX.
int rand()	Returns pseudo-random number in range 0 to RAND_MAX.
void srand(unsigned int seed)	Uses seed as seed for new sequence of pseudo-random numbers. Initial seed is 1.
void* calloc(size_t nobj, size_t size)	Returns pointer to zero-initialized newly-allocated space for an array of nobj objects each of size size, or NULL if request cannot be satisfied.
void* malloc(size_t size)	Returns pointer to uninitialized newly-allocated space for an object of size size, or NULL if request cannot be satisfied.
void* realloc(void* p, size_t size)	Changes to size the size of the object to which p points. Contents unchanged to minimum of old and new sizes. If new size is larger, new space is uninitialized. Returns pointer to the new space or, if request cannot be satisfied NULL leaving p unchanged.
void free(void* p)	Deallocates space to which p points. p must be NULL, in which case there is no effect, or a pointer returned by calloc, malloc or realloc.
void abort()	Causes program to terminate abnormally, as if by raise(SIGABRT).

(contd.)

Table 7.12 (*contd.*)

Function Prototype	*Description*
void exit(int status)	Causes normal program termination. Functions installed using atexit are called in the reverse order of registration, open files are flushed, open streams are closed and control is returned to environment. Status is returned to environment in implementation-dependent manner. Zero indicates successful termination and the values EXIT_SUCCESS and EXIT_FAILURE may be used.
int atexit(void (*fcm)(void))	Registers fcm to be called when program terminates normally. Non-zero returned if registration cannot be made.
int system(const char* s)	Passes s to environment for execution. If s is NULL, non-zero returned if command processor exists; return value is implementation-dependent if s is non-NULL.
char* getenv(const char* name)	Returns (implementation-dependent) environment string associated with name, or NULL if no such string exists.
void* bsearch(const void* key, const void* base, size_t n, size_t size, int (*cmp)(const void* keyval, const void* datum))	Searches base[0] ... base[n – 1] for item matching *key. Comparison function cmp must return negative if first argument is less than second, zero if equal and positive if greater. The n items of base must be in ascending order. Returns a pointer to the matching entry or NULL if not found.
void qsort(void* base, size_t n, size_t size, int (*cmp)(const void*, const void*))	Arranges into ascending order the array base[0]...base[n–1] of objects of size size. Comparison function cmp must return negative if first argument is less than second, zero if equal and positive if greater.
int abs(int n)	Returns absolute value of n.
long labs(long n)	Returns absolute value of n.
div_t div(int num, int denom)	Returns in fields quot and rem of structure of type div_t as the quotient and remainder of num/denom.
ldiv_t ldiv(long num, long denom)	Returns in fields quot and rem of structure of type ldiv_t as the quotient and remainder of num/denom.

<string.h>

This file contains functions related to string functions. The following functions (Table 7.13) are defined.

Table 7.13

Function Prototype	*Description*
char* strcpy(char* *s*, const char* *ct*)	Copy *ct* to *s* including terminating NULL. Return *s*.
char* strncpy(char* *s*, const char* *ct*, int *n*)	Copy at most *n* characters of *ct* to *s* Pad with NULLs if *ct* is of length less than *n*. Return *s*.
char* strcat(char* *s*, const char* *ct*)	Concatenates *ct* to *s*. Appends *ct* string at the end of *s* string. Return *s*.
char* strncat(char* *s*, const char* *ct*, int *n*)	Concatenates at most *n* characters of *ct* to *s*. Terminate *s* with NULL and return *s*.
int strcmp(const char* *cs*, const char* *ct*)	Compare *cs* and *ct*. Return negative if *cs* < *ct*, zero if *cs* == *ct*, positive if *cs* > *ct*.
int strncmp(const char* *cs*, const char* *ct*, int *n*)	Compare at most n characters of *cs* and *ct*. Return negative if *cs* < *ct*, zero if *cs* == *ct*, positive if *cs* > *ct*.
char* strchr(const char* *cs*, int *c*)	Return pointer to first occurrence of *c* in *cs*, or NULL if not found.
char* strrchr(const char* *cs*, int *c*)	Return pointer to last occurrence of *c* in *cs*, or NULL if not found.
size_t strspn(const char* *cs*, const char* *ct*)	Return length of prefix of *cs* consisting entirely of characters in *ct*.
size_t strcspn(const char* *cs*, const char* *ct*)	Return length of prefix of *cs* consisting entirely of characters not in *ct*.
char* strpbrk(const char* *cs*, const char* *ct*)	Return pointer to first occurrence within *cs* of any character of *ct*, or NULL if not found.
char* strstr(const char* *cs*, const char* *ct*)	Return pointer to first occurrence of *ct* in *cs*, or NULL if not found.
size_t strlen(const char* *cs*)	Return length of *cs*.
char* strerror(int *n*)	Return pointer to implementation-defined string corresponding with error *n*.
char* strtok(char* *cs*, const char* *ct*)	A sequence of calls to `strtok` returns tokens from *cs* delimited by a character in *ct*. Non-`NULL` *cs* indicates the first call in a sequence. *ct* may differ on each call. Returns `NULL` when no such token found.
void* memcpy(void* *s*, const void* *ct*, int *n*)	Copy *n* characters from *ct* to *s*. Return *s*. Does not work correctly if objects overlap.
void* memmove(void* *s*, const void* *ct*, int *n*)	Copy *n* characters from *ct* to *s*. Return *s*. Works correctly even if objects overlap.
int memcmp(const void* *cs*, const void* *ct*, int *n*)	Compare first *n* characters of *cs* with *ct*. Return negative if *cs* < *ct*, zero if *cs* == *ct*, positive if *cs* > *ct*.

(*contd.*)

Table 7.13 (*contd.*)

Function Prototype	*Description*
void* memchr(const char* *cs*, int *c*, int *n*)	Return pointer to first occurrence of *c* in first n characters of *cs*, or NULL if not found.
void* memset(char* *s*, int *c*, int *n*)	Replace each of the first *n* characters of *s* by *c*. Return *s*.

<time.h>

This file contains functions related to time functions. Data types/data found in Table 7.14 are defined for use with time functions.

Table 7.14

Name	*Description*
clock_t	An arithmetic type representing time.
CLOCKS_PER_SEC	The number of clock_t units per second.
time_t	An arithmetic type representing time.
struct tm	Represents the components of calendar time int tm_sec; => seconds after the minute int tm_min; => minutes after the hour int tm_hour; => hours since midnight int tm_mday; => day of the month int tm_mon; => months since January int tm_year; => years since 1900 int tm_wday;=> days since Sunday int tm_yday; => days since January 1 int tm_isdst; => Daylight Saving Time flag: is positive if DST is in effect, zero if not in effect, negative if information unavailable

The following functions (Table 7.15) are defined:

Table 7.15

Function Prototype	*Description*
clock_t clock();	Returns processor time used by program or –1 if not available.
time_t time(time_t* *tp*);	Returns current calendar time or –1 if not available. If tp is non-NULL, return value is also assigned to **tp*.

(*contd.*)

Table 7.15 (*contd.*)

Function Prototype	*Description*
double difftime(time_t *time2*, time_t *time1*);	Returns the difference is seconds between *time2* and *time1*.
time_t mktime(struct tm* *tp*);	Returns the local time corresponding to **tp*, or –1 if it cannot be represented.
char* asctime(const struct tm* *tp*);	Returns the given time as a string of the form: Sun Jan 3 14:14:13 1988\n\0
char* ctime(const time_t* *tp*);	Converts the given calendar time to a local time and returns the equivalent string. Equivalent to:asctime(localtime(tp))
struct tm* gmtime(const time_t* *tp*);	Returns the given calendar time converted into Coordinated Universal Time, or NULL if not available.
struct tm* localtime(const time_t* *tp*);	Returns calendar time **tp* converted into local time.
size_t strftime(char* *s*, size_t *smax*, const char* *fmt*, const struct tm* *tp*);	Formats **tp* into *s* according to *fmt*.

SUMMARY

The key concepts introduced in this chapter are as follows:

- A couple of library functions are available in standard C language. C++, being a superset of C, all standard library available in C are available in C++, as well.
- assert.h file contains functions related to diagnostics.
- ctype.h file contains functions related to character class tests.
- errno.h file defines the system-wide error numbers (set by system calls).
- float.h file contains implementation-defined floating-point limits giving the range and other characteristics of the double and float data types.
- limits.h file contains implementation-defined limits for integral data-types giving the range and other characteristics of the integer data types.
- math.h file contains functions related to mathematical functions.
- setjmp.h file contains functions related to non-local jump instructions.
- signal.h file contains functions related to handling of signals in exceptional conditions.

- stdarg.h file contains functions related to facilities for stepping through a list of function arguments of unknown number and type.
- stdio.h file contains functions related to Input and Output.
- stdlib.h file contains functions related to utility functions.
- string.h file contains functions related to string functions.
- time.h file contains functions related to time functions.

REVIEW QUESTIONS

1. Write a C program that will enter a line of text, store it in an array, and then write it backwards.

2. Using functions for files as in stdio.h, write a program to copy the information from input file to output file by reducing the spaces in the input file.

3. Explain the usage of the functions strncpy, strcpy, strncmp, strcmp in the context of strings.

4. Illustrate the usage of variable number of arguments in function calls with suitable example.

5. Write a program to read data relating to 1000 books and to print them. Use structure declaration for every book, for fields—Title and author, each having 20 characters, accession number in integer and cost in float.

6. Explain the C-language features for Input/Output of data using files.

7. What is the difference of memcpy and strcpy?

8. Write a program that emulates the Copy system command. It should copy contents of a text file to another file. Invoke the program for two command-line arguments, the source file and destination file. In the program check that the user has typed the correct number of command-line arguments and that the files specified can be opened.

9. What is the function of the exit library function?

10. Write a program with an array of pointers to strings representing the days of the week. Provide functions to sort the strings in ascending alphabetical order. While sorting, sort the pointers to the strings, not the actual strings.

11. Write a function that takes variable number of arguments and averages the parameters passed through the function.

8 Data Abstraction through Classes and User Defined Data Types

The task of composition of operations is often considered the heart of the art o
programming. ... However, it will become evident that the appropriate
composition of data is equally fundamental and appropriate
—N. Wirth

LEARNING OBJECTIVES

The objective of this chapter is to acquaint you with:

- C-struct and defining user-defined data types through typedef
- Class, Object and members of a class
- Constructor and Destructor
- Dynamic memory management using new and delete operator (C++) or malloc and free (C-way)
- The *this* pointer
- Static members of a class
- Additional scope of variables

INTRODUCTION

Encapsulation is the process of forming objects. An encapsulated object is often called an abstract data type. We need encapsulation because we, as humans, do mistakes. Encapsulation helps building an impenetrable wall to protect the contained code from accidental modification, whether willingly or unwillingly. We also tend to isolate errors to small sections of code to make them easier tc find and fix.

C-Structure

A C++ class is a mechanism for creating user-defined data types. It is very similar to the structure as in C-language. A C-language structure has a set of data members. In C, user-defined data type can be defined using a structure with a template that serves to define its member data components. A variable of that user-defined data type can be used similar to using normal built-in type declaration. For example, a FRACTION structure type having two integer member components named numerator and denominator can be declared as:

```
struct FRACTION
{
   int numerator;
   int denominator;
};
```

In C, declaring a structure means declaring a user-defined data type and specifying a sequence of members or fields of different types inside the structure. C declaration of structure has the provision of an optional identifier, called a *tag* that gives the name of the structure type. A tag can be used in subsequent references to the structure type. Declaring a variable of a structure type holds the entire sequence of member data defined within that structure type. A structure declaration in C takes the following form:

```
struct structure-type-name
{
   data type member1;
   data type member2;
   ...
} variable-name;
```

structure-type-name is the name of the structure (user defined type). Field variable-name is optional. It can contain one or more valid variable identifiers. The declaration body (within the braces) may contain data members.

The declaration of a structure type does not allocate space for a structure. It works just as a declaration of the type, so that it can be used as a template for later declarations of structure variables. When actual variable names are declared of the structure datatype, then only space is allocated for the structure. Members of a structure variable can be accessed through dot (.) notation, and the same can be accessed through -> notation in case of pointer to structure. An example follows:

```
// FRACTION is a structure type (tag)
// which does not allocate a storage
struct FRACTION
{
  int numerator;
  int denominator;
} a, b; // variable "a" and "b" require space to store
struct FRACTION c; // variable "c" requires space to store
int main()
{
   // assigns 1 to both the members of structure
   // variable 'a' (using dot notation)
   // pa is initialised as pointer to structure variable 'a'

   struct FRACTION *pa = &a;
   a.numerator = a.denominator = 1;

   // has the same effect as above
   pa->numerator = pa -> denominator = 1;

   return 0;
}
```

A previously defined structure-type (tag) can be used to refer to a structure type defined elsewhere without re-declaring the members again. Declarations of pointers to structures and typedefs (to be discussed in subsequent subsection) for structure types can use the structure tag before defining the structure type. Otherwise, the structure definition must be encountered prior to any actual use of the structure where the size of the fields is required. Thus, a member cannot be declared to have the type of the structure in which it appears. However, as long as the structure type has a tag, a member can be declared as a pointer to the structure type in which it appears. This allows to create linked lists of structures. For example,

```
// NODE structure has a pointer to NODE and a integer data member
struct NODE
{
  int data;
  struct NODE * next;
};
struct NODE n; // variable "n" is of structure type NODE
```

Structures follow the same scoping as other identifiers. Structure identifiers must be distinct from other structure, union, and enumeration tags with the same visibility. Nested structures can also be accessed as though they were declared at the file-scope level. For example, here's a declaration:

```
struct A
{
  int a;
  struct B
  {
    int b;
  } s2;
} s1;
// variables a1 and s2 are of structure type A and B respectively
struct A s3; // declares variable s3 of structure type A
struct B s4; // declares variable s4 of structure type B
```

The most important limitation of C structure is that it does not permit data hiding. A structure member can be directly accessed by the structure variable from any function, from anywhere within the scope.

typedef

C++ allows us to define our own types based on other existing data types. It takes the form as

```
typedef already_available_type new_type_name;
```

A typedef declaration lets one define one's own identifiers, which can be used in place of built-in-type specifiers, e.g. int, float, and double or an existing user defined data type. A typedef declaration does not reserve storage. The declarator becomes a new type. One can use typedef declarations to construct shorter or more meaningful names for types built-in in the language or for user defined types. typedef names allow to encapsulate implementation details that can be changed at a later point of time. This does not affect those functions, which use the type without accessing the inner members.

A typedef declaration does not create types. It creates synonyms for the existing types, or names for types that could be specified in other ways. When a typedef name is used as a type specifier, it can be combined with certain type specifiers, but not others. Acceptable modifiers include ***const*** and ***volatile***.

The ***volatile*** keyword is a type qualifier used to declare that an object can be modified in the program by something other than statements, such as the operating system, the hardware, or a concurrently executing thread. The following example declares a ***volatile*** integer n whose value can be modified by external processes:

```
int volatile n;
```

The ***volatile*** qualifier maintains consistency of memory access to data objects. It tells the compiler that the variable should always contain its current value even when optimized. This is necessary, so the variable can be queried when an exception occurs. Volatile variables are read from memory each time their value is needed, and written back to memory each time they are changed. The volatile qualifier is useful for data variables that have values that can change in ways unknown to the program (such as the system clock). The portions of an expression that reference ***volatile*** objects should not be changed or moved.

The following statements declare INTEGER as a synonym for int and then use this typedef to declare age, height, and weight as integral variables:

```
typedef int  INTEGER;
INTEGER age, height, weight;
```

The following declarations are equivalent to the above declaration:

```
int  age, height, weight;
```

Some more examples of this kind are:

```
#define MAX 100
typedef char CHAR;
typedef unsigned int UINT;
typedef char * PCHAR;
typedef char CHARARRAY [MAX];
```

In this case we have defined four new data types: CHAR, UINT, PCHAR and CHARARRAY as char, unsigned int, char * and char[MAX] i.e. char[100] respectively, that can be used later as valid types for example:

```
CHAR            a, b, c;
UINT            uiMax;
PCHAR           pch;
CHARARRAY       name;
```

For typedef of a structure, we can use something like this:

```
typedef struct
{
   int numerator;
   int denominator;
}FRACTION;
```

One can then use the structure FRACTION in the following declarations:

```
FRACTION f1, f2;
```

A member can be declared as a pointer to the typedef structure type in which it appears, as long as the structure type has a tag, for example,

```
// NODE structure has a pointer to itself (i.e. _NODE)
// and a integer data member
typedef struct _NODE // _NODE is the tagname
{
  int data;
  _NODE * next;
} NODE;

// variable "n" is of type NODE, struct NODE is not required
NODE n;
```

typedef names can be used to improve code readability.

A particularly complicated use of typedef is to define a synonym for a "pointer to a function that returns type T." For example, a typedef declaration that means "pointer to a function that takes no arguments and returns type void" uses the code `typedef void (*PVFN)();`

The synonym can be handy in declaring arrays of functions that are to be invoked through a pointer as given in Example 8.1.

EXAMPLE 8.1:

```
#include <iostream.h>
#include <stdlib.h>
// declares four functions which are assumed
// to be defined elsewhere
extern void func1();
extern void func2();
extern void func3();
extern void func4();
// Declare synonym for pointer to function that
// takes no arguments and returns void type
typedef void (*PVFN)();
int main(int argc, char * argv[])
{
   // Declare an array of pointers to functions.
   PVFN pvfn1[] = {func1, func2, func3, func4};

   // Invoke the function specified on the command line
   // first arg 1 => 1st function is called

   if ((argc > 0) && (*argv[1] > '0') && (*argv[1] <= '4'))
      (*pvfn1[*argv[1] - '1'])();
   return 0;
```

CLASS

A C++ class is a mechanism for creating user-defined data types. In C++, a class is a mechanism to organize data and functions together in a same structure. A class is a way to bind the data and its associated behaviour together. Class means, State + Behaviour. Class specification has two parts: Class declaration and Member Function definition. Class declaration indicates the type and scope of its members (data and function). Member Function definition tells how the member functions within the class are implemented. C++ classes are far more powerful than the user-defined types created in C. In C++, one can specify the functionality of the type mechanisms of the underlying language. This allows new types to have all the expressive capabilities possessed by the built-in-types, as available in C. Thus, a class is much more integrated with the language, than the concept of modules (that package types and operations). For languages with modules, the types and operations included in the module are not seamlessly integrated with the language. So, it may become very cumbersome to use them. Polymorphism is supported through classes with virtual functions.

An *object* has the same relationship to a class that a variable has to a data type. An instance of a class is an object, rather than a variable. An object occupies space in memory, whereas a class does not. A class is declared using the keyword ***class***, whose functionality is similar to one of the C keyword ***struct***, but with the possibility of including functions as well. This takes the form shown in Example 8.2:

EXAMPLE 8.2:

```
class classname
{
   access_right_1:
      member1;
   access_right_2:
      member2;
      ...
} objectname;
```

where, classname is the name for the class (user defined type) and the field objectname is optional, containing one or more valid object identifiers. The declaration body (within the braces) may contain members, which may either be data or function declarations. The data members are called *instance data* and function members are called *member functions*. There can be also optional access right labels which, may be any of these three keywords: *private, public* or *protected.*

The access right labels indicate the following:

- **private** members of a class are accessible only from other members of its same class or from its "friends".
- **protected** members are accessible, in addition to from members of its same class and friends, and also from members of its derived classes.
- **public** members are accessible from anywhere where the class is visible. This holds true till another access right label appears in the block.

Using the class type, one can declare one or more objects of that class type see Example 8.3).

EXAMPLE 8.3:

```
class X
{
/* define class members (data and/or functions here)*/
};
int main()
{
  X xobj1; //creates an object instance of class type X
  X xobj2; //creates another object instance of class type X
  return 0;
}
```

Another example follows in Program Source Code 8.1.

Program Source Code 8.1

```
// A simple class example
#include <iostream.h>
class SimpleClass
{
   private:
      int IntegerData;
   public:
      void SetData(int d)
      {
         IntegerData = d;
      };
      void ShowData()
      {
         cout << "\n Data is " << IntegerData;
      };
};
```

(contd.)

Program Source Code 8.1 *(contd.)*

```
int main()
{
    SimpleClass s1, s2;
    s1.SetData(1000);
    s2.SetData(2000);
    s1.ShowData();
    s2.ShowData();
    return 0;
}
```

Output 8.1

```
Data is 1000
Data is 2000
```

In this program, class SimpleClass contains one data item and two member functions. Placing data and functions together into a single entity is the central idea of object-oriented programming. Functions provide the only interface (being declared as public) from outside the class to the class, to access the privately declared data item. The first member function `SetData` sets the data item to a value, and the second member function `ShowData` displays the stored value. In the example, the class whose name is "SimpleClass" is specified in the first part of the program. Later, in main program, we define the objects, s1 and s2, that are instances of the class SimpleClass. Remember, the specification for the class does not create any object. It only describes how they will look when they are created. It is the definition that actually creates objects that can be used by the program. Defining an object is similar to defining a variable of any data type. Space is set aside for it in memory. The next two statements in `main()` function call the member function SetData();

```
s1.SetData(1000);
s2.SetData(1000);
```

These statements don't look like normal function calls. Notice that, the object names s1 and s2 are connected to the function names with a period. This syntax is used to call a member function that is associated with a specific object. SetData() is a member function of the SimpleClass class and so, it must always be called in connection with an object of this class. Member functions of a class can be accessed only through an object of that class.

To use a member function, the **dot** operator (the period) connects the object name and the member function. The syntax is similar the way we refer to structure member. The **dot** operator is also called the class member access operator.

In C++, one can also declare a class type with the keywords ***union, struct***. A union object can hold any one of a named member set. Structure and class objects hold a complete set of members. Each class type represents a unique set of class members that include data members, member functions, and other type names. The default access for members depends on the class key, such as

1. The members of a class that is declared with keyword ***class*** are private by default. A class is inherited privately by default.
2. The members of a class declared with keyword ***struct*** are public by default. A structure is inherited publicly by default.
3. The members of a union declared with the keyword ***union*** are public by default. One cannot use a union as a base class in derivation.

As stated already, the body of the class contains three keywords: *protected*, *public* and *private*. A key feature of object-oriented programming is data hiding. The primary mechanism for hiding data is to put it in a class and declare it as private. Private data and functions can only be accessed from within the class. Public data or functions are accessible from within as well as outside the class (Illustration is provided in Figure 8.1).

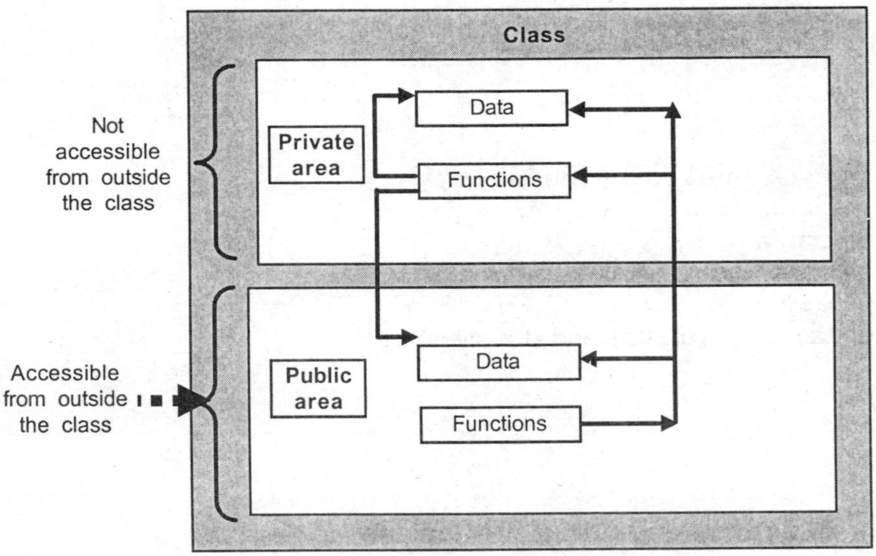

Figure 8.1 Access specifier as public or private.

By default, unless explicitly specified, all data and function members of a class are hidden (private). The data members of a class are, of course, usually hidden. Parts of a class can be hidden or made explicitly available by use of private and public declarations in the class.

Classes and Structures

The C++ class is an extension of the C-language structure. The only difference between a structure and a class is that structure members have public access by default, and class members have private access by default. Consequently, one can use the keywords class or struct to define equivalent classes. In the following code fragment (Example 8.4), the class X is equivalent to the structure Y:

EXAMPLE 8.4: Here, class A is equivalent to struct B

```
class A
//In this example, class A is equivalent to struct B
class A
{
     int a;  //private by default
   public:
     // public member function f() returns a copy of
     // instance data "a" (which is private)
     int f()
     {
        // assigns 5 to a then returns a (by value)
        return a = 5;
     }
};
struct B
{
     int f() // public by default
     {
        return a = 5;
        }
     private:
        int a; //  private data member
};
int main()
{
   A x;
   B y;
   x.a =0; // syntax error: a cannot be accessed
           // since a is private in class A
   y.a =1; // syntax error: a cannot be accessed
           // since a is private in struct B
   return 0;
```

If one defines a structure and then declare an object of that structure using the keyword class, the members of the object are still public by default. In the example Source Code 8.2, `main()` has access to the members of X even though X is declared as using the keyword class:

Program Source Code 8.2

```
//This example declares a structure, then declares a class
that is an object of the structure.
#include <iostream.h>
struct X
{
    int a;
    int b;
};
class X x; // X becomes the name of the class, x is the name of
the object instance
int main()
{
    x.a =0; // a can be accessed since a is publicly accessible
    in struct X
    x.b =1; // b can be accessed since b is publicly accessible
    in struct X
    cout <<"x.a= "<<x.a<<", x.b="<<x.b<<endl;
    return 0;
}
```

Output 8.2

```
x.a=0,x.b=1
```

Class Members

An optional member list declares sub-objects called *class members*. Class members can be data, functions, classes, enumeration, bit fields, and typedef names. A member list is the only place to declare class members within the class declaration braces. Declarations for friends must appear in member lists, even though they are not class members. Member declarations can contain access specifiers, member declarations, and member definitions. The members can be accessed by using the class access operators: **dot** (.) and **arrow** (–>) operators. A member declaration declares a class member for the class that contains the declaration.

An access specifier is one of the following:

- public
- private
- protected

A member declarator declares an object, function, or type within a declaration. It cannot contain an initializer. One can initialize a member by using a constructor. If the member belongs to an aggregate class, one can initialize it by using a brace initializer list in the declarator list. A brace initializer list is one that is surrounded by braces ({}). One must explicitly initialize a class that contains constant or reference members with a brace initializer list; or one can initialize it explicitly with a constructor.

Data members include members that are declared with any of the built-in types as well as other types, including pointer, reference, array types, and user-defined types. One can declare a data member the same way as a variable. However, one cannot place explicit initializers inside the class definition. If an array is declared as a nonstatic class member, all the array dimensions must be specified.

A class X cannot have a member that is of type X. It can, however, contain pointers to X, references to X, and static objects of X . Member functions of X can take arguments of type X and have a return type of X . For example,

```
class X
{
   X();
   X *xptr;
   X &xref;
   static X xcount;
   X xfunc(X);
};
```

We will now construct a class Fraction which can store the numerator and denominator. Let's first declare a class Fraction which is contained in the header file of the class namely fract.hpp. The class declaration shows all the interface of the class and the definitions of the function members are called the class implementation. Suppose, class implementation is given in file fract.cpp, then the contents of the header file FRACT.HPP will be as given in Program Source Code 8.3.

Program Source Code 8.3

```
FRACT.HPP
class Fraction
{
   private:       // encapsulated data portion
      int num;    // numerator
      int denom;  // denominator
   public:        // public interface functions
      void SetValue(int, int); // sets a value of the fraction
      void GetValue(int &, int &);
};
```

The data fields in this class are numerator and denominator, both of which are of integer type. The data members are declared as private, which means that they can be accessed only from members of its same class Fraction or from its friends. They can be manipulated by the publicly accessible interface functions SetValue and GetValue.

It should be noted that even if the data members are not explicitly declared as private, they are, by default, assumed to be declared as private. We could have declared class as similar construct to struct. The difference is that members of a class are private by default, whereas members of a struct are public by default.

Now, let's see the implementation of SetValue and GetValue functions. Member functions can be defined inline or external to the class declaration. They may have default parameter declarations, as well. When a member function is implemented outside the class declaration, then a scope resolution operator (::) is required. The scope resolution operator prefixed with a class name and followed by the member function name indicates for which class the member function is defined. Now, look at the contents of `FRACT.CPP` (Program Source Code 8.3a). The `main()` function can be written in a different file called `TESTFR.CPP` where we declare a Fraction object f and then set value and get value by calling appropriate functions. The member functions are publicly accessible, so the main function can access them. If main() function would require to access the data members num and denom directly as f.denom or f.num, the compiler will issue error, as these data members are declared as private, and therefore not accessible from the main function.

Program Source Code 8.3a

FRACT.CPP

```
#include "fract.hpp"
void Fraction :: SetValue(int a, int b)
{
   num = a;
   denom = b;
}
void Fraction :: GetValue(int & a, int & b)
{
   a = num;
   b = denom;
}
```

TESTFR.CPP

```
#include <iostream.h>
#include "fract.hpp"
int main()
{
   Fraction f;
   int n, d;
   cout << "Please enter the value of"
         << "numerator and denominator : ";
   cin >> n >> d;
   f.SetValue(n,d);
   cout << "numerator value set = "<< n << endl;
   cout << "denominator value set = " << d << endl;
   f.GetValue(n, d);
   cout << "numerator value retrieved = "<< n << endl;
   cout << "denominator value retrieved = " << d << endl;
   return 0;
}
```

Output 8.3

```
Please enter the value of numerator and denominator : 3 4
numerator value set = 3
denominator value set = 4
numerator value retrieved = 3
denominator value retrieved = 4
```

Constructor and Destructor

Constructors and destructors are special member functions of classes (structs as well) that are used to construct and destroy objects. Construction of an object involves memory allocation and initialization for the object. Destruction of an object involves cleanup and deallocation of memory for the object. Like all other member functions, constructors and destructors are declared within a class declaration. They can be defined inline or external to the class declaration. Constructors can have default arguments. Similar access rules (private, protected or public) are applicable to constructor or destructor as well. Unlike other member functions, constructors can have member initialization lists.

There are some restrictions to constructors and destructors, which are as follows:

1. Constructors and destructors do not have return types (not even voids) nor can they return values.
2. Although constructor and destructor are also functions, one cannot use references and pointers on constructors and destructors, because one cannot take their addresses.
3. One cannot declare constructors with the keyword virtual.
4. One cannot declare constructors and destructors as static, const, or volatile.
5. Unions cannot contain class objects that have constructors or destructors.

The constructor member function has, by definition, the same name as the corresponding class. The C++ run-time system ensures that the constructor of a class is called when an object instance is created. If no constructor is declared and defined for a class, compiler provided default constructor is used instead. The actual generated code of the compiler of course depends on the compiler. A compiler-supplied constructor in a class, which contains composed objects, will 'automatically' call the member initializers.

Constructor

Sometimes, it is convenient if an object can initialize on itself when it is first created, without the need to make a separate call to a member function. When the representation of a type is hidden, some mechanism must be provided to initialize variables of that type. Requiring an explicit function to initialize the variable may result in error. For example, in the earlier example of FRACTION class, if compiler provided default constructor provision is absent, then we cannot use/call GetValue function before the SetValue function is called for a Fraction object. In that case we would have retrieved all garbage values as numerator and denominator stored in a Fraction object (unless SetValue is called before). It would have been better if the designer of the type provides a distinguished function to do the initialization. Given such a function, allocation and initialization of a variable becomes an atomic operation (often called instantiation) instead of having separate function call. Such an initialization function is called *constructor*. Constructor is a special member function meant to carry out automatic initialization. A constructor is a member function that gets executed automatically whenever an object is created.

An example program is provided as Program Source Code 8.4:

Program Source Code 8.4

```
// A simple constructor example
#include <iostream.h>
class SimpleClass
{
   private:
      int IntegerData;
   public:
      SimpleClass()
      {
         IntegerData = 500;
      }
      void SetData(int d)
      {
         IntegerData = d;
      };
      int GetData()
      {
         return IntegerData;
      };
};

int main()
{
   SimpleClass s1, s2;
   cout << "\n s1 has data : " << s1.GetData();
   cout << "\n s2 has data : " << s2.GetData();
   s1.SetData(1000);
   s2.SetData(2000);
   cout << "\n s1 has data : " << s1.GetData();
   cout << "\n s2 has data : " << s2.GetData();
   return 0;
}
```

Output 8.4

```
s1 has data : 500
s2 has data : 500
s1 has data : 1000
s2 has data : 2000
```

In this example program, it is more convenient, especially when there are a great many objects of a given class, to cause each object to initialize itself. In the SimpleClass class, the constructor SimpleClass() does this. This function is called automatically, whenever a new object of type SimpleClass is created. Thus, in the main function, the statement

```
SimpleClass s1, s2;
```

creates two objects s1 and s2 of type SimpleClass. As each is created, its constructor SimpleClass() is executed. This function sets the IntegerData variable to 500. So, the effect of this single statement is not only to create two objects s1 and s2, but also to initialize their respective IntegerData variables to 500.

Overloaded Constructors

A class can have more than one constructor (overloaded). If there are two constructors within the same name SimpleClass, we say the constructor is overloaded. Which of the two constructors is executed when an object is created, depends on the order, number and type of the arguments used in the definitions available(as in function overloading). Let's look at an example (Program Source Code 8.5).

Program Source Code 8.5

```
#include <iostream.h>
class SimpleClass
{
   private:
     int IntegerData;
   public:
     SimpleClass()
     {
        IntegerData = 500;
     }
     SimpleClass(int data)
     {
```

(contd.)

Program Source Code 8.5 *(contd.)*

```
        IntegerData = data;
    }
    void SetData(int d)
    {
        IntegerDat  = d;
    };
    int GetData()
    {
        return IntegerData;
    };
};

int main()
{
   SimpleClass s1, s2;  // constructor call with no argument
   SimpleClass s3(400); // constructor call with one argument
   SimpleClass s4=600;  // constructor call with one argument

   cout << "\n s1 has data: " << s1.GetData();
   cout << "\n s2 has data: " << s2.GetData();
   cout <<"\n s3 has data: " << s3.GetData();
   cout <<"\n s4 has data: " << s4.GetData();

   return 0;
}
```

Output 8.5

```
s1 has data : 500
s2 has data : 500
s3 has data : 400
s4 has data : 600
```

Here, SimpleClass class has two constructors, one without any argument, and another with one integer argument. The first constructor initializes its IntegerData member to a default value 500, and the second one takes an argument with the constructor and initializes its data member to the value passed for initialization. As such, in the main program, s1, s2 objects are initialized with constructor, with no argument, i.e. they contain the values 500 each. Objects s3 is initialized with 400 and s4 with 600 through the constructor call with one argument. Note the differences in the usage, s3 object is used as

"SimpleClass s3(400)" and "SimpleClass s4=600", both causing the same effect of initialization.

Now, let's reexamine the Fraction class with two constructors and one destructor in Program Source Code 8.6. Fraction constructor having two arguments initialize the Fraction object from the given arguments supplied. Fraction constructor without any argument (called default constructor; if not provided, compiler provides one, however, the intended implementation is not guaranteed) initialize Fraction object as numerator = 1 and denominator = 0.

Program Source Code 8.6
FRACT.HPP

```
class Fraction
{
  private:      // encapsulated data portion
    int num;    // numerator
    int denom; // denominator
  public:         // public interface functions
    Fraction(int, int); // Constructor
    Fraction(); // Default constructor
    ~Fraction(){}; // Destructor
    void SetValue(int, int); // sets a value of the fraction
    void GetValue(int &, int &);
};
```

FRACT.CPP

```
#include <iostream.h>
#include "fract.hpp"
Fraction :: Fraction(int a, int b)
{
  num = a;
  denom = b;
  cout << "numerator set inside constructor = "<< num << endl;
  cout << "denominator set inside constructor = "<< denom << endl;
}
Fraction :: Fraction()
{
  num = 0;
  denom = 1;
  cout << "numerator set inside constructor = 0" << endl;
  cout << "denominator set inside constructor = 1" << endl;
}
```

(*contd.*)

Program Source Code 8.6 *(contd.)*

```
void Fraction :: SetValue(int a, int b)
{
   num = a;
   denom = b;
}
void Fraction :: GetValue(int & a, int & b)
{
   a = num;
   b = denom;
}
```

In this source code, the main function takes values of numerator and denominator from user and then creates a Fraction object with the given values (through constructor call). This avoids explicit call made to SetValue to do the initialization as a separate step after declaring the Fraction object variable. However, C++ runtime engine ensures that if we declare a variable as say, Fraction f; then the default constructor will be called for the object to do the initialization. And also, if we don't provide the default constructor, compiler provides one but that may not have the intended implementation. As such, it is always recommended to provide your own constructors and other functions (which may be provided by the compiler if you don't provide one). Constructor is automatically called when an object is declared or when a pointer to object is allocated using specific call to *new* operator. A test program for Program Source Code 8.6 is provided as Source Code 8.6a.

Program Source Code 8.6a
TESTFR.CPP

```
#include <iostream.h>
#include "fract.hpp"
int main()
{
   int n, d;
   cout << "Please enter value of the "
        << "numerator and denominator: ";
   cin >> n >> d;
// instead of writing two statements
// Fraction f; followed by f.SetValue(n,d), we call
   Fraction f(n,d);
f.GetValue(n, d);
   cout << "numerator value retrieved = "<< n << endl;
   cout << "denominator value retrieved = "<< d << endl;
   return 0;
}
```

(contd.)

```
Output 8.6a (contd.)
```

```
Please enter value of the numerator and denominator : 3 4
numerator set inside constructor = 3
denominator set inside constructor = 4
numerator value retrieved = 3
denominator value retrieved = 4
```

A default constructor is a constructor that either has no arguments, or, if it has arguments, all the arguments have default values. Thus, we could have declared just one constructor having default arguments as numerator = 0 and denominator = 1, as given in the modified header filer FRACT.HPP as in Program Source Code 8.7.

```
Program Source Code 8.7
FRACT.HPP
```

```
class Fraction
{
     // data/code as in code 8.6
   public: // public interface functions
     // we provide Constructor with default values
     // so, we don't need any default Constructor
     Fraction(int = 0, int = 1);
     // Fraction();-- not needed
     // rest of the code goes here as in 8.6
};
```

And then, the implementation for the constructor without any argument is not needed any more. This is explicit in Program Source Code 8.7a.

```
Program Source Code 8.7a
FRACT.CPP
```

```
#include <iostream.h>
#include "fract.hpp"
Fraction :: Fraction(int a, int b)
{
   num = a;
   denom = b;
   cout  << "numerator set inside constructor = "
         << num << endl;
   cout  <<  "denominator set inside constructor = "
         <<  denom << endl;
}
```

(*contd.*)

Program Source Code 8.7a (*contd.*)

```
/* The following default constructor not needed
   anymore, that's why within commented block
Fraction :: Fraction()
{
   num = 1;
   denom = 0;
   cout  << "numerator set inside constructor = 1"<< endl;
   cout  << "denominator set inside constructor = 0" << endl;
}
*/
// rest of the source code for SetValue, GetValue
// as in Program Source Code 8.6
```

A main function is given in Program Source Code 8.7b, with Fraction object created with zero, one or more arguments.

Program Source Code 8.7b
TESTFR.CPP

```
#include <iostream.h>
#include "fract.hpp"
int main()
{
   int n, d;
   cout  << "Please enter the value of the "
         << "numerator and denominator: ";
   cin >> n >> d;
   Fraction f(n,d); // calls constructor with 2 arguments
   f.GetValue(n, d);
   cout << "numerator value retrieved = "<< n << endl;
   cout << "denominator value retrieved = " << d << endl;

   cout << "Please enter the value of the numerator only: ";
   cin >> n;
   Fraction f1(n); // calls constructor: denominator
                   // defaulted to 1
   f1.GetValue(n, d);
   cout  << "numerator value retrieved = "<< n << endl;
   cout  << "denominator value retrieved = " << d << endl;

   cout  << "Ok..now I will create a fraction-no input please"
         << endl;
   Fraction f2;  // calls constructor:numerator=0,
                 // denominator = 1(default)
```

(*contd.*)

Program Source Code 8.7b (*contd.*)

```
    f2.GetValue (n, d);
    cout << "numerator value retrieved = "<< n << endl;
    cout << "denominator value retrieved = " << d << endl;

    return 0;
}
```

Output 8.7b

```
Please enter the value of the numerator and denominator: 3 4
numerator value set inside constructor = 3
denominator value set inside constructor = 4
numerator value retrieved = 3
denominator value retrieved = 4
Please enter the value of the numerator only: 3
numerator value set inside constructor = 3
denominator value set inside constructor = 1
numerator value retrieved = 3
denominator value retrieved = 1
Ok..now I will create a fraction-no input please
numerator value set inside constructor = 0
denominator value set inside constructor = 1
numerator value retrieved = 0
denominator value retrieved = 1
```

Copy Constructor

A copy constructor is used to make a copy of one object from another object of the same class type. A copy constructor is called with a single argument that is a reference to its own class type (parameter passing by value cannot be used here). If a user-defined copy constructor does not exist for a class, the compiler creates a copy constructor with public access, for that class. For example, the following code fragment shows usage of copy constructor. We have used constant reference of the argument passed to the copy constructor, so as to prevent any accidental or intentional modification of the argument being passed (a non-const reference argument can be modified from within a function). The argument, if allowed to pass by value, would have tried to create a clone copy first, before even entering the copy constructor call (call by value requires creation of a copy of the variable called with, to pass as argument). This requires the call of copy constructor again (which creates a copy from its own, i.e. cloning). This would have ended up with infinite recursion, thereby causing stack overflow. As such, parameter passing by value is not allowed in case of a copy constructor. An example is provided in Program Source Code 8.8.

Program Source Code 8.8

FRACT.HPP

```
class Fraction
{
    // other data/code goes here
  public: // public interface functions
    // other code goes here
    Fraction(const Fraction &); // copy constructor
    // other code goes here
};
```

FRACT.CPP

```
#include <iostream.h>
#include "fract.hpp"
// other code goes here
Fraction :: Fraction (const Fraction & AnotherFraction)
{
  num = AnotherFraction.num;
  denom = AnotherFraction.denom;
}
// other code goes here
```

TESTFR.CPP

```
#include <iostream.h>
#include "fract.hpp"
int main()
{
  int n, d;
  cout << "Please enter the value of the numerator and denominator: ";
  cin >> n >> d;
  Fraction f(n, d);
  f.GetValue(n, d);
  cout << "numerator value retrieved = "<< n << endl;
  cout << "denominator value retrieved = " << d << endl;
  cout << "Now a second clone copy is being created :" << endl;
  Fraction f1 = f;
  f1.GetValue(n, d);
  cout << "clone's numerator value retrieved = "
       << n << endl;
  cout << "clone's denominator value retrieved = "
       << d << endl;

  return 0;
}
```

```
Output 8.8
Please enter the value of the numerator and denominator: 5 6
numerator value set inside constructor = 5
denominator value set inside constructor = 6
numerator value retrieved = 5
denominator value retrieved = 6
Now a second clone copy is being created:
clone's numerator value retrieved = 5
clone's denominator value retrieved = 6
```

Copy constructor is invoked in the following cases:

1. Object initialization, by declaring the object variable and at the same time, assigning a value using another object. When we initialize an integer, we can do this using any of the following:

   ```
   int x = 10;
   or
   int x(10);
   ```

   For the object type Fraction, the following statements are applicable:

   ```
   Fraction f; // default constructor Fraction::Fraction()
               // is called to initialize f.
   Fraction f(); // same as the above statement
   Fraction f(3); //constructor Fraction::Fraction(int,int)
                  // called with 2nd argument defaulted
   Fraction f = 3; // creating Fraction f and initializing f
                   // from int through constructor call
   Fraction f1 = f; // calling copy constructor that creates
                    //and initializes a copy f1 from f
   Fraction f1(f);  // same as the above statement
   ```

2. Whenever we pass an object to a function by value. We have stated earlier that whenever we pass a variable "by value" to a function, a copy of that variable is created for the function, and that there are really two separate variables occupying different memory locations: one in the function and one in the code that calls the function. The copy constructor is responsible for this copying process (precisely for this reason, a copy constructor declaration or implementation cannot pass parameter by value, resulting in an infinite recursion).

   Here we are initializing (declaration + assignment) the fraction "f1" in terms of a previously declared fraction "f" (it is not important that we initialize "f" an explicit value before initializing "f1", "f1" will be assigned whatever value "f" has). So, if we write like the following:

```
Fraction f; // default initialization
f.SetValue(5,6); // sets explicit value of 5/6
Fraction f1 = f; // f1 gets created with it's
                 // initialization done from f.
```

When we do this, the "Copy Constructor" is making a copy of "f".

3. Whenever we have a function that returns an object by value. Again, there are two distinct copies of objects being returned: one defined inside the function and one in the code that calls the function. The function would have a prototype that looks something like this:

```
class1 functionname()
{
   class1 object1;
   ..............................
   return (object1);  // object1 is defined within
                      // local scope of function
}
```

and the calling statement might look something like this:

```
int main()
{
   class1 object2;
   // object2 is assigned to the value returned
   object2 = functionname();
   ..........
}
```

Again, it is the copy constructor that is responsible for copying the return value from the function to "object2" in the above example.

Destructor

A destructor is a special member function with the same name as its class that is prefixed by a ~(tilde). A destructor takes no arguments and has no return type (not even void). One cannot take its address. One cannot declare destructors as const, volatile. One can declare a destructor as virtual or pure virtual. A union cannot have as a member, an object of a class with a destructor. Destructors are used to deallocate memory and do other cleanup for an object and its members when the object is destroyed. Destructor is called for an object when that object goes out of scope or explicitly deleted through delete call.

The destructor is responsible for cleaning up when a class object is no longer needed, deallocating any memory that the object used. When a program ends execution, any object created should be deleted. Likewise, if a function creates an object, that object should be deleted when the function exits. For many classes, the compiler supplied destructor will be sufficient. However, similar to the copy constructor, the destructor will only delete the member variables of the class. Destructor is automatically called when an object goes out of scope, or when a pointer to object is deallocated using specific call to *delete* operator.

DYNAMIC MEMORY MANAGEMENT

Earlier, we had introduced the concept of single variable and array of data. When these are declared, the size of the data is known at the compile time. Quite often, it is not possible to declare an array of a fixed size in advance. Then, the size of that data is impossible to estimate beforehand, and one may choose to have an optimum size of array to declare, based on dynamic or runtime situations. This requires the support of allocating or deallocating memory at runtime.

Operators New and Delete

Operator New

The ***new*** operator provides dynamic memory allocation. The call to *new* operator is required to be followed by a data type and optionally followed by (i) the number of elements required within square brackets [] and/or (ii) initializer expression placed within parantheses (). The call to new operator for a particular data type returns a pointer to the initial element in the array, i.e. the beginning of the new block of assigned memory. The data type can be built-in data types, *typedef* types, *class* or *struct* types. The lifetime of an object created by new is not restricted to the scope in which it is created. Repeated calls to new operator for same or different pointer return pointers to different objects because of separate memory allocations. It takes the following form:

```
pointer = new data type;
     or
pointer = new  data type (initializer_expression);
     or
pointer = new data type [number_of_elements];
     or
pointer = new data type [number_of_elements]
                         (initilaizer_expression);
```

For example,

```
// allocates storage for a single uninitialized character
char *pc1 = new char;

// allocates storage for a single character
// initialized with 'a'
char *pc2 = new char('a');

// allocates storage for 10 uninitialized integers
int *pi1 = new int[10];

// allocates storage for 10 integers each of
// which is initialized to 4
int *pi2 = new int[10](4);
```

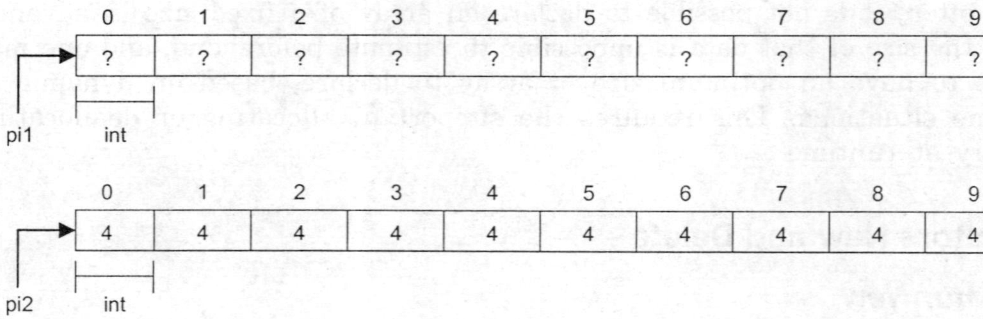

As for the creation of the Fraction object,

```
Fraction *pf = new Fraction;
```

the statement allocates storage for a single Fraction object and initializes the newly created object through the default constructor (constructor without any parameter or constructor with default arguments so that call with no parameter is supported).

The above statement is equivalent to the optional parentheses following new Fraction call, shown as under:

```
Fraction *pf = new Fraction();
```

However, for the following call,

```
Fraction *pf = new Fraction(3);
```

the object is allocated as well as initialized in the single statement through the appropriate constructor call (i.e. constructor with one argument, or two arguments where the last argument is defaulted).

There is a major difference between declaring a conventional array and dynamically allocating memory through a pointer. The difference is, in case of array, the size must be a constant value. This means that its size is decided at compile time before its execution. On the other hand, the dynamic memory allocation allows assigning memory during runtime, so the decision on the size of the dynamic array can be decided at runtime just before allocation. Also, array once defined has a fixed or constant starting address given by the compiler and that address connot be changed theirafter by assigning to any other pointer.

While allocating memory dynamically, it may so happen that the memory is exhausted, so that dynamic memory allocation fails. Then, a NULL pointer will be returned. As such, it is always recommended that one checks for the returned pointer from new call, whether it is NULL or not, before using the pointer to avoid unintended crash. The following example clarifies this idea:

```
int * pi;
pi = new int [10];
if (pi == NULL)
{
   // dynamic memory allocation failed,
   // appropriate measures should be taken.
}
```

In some circumstances, corrective action needs to be taken when dynamic memory allocation fails. When global new operator fails to allocate storage to create a new object, it calls a new handler function if one has been installed by a call to a function named _set_new_handler(..) (defined in <new.h>). The function _set_new_handler(..) can be used to call a user defined new handler or the default new handler can be used instead. The function _set_new_handler(..) takes an argument as a pointer to a function (the user defined new handler function), which takes the form of one argument of type size_t stating size of the memory allocation and returns integer. The call _set_new_handler(..) returns a pointer to the previous new handler function. If user-defined function is not specified through _set_new_handler(..) function, operator new returns the NULL pointer.

The next program fragment (Program Source Code 8.9) shows how the function set_new_handler() can be used to take appropriate measures, if the new operator fails to allocate storage.

Program Source Code 8.9

```
#include <iostream.h>
#include <new.h>
int MyNewHandler(size_t s)
```

(contd.)

Program Source Code 8.9 *(contd.)*

```
{
   /* prints appropriate error message on cerr object and then exit
   /* from program as it is felt that it's no point to continue
   further, alternately, some measures could have been taken to
   free some part of memory somehow if possible and continue
   further */
  cerr <<"Sorry: operator new failed to allocate memory" << endl;
  exit(1); // exiting from program with error code 1
  return 0;
}
  int main()
{
  // sets user defined new handler _set_new_handler(MyNewHandler);
  //Rest of program ...
}
```

Output 8.9

```
Sorry: operator new failed to allocate memory
```

If the program fails because operator new cannot allocate storage, the program exits with the message as shown in Output 8.9.

Operator Delete

The *delete* operator destroys the object created with operator *new* by deallocating the memory associated with the object. If a dynamically allocated memory is no longer needed, it is freed, so that the occupied memory blocks become available for future requests of dynamic memory allocations. The *delete* operator has a *void* return type. It has the following syntax:

```
delete pointer;
or
delete [] pointer;
```

The first expression should be used to *delete* memory allocated for a single element, and the second one for memory allocated for multiple elements (dynamic arrays created through new call).

The operand of *delete* must be a pointer returned by operator *new* call, and cannot be a pointer to constant. If operator *new* call fails, the pointer returned by *new* will have a zero value(NULL). However, it can still be used with *delete*. Deleting a null pointer has no effect.

In general, the NULL pointer is defined as

```
#define NULL 0
```

It is indifferent to put 0 or NULL when you check pointers, but the use of NULL with pointers is widely extended and its use is recommended for greater legibility. The reason is that, it is very rare to compare a pointer is or set directly to a numerical literal constant, and thus this action is symbolically masked.

If you have defined a destructor for a class, *delete* invokes that destructor. Whether a destructor exists or not, *delete* frees the storage pointed by calling the function operator *delete()* of the class, if one exists. If users do not provide destructor for a class, then the compiler generates a default destructor. However, the generated destructor may not have the intended memory deallocations.

Now, we can modify the previously shown example of FRACTION to work in a different way (Program Source Code 8.10).

Program Source Code 8.10
FRACT.HPP

```
class Fraction
{
  private:       // encapsulated data portion
    int *num;    // numerator pointer to int
    int *denom;    // denominator pointer to int
  public:        // public interface functions
    Fraction(int = 0, int = 1); // Constructor
    Fraction(const Fraction &); // copy constructor
    ~Fraction(); // Destructor
}
```

FRACT.CPP

```
#include <iostream.h>
#include "fract.hpp"
Fraction :: Fraction (const Fraction & AnotherFraction)
{
  // allocate space for the pointers num and denom
  num = new int();
  denom = new int; // new int() also could have been written
  *num = *(AnotherFraction.num);
  *denom = *(AnotherFraction.denom);
```

(contd.)

Program Source Code 8.10 *(contd.)*

FRACT.CPP

```
    cout << "copy constructor sets numerator = "<< *num
         << ", denominator = " << *denom << endl;
}
Fraction :: Fraction(int a, int b)
{
    // allocate space for the pointers num and denom
    // (showing different ways of initializing data members)
    // allocate num through new operator and initialize with a
    num = new int(a);
    // allocate denom through new operator and
    // then assign *denom to b;
    denom = new int;
    *denom = b;
    cout << "constructor sets numerator = "<< *num
         << ", denominator = " << *denom << endl;
}
Fraction :: ~Fraction()
{
    cout << "destructor deallocates numerator = "<< *num
         << ", denominator = " << *denom << endl;
    // deallocate space for the pointers num and denom
    delete denom;
    delete num;
}
```

TESTFR.CPP

```
int main()
{
    int n, d;
    cout << "Please enter values of numerator, denominator: ";
    cin  >> n >> d;
    cout << "Creating fraction f : " << endl;
    Fraction f(n, d); // automatic call to constructor

    cout << "\nPlease enter another set of "
         << "numerator, denominator : ";
    cin >> n >> d;
    // manual allocation through new operator call
    // (constructor called automatically)
    cout << "Creating fraction *pf : " << endl;
    Fraction *pf = new Fraction (n, d);
```

(contd.)

Program Source Code 8.10 *(contd.)*
FRACT.CPP

```
    cout << "\nNow a clone copy (f2) created "
         << "from *pf:" << endl;
    // f2 gets a copy from *pf through copy constructor
    Fraction f2 = *pf;

    cout << "\nNow another clone copy (*pf2) "
         << "created from f:" << endl;
    // pf2 is allocated through new operator and then
    // *pf2 gets a copy from f through copy constructor
    Fraction *pf2 = new Fraction(f);

    // objects f and f2 automatically destroyed when returned from
    // function (destructor call also will be automatic)
    // pf and pf2 have to be specifically destroyed
    cout << "\n*pf2 is being destroyed:" << endl;
    delete pf2;
    cout << "\n*pf is being destroyed:" << endl;
    delete pf;
    cout << "\nnow objects f2 and f automatically destroyed :"
    << endl;
    return 0;
}
```

Output 8.10

```
Please enter values of numerator, denominator: 3 4
Creating fraction f:
constructor sets numerator = 3, denominator = 4

Please enter another set of numerator, denominator: 5 6
Creating fraction *pf:
constructor sets numerator = 5, denominator = 6

Now a clone copy (f2) created from *pf:
copy constructor sets numerator = 5, denominator = 6

Now another clone copy (*pf2) created from f:
copy constructor sets numerator = 3, denominator = 4

*pf2 is being destroyed:
destructor deallocates numerator = 3, denominator = 4

*pf is being destroyed:
destructor deallocates numerator = 5, denominator = 6

now objects f2 and f automatically destroyed:
destructor deallocates numerator = 5, denominator = 6
destructor deallocates numerator = 3, denominator = 4
```

Malloc and Free

Operators ***new*** and *delete* are exclusive of C++ and they are not available in C language. In C language, dynamic memory allocations and deallocations can be done through ***malloc*** and ***free*** functions (defined in stdlib.h), respectively. Let's first take a C example (memory allocations and deallocations through malloc and free) and it's C++ counterpart example (memory allocations and deallocations through operator new and delete).

In the following program (Program Source Code 8.11), we have two string variables: (i) a pointer variable szStr which is declared as pointer to character initialized to NULL (a placeholder for dynamically allocated character array) (ii) a character array chArr which can hold a fixed sized array (array size bounded by a constant named MAX_SIZE), which will be used to take input from user. MAX_SIZE is defined to be 61 (considering maximum size of character string of 60 characters and a null terminator). We also define a function called MemFail, which will be called if memory allocation fails for some reason. The program works as follows. User input is taken in the fixed size character array named chArr, and depending on the length of the string, we allocate required number of characters (including the NULL character as string terminator) for szStr through malloc function or new operator. It can be noted that malloc function call requires number of bytes as parameters. As such ***nChar***(number of characters) * ***sizeof***(char) is used as parameter to malloc. We know that size of a character is usually one byte, but it may be two bytes, and the number of characters should be multiplied by size of one character to get number of bytes to be allocated. It should be also noted that malloc-free are the memory allocation-deallocation pairs in C (which can be used in C++ as well for non-class or struct type of data, as they don't call constructor-destructor pair respectively). In C++, operator new and operator delete are the memory allocation-deallocation pairs (for class or struct type of data, they also mean call to constructor-destructor pair respectively for initialization-cleanup). Also, operator new takes number of data types to be created in square brackets ([ ]), not number of bytes. printf-scanf have been used for output-input in C, which has been equivalently used in C++ example through insertion (<<) operator and extraction (>>) operator. We have also used new handler for automatic call of new handler routines in case of dynamic memory fails.

Program Source Code 8.11
C program example

```
#include <stdio.h>
#include <stdlib.h>
#include <string.h>
```

Program Source Code 8.11 *(contd.)*

```
int MemFail(size_t s)
{
   printf("Sorry: unable to allocate memory\n");
   exit(1); // exiting from program with error code 1
   return 0;
}
/* MAX_SIZE defines maximum possible size of input
   as 60 + 1character */
#define MAX_SIZE 60 + 1
int main()
{
   char *szStr = (char *) NULL;
   char chArr[MAX_SIZE];
   int nChar;

   /* Take input */
   printf("Please input a string (60 character max.): ");
   scanf("%s", chArr);

   /* Allocate required space for character string szStr */
   nChar = strlen(chArr)+1;
   szStr = (char *) malloc(nChar * sizeof(char));
   if (szStr == NULL)
   {
      MemFail();
   }
   else
   {
      printf("%s %d characters\n",
              "Required memory space allocated for",
             nChar);
      strcpy(szStr, chArr);
      printf("%s : %s\n",
               "String copied in allocated space",
              szStr);
      free( szStr );
      printf("Memory space deallocated\n");
   }
   return 0;
}
```

Equivalent C++ program example

```
#include <iostream.h>
#include <stdlib.h>
#include <string.h>
#include <new.h>
int MemFail(size_t s)
```

(contd.)

Program Source Code 8.11 *(contd.)*

```
{
   cerr << "Sorry: unable to allocate memory" << endl;
   exit(1); // exiting from program with error code 1
   return 0;
}
/* MAX_SIZE defines maximum possible size of input
   as 60 + 1character */
const int MAX_SIZE = 60 + 1;
int main()
{
   char *szStr = (char *) NULL;
   char chArr[MAX_SIZE];
   int nChar;
// sets user defined new handler
   _set_new_handler(MemFail);
   /* Take input */
   cout << "Please input a string (60 character max.): ";
   cin >> chArr;
   /* Allocate required space for character string szStr */
   nChar = strlen(chArr)+1;
   szStr = new char [nChar];
   cout  << "Required memory space allocated for "
         << nChar << " characters" << endl;
   strcpy(szStr, chArr);
   cout  << "String copied in allocated space : "
         << szStr << endl;
   delete [] szStr;
   cout << "Memory space deallocated" << endl;
   return 0;
}
```

Output 8.11 (Same for both the programs)

```
Please input a string (60 character max.): Hello
Required memory space allocated for 6 characters
String copied in allocated space: Hello
Memory space deallocated
```

Advantage of operator *new* over *malloc* function

Operator new has some advantages over malloc functions. They are as follows:

(i) Operator *new* automatically computes the size of the data objects without using ***sizeof*** operator.

(ii) It automatically returns the right pointer type without the need of type cast.
(iii) While allocating the memory it is possible to initialize the object.
(iv) Operator *new* and *delete* can be overloaded like other operators.

This Pointer

The keyword ***this*** identifies a special type of pointer. When a nonstatic member function is called, the ***this*** pointer remains a constant (i.e. const means nonmodifiable) pointer to the object for which the function was called. One cannot declare the pointer or make assignments to it. The type of the ***this*** pointers in some class, say X is provided in Table 8.1.

Table 8.1

Type of Member Function	*Type of this Pointer*
nonstatic member function	X * const
nonstatic member function with const qualifier	const X * const
static member function	not used

The ***this*** pointer is passed as an extra argument (hidden) to all nonstatic member function calls. It is available as a local variable within the body of all nonstatic functions. Member data is addressed by evaluating the expression this–>member-name (implicit even without using this–>, this–> is not required explicitly). Some previous code examples are provided as example in Program Source Code 8.12. It makes explicit use of ***this*** pointer, which is within a nonstatic member function pointer to the object for which the function was called.

```
Program Source Code 8.12
FRACT.HPP
class Fraction
{
   private:       // encapsulated data portion
      int num;    // numerator
      int denom;  // denominator
   public:        // public interface functions
      Fraction(int = 0, int = 1); // Constructor
      ~Fraction(){}; // Destructor
      void GetValue(int &, int &) const;
};
```

(*contd.*)

Program Source Code 8.12 *(contd.)*

FRACT.CPP

```
#include <iostream.h>
#include "fract.hpp"
Fraction :: Fraction(int a, int b)
{
   this-> num = a; // explicit use of this pointer
   denom = b; // implicitly equivalent to this->denom = b;
   // cannot assign this to anything else,
   // as 'this' is a constant
}
void Fraction :: GetValue(int & a, int & b) const
{
   a = this-> num;      // explicit use of this pointer
   b = this-> denom;    // explicit use of this pointer
   // cannot write this->somemember as lvalue, like
   // this->num = 20;
   // as this is not allowed for const member funtion.
}
```

TESTFR.CPP

```
#include <iostream.h>
#include "fract.hpp"
int main()
{
   int n, d;
   // within the constructor, this assigns to &f
   Fraction f(4, 5);
   f.GetValue(n, d); // Within GetValue, this assigns to &f
   return 0;
}
```

Static Member

One can declare class members as static. All the objects of a class in a program share only one copy of the static member, whereas nonstatic member data is per object and nonstatic member function is per class. As such, static member of a class does not contribute to the size of the object occupying space in memory. Static data members of a class are also known as "class variables", because their content does not depend on any object. A typical use of static members is for recording data common to all objects of a class. For example, we can use a static data member as a counter to store the number of live FRACTION objects created. Each time a new object is created through constructor, this static data member can be incremented to track the total number of objects created so far. The destructor can decrement the counter, so that at any point of time, number of live FRACTION objects can be found. The declaration of a static member in the member list of a class is not a definition. The definition of a static member is equivalent to an external variable definition. One must define the static member outside class declaration. For example;

```
class X
{
   public:
      static int i;
};
int X::i =0; // definition outside class declaration
```

One can access a static member from outside its class only if it is declared as public. The member can be accessed by qualifying the class name using the ::(scope resolution) operator. In the following example, You can see the static member f()of class type X as X::f():

```
class X
{
   public:
      static int f();
};
int main ()
{
   X::f();
}
```

One cannot declare a static member function with the keyword **virtual**. A *static* member function can access only the names of static members, enumerators, and nested types of the class in which it is declared.

Scope of Class Names

A class declaration introduces the class name into the scope where it is declared. Any class, object, function or other declaration of that name in an enclosing scope is hidden. For example, if a class name is declared in a scope where an object, function, or enumerator of the same name is also declared. In this case, one can only refer to the **class** by using the elaborated type specifier.

The class key (***struct***, or ***union***) must precede the class name to identify it. Look at the following example (8.5).

EXAMPLE 8.5:

```
//This example shows the scope of class names.
claas X {int a;};
X xGlobal; // global
int X(class X*)// redefine X to be a function
{
   return 0;
}
//use keyword class to define a pointer to the
// class type X as the function argument
int main()
{
   class X* px;   // use keyword class to define
                  // a pointer to class type X
   px = &xGlobal; // assign pointer
   X(px); // call function X with pointer to class X
   return 0;
}
```

Scope of Variables

The scope of an identifier is the portion of the program in which the identifier is defined and can be referred to. There are three types of scope:

1. File scope: Global
2. Block scope: Local
3. Class scope: Members of a class

Member functions are always within the scope of their class. Because of this, members of the class objects on which a member function is operating, can be referred to without using the scope resolution operator **::** . For accessing any member function outside the scope of a class, the member name must be qualified to indicate the class whose member is being referred to. This is the case, for example, when one initializes static variables outside member function of a class.

C++ is also a block-structured language. Blocks and scopes can be used in constructing programs. A variable declared inside the block is said to be local to the block. Global variables can be referred anywhere in the code, even within functions, whenever it be after its declaration. The scope of local variables is limited to the code level in which they are declared. If they are declared at the beginning of a function, its scope is the whole main function. In C++ the scope of a variable is given by the block in which it is declared (a block is a group of instructions grouped together within key brackets {} signs).

```
   .........
{
   int i = 10;
   ..........
   {
      int i = 20; // hides previous i
      ..........
   }
}
```

In C++ , variable in outer block can be accessed from within the inner block by an operator :: called the scope resolution operator. It takes the form of ::variable_name, for example:

```
int a = 10;
{
   int a = 20;
   cout << a; // prints 20
   cout << ::a; // prints 10
}
cout << a; // prints 10
```

If a variable is declared within a function, it will be a variable with function scope. If a variable is declared in a loop its scope will be only the loop. In addition to local and global scopes exists the external scope, that causes a variable to be visible not only in the same source file but in all other files which will be linked with.

An example program follows (Program Source Code 8.13) where we have used same variable name in different scope.

Program Source Code 8.13

```
#include <iostream.h>
int a = 10; // global a
class X
{
   public:
      int a;
```

(contd.)

Program Source Code 8.13 *(contd.)*

```
     static int sa;
     void f();
};
int X:: sa = 20; // initializing static member a of X
void X::f()
{
   int a = 30; // local variable a

   cout << "global a = " << ::a << endl;
   cout << "local a = " << a << endl;
   cout << "nonstatic member a = " << this->a << endl;
   cout << "static member sa = " << X::sa << endl;
}
int main()
{
   X aXObj;
   aXObj.a = 40; // initializing nonstatic member
   aXObj.f();
   return 0;
}
```

Output 8.13

```
global a = 10
local a = 30
nonstatic member a = 40
static member sa = 20
```

It should be noted that an object created by *new* operator gets a lifetime of the object directly under control of the programmer. This is not related to the block structure of the program. If we create an object within a block by using *new* operator, it will remain in life until and unless it is destroyed explicitly by using *delete* operator.

SUMMARY

The key concepts introduced in this chapter are as follows:

- In C, user-defined data type can be defined using a structure with a template that serves to define its member data components.

- A typedef declaration lets one define own identifiers, which can be used in place of built-in-type specifiers, e.g. int, float, and double or an existing user-defined data type.
- The ***volatile*** keyword is a type qualifier used to declare that an object can be modified in the program by something other than statements, such as the operating system, the hardware, or a concurrently executing thread.
- In C++, a class is a mechanism to organize data and functions together in the same structure. Class members can be data, functions, classes, enumeration, bit fields, and typedef names.
- An instance of a class is an object, rather than a variable. An object occupies space in memory whereas a class does not.
- There can be access right labels for data or functions within a class as any of these three keywords: private, public or protected.
- In C++, one can also declare a class type with the keywords union and struct. The only difference between a structure and a class is that structure members have public access by default and class members have private access by default.
- Constructors and destructors are special member functions of classes (structs as well) that are used to construct and destroy objects. A copy constructor is used to make a copy of one object from another object of the same class type.
- The C++ *new* operator provides dynamic memory allocation. The C++ *delete* operator destroys the object created with operator new by deallocating the memory associated with the object. In C language, dynamic memory allocations and deallocations can be done through *malloc* and *free* functions (defined in stdlib.h) respectively.
- When a nonstatic member function is called, the *this* pointer is a constant pointer to the object for which the function was called.
- Static data members of a class are also known as "class variables", because their content does not depend on any object.

REVIEW QUESTIONS

1. If adequate memory is not available to allocate a new variable by using new operator, what measures can you take so that every time you don't have to check whether the memory allocation has failed or not?

2. In C++, what happens if a constructor or destructor assigns a value to the pointer 'this'? Explain what precautions must be taken when writing such a constructor to ensure that it can correctly initialize both free store and automatic objects.
3. Explain about 'this' pointer. What is meant by overriding? Where is it used? Explain with an example.
4. Define constructor. What are the characteristics of a constructor?
5. Can we have more than one constructor in a class? If yes, explain the need for such situation.
6. What is the scope resolution operator (::) in C+?
7. Explain how constructor and destructor differ from normal functions.
8. A book shop maintains the inventory of books that are being sold at the shop. The list includes details such as author, title, publisher, cost and stock position. Whenever a customer wants a book, the sales person inputs the title and author and the system searches the list and displays whether it is available or not. If it is not, an appropriate message is displayed. If it is, then the system displays the book details and requests for the number of copies required. If the required copies are available, the total cost of the requested copies is displayed, otherwise, the message "required copies not in stock" is displayed. Design a system using a class called "book" with suitable member functions and construction.
9. What is default constructor? What is its advantage?
10. What do you mean by dynamic initialization of objects?
11. What is the scope of a variable?
12. Imagine a toll booth and a bridge. Cars passing by the booth are expected to pay an amount of Rs. 50/- as toll tax. Mostly they do, but sometimes a car goes by without paying. The toll booth keeps track of the number of the cars that has passed without paying, the total number of cars passed by, and the total amount of money collected. Execute this with a class called tollbooth and print out the result as follows:
    (a) the number of cars passed by without paying
    (b) total number of cars passed by
    (c) total cash collected.
13. What do you mean by constructor overloading? Describe with an example.

14. What will be printed by the following program? Explain why.

```
#include <iostream.h>
class A {
public:
   static int n;
   A () { n++; };
   ~A () { n--; };
};
int A::n=0;

int main () {
   A a;
   A b[5];
   A * c = new A;
   cout << a.n << endl;
   delete c;
   cout << A::n << endl;
   return 0;
}
```

15. What is the implication of putting a 'const' after a member function declaration say, class X?

```
{
     :
     void f() const;
};
```

16. If same variable name is used as a global data, as a non-static member data, and a local variable, how do you distinguish each from the others, while accessing from within a member function?

9 *Operator Overloading*

Operator overloading is just "syntactic sugar," which means it is simply another way for you to make a function call.

—Bruce Eckel

LEARNING OBJECTIVES

The objective of this chapter is to acquaint you with:

- Operator overloading techniques and restrictions
- Overloading unary and binary operators
- Overloading function operator, index operator, class member access and cast operator
- User defined conversions through constructors or cast operators
- Overloaded non-member operators outside the class
- Overloading new and delete operators

INTRODUCTION

C++ operators can be defined to behave similarly or differently in user-defined ways when they are applied to operands of class type. Language defined operators can be overloaded by redefining them to perform a particular operation when applied to an object of a particular class. In function overloading, function name remaining same, the functions differ from one another by differing number, order, or type of operands (not the return type). In addition, overloaded operators must have at least one argument of a class type. Also, arity of the overloaded operators should be same as defined by the language and as applicable to same operators for built-in data types. By arity, we mean number of operands (that defines binary or unary-ness). For example, the language defined += operator is a binary operator (i.e. it can take two operands, arity is two), as such, while overloading += operator for a user-defined class, we have to retain the binary-ness (arity two) of the operator. Operator overloading allows one to define own meanings (semantics) for the built-in C++ operators when applied to class types. An overloaded operator implementation is similar to a function call and is declared with the keyword ***operator*** preceding the operator. To overload an operator as a member of a class, we need to write, as in the case of a class member function, where name of the function is keyword operator preceding the operator symbol intended for overloading. This takes the following form:

```
return-data type operator operator-symbol (arguments);
```

The following operators can be overloaded in C++:

```
+     -     *     /     %     |     &     |     ~
!     =     <     >     +=    -=    *=    /=    %=
|=    &=    |=    <<    >>    <<=   >>=   ==    !=
<=    >=    &&    ||    ++    --    ,     ->    *->
( )   [ ]   new   delete
```

Operator overloading is needed for better representation, e.g. we could have defined member functions of a class Fraction called Plus, Product and so on and then could use something like:

```
Fraction a, b, c, d, e, f;
a = Prod(Prod(Plus(b, c), Plus(d, e)), f);
```

Using operator overloading, we could have used like:

```
Fraction a, b, c, d, e, f;
a = (b + c)*(d + e) * f;
```

This has indeed better readability.

Let's see an example of two overloaded operators: operator + and operator =. We will add two fraction objects a (=3/4) and b (=5/6), whose result sum fraction object(=19/12) is stored in another fraction object c as follows:

$$c = a + b = \frac{3}{4} + \frac{5}{6} = \frac{3*3+5*2}{12} = \frac{19}{12}$$

The declaration of the overloaded operator + and operator = have been defined in the Program Source Code 9.1.

Program Source Code 9.1

```
#include <iostream.h>
int gcd(int a, int b)
{
   int c;
   if (a > b)
```

(*contd.*)

Program Source Code 9.1 *(contd.)*

```
   {
      // swap and b to ensure a <= b
      c = a;
      a = b;
      b = c;
   }
   c = b % a; // c is the remainder of b divided by a
   while (c != 0)
   {
      // new dividend becomes the previous divisor
      // new divisor becomes the remainder
      b = a;
      a = c;
      c = b % a;
   }
   return a; // a is the gcd
}

int lcm(int a, int b)
{
   int g, l;
   g = gcd(a,b);
   l = g * (a/g) * (b/g);
   return l;
}

class Fraction
{
   private:
      int num;
      int denom;
   public:
      Fraction(int = 0, int = 1); // constructor
      Fraction(const Fraction &);// copy constructor
      ~Fraction();         // destructor
      Fraction operator + (Fraction); // + operator
      Fraction operator = (Fraction); // = operator
};
```

(contd.)

Program Source Code 9.1 *(contd.)*

```
Fraction :: Fraction (const Fraction & AnotherFraction)
{
   this->num = AnotherFraction.num;
   this->denom = AnotherFraction.denom;
   cout<< "Fraction object (" << this->num
      <<"/" << this->denom << ") created(copy)" << endl;
}

Fraction :: Fraction(int a, int b)
{
   this->num = a;
   this->denom = b;
   cout  << "Fraction object (" << this->num
         <<"/" << this->denom << ") created" << endl;
}

Fraction :: ~Fraction()
{
   cout<< "Fraction object (" << this->num
      <<"/" << this->denom << ") destroyed" << endl;
}

Fraction Fraction :: operator + (Fraction operand2)
{
   Fraction tmp;
   int g, l;
   l = lcm(this->denom, operand2.denom);
   tmp.num =  this->num * (l/this->denom) +
            operand2.num * (l/operand2.denom);
   tmp.denom = l;
   g = gcd(tmp.num, tmp.denom);
   tmp.num /= g;
   tmp.denom /= g;
   cout  << "In overloaded Fraction::operator + : ("
         << this->num << "/" << this->denom << ") + ("
         << operand2.num << "/" << operand2.denom << ") = ("
         << tmp.num << "/" << tmp.denom << ")" << endl;
   return tmp;
}
```

(contd.)

Program Source Code 9.1 *(contd.)*

```
Fraction Fraction :: operator = (Fraction rval)
{
   this->num = rval.num;
   this->denom = rval.denom;
   cout<< "In overloaded Fraction::operator = : ("
      << rval.num <<"/" << rval.denom << ") -> ("
        << this->num <<"/" << this->denom << ")" << endl;
   return *this;
}

int main()
{
   int n, d;
   cout  << "Please enter values of "
         << "numerator, denominator: ";
   cin >> n >> d;
   Fraction f1(n,d); // automatic call to constructor

   cout  << "Please enter another set of "
         << "numerator, denominator : ";
   cin >> n >> d;
   Fraction f2(n,d);

   Fraction f3;

   f3 = f1 + f2;

   return 0;
}
```

Output 9.1

```
Please enter values of numerator, denominator: 3 4
Fraction object (3/4) created
Please enter another set of numerator, denominator: 5 6
Fraction object (5/6) created
Fraction object (0/1) created
Fraction object (5/6) created(copy)
Fraction object (0/1) created
In overloaded Fraction::operator + : (3/4) + (5/6) = (19/12)
```

(contd.)

Output 9.1 *(contd.)*

```
Fraction object (19/12) created(copy)
Fraction object (19/12) destroyed
Fraction object (5/6) destroyed
In overloaded Fraction::operator = : (19/12)->(19/12)
Fraction object (19/12) created(copy)
Fraction object (19/12) destroyed
Fraction object (19/12) destroyed
Fraction object (19/12) destroyed
Fraction object (5/6) destroyed
Fraction object (3/4) destroyed
```

Here, each of the two overloaded binary operators + and = is a member function of class Fraction. C++ matches the first operand against the object for which the operator was called, and the second operand is taken against the argument in the overloaded operator call. Thus, f1+f2 implies f1.operator +(f2), that is member operator + is called for the object f1 (first operand) and object f2 is the second operand. As such, when we look inside the implementation of the operator +, the first operand is taken as the current object referred to by the ***this*** pointer, and the second operand is taken as the argument passed. Within the operator + implementation, we perform addition of two fractions. The new denominator becomes the LCM (least common multiplier) of the denominators, of the first and second operands and new numerator becomes (first numerator * new denominator/first denominator) plus (second numerator * new denominator/second denominator), for example, if there are two fractions a/b and c/d which are added so that a/b is the first operand and c/d is the second operand and say, LCM of c and d is m, so that m = b * p = d * q then, (a/b) + (c/d) will yield a fraction (g/h) where,

```
g = a * p + c * q    and    h = m
```

The result of the addition is stored in a local temporary variable called tmp and is returned by value.

In case of = operator, when we write statements like a = b, then it is interpreted as a.operator = (b) where a is the first operand (*lvalue*) and b is the second operand (*rvalue*), i.e. the return value of the equality operator is the *lvalue* itself. For example, the following expression

```
a = 20 + (b = 10);
```

is equivalent to:

```
b = 10;
```

and then

```
a = 20 + b;
```

This implies that first 10 is assigned to b and then a is assigned the value of 20 plus the result of the previous assignation of b (i.e. 10), thus a gets the value of 30. Thus, we can also write statements like:

```
a = b = c = 10;
```

This assigns integer value 10 to each of the three variables a, b and c.

Thus, within the implementation of the operator =, the first operand is the current object for which the operator is called (*lvalue*) as pointed to by the ***this*** pointer, second operand as passed through the argument. The implementation, as you see, modifies the current object by the contents of the argument object, i.e. copies the contents of the argument object to contents of itself. This is very different from copy constructor, where we create a clone object from the copy of the argument passes in a similar way, but in copy constructor, we create an object and initialize the contents from another similar object, and in case of = operator, the object, is already there; we just assign it to new contents as given by the argument(*rvalue*). Copy constructor does not return anything, it just creates the object. Operator = returns itself, i.e. the object itself (*lvalue*) referred to as **this* from within the = operator. And that's what is expected, as we understand the behaviour of the assignment operator. Right? It should return the *lvalue* itself, and that's why we can write

```
a = 20 + (b = 10);
```

Now, let's analyze the output step-by-step:

- The main program starts with declaring two integer variables n and d. These are placeholders for numerator and denominator to read from user input.
- Next, the message `"Please enter values of numerator, denominator:"` is printed to wait for the inputs for numerator and denominator. User keys in the input as 3 and 4 for values of numerator variable n and denominator variable d respectively.
- Next line, it calls "Fraction f1(n, d);" to create a Fraction object f1 from n and d by calling the constructor that takes two integer arguments. f1 is created with the message printed from within the constructor as `"Fraction object (3/4) created"`.
- Next set of user input is taken for another set of numerator and denominator by printing the message `"Please enter another set of numerator, denominator :"` and the above cycle continues. The user keys in input as 5 and 6 for corresponding values of n and d.

- Fraction object f2 is created through the constructor and the message from within the constructor prints as `"Fraction object (5/6) created"`.
- Now another object f3 is created without any argument. This means, the default constructor will be called to initialize f3. In this case, the constructor having two arguments (both of them defaulted allowing 0-parameter or 1-parameter or 2-parameter calls) is called with the arguments defaulted to 0 for the numerator and 1 for the denominator. Thus, the message `"Fraction object (0/1) created"` is printed.
- Next line, we write f3 = f1 + f2; Before calling the assignment operator, the operator + needs to be called (*rvalue* is evaluated first before *lvalue*). Thus, f1 + f2 => f1.operator+ is called passing f2 as an argument. As operator + is defined as a member function of Fraction class, the parameter is passed as a value. As such, before entering the operator+ function, f2 is copied to a new variable called operand2 (since called by value). This is done by calling the copy constructor to create operand2 object from f2 object. As such, the line `"Fraction object (5/6) created(copy)"` is printed from within copy constructor and since f2 contained 5/6, the new object created operand2 also contains 5/6.
- Just after entering the operator + implementation, a variable tmp is created. This again requires the 2-parameter constructor call with both of its parameters defaulted. As such, the next line is printed as `"Fraction object (0/1) created"`.
- Now, the actual implementation of operator + is done with the help of other supporting functions like lcm etc. Before returning from the operator +, we print the message `"In overloaded Fraction:: operator + : (3/4)+(5/6)=(19/12)"` to indicate the contents of the variable tmp that contains 19/12 resulted from an addition of the current object pointed to by the ***this*** pointer, having the value of 3/4 and the argument passed which is operand2 object having the value of 5/6. The operator + now returns to the caller and the return is by value. The return value from the + operator goes in as *rvalue* of the = operator. A new object has to be created from the local variable tmp, which is returned by value.
- This creation of new temporary (managed by the compiler, say the new variable thus created is named tmp10, tmp10 is automatically created while returning by value). Thus, a copy constructor is called to create tmp10 from tmp (which contains the value 19/12). As such, from within the copy constructor for tmp10, the message is printed as `"Fraction object (19/12) created(copy)"`.

- After the return is done, the local variable tmp (local within operator + function body) goes out of scope. So, tmp faces an automatic destruction through the destructor call from within which the message is printed as `"Fraction object (19/12) destroyed"`.
- Another local variable operand2 (which was the parameter to the operator + function, containing the value 5/6) goes out of scope. Since the parameter passing was done as call by value, the parameter named argument2 was created as cloned copy at the time of the call. Now, argument2 variable gets destroyed through the destructor thereby printing the message `"Fraction object (5/6) destroyed"`.
- Now is the turn for the *lvalue* of the statement f3 = f1 + f2; i.e. now, operator = is called. The parameter named *rval* is passed as *rvalue* taken from the result of f1 + f2, i.e. having the value 19/12. From within the operator =, actual copying or assignment is done by copying to the current object pointed to by ***this*** pointer from the argument named as rval. The statement prints as `"In overloaded Fraction::operator =: (19/12)->(19/12)"`.
- Since the return value from an assignment operator is the *lvalue* itself which is the current object, ***this*** is returned from the operator =. The return is made by value. So, a new object has to be created from the current object, i.e. ***this***, which is returned by value. This creation of new temporary (managed by the compiler, say the new variable thus created is named tmp11) is automatically created while returning by value. Thus, a copy constructor is called to create tmp11 from ***this*** (which contains the value 19/12). As such, from within the copy constructor for tmp11, the message is printed as `"Fraction object (19/12) created(copy)"`.
- After the return is done, the temporary variable tmp10 and tmp11 (created automatically) goes out of scope, thereby needing destruction of these variables through destructor call. As such, from within destructor, the message is printed as `"Fraction object (19/12) destroyed"` for tmp11 destruction and `"Fraction object (19/12) destroyed"` for tmp10 destruction.
- Now, the main program returns, thereby causing destructor calls for the local variables f3, f1, f2 since they are out of scope. Three destructor calls occur in sequence thus printing the messages : `"Fraction object (19/12) destroyed"` for f3, `"Fraction object (5/6) destroyed"` for f2 and `"Fraction object (3/4) destroyed"` for f1.

Now, let's optimize the program to some extent by utilizing call by reference instead of using call by value, wherever possible. A parameter can be passed as constant reference for two reasons:

1. reference to save the need for creating new space for the argument (required in case of call by value) and
2. constant to protect the variable from being updated from within the implementation of the function (call by value protects that as that works on a copy of the original variable passed as value).

Similar reason holds for returning from function.

Return from function should be by reference wherever possible (see Program Source Code 9.1a). We cannot return a reference of a local variable, though. However, we can make changes (shown in source code as bold letters) in the implementation of operator + and operator =. We have passed arguments in the operator + and the operator = as constant reference, thereby reducing the need for extra object creations (which were otherwise required in case of call by value). Operator + returns by value (as local variable tmp cannot be returned as a reference and the current object referred to by this pointer cannot be changed), whereas operator = returns by reference. This is because, operator = changes the current object referred to by ***this*** pointer and since the current object does not go out of scope when operator = function returns, ****this*** i.e. the current object can be returned as reference. This will reduce the number of Fraction object creations. This is shown in the Output 9.1a. The differences from previous Output (9.1) is shown as strikeouts.

Program Source Code 9.1a

```
#include <iostream.h>
int gcd(int a, int b)
{
   ..........
}

int lcm(int a, int b)
{
   ...........
}
class Fraction
{
   ......
   public:
      Fraction operator + (const Fraction &); // + operator
      Fraction& operator = (const Fraction &); // = operator
};
```

(*contd.*)

Program Source Code 9.1a *(contd.)*

```
............
Fraction Fraction :: operator + (const Fraction & operand2)
{
   ........
}
Fraction& Fraction :: operator = (const Fraction & rval)
{
   ........
}
int main()
{
   ........
}
```

Output 9.1a

```
Please enter values of numerator, denominator : 3 4
Fraction object (3/4) created
Please enter another set of numerator, denominator : 5 6
Fraction object (5/6) created
Fraction object (0/1) created
Fraction object (5/6) created(copy)
Fraction object (0/1) created
In overloaded Fraction::operator + : (3/4)+(5/6)=(19/12)
Fraction object (19/12) created(copy)
Fraction object (19/12) destroyed
Fraction object (5/6) destroyed
In overloaded Fraction::operator = : (19/12)->(19/12)
Fraction object (19/12) created(copy)
Fraction object (19/12) destroyed
Fraction object (19/12) destroyed
Fraction object (19/12) destroyed
Fraction object (5/6) destroyed
Fraction object (3/4) destroyed
```

Restrictions

It's very tempting to overload operators. However, there are some restrictions, such as the following:

1. One cannot extend the language by inventing new operator, e.g. one cannot create own "exponentiation" operator using the character **. One must limit oneself to existing language provided operators.

2. An operator's arity cannot be changed, e.g. negation(~) operator cannot be used as a binary operator. `a = ~b` is ok, however, `a = b ~ c` is not correct.
3. Operator precedence cannot be changed. Multiplication operator has a higher precedence than the addition operator, e.g.

   ```
   a = b + c * d; // same as a = b + (c * d);
   // parentheses takes control on order of evaluation
   a = (b + c) * d;
   ```

   As such, the operator you choose may not have the precedence appropriate for the intended meaning, e.g. the ^ operator may seem an appropriate choice to perform exponentiation, but its precedence is lower than that of addition.
4. Operator's associativity cannot be changed. Addition and subtraction operators are both left-associative (expression is evaluated left-to-right) and one cannot change the rule. Therefore, a = b + c – d; is interpreted as normal interpretation which is a = (b + c) – d; even if you like to have right to left associativity say, a = (b) + (c – d); unless you parenthesize to take control on order of evaluation.
5. One cannot change operators for built-in data types like ***int***, ***char***, ***float***. At least one operand of overloaded operators must be user-defined type.
6. Following operators cannot be overloaded:

.	class member operator
.*	pointer to member operator
::	scope resolution operator
?:	conditional expression operator

Note:

1. Just because you can overload an operator does not necessarily mean that's a good idea.
2. You should not change the usual meaning of the operator even if you can.

When not to Overload Operators

Operators should be overloaded only when the meaning of the operator is clear and unambiguous. The arithmetic operators like + and * are meaningful when applied to numeric type classes, e.g. complex numbers, fractions, and so on but not to everything like

```
laterDate = TodaysDate + someOtherDate ; // meaning is not clear
```

If the interpretation of the addition of two dates resulting in another date is not clear or is ambiguous.

Many programmers overload the + operator for a String class to perform concatenation of two String objects. However, conditional relational operators for String class need necessarily be unambiguous. For example,

```
String a("abc"), b("aBc");
if (a == b) // case sensitive or not -- not very clear
            // ....

Set s1, s2, s3;
s3 = s1 && s2; // union or intersection?
```

Overloading Unary Operators

A unary operator can be overloaded by declaring a nonmember function that takes one argument, or a nonstatic member function of a class that takes no arguments (means argument taken from the object for which the operator is called). If an object is prefixed with an overloaded unary operator, it's interpreted as the function call, e.g. –x is interpreted as: x.operator –() (if unary operator – is declared as a nonstatic member operator) or operator –(x) (in case it's defined as a non-member operator). Study the following example (9.1).

EXAMPLE 9.1:

```
class Fraction
{
   ......
   Fraction operator - ();
};
int main ()
{
   Fraction x, y;

   // y is assigned a value as returned from
   // overloaded unary operator - applied on x
   y = -x;
   return 0;
}
```

The operator can be overloaded for Fraction class as follows:

```
Fraction Fraction :: operator - ()
{
   Fraction tmp;
   tmp.num = -this->num;
   tmp.denom = this->denom;
   return tmp;
}
```

Other unary operators are:

```
*  &  +  -  !  ~
```

The interpretaions or semantics of these operators are described below. These semantics will help to write the proper implementations if overloading these operators are felt necessary.

*	=>	Indirection, expression must be a pointer. Result is an lvalue referring to the object to which the expression points.
&	=>	Result of unary & is a pointer to its operand.
+	=>	Operand of unary + operator must have arithmetic or pointer type and result is the value of the argument. Unary + is a historical accident and is generally useless.
–	=>	The operand of the unary – operator must have arithmetic type and the result is the negation of the operand.
!	=>	Logical negation operator, it's value is 1 if operand value is 0 and value is 0 if operand value is 1.
~	=>	Operand of ~ must have integral type. Result is one's compliment of its operand.

Overloading Binary Operators

One can overload a binary operator by declaring a nonmember function that takes two arguments, or a nonstatic member function that takes one argument. When one uses an object with an overloaded binary operator (see Example 9.2) you can interpret the operator function call x*y as:

```
x.operator*(y)
or
operator*(x,y)
```

depending on the declarations of the operator function.

EXAMPLE 9.2:

```
class Fraction
{
   ......
   Fraction operator * (const Fraction &); // member
   // or as non-member like
   // friend Fraction operator *(const Fraction &,
                 const Fraction &);
   .......
};
int main ()
{
   Fraction  x(3,4);
   Fraction y =10;
   x*y; //overloaded binary operator
   return 0;
}
```

Overloaded Function Calls

The operands are names of functions and optionally a list of expressions. The function operator() must be defined as a nonstatic member function. One cannot declare an overloaded function call operator that is a nonmember function. The function opereator takes the following form:

functionname(expressionlist$_{optional}$)

This is considered a binary operator with the function name as first operand and possibly employ expression-list as the second. The name of defining the function is operator (). Thus, the call X(arg1, arg2, arg3) is interpreted as X.operator()(arg1,arg2.arg3) for a class object X, as in Example 9.3.

EXAMPLE 9.3:

```
class SubString;

class String
{
    char * szStr;
    int size;
    friend SubString;
  public:
    String(const char *s)
```

```
    {
        szStr = new char[(size=strlen(s)) + 1];
        strcpy(szStr, s);
    }
    ~String()
    {
        delete [] szStr;
    }
    SubString operator ()(int position, int length);
};

class SubString
{
    char *pStartChar;
    int  size;
  public:
    SubString(char *p, int s)
    {
       pStartChar = p;
       size = s;
    }
    SubString & operator = (const String &arg)
    {
       strncpy(pStartChar, arg.szStr, size);
       return *this;
    }
    ~SubString()
    {
       // does nothing
    }
};

SubString String :: operator () (int position, int length)
{
  SubString tmp (szStr + position, length);
  return tmp;
}

int main()
{
  String x = "String";
  x(3,1) = "o"; // x becomes "Strong"
  return 0;
}
```

Function operator call returns a substring describing x(3,1), i.e. one character at position 3(first position is 0) of the value of string variable x. The assignment is then resolved to a call of substring's assignment operator with the operand string("o") to place "o" in the part of the variable x described by the substring x(3,1) so variable, x finally gets the value "Strong".

Overloaded Subscripting

An expression that contains the subscripting operator has the following syntax in the form of a binary operator

```
identifier [expression]
```

The operands are identifiers and expressions. The operator function operator [ ] must be defined as a nonstatic member function. One cannot declare an overloaded subscript operator that is a nonmember function.

x[y] is interpreted as x.operator[](y). It is not interpreted as operator [](x,y) because it is defined as a nonstatic member function. Here's an example (9.4).

EXAMPLE 9.4:

```
class IntArray
{
        int length;
        int *array;
    public:
        int& operator [](int index);
}

int & IntArray :: operator [](int index)
{
    static int dummy = 0;
    if ((index >= 0) && (index < length))
        return array[index];
    else
    {
        cout << "Error: out of range" << endl;
        return dummy;
    }
}
```

And we could use :

```
int main()
{
    IntArray number(10);
```

```
    for (i=0; i < 10; i++)
        number[i] = i; // calls number.operator [](i)
    return 0;
}
```

The intention, in this example, to initialize the array elements will not work if the overloaded [] operator returns by value instead of returning by reference. Why? If return by value was used then a copy of the individual elements would have been returned, and therefore the *lvalue* in the expression number[i] = i would have been a copy of number[i] and not number[i] itself. Also, in the implementation of the overloaded index operator, we have checked whether the index passed to access the array elements crosses the boundary. This checks whether the index is lower than the lowest permissible index value, 0 and higher than the highest possible index value, 9 in the above example. In case it crosses the boundary, we print an error message and continue by returning a dummy value. We could also have decided to exit from the program in case of array boundary overflow or underflow. This could have been done by calling exit(1) thereby causing program termination with error code 1 returned to the operating system that invoked execution of the executable file.

Overloaded Class Member Access

An expression containing the class member access ->(arrow) operator has the following syntax, and is considered a unary operator:

```
identifier ->name-expression
```

The operator function operator->() must be defined as a nonstatic member function.

The following restrictions apply to class member access operators:

1. An overloaded arrow operator cannot be declared as a nonmember function.
2. The class member access .(dot) operator cannot be overloaded.

Now, let's say, we overload the ->(arrow) operator, as in Example 9.5.

EXAMPLE 9.5:

```
class Y
{
    public:
        void f();
};
```

```
class X
{
   public:
      Y*operator->();
};

int main()
{
   X x;
   //.
   //.
   //.
   x->f();
   return 0;
}
```

Here x–>f() is interpreted as:

```
(x.operator->())->f()
```

x.operator–>() must return either a reference to a class object, or a class object for which the overloaded operator–>function is defined, or a pointer to any class. If the overloaded operator–>function returns a class type, the class type must not be the same as the class that declares the function. The class type that is returned, must contain its own definition of an overloaded ->operator function.

Cast Operator

The cast operator is used for explicit type conversions (see Example 9.6).

EXAMPLE 9.6:

```
class Fraction
{
      ...
        int num;
        int denom;
     public:
        operator float();
};

Fraction::operator float()
{
   return ((float) this->num )/ ((float) this->denom);
}
```

A class can have multiple cast operators defined for a class, so the objects belonging to the class can be typecasted to similar or equivalent classes or data types.

User-defined Conversions

User-defined conversions allow to specify object conversions with constructors or with conversion functions. C++ implicitly uses user-defined conversions, in addition to standard conversions, for conversion of initializers, functions arguments, function return values, expression operands, expressions controlling iteration, selection statements, and explicit type conversions. There are two types of user-defined conversions:

- Conversion by constructor
- Conversion operators or cast operators.

Conversion by Constructor

One can call a class constructor with a single argument to convert from the argument type to the type of the class, as shown in Example 9.7.

EXAMPLE 9.7:

```
class Storage
{
      int a,b;
      char* c;
   public:
      Storage(int i);
      Storage(const char*n,int j = 0);
};
void func1(Storage);
int main ()
{
   Storage o1 = 2;   //o1 = Storage(2)
   Storage o2 = "string"; //o2 = Storage("string",0)
   o1 = 10; //o1 = Storage(10)
   func1(5); //func1(Storage(5))
   return 0;
}
```

At the most, one user-defined conversion—either a constructor or conversion operator—is allowed to a class object. Assume you call a constructor with an argument, and you have not defined a constructor that accepts that argument type. In such a situation, standard conversions are used to convert the argument to another argument type that is acceptable to a constructor for that class. It does not call other constructors or conversion functions to convert the argument to a type that is acceptable to a constructor that is defined for that class.

Conversion by Cast Operators

One can define a member function of a class that is called a cast operator. A cast operator converts from the type of its class to another specified type. Function specifies a conversion from the class type of which the cast operator is a member, to the type specified by the name of the cast operator. Classes, enumerations, and typedef names cannot be declared or defined as part of the function name. The following code fragment (Example 9.8) shows a cast operator called operator int():

EXAMPLE 9.8:

```
class Y
{
        int b;
    public:
        operator int();
};
Y :: operator int(){return b;}
void f(Y obj )
{
    // each value assigned is converted by Y::operator int()
    int i = int(obj);
    int j = (int)obj;
    int k = i+obj;
}
```

Cast operators take no arguments, and the return type is implicitly the conversion type. C++ implicitly applies only one user-defined conversion to a single value. User-defined conversions must be unambiguous, or C++ compiler does not call them. If you declare a conversion function (cast operator) with the keyword ***const***, the keyword does not affect the function, except when it acts as a tiebreaker when there is more than one conversion function that you could apply. Specifically, if more than one conversion function could be applied, C++ environment compares all of these functions. If you declare any of these functions with the keyword const, the constness is ignored for the purposes of this comparison. If one of these functions is a best match, it is applied.

Overloaded Increment and Decrement

One can overload the prefix increment operator (++) for a class type by declaring a nonmember function operator with one argument of class type or a reference to class type. One can also overload it by declaring a member function operator with no arguments. One can overload the postfix increment operator ++ as well for a ***class*** type, by declaring a nonmember function operator ++() with two arguments. The first argument has class type, and the second has ***int*** type. Alternatively, a member function operator can be declared as operator++() with one argument having type ***int***. The compiler uses the int argument to distinguish between the prefix and postfix increment operators. For implicit calls, the default value is zero. Here is an example (9.9) to illustrate an overloaded prefix increment operator.

EXAMPLE 9.9:

```
class X
{
      int a;
   public:
      X operator++(); // prefix increment operator
      X operator++(int); // postfix increment operator
};
int main()
{
   X x;
   ++x; // call x.operator++()
   x++; // call x.operator++(int)
   x.operator++(); // explicit call like ++x
   x.operator++(0); // explicit call like x++
   return 0;
}
```

The operators ++(pre and post) can be implemented for the Fraction class as follows:

```
Fraction& Fraction::operator ++()
{
   // preincrement operator, increment current object
   // before returning itself
   this->num = this->num + this->denom;
   return *this;
}
```

```
Fraction Fraction::operator ++(int a)
{
   // postincrement operator, increment current
   // object after returning itself
   Fraction tmp(*this); // tmp object created as a cloned
                       // copy of the current object
   this->num = this->num + this->denom;
   return tmp;
}
```

Note the differences here. Originally, C++ did not provide a way of specifying separate functions for prefix and postfix operators for ++ and −−. Later, it was decided that a function called operator ++ taking one argument would define the prefix increment operator ++ and a function called operator ++ taking two arguments would define the postfix increment operator. For postfix increment operator ++, the second argument must be of type int and the compiler while generating code will ensure that the postincrement operator ++() is called with the second argument 0 when invoked by a postfix increment expression.

All other unary operators are prefix (like unary +, unary −, ~, !, & etc.) in nature and are overloaded by a function taking one argument. As such, when these unary operators are overloaded as a member function of a class, then the implicit *this* pointer (i.e. pointer to the current object for which the operator is called) is the first or only argument. As such, preincrement(++) or predecrement(−−) operators follow the same pattern of using the implicit ***this*** pointer as the first and only argument. The implementation for the preincrement operator therefore modifies (increments) itself and then returns ***this** as the *lvalue*. The return from a preincrement operator is the object itself after increment is done. Since ***this** does not go out of scope at the time of return, the return type can use by reference (instead of by value). In case of postincrement (++) or postdecrement (−−) operator the first argument is implicitly the ***this*** pointer, i.e. pointer to the current object and the second argument is taken as ***int*** (compiler ensures that second argument's value gets zero value at the time of invocation). This dummy second argument is just to distinguish the prefix and postfix versions of the increment and decrement operators. This gives an interesting observation. Let's see a program example (Program Source Code 9.2).

Program Source Code 9.2

```
#include <iostream.h>
class INTEGER
{
        int i;
    public:
        // constructor with one default argument
        INTEGER(int a=0):i(a){};
        ~INTEGER(){}; // destructor
        INTEGER(const INTEGER &); // copy constructor
        INTEGER& operator = (const INTEGER &); // = operator
        INTEGER operator + (const INTEGER &); // + operator
        INTEGER& operator ++ (); // preincrement operator
        INTEGER operator ++ (int); // postincrement operator
        operator int(); // cast operator to int
};
INTEGER :: INTEGER (const INTEGER &arg)
{
    // copy constructor
    this->i = arg.i;
}
INTEGER& INTEGER :: operator = (const INTEGER &arg)
{
    // assignment operator
    this->i = arg.i;
    return *this;
}
INTEGER INTEGER :: operator + (const INTEGER &arg)
{
    // addition operator
    INTEGER tmp;
    tmp.i = this->i + arg.i;
    return tmp;
}

INTEGER INTEGER :: operator ++ (int arg)
{
    // postincrement operator, the second argument is ignored
    INTEGER tmp = *this; // create a cloned copy from itself
    this->i++; // increment itself
    // return the previous cloned copy containing
```

(*contd.*)

Program Source Code 9.2 *(Contd.)*

```
    // value before increment (return is by value)
    return tmp;
}

INTEGER & INTEGER :: operator ++ ()
{
    // preincrement operator, increment itself and
    // return as reference
    this->i++;
    return *this;
}

INTEGER :: operator int()
{
    // cast operator to int, return by value (default)
    // no explicit return type needs to be specified
    // cast operator name defines the implicit return type
    return this->i;
}

int main()
{
    int a = 5;
    INTEGER b = 5;

    a = ++a + a++;
    b = ++b + b++;

    cout << "a = " << a << endl;
    cout << "b = " << (int)b << endl;
    return 0;
}
```

Output 9.2

```
a = 13
b = 12
```

Can you analyze the differences? The variable *a* was declared as a built-in data type ***int***, and variable *b* has been declared as a user-defined data type

INTEGER. The usage is similar, still, we are getting different results. Let's see why it is.

We know that in terms of operator precedence, postincrement has higher precedence over preincrement. And associativity of unary post- and pre-increment operators is right to left. Binary + and – operators have lower priority than pre or post increment and associativity of + operator is left to right.

In case of built-in type ***int***, the statement:

```
a = ++a + a++
```

is interpreted as the following sequences:

1. a++ => unary postincrement operator has higher precedence over unary preincrement as well as binary + operator, that's why is executed first causing the value of 'a' changed to 6(previous value was 5), this becomes the second argument of binary + operator.
2. ++a => a is preincremented getting the value 7 (previous value was 6), this becomes the first argument of binary + operator.
3. Now the binary + operator takes place with two arguments as 7 and 6 causing the resulting value as 13.

In case of user-defined type INTEGER, the statement:

```
b = ++b + b++
```

is interpreted as the following sequences:

1. b++ => overloaded binary postincrement operator has higher precedence over binary + operator as well as uanry preincrement operator. Therefore, the second operand of the binary + operator becomes 5 (current value of b) and b gets itself changed to 6 (that's how the postincrementer operator for INTEGER was implemented).
2. ++b => b is preincremented using the overloaded unary preincrement operator which has higher precedence over binary + operator, thereby getting the value 7 (previous value of b was 6 as set in the overlaoded postincrement operator), this becomes the first argument of binary + operator.
3. Now the binary + operator takes place with two arguments as 7 and 5 causing the resulting value as 12.

Overloaded Non-member Operator

The overloaded operators may be members of a class or non-members. For example, a non-member binary + operator for a class Fraction can be declared as a friend (friends of class X can access private as well as protected members of class X). Also, the non-member binary operator + has been declared to take two explicit operands. In case of member operator, the first operand is implicitly taken as the current object referred to by ***this*** pointer. Here, being a non-member, no implicit argument can be taken, and the arguments are declared explicitly. The declaration of a non-member binary + operator is as follows:

```
class Fraction
{
    .......
    public:
    friend Fraction operator + (const Fraction &operand1,
    const Fraction & operand2);
    ......
};
```

A member operator declaration will take higher precedence than nonmember operator (if both are defined). In case a member operator is not defined, a non-member operator performs the equivalent role. Thus, if we use the following:

```
Fraction f1, f2, f3;
f1 = f2 + f3;
```

then f2 + f3 can be interpreted as f2.operator+(f3) in case the binary + operator has been defined as a member function of the Fraction class. And, f2 + f3 is interpreted as operator+(f2,f3) in case the binary + operator has been defined as a non-member and has been declared as a friend of the Fraction class (see Example 9.10).

EXAMPLE 9.10:

```
Fraction operator + (const Fraction &operand1,
                     const Fraction & operand2)
{
  Fraction tmp;
  int g, l;
  l = lcm(operand1.denom, operand2.denom);
  tmp.num =  operand1.num * (l/operand1.denom) +
             operand2.num * (l/operand2.denom);
  tmp.denom = l;
  g = gcd(tmp.num, tmp.denom);
  tmp.num /= g;
  tmp.denom /= g;
  return tmp;
}
```

As we see here, a member operator and a non-member operator does not make much of a difference (other than the mode of declaration as member or non-member) if the first operand (left hand operand) is a class object. When the first or left hand operand is an object of some other class and operator cannot be overloaded for that class, then it's a good idea to overload operator as non-member. For example, the overloaded insertion (<<) operator and extraction (>>) operator should be non-members. Here, the first argument should be cin in case of extraction (>>) operator and cout in case of insertion (<<) operator. Both these overloaded operators are shown in Program Source Code 9.3.

Program Source Code 9.3

```
#include <iostream.h>
class Fraction
{
   private:
      int num;
      int denom;
   public:
      Fraction(int = 0, int = 1); // constructor
      ~Fraction();         // destructor
      friend ostream& operator << (ostream&, const Fraction &);
      friend istream& operator >> (istream&, Fraction &);
};

Fraction :: Fraction(int a, int b)
{
   this->num = a;
   this->denom = b;
   cout << "Constructor call : Fraction object ("
        << this->num <<"/" << this->denom
        << ") created" << endl;
}

Fraction :: ~Fraction()
{
   cout << "Fraction object (" << this->num
        <<"/" << this->denom << ") destroyed" << endl;
}

ostream& operator << (ostream& os, const Fraction & arg)
```

(contd.)

Program Source Code 9.3 *(contd.)*

```
{
   os << "The fraction is: "
      << arg.num << "/" << arg.denom << endl;
   return os;
}

istream& operator >> (istream& is, Fraction & arg)
{
   is >> arg.num >> arg.denom;
   return is;
}

int main()
{
   Fraction f1;
   cout  << "Please enter values of "
         << "numerator, denominator : ";
   cin >> f1; // uses overloaded extraction operator
   cout << f1; // uses overloaded inserton operator
   return 0;
}
```

Output 9.3

```
Constructor call: Fraction object (0/1) created
Please enter values of numerator, denominator: 3 4
The fraction is: 3/4
Fraction object (3/4) destroyed
```

Overloaded *new* and *delete*

One can implement own memory management scheme for a class by overloading the operators *new* and *delete*. The overloaded operator *new* must return a *void**, and its first argument must have type ***size_t***. The overloaded operator *delete* must return a *void* type, and its first argument must be *void**. The second argument for the overloaded delete operator is optional, and if present, it must have type ***size_t***. One can only define one *delete* operator function for a class. Type ***size_t*** is an implementation dependent unsigned integral type defined in <stddef.h>. When *new* and *delete* are overloaded within a class declaration, they are static member functions whether they are declared with the keyword static or not. They cannot be virtual functions (to be discussed later). One can access the standard, nonoverloaded versions of new and *delete* within a class scope containing the overloading *new* and *delete* operators by using the :: (scope resolution) operator to provide global access. An example program follows as Program Source Code 9.4:

Program Source Code 9.4

```
#include <stdlib.h>
#include <stdio.h>

void *AllocateMem(size_t sz)
{
   void* pm = malloc(sz);
   if (pm == NULL)
   {
      printf("Failed to allocate memory\n");
      exit(1);
   }
   else
   {
      printf("Memory successfully allocated\n");
   }
   return pm;
}

void FreeMem(void * m)
{
   free(m);
}

void* operator new(size_t sz)
{
   // Global overloaded new operator
   printf("Global operator new called to ");
   printf("allocate % d bytes\n", sz);
   return AllocateMem(sz);
}

void operator delete(void * m)
```

(*contd.*)

Program Source Code 9.4 *(contd.)*

```
{
   // Global overloaded delete operator
   printf("Global operator delete called\n");
   FreeMem(m);
}

class Fraction
{
   private:
    int num;
    int denom;
   public:
    Fraction(int = 0, int = 1);   // constructor
    ~Fraction();       // destructor
     // overloaded member new and delete operator
     void* operator new(size_t);
     void operator delete(void *);
};

void* Fraction :: operator new( size_t sz)
{
   //overloaded member new operator of Fraction class
   printf("Fraction::operator new called to ");
   printf("allocate % d bytes\n", sz);
   return AllocateMem(sz);
}

void Fraction :: operator delete( void* m)
{
   // overloaded member delete operator of Fraction class
   printf("Fraction::operator delete called\n");
   FreeMem(m) ;
}

Fraction :: Fraction(int a, int b)
{
   this->num = a;
   this->denom = b;
   printf("Constructor call : Fraction object ");
   printf("(%d/%d) created\n",
         this->num, this->denom);
```

(contd.)

Program Source Code 9.4 *(Contd.)*

```
}

Fraction :: ~Fraction()
{
   printf("Fraction object (%d/%d) destroyed\n",
           this->num, this->denom);
}

int main()
{
   Fraction *pf1, *pf2;

   // allocate four Fraction objects
   pf1 = new Fraction[4];
   pf2 = new Fraction;

   delete pf2; // deallocate object pf2
   delete [] pf1; // deallocate objects pointed to by pf1

   return 0;
}
```

Output 9.4

```
Global operator new called to allocate 36 bytes
Memory successfully allocated
Constructor call : Fraction object (0/1) created
Constructor call : Fraction object (0/1) created
Constructor call : Fraction object (0/1) created
Constructor call : Fraction object (0/1) created
Fraction :: operator new called to allocate 8 bytes
Memory successfully allocated
Constructor call : Fraction object (0/1) created
Fraction object (0/1) destroyed
Fraction :: operator delete called
Fraction object (0/1) destroyed
Fraction object (0/1) destroyed
Fraction object (0/1) destroyed
Fraction object (0/1) destroyed
Global operator delete called
```

This shows that global operator *new* and *delete* were called for array allocations and deallocations, whereas member operator *new* and *delete* were called for creation and destruction of a single object. Another interesting observation is that while allocating single Fraction object memory allocated was 8 bytes (allocation for two integers each of 4 bytes). However, allocation of 4 Fraction objects was 36 bytes. This is because 4 Fraction objects require 4 * 8 = 32 bytes, and an additional 4 bytes are required to store the array size so that at the time of deletion, destructor can be called so many times.

SUMMARY

The key concepts introduced in this chapter are as follows:

- Language-defined operators can be overloaded by redefining it to perform a particular operation when applied to an object of a particular class.
- A unary operator can be overloaded by declaring a non-member function that takes one argument, or a nonstatic member function of a class that takes no arguments.
- One can overload a binary operator by declaring a non-member function that takes two arguments, or a nonstatic member function that takes one argument.
- Function operator () can be overloaded as a binary operator with the function-name as first operand and possibly empty expression-list as the second.
- Index operator [ ] can be overloaded as a binary operator with the object for which it is applicable as the first operand and an integer index as the second. Overloading index operator helps to check whether the index crosses the array boundary.
- The cast operator is used for explicit type conversions.
- Not all operators can be overloaded, exceptions are ., .*, :: , ?: operators.
- User-defined conversions allow to specify object conversions with constructors or with cast operators.
- Prefix and Postfix form of increment as well as decrement operators can also be overloaded.
- Overloaded non-member operator has been illustrated.
- One can implement own memory management scheme for a class by overloading the operators *new* and *delete*.

REVIEW QUESTIONS

1. The overloaded index [] operator returns by reference. What implications will be there if it returns by value? Comment and justify.

2. Can an overloaded binary + operator return by reference?
3. Implement the following overloaded operators for Fraction class:
   (a) +=, *= for Fraction class
   (b) Relational operator like ==, >= for Fraction class
   (c) new operator for Fraction class (Hint: use malloc inside implementation)
   (d) unary and binary – operator
4. Which operators cannot be overloaded?
5. Write a program that has a class called POINT which stores co-ordinates in (x,y) form. Define constructor, destructor and overloaded '–' operator to calculate distance between two points.
6. Define and implement a FRACTION class to support the following main function.

```
int main()
{
    FRACTION f(3,4), f1(2), f2;
    f2 = f + f1;
    f2.showdata();
}
```

7. You are given a main program. Design and Implement suitable classes to support the given main program:

(a)
```
int main()
{
    Integer a = 4;
    Integer b = a;
    Integer c;
    c = a + b++;
    int i = a;
    cout << a << b << c;
    return 0;
}
```

(b)
```
int main()
{
    IntArray i(10); // i is an array of 10 integers
    for (int k = 0; k < 10; k++)
       i[k] = k;
    cout << i;
    return 0;
}
```

(c)
```
int main()
{
    // Centigrade and Farenheit are two temperature
```

```
        // types with the relation C/5 = (F-32)/9
        Centigrade c = -40;
        Farenheit f = c;
        cout << f;
        if (c == f)
           cout << "equal";
        else
           cout << "not equal";
        return 0;
     }
```

(d)
```
int main()
     {
        Complex a(3,4); // a= 3 + 4.i, i = sqrt(-1)
        Complex b = a;
        a += b;
        cout << a << b;
        return 0;
     }
```

8. What will be printed by the following program? Explain why.

```
#include <stdio.h>
class X
{
    public:
    X(){printf("1");};
    X(const X& a){printf("2");};
    ~X(){printf("3");};
    X& operator = (const X& a)
    {printf("4"); return *this;};
    X operator + (const X& a);
 };
 X X :: operator + (const X& a)
 {
    X t;
    printf("5");
    return t;
};
int main()
{   X x;
    x = x + x;
    return 0;
}
```

9. How many ways type conversion (user-defined conversions) of class instances be specified? Explain with examples.

10 Class Relationships

C++: Where friends have access to your private members.
—Gavin Russel Baker

LEARNING OBJECTIVES

The objective of this chapter is to acquaint you with:

- The concept of inheritance—single and multiple
- Constructor and destructor calling sequences
- Virtual base class
- Accessibility in friends and derived classes
- Virtual function and operator
- Linking C file in C++ program

INTRODUCTION

OOP is a relatively new programming paradigm that helps organize programs around "objects" rather than "actions". One of the first object-oriented computer languages was called Simula. After that, Smalltalk, Eiffel, C++ and Java have emerged as powerful object-oriented languages. Traditionally, procedural programming paradigm used to work for data processing, to process input data as to produce output data. The programming challenge was on how to write the procedure at the top of the underlying data. OOP takes the view that what we really care about are the objects we want to manipulate rather than the procedures required to manipulate them. This requires implementations based on object interfaces by hiding the implementation details from the users of an object.

Characteristics of OOP

Abstraction helps to design good software. Historically, computer programming has moved from low level machine code to more abstract assembly languages and to higher level of abstractions through high-level programming languages like C and Pascal. Thus, programmers have learnt to code using high level of abstractions to concentrate on the algorithm rather than on the details of its machine code format. Abstract Data Types (ADT) help programmers to concentrate on "what" can be done with the data rather than on data representation. Low-level details of the implementations of a service are hidden from the users of the service.

OOP helps to hide implementation details from the users by encapsulating implementation details within an object. Traditionally, procedural programming used to concentrate on the "how" part of a program than on procedural details which transform data.

Data hiding is an important characteristic of OOP. An object should only "know" about the data it needs to know about. That will prevent the situation that someone maintaining the code may inadvertently point to or otherwise access the wrong data unintentionally. Thus, all data not required by an object should be "hidden" from it.

Inheritance defines a class for specialization from a generalized existing class through IS-A relationship. The subclass or derived class inherits definitions from one or more general classes called super class or base class. Thus, a subclass need not carry its own definition of data and methods that are generic to the super class (or super classes). It reduces development time, and ensures more accurate coding.

Relationships

Objects are conceived as data and associated procedures together. The first step in OOP is to identify all the objects we would like to manipulate and find out how they relate to each other. Once we identify an object, we generalize it as a class of objects and define the kind of data it contains and list of procedures that can manipulate it. Each distinct procedural sequence is known as a method. An instance of a class is called an "object" or, in some environments, an "instance of a class." The object or class instance is what is run or used at runtime in the computer. Its methods provide computer instructions while class object characteristics provide relevant data. User communicates with objects, and they in turn communicate with each other with well-defined interfaces called messages or methods or member functions. As such, an object is a self-contained entity with well-defined charateristics and behaviour. Take for example, some of the common place objects, as depicted in Figure 10.1.

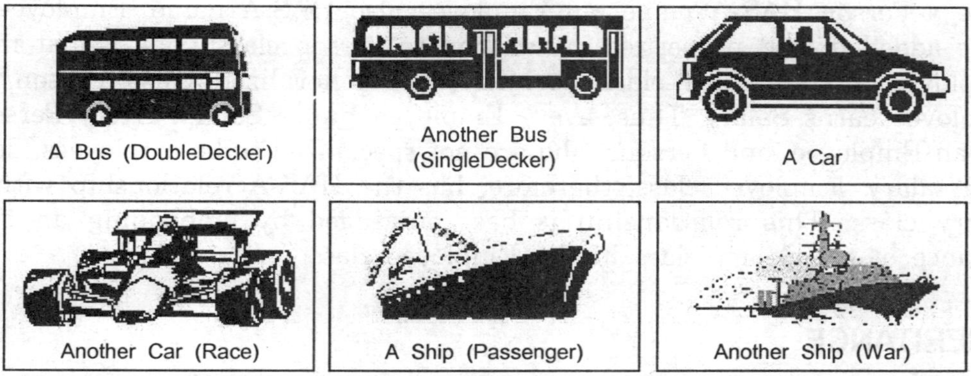

Figure 10.1 Objects—Some examples.

These are some examples of some objects of different categories, e.g. Bus, Car, Ship. The categories can be classes of which objects are instances. For example, there can be a generalized Vehicle class defined, which is more of an abstract class than of a concrete class. An abstract class cannot have an instance. Bus, Car, Ship can be derived (inherited) or specialized from Vehicle class. This is because, Bus is–a Vehicle, Car is–a Vehicle, ship is–a vehicle. Now, DoubleDeckerBus is–a Bus.

SingleDeckerBus is–a Bus, too. As such, DoubleDeckerBus and SingleDeckerBus can be inherited from a generalized Bus class. Similarly, genaralized Car class can be inherited to specialized class called RacingCar or say, passenger Car. There can be many such arguments stating the relationship among these objects and classes to which they belong.

Let's take another debate of class relationships. Let's consider an Asset class, Building class, Vehicle class, and CompanyCar class. All CompanyCars are vehicles. Some CompanyCars are Assets because the organizations own them. Others might be leased. Not all assets are vehicles. MoneyAccounts are assets. RealEstateHoldings are Assets. Some RealEstateHoldings are Buildings. Not all Buildings are Assets—*ad infinitum.*

A specialized class <u>**is**</u> a specialization of another generalized class and, we say that the specialized class (or derived class or subclass) has the **IS-A** relationship with the generalized class (or base class or superclass). For example, an Employee is-a Person. This relationship is best envisaged through inheritance. Class Employee is derived from class Person. Employee is the subclass or derived class. Person is the superclass or base class. A class may have an object instance (instance of another class) as a data member. For example, a Person **has** a name, therefore, the Person class has the HAS-A relationship with the Name class. Through inheritance or is-a relationship, Employee class derives properties from the generalized class Person. Thus, since a Person HAS-A name, an Employee also HAS-A name. Employee has some added (extra) properties in addition to Person class, that's what makes Employee a specialized class derived from generalized class Person, like Employee earns Salary. Thus, every Employee **has** a Salary. Every Person is not an Employee, and Persons who are not specialized to be employees, do not earn salary. Employee class, therefore, has the HAS-A relationship with the Salary class. This relationship is best envisaged by embedding an object instance of the Salary class in the Employee class.

INHERITANCE

Inheritance is one of the most important notions of OOP. Inheritance allows creating classes from existing classes through an IS-A relationship. When members (data and/or functions) are inherited, they can be used in the derived class as if they are members of the derived class that inherits them, provided, the base class permits the derived class to do so. If class B inherits from class A, then B is called the specialization of generalized class A. Class A is called the base or super class and class B is called the derived or sub class. A derived class inherits the properties that include data and function members of its base class. Thus, all the code, which is written to work with objects of the base class, will work with the objects of derived classes. This makes class definitions for subclasses much smaller and neater and makes it possible to write code, which works with objects of different types, on the right level of generality. One can also add extra data members as well as member functions to the derived class. One can also modify the implementation of existing member functions or data by overriding base class member functions or data in the newly derived class. A class can be derived from one or more base classes.

If we draw a class inheritance hierarchy (who derives from whom) tree, more general and abstract notions are at the top of the tree; they get specialized as we go further down the tree (see Figure 10.2).

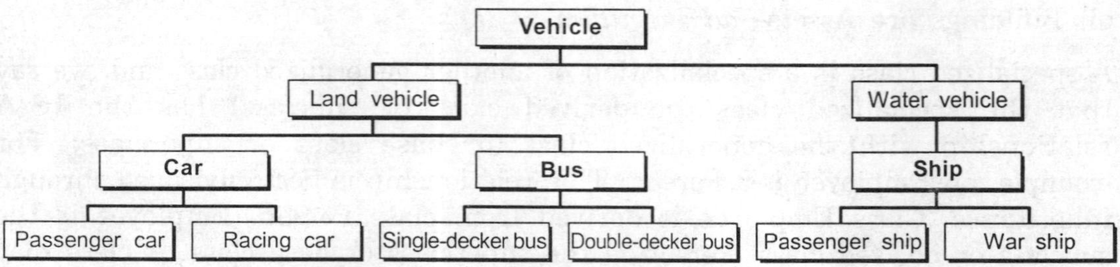

Figure 10.2 Vehicle class hierarcy.

The same can be used in a programming language as follows:

Say, class X is the base class and class Y is the subclass. This takes the following form:

```
           ⎧private(default)⎫
Class Y:  ⎨protected        ⎬ X
           ⎩public          ⎭
{
................
};
```

Depending on the usage of private (if nothing is mentioned, by default, private is taken), protected or public, we mean that class X is private or protected or public base class with respect to the derived class Y. If one class derives from multiple base classes, we call this as *multiple inheritance*, and the declaration of such class takes the following form:

```
(Y derives from X as public and W as protected, say)
class Y: public X, protected W
{
   .......
};
```

The comma (,) in the list indicates multiple inheritance with the appropriate access specifiers (private, protected or public).

Thus, through inheritance, we define a composite type as specialization from one or more generalized types. When using inheritance, the inherited class is called the *base class* or *superclass*, and the inheriting class is called the *subclass* or *derived class*. Inheritance is used to accomplish two programming goals:

1. ***code reuse***—much of the functionality needed are defined in the base classes, and derived classes can add additional functionality.
2. ***subtyping***—the derived class is a "subtype" of a more "abstract" base class thereby providing means for specialization from an existing class.

For example, a Vehicle type is abstract, but can be specialized (made more concrete) by deriving a LandVehicle type, or a WaterVehicle type. A LandVehicle type can be further specialized as Bus, Car and so on.

C++ implements three forms of *polymorphism*:

1. ad hoc polymorphism or operator overloading
2. parametric polymorphism or template classes/functions
3. subtype polymorphism or subtyping using inheritance and "virtual functions"

Operator overloading, templates, as well as inheritance are the forms of static or compile-time mechanism of polymorphism but virtual functions and parametric polymorphism are the forms of dynamic or run-time mechanism of polymorphism.

Using superclass member functions, one can

1. inherit a superclass's member function as-it-is and call it as if it were one of the subclass's member functions;
2. overload a member function with a new implementation in the subclass; and
3. extend with a member function of the same name that calls the inherited method from superclass plus does something else.

Suppose, we declare a class as a forward reference as class A; and try to write a declaration of a derived class as follows:

```
class B: public A   // error : Base class A undefined,
                    // need complete definition of A prior B
{
   A  a;            // error: a uses undefined class A,
                    // needs prior full definition
   static  A  sa;   // ok: 'static A' is not a definition
};
```

Unless redefined in the subclass, members of a superclass can be referred to as if they were members of the subclass. Scope resolution operator (::) can be used to refer to a superclass member explicitly. (See Example 10.1)

EXAMPLE 10.1:

```
class Super                    class Sub: public Super
{                              {
   public:                        public:
      int a;                         int b;
      int b;                         int c;
};                             };
```

```
void f()
{
   Sub  d;
   d.a = 1;
   d.b = 2; // d.b => Sub's b overrides that of Super
           //(although occupies different memory locations)
   d.Super::b = 3;  // d.Super::b refers to 'b' of
                    // Super subobject of d(instance of Sub)
   d.c = 4;
   Super *pS = &d;  // standard conversion:
                    // subclass * to superclass *
}
```

Direct and Indirect superclasses

A class X is called a direct superclass, if it is mentioned in the list of superclasses of the subclass declaration of class Y. A direct base class is analogous to a parent in a hierarchical graph. Class X is called an indirect superclass if it is not a direct superclass of Y but it is a superclass of one of the indirect or direct superclasses mentioned in the list of superclasses of Y. An indirect base class is analogous to a grandparent or great grandparent or great-great grandparent in a hierarchical graph. For a given class, all base classes or superclasses that are not direct superclasses are indirect superclasses. In the classname :: name notation, name must be a name of a member of a direct or an indirect superclass so as to specify where from to start looking for a name. Study the following example (10.2).

EXAMPLE 10.2:

```
class X
{
   public:
      void f();
};
```

```
class Y: public X
{
};
```

```
class Z: public Y
{
   public:
      void f();
};
```

```
void Z :: f()
{
   f();  // calls Z:: f(), because Z's f() supercedes
         // Y::f()
   X::f(); // calls X's f(), since X is an indirect superclass of Z
   Y::f(); // calls Y's f() since
           // Y is an direct superclass of Z
}
```

Protected Members

The protected members (data or function) are accessible by member functions and friends of the class in which they are declared by member functions and friends of the derived class or subclasses. See the example (10.3) on access rights.

EXAMPLE 10.3:

```
class Super
{
  private:
     int topsecret;
```

```
   protected:
      int secret;
   public:
      int opensecret;
};
class Sub: public Super
{
   private:
      void f();
};
void Sub :: f()
{
   topsecret = 1; // Error: cannot access private member
                  // declared in class 'Super'
   secret = 1;    // Ok: can access protected member
                  // declared in class 'Super'
   opensecret = 1;  // Ok: can access public member
                    // declared in class 'Super'
}
int main()
{
   Super aSuperObj;// compiler generated constructor called
   Sub aSubObj; // compiler generated constructor called
   // can't access private and protected members of
   // class 'Super', can only access public members
   // of class 'Super'
   aSuperObj.topsecret = 1; // error : private data
   aSuperObj.secret = 1; // error : protected data
   aSuperObj.opensecret = 1; // Ok: public data
   // similarly, can't access private and protected
   // members of class 'Sub', can only access public
   // members of class 'Sub'
   aSubObj.topsecret = 1; // error: private data
      aSubObj.secret = 1; // error: protected data
      aSubObj.opensecret = 1; // Ok: public data
      return 0;
   }
```

Here you can observe the access mechanism for private, protected or public data from member functions of same class, member functions of subclass, and non-member isolated function like main(). We have purposely omitted constructor and destructor for these classes, and if otherwise successfully compiled, compiler will generate default constructor and destructor. However, it is recommended that you always declare your own constructor as well as destructor without depending on the compiler generated defaults.

Constructor and Destructor Calling Sequence

When an object belonging to the subclass is constructed, the superclass constructor is called prior to the subclass constructor. That is, objects are constructed from the base down the inheritance hierarchy. Thus, the subclass constructor can pass arguments to the superclass constructor using the list of initializers. Usually, destruction goes in a reverse way; a derived class destructor is executed before a base class. An example is given in Program Source Code 10.1.

Program Source Code 10.1

```
#include <iostream.h>

class Super
{
   private:
     int   a;
   //protected data and methods only visible to subclasses
   protected:
     void printInfo();
   public:
      Super(int x = 0): a(x)
      {
         cout << "Super Constructor called" << endl;
      };
      ~Super()
      {
         cout << "Super Destructor called" << endl;
      };
      void print();
};

class Sub : public Super //default is private inheritance
                         //if public not specified
```

(*contd.*)

Program Source Code 10.1 *(contd.)*

```
{
  private:
    int b;
  public:
    Sub(int y = 0) : Super(y),  b(y+10)
    {
      cout << "Sub Constructor called" << endl;
    };
    ~Sub() {cout << "Sub Destructor called" << endl;};
    void printInfo();
};

void Super :: printInfo()
{
  cout  << "a = " << this->a ;
  cout  << " ,size of data component of Super class is:"
        << sizeof(this->a) << endl;
}

void Super :: print()
{
  /* this function in turn calls printInfo(),
     Super::print() is a public interface, callable by
     anybody whereas, Super::printInfo() is protected
     interface, therefore callable by subclass's
     member functions and friends                   */

  //this-> is optional here, shown for alternate syntax
  this->Super::printInfo();
}

void Sub :: printInfo()
{
  Super::printInfo();
  cout << "b = " << this->b ;
  cout << " ,size of data component of Sub class is:"
       << sizeof(this->b) << endl;
}

int main()
```

(contd.)

Program Source Code 10.1 *(contd.)*

```
{
   Super super1(100); //super1 is an instance of class Super
   Sub sub1(200); //sub1 is an instance of class Sub

   // super1.printInfo();  //cannot call since printInfo()
                           //is protected in Super
   super1.print(); //can call publicly accessible
                   //Super::print()
   cout << endl; //a line separator is printed
                 //for output clarity
   sub1.printInfo();  //can call since printInfo()
                      //is public in Sub class

   cout << endl; //a line separator is printed
                 //for output clarity

   cout << "size of super1 is: " << sizeof(super1) << endl;
   cout << "size of sub1 is: " << sizeof(sub1) << endl;
   return 0;
}
```

Output 10.1

```
Super Constructor called
Super Constructor called
Sub Constructor called
a = 100 ,size of data component of Super class is:4

a = 200 ,size of data component of Super class is:4
b = 210 ,size of data component of Sub class is:4

size of super1 is: 4
size of sub1 is: 8
Sub Destructor called
Super Destructor called
Super Destructor called
```

In this program, we have two classes as follows:

1. Super as a generalized class having
   a. one private data member named a (of built-in integer type) (means only accessible to the member functions of class Super and its friends, if any);
   b. one protected function named printInfo() returning void. Being protected, this function is callable by the members of the class Super and its derived class named Sub(we have one derived class of Super named Sub). This function, when called, prints the contents of the current object (for which the function is called) and size of its data component with appropriate meaningful messages;
   c. three public functions (anybody can call these):
      (i) one constructor, which can take zero or one argument of built-in integer type. If no argument is passed, then it is defaulted to zero. If one argument is passed then that is used to initialize the data member named a. We could have also written the constructor as Super(int x = 0) {a=x;}; This would mean that the data component x will be initialized first with some default value (as decided by the compiler, since it is of ***int*** type, constructor is called if the data component is object instance of some class) and then assigned the variable a with the value of x.
      (ii) one destructor, which does nothing (no deallocation of data component is necessary).
      (iii) one function print() returning void, which, in turn, calls printInfo() function.
2. Sub as a specialized class (derived from class Super) having.
   a. one private data member named b (of built-in integer type) (means only accessible to the member functions of class Sub and its friends, if any); and
   b. three public functions (anybody can call these):
      (i) one constructor, which can take zero or one argument of built-in integer type. If no argument is passed, then it is defaulted to zero. The argument passed is used to initialize the superclass object (through the constructor call of class Super passing appropriate parameter) and to initialize its own data member named b. We could have also written the constructor as: Sub(int y = 0): Super(y){b=y+10;}; This would mean that the data component y will be initialized first with some default

value (as decided by the compiler since it is of ***int*** type, constructor is called if the data component is object instance of some class) and then assigned the variable b with the computed value of y+10.

(ii) one destructor, which does nothing (no deallocation of data component is necessary).

(iii) one function printInfo() returning void, which, when called, calls superclass's printInfo() function (Super::printInfo()) and then prints the contents of the current object (for which the function is called) and size of its data component with appropriate meaningful messages).

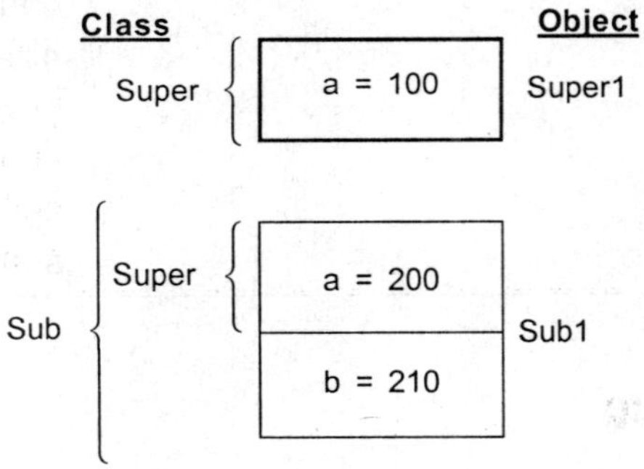

In the main function, we can observe that super1 is an object instance of class Super and sub1 is an object instance of class Sub.

From within main function we cannot call super1.printInfo(), as printInfo is a protected function in class Super. So, we call super1.print() which is allowed as it is declared in public section of class Super. We can also observe that the size of a class is equal to the composite size of its data components (this statement does not necessary hold true if there is a virtual function).

If we assume that sizeof(int) = 4 (assuming 32-bit machine), then,

```
sizeof(super1) = sizeof(Super)
               = sizeof(a)
               = sizeof(int)
               = 4
     and
sizeof(sub1)  = sizeof(Sub)
              = sizeof(Super) + sizeof(b)
              = 4 + sizeof(int)
              = 4 + 4 = 8
```

The program output can be explained as in Table 10.1:

Table 10.1

Program Output	*Reasons*
Super Constructor called	super1 object created
Super Constructor called	sub1 object creation, constructor
Sub Constructor called	called topdown
a = 100, size of data component of Super class is:4	super1.print() is called
	cout << endl; prints an empty line
a = 200, size of data component of Super class is:4	sub1.print() is called
b = 210, size of data component of Sub class is:4	
	cout << endl; prints an empty line
size of super1 is: 4	sizeof(super1) is printed
size of sub1 is: 8	sizeof(sub1) is printed
Sub Destructor called	sub1 object destroyed, destructor
Super Destructor called	called bottomup
Super Destructor called	super1 object destroyed

Multiple Inheritance

Multiple inheritance allows declaring a derived class or subclass that inherits properties from more than one base class or superclass. In the following example, Super1, Super2 and Super3 are direct base classes of class Sub. The order of derivation is not significant and the order in which storage is allocated for base classes is implementation dependent. Some compilers do follow the rule that the order of derivation determines the order of default initialization by constructors and clean up by destructors.

```
class Super1 { };
class Super2 { };
class Super3 { };
class Sub :public Super1,
           public Super2,
           public Super3
{
};
```

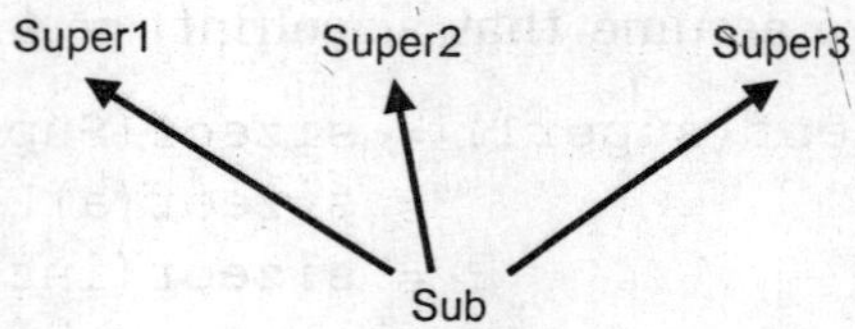

Same class cannot be specified as direct base class multiple times. Thus, the following declarations are incorrect:

```
class Super {public : int s;};

// error: Super is already a base class, can't be twice
class Sub: public Super, public Super {   };
```

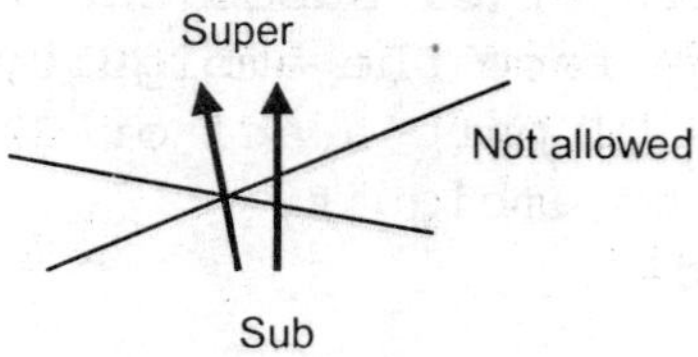

The reason that a given class may not appear more than once in a list of direct base classes is that every reference to it or its members would be ambiguous then (member of which class, even the scope resolution operator won't be able to resolve this). For example, if for debate sake we assume that this would be allowed to have same direct base class more than once, then we write a function as follows:

```
void f(Sub * p)
{
   //ambiguity is to decide which s?
   //if we say, Super::s, even then it is ambiguous
   p->s = 10;
}
```

However, same class can be specified as indirect base class multiple times. Thus, the following declarations are acceptable:

```
class C1  { public : int ac1; };
class C21 : public C1 { };
class C22 : public C1 { };
class C3  : public C21, public C22
{
   public :
     void fc3();
};
```

Here, object instance of class C3 has two sub-objects of class C1.

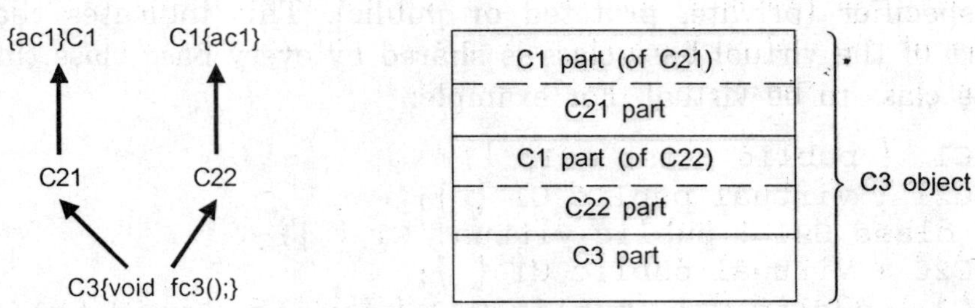

Class C1 has a member int a; If a function void C3::f() is written a follows:

```
void C3 :: fc3()
{
   // we have two copies of C1 subobject in C3,
   // to access ac1, we face the ambiguity,
   // which ac1? C21's C1 part's ac1 or C22's C1 part's
   // ac1? This leads to ambiguity
   ac1 = 0: // which ac1?
}
```

However, if we write,

```
void C3 :: fc3()
{
   C21:: ac1 = C22 :: ac1 = 0: // Now it is ok
}
```

If we write in a main function, say, like the following:

```
int main()
{
   C3 * pC3 = new C3;
   C1 * pC1 = pC3; // ambiguous : pC1 is pointer to which
                   // C1 object? C21's or C22's?
   pC1 = (C1 *) pC3; // even the forced casting will not help
   pC1 = (C1 *) (C21 *) pC3; // ok, C21's C1, explicit.
   pC1 = (C1 *) (C22 *) pC3; // ok, C22's C1, explicit.
   return 0;
}
```

Virtual Base Classes

In the following example, an object instance of class C3 has two distinct objects of class C1, one through class C21, and another through class C22 . The ***virtual*** keyword can be used in front of the base class specifiers in the base lists of classes C21 and C22. The virtual keyword can appear before or after the access specifier (private, proteted or public). This indicates that a single subobject of the virtual base class is shared by every base class that specified the base class to be virtual. For example:

```
class C1  { public : int ac1; };
class C21 : virtual public C1 { };
// or, class C21 : public virtual C1 { };
class C22 : virtual public C1 { };
class C3 : public C21, public C22 { public : void fc3();};
```

Here, object instance of class C3 has single shared sub-object of class C1.

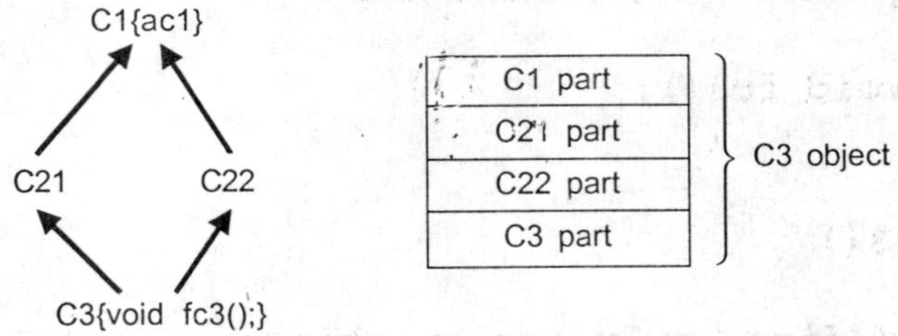

A class can have both virtual as well as nonvirtual base classes, for example,

```
class C1  {public : int ac1;};
class C21 : virtual public C1 { };
class C22 : virtual public C1 { };
class C23 : public C1 {};
class C3  : public C21, public C22, public C23 {};
```

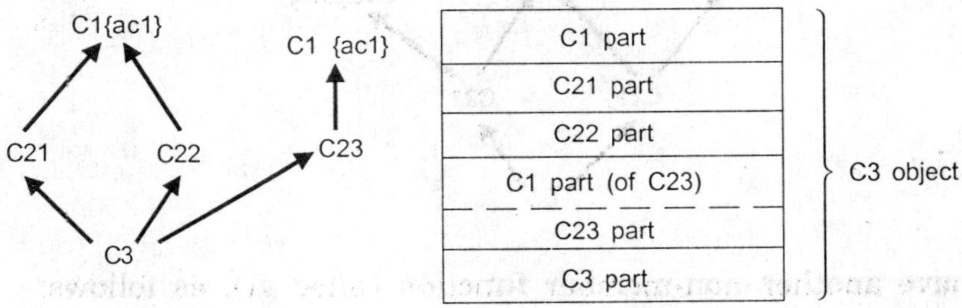

In the above example, class C3 has two subobjects of class C1. One is shared by classes C21 and C22, and another is through class C23. If any member function wants to access data ac1 of C1, it should be unambiguously referred as either of (C21::ac1 or C22::ac1) or C23::ac1 as the case may be. In case of any ambiguity to access any name of a member, it should be qualified with appropriate class name with scope resolution operator so that the access can be unambiguous, as in Example 10.4.

EXAMPLE 10.4:

```
class C11 {public : int ac11;};
class C12 {public : int ac12;};
class C21 : public C12, public virtual C11
{
};
class C22 : public C12, public virtual C11
{
```

```
};
class C3  : public C21, public C22
{
   public: void fc3();
};

void C3::fc3()
{
   ac11++;  //fine, only one unambiguous 'ac11'
   ac12++;  //ambiguous, which ac12? C3 has two copies
            //of ac12, one via C21, other via C22
}
```

To resolve the ambiguity, the name b should be qualified as C::b or D::b.

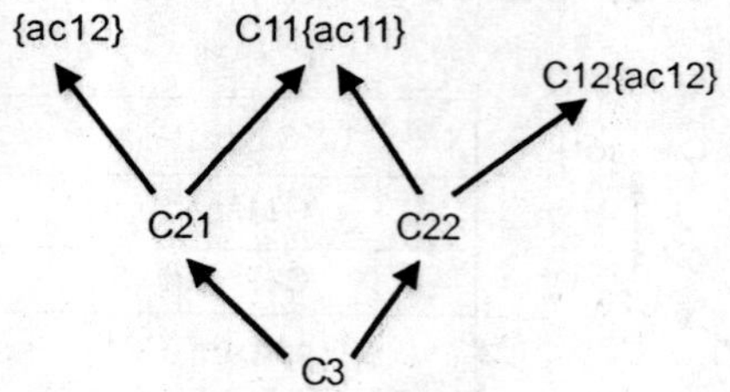

Also, if we have another non-member function called g(), as follows:

```
void g()
{
   C3   ac3;
   // conversion of derived * to base * is allowed,
   // as long as it is unambiguous
   C21 * pc21 = &ac3;
   C22 * pc22 = &ac3;
   C11 * pc11 = &ac3;

   C12 * pc12 = &ac3; // Ambiguous conversion, as have two
                      // copies of C12, which C12?
                      // C21::C12 or C22::C12? Need to resolve
   C12 * apc12 = (C22 *)&ac3; // now unambiguous
}
```

A name B::f dominates a name A::f if class B has A as its base class. If a name dominates another, no ambiguity exists between the two; the dominant name is used when there is a choice, as we have in

```
class A {public : int a; int f()};
class B: public virtual A {public: int a; int f();};
class C: public virtual A { };
class D: public B, public C {public : void g();};

void D::g()
{
   a ++ ; // ok, B::a dominates A::a
   f(); // ok, B::f dominates A::f()
}
```

Here, object instance of class D has single shared sub-object of class A.

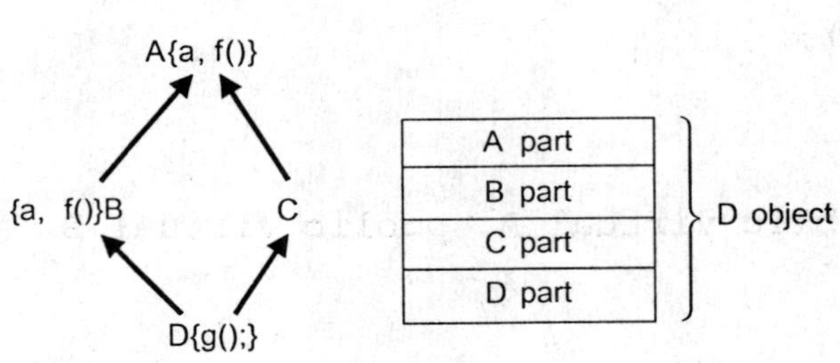

Now we will see the constructor calling sequence in case of virtual base classes.

Constructor and Destructor Calling Sequence

Suppose we have the following class hierarchy (represented by Directed Acyclic Graph (DAG)):

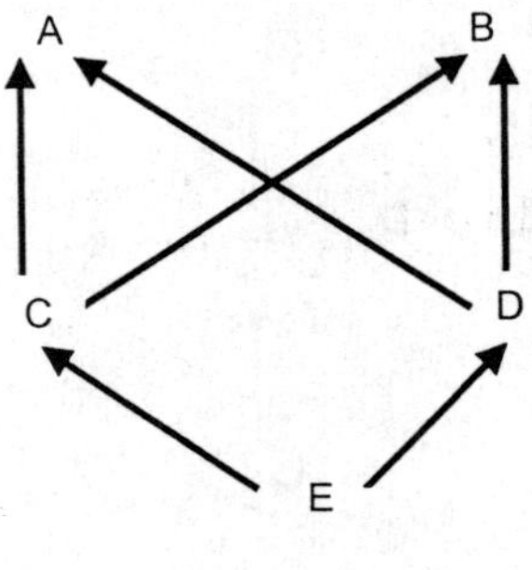

This can be incorporated in a program as in Program Source Code 10.2.

Program Source Code 10.2

```
#include <iostream.h>

class A
{
   int a;
   public:
      A(int);
      ~A();
};

class B
{
   int b;
   public:
      B(int);
      ~B();
};

class C: public virtual A, public virtual B
{
   int c;
   public:
      C(int);
      ~C();
};

class D: public virtual A, public virtual B
{
   int d;
   public:
      D(int);
      ~D();
};

class E: public C, public D
{
   int e;
   public:
      E(int);
      ~E();
};
```

(contd.)

Program Source Code 10.2 *(Contd.)*

```
A :: A (int x) : a(x + 10)
{
   cout << "A Constructor called -- A::a = " << a << endl;
}

A::~A()
{
   cout << "A Destructor called" << endl;
}

B :: B (int x) : b(x + 20)
{
   cout << "B Constructor called -- B::b = " << b << endl;
}

B::~B()
{
   cout << "B Destructor called" << endl;
}

C :: C (int x) : c(x + 30), A(x + 40), B(x + 50)
{
   cout << "C Constructor called -- C::c = " << c << endl;
}

C::~C()
{
   cout << "C Destructor called" << endl;
}

D :: D (int x) : d(x + 60), A(x + 70), B(x + 80)
{
   cout << "D Constructor called -- D::d = " << d << endl;
}

D::~D()
{
   cout << "D Destructor called" << endl;
}

E :: E (int x) : e(x + 90), A(x + 100), B(x + 110),
                 C(x + 120),  D(x + 130)
```

(contd.)

Program Source Code 10.2 *(Contd.)*

```
{
   cout << "E Constructor called -- E::e = " << e << endl;
}

E::~E()
{
   cout << "E Destructor called" << endl;
};

int main()
{
   E  anEObj(1000);
   return 0;
}
```

Output 10.2

```
A Constructor called -- A::a = 1110
B Constructor called -- B::b = 1130
C Constructor called -- C::c = 1150
D Constructor called -- D::d = 1190
E Constructor called -- E::e = 1090
E Destructor called
D Destructor called
C Destructor called
B Destructor called
A Destructor called
```

In this program anEObj constructor calls the following constructors in sequence (top down):

1. A::A constructor through E constructor directly (not via C nor via D)
2. B::B constructor through E constructor directly (not via C nor via D)
3. C::C constructor through E constructor (C::C constructor does not in turn call A::A or B::B constructor as these subobjects have been already created).
4. D::D constructor through E constructor (D::D constructor does not in turn call A::A or B::B constructor as these subobjects have been already created).
5. E::E constructor.

While this is so, the destructor calling sequence is just the reverse bottom upwards.

A complete object is an object that is not a sub-object representing a base class. Its class is said to be the most derived class of the object. All subobjets for virtual base classes are initialized by the constructor of the most derived class. If a constructor of this class does not specify a memory initializer for a virtual base class then that virtual base class must have a default constructor or no constructors (compiler generated one will be used then). Any memory initializers for virtual classes specified in a constructor for a class that is not the class of the complete object are ignored. Destructor calling sequence is automatic, i.e. bottom-up.

Friend

If a class X declares a friend in order to grant the access privileges same as that of members of class X, it means a friend of class X can access all the members (data or function, declared as private, protected or public) of the class X which has granted friendship. Friendship is granted by a class X to another class Y, or to a member function of another class Y, or to a single isolated non-member function. However, neither a constructor nor a destructor of a class can be a friend function to another class. A class X grants friendship, by explicitly declaring the friend inside the structure declaration of class X. A class Y must be defined before any of the member function of class Y can be granted friendship by another class X. This in effect, opens a small hole in the protective shield of data abstraction of the class, and so it should be used sparingly with extreme caution.

Assume that we have a Fraction class with private data members and constructor, destructor as usual and now with two publicly accessible member functions named printFraction and setFractionToZero both returning void. Both these functions, being non-static member functions of Fraction class, work on Fraction object type (which becomes the first and only argument of the functions and the argument is accessible through implied parameter *this*). The goal of the function printFraction is to print the contents of the Fraction object (for which it is called). And the goal of the setFractionToZero is to set the fraction object (for which it is called) to zero value, i.e. numerator = 0 and denominator = 1.

Now, we have two more classes called Aclass and Bclass both having no data members, but each having an empty constructor and destructor. Both of these classes now have two member functions defined, named setFractionToZero, and printFraction both returning void and both taking one Fraction object type parameter passed as reference. In the printFraction function, the Fraction object is passed as a constant reference, so that it is not modifiable from within the printFraction implementation. In the setFractionToZero function, the Fraction object is passed as a non-constant reference, so that it is modifiable from within the setFractionToZero implementation. The objective of these two functions are similar to the same named member functions of Fraction class, i.e. setFractionToZero will set the Fraction object passed to zero. And printFraction will print the contents of the Fraction object passed. We have also defined two non-member isolated functions named setFractionToZero and printFrcation with the similar signature (return type, number and type of parameters) as those of Aclass or Bclass members. These two functions have been defined outside any class (that's why non-member and isolated) with similar intentions as those of same named member functions of Aclass or Bclass.

Now, Aclass and Bclass are outsiders with respect to class Fraction. As such, the members of Aclass and Bclass as well as any other isolated non-member functions cannot access the private and protected members (data or function) of class Fraction, unless class Fraction grants friendship. In this example, class Fraction grants friendship to (i) entire class Aclass, (ii) printFraction member function of class Bclass (iii) non-member function setFractionToZero. By virtue of friendship, all the members (data or functions, private, protected or public) of class Fraction are granted free access by: (i) each member function of Aclass, (ii) printFraction member function of class Bclass (no other member function of Bclass is allowed to this privilege) and (iii) non-member function setFractionToZero. If you now see the implementations of these functions and other functions in more detail, you will notice that:

1. Both the member functions of Aclass named printFraction and setFractionToZero can access private data members of Fraction object passed as parameter.
2. Bclass::printFraction accesses private data members of Fraction object passed as parameter to print the fraction. Bclass::setFractionToZero shows commented statements as those intentions (that's why, commented) cannot be accomodated. This function, when called, prints an appropriate message stating its inability to carry out the intention.
3. Non-member function setFractionToZero accesses private data members of Fraction object passed as parameter to set it to zero. However, non-member function printFraction shows commented statements as those intentions (that's why, commented) cannot be accomodated. This function, when called, prints an appropriate message stating its inability to carry out the intention.

Let us study the Program Source Code (10.3) to illustrate this:

Program Source Code 10.3

```
#include <iostream.h>

class Fraction;
class Aclass
{
   public:
      AClass(){};
      ~AClass(){};
      void printFraction(const Fraction &);
      void setFractionToZero(Fraction &);
};

class BClass
{
   public:
      BClass(){};
      ~BClass(){};
      void printFraction(const Fraction &);
      void setFractionToZero(Fraction &);
};
void printFraction(const Fraction &);
void setFractionToZero(Fraction &);

class Fraction
{
      int num;
      int denom;

      friend class AClass;
      friend void BClass::printFraction(const Fraction &);
      friend void setFractionToZero(Fraction &);
   public:
      Fraction(int = 0, int = 1); // constructor
      ~Fraction();          //destructor
      void printFraction();
      void setFractionToZero();
};
```

(*contd.*)

Program Source Code 10.3 *(contd.)*

```
Fraction :: Fraction(int a, int b)
{
   this->num = a;
   this->denom = b;
}

Fraction :: ~Fraction()
{
}

void Fraction :: printFraction()
{
   cout << "Function Fraction::printFraction"
        << "prints fraction: ";
        << this->num << "/"
        << this->denom << endl;
}

void Fraction :: setFractionToZero()
{
   this->num = 0; this->denom = 1;
   cout << "Function Fraction::setFractionToZero"
        << "sets fraction to zero" << endl;
}

void AClass :: printFraction(const Fraction &f)
{
   cout << "Function AClass::printFraction"
        << "prints fraction: " << f.denom << endl;
        << f.num << "/"
}

void AClass :: setFractionToZero(Fraction &f)
{
   f.num = 0; f.denom = 1;
   cout << "Function AClass::setFractionToZero"
        << "setsfraction to zero" << endl;
}
void BClass:: printFraction(const Fraction &f)
```

(contd.)

Program Source Code 10.3 *(contd.)*

```
{
   cout << "Function BClass::printFraction
        << "prints fraction: "
        << f.num << "/" << f.denom << endl;
}

void BClass:: setFractionToZero(Fraction &f)
{
/* ---- BClass :: setFractionToZero is not a
   friend of Fraction, as such,cannot access private
   member(num,denom) declared in class 'Fraction' */

// f.num = 0; f.denom = 1; -- cannot access
cout << "Function BClass::setFractionToZero CANNOT"
      << "CAN'T set fraction to 0" << endl;
}

void printFraction(const Fraction &f)
{
/* ---- printFraction is not a friend of Fraction,
   as such, cannot access private member(num,denom)
   declared in class 'Fraction'*/
// cout << "Function printFraction prints fraction: "
//       << f.num << "/" << f.denom << endl;
   cout << "Function printFraction CANNOT print"
        << "fraction" << endl;
}

void setFractionToZero(Fraction &f)
{
   f.num = 0; f.denom = 1;
   cout << "Function setFractionToZero sets fraction"
        << "to zero" << endl;
}

int main()
{
   AClass aobj; // aobj is an object instance of AClass
   BClass bobj; // bobj is an object instance of BClass
   int n, d;
```

(contd.)

Program Source Code 10.3 (*contd.*)

```
cout << "Please enter values of numerator, denominator : ";
cin >> n >> d;
Fraction f1(n,d); // automatic call to constructor

f1.printFraction();
f1.setFractionToZero();
cout << endl;

aobj.printFraction(f1);
aobj.setFractionToZero(f1);
cout << endl;

bobj.printFraction(f1);
bobj.setFractionToZero(f1);
cout << endl;

printFraction(f1);
setFractionToZero(f1);
cout << endl;
return 0;
}
```

Output 10.3

```
Please enter values of numerator, denominator: 4 5
Function Fraction::printFraction prints fraction: 4/5
Function Fraction::setFractionToZero sets fraction to zero

Function AClass::printFraction prints fraction: 0/1
Function AClass::setFractionToZero sets fraction to zero

Function BClass::printFraction prints fraction: 0/1
Function BClass::setFractionToZero CAN'T set fraction to 0

Function printFraction CAN'T print fraction
Function setFractionToZero sets fraction to zero
```

Now, if you follow the main program, we have objects aobj (instance of Aclass), bobj (instance of Bclass), and f1 (instance of Fraction). We call the pair of functions printFraction and setFractionToZero as member functions for f1, aobj, bobj and the non-member functions as well. And if you follow the output, we can see the messages like Function BClass::setFractionToZero and printFraction CANNOT set fraction to zero and in all other cases, the functions can perform the intentions.

And here are some more points which should be noted for using friends:

1. A friend declaration has to appear in the declaration of the class which is granting the friendship.
2. Friendship, like all other access, is granted, not grabbed. e.g.

   ```
   class X{.... friend void f(); .......};
   ```

   Here, function f() can access private and protected members of class X, because X is granting friendship to function f(). It is, however, not granting friendship to any other overloaded variation to it, like say not to void f(int).
3. A function can be a friend of two different classes, e.g.

   ```
   class Fraction;
   class Integer
   {
       ......
       friend Integer operator + (const Fraction&, const
                                      Integer&);
       ......
   };
   class Fraction
   {
       .......
       friend Integer operator + (const Fraction&, const Integer&);
       ......
   };
   Integer operator + (const Fraction& a, const Integer& b)
   {
       // common friend of Integer as well as Fraction
       // implementation goes here
   }
   ```

   This is better since it avoids complicating the interface by unnecessarily making interface for all (as public), rather, via controlled interface through friendship.
4. Friend allows user-defined conversions to be used for its first argument, where member functions do not, as for example,

   ```
   class Fraction
   {
   ```

```
    Fraction operator - (Fraction);
    friend Fraction operator + (Fraction, Fraction);
};
```

Here, Fraction::operator – requires a fraction lvalue as its first argument, so 10 – x is in error, where x is a Fraction object. On the other hand, the friend operator +(Fraction, Fraction) accepts any value that is a Fraction object or can be converted to one Fraction object; so, 1 + x is allowed, 1 + x will be taken as Fraction (1) + x

5. When a friend declaration refers to an overloaded name or operator, only the function matching the signature (number type and order of arguments) becomes a friend.
6. Friends also help to provide access to the representation of a class of functions that cannot be member functions because they will be called from another language, e.g.

```
class X;
// the function drawCircle was compiled through
// C(not C++) compiler
extern "C" void drawCircle(X *);
class X
{
    friend void drawCircle(X *);
};
```

7. There can be mutual friendships between two classes, such as

```
class X
{
    friend class Y;
    .......
};
class Y
{
    friend class X;
    .......
};
```

Some more examples follow:

```
class X
{
 enum {a = 100};
 friend class Y;
};
```

```
class Y
{
    // Y is a friend of class X, so, can access
    // private data of X, X::size
       int vect [X:: size]; // ok

};

class Z
{
   int vect[X::size];   // error: X::size is private,
                        // so inaccessible to Z

};
```

Per Class Protection

In C++, class is the basic unit of protection. For example,

```
class Fraction
{
        :
   public:        // public interface functions
        :
        Fraction(const Fraction &); // copy constructor
        :
};
Fraction :: Fraction (const Fraction & AnotherFraction)
{
   this->num = AnotherFraction.num;
   this->denom = AnotherFraction.denom;
}
```

Here, accessing private data members num and denom of AnotherFraction object is allowed by a different object for which the copy constructor is called. This is because, C++ provides protection per class, not per object. This means, object instances of a particular class cannot access private or protected data or function members of objects of another class (unless friendship is granted by the later class). However, objects belonging to the same class can access private or protected data or function members of each other.

Virtual Function

A virtual function is a member function in a class such that it is expected to be redefined in the derived classes. If a virtual function is called through a pointer to a base class, the derived class's version of the function is executed. A virtual function is declared by placing ***virtual*** keyword in the base class function declaration, and not necessarily in the declarations in the derived classes (no harm in saying it virtual again in derived classes but not required) (see Example 10.5)

EXAMPLE 10.5:

```
class A
{
   public:
      virtual void f(int);
      virtual void g(int);
      virtual void h(int);
      void k(int);
};
class B: public A
{
   public:
      int b;
      void g(int);
};
class C: public B
{
   public:
      int c;
      void h(int);
      void k(int);
};
```

Suppose, a C object is created as

```
A * pa = new C;
```

and then we call,

```
pa->g(2);
```

then, it implies call of B::g function since function g was declared as virtual function in A class. Suppose, we have a main function as follows:

```
int main ()
{
   C c;
   A* aptr =&c; // or pa = new C; is called
```

```
    aptr->f(); //calls A::f() because f() is virtual in A
               // but not redefined in B or C
    aptr->g(); //calls B::g() because g() is virtual in A
               //but redefined in B
    aptr->h(); //calls C::h() because h() is virtual in A
               // but redefined in C
    aptr->k(); //calls A::k() because k() is nonvirtual
               // in A evenif it is redefined in C
    return 0;
}
```

At compile time, the compiler cannot identify the function to be called by the statement aptr->g(). At runtime, the statement is evaluated depending on the type of the object created or referred at runtime. This method of dynamic decision of call to a particular function depending on the type of object created is called *dynamic binding*. Internally, it maintains a virtual function table (called vtbl) stores a table of function pointers, which have been declared as virtual. This pointer to the **vtbl** called **vptr** resides in the storage of the object. As such, the size of an object is not necessarily sum total of the sum of size of its data members (because a vptr may be present in each object whose class has declared at least one virtual function). Depending on the type of the object created (irrespective of the type of the object declared), the virtual function table is created in a bottom-up approach where to find the function when the named function is called.

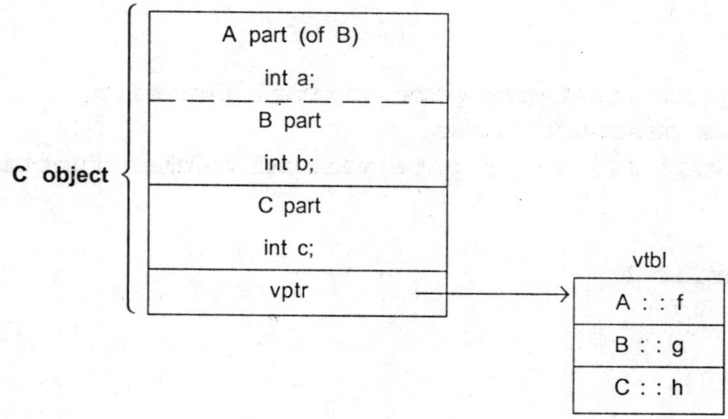

Functions in derived classes override virtual functions in base classes only if their type that is, number of arguments, type of arguments, and order of arguments are the same. A function in a derived class cannot differ from a virtual function in a base class in its return type only; the argument list must differ as well. When calling a function using pointers or references, the following rules apply:

1. A call to a virtual function is resolved according to the underlying type of object for which it is called.
2. A call to a nonvirtual function is resolved according to the type of the pointer or reference.

A virtual function cannot be global or static. By definition, a virtual function is a member function of a base class and relies on a specific object to determine which implementation of the function is called. A virtual function can be declared a friend of another class.

Abstract Class

An abstract class is a class that is designed to be specifically used as a base class (not to be instantiated to create an object instance). An abstract class contains at least one pure virtual function. Pure virtual functions are inherited. One can declare a function to be pure by using a pure specifier in the declaration of the member function in the class declaration. A function is declared pure if it has no definition, and cannot be executed. Study the following example (10.6).

EXAMPLE 10.6:

```
class A
{
   public:
   // Having at least one pure virtual function,
   // A is an abstract class
   virtual void f()=0; // pure virtual member function
};

class B: public A
{
   public:
      void f()
      {
         cout << "Hi there" << endl;
      };
};

int main ()
```

```
{
   B b;
   b.f(); // ok: calls B::f()
   A a;    // error, cannot instantiate an object of an abstract class type
   return 0;
}
```

Attempting to call a pure virtual function that has no implementation is undefined. One cannot create objects of an abstract class. If a derived class does not define or provide implementation of a function which is declared as pure virtual function in the base class, then by virtue of inheritance, pure virtual function is inherited. Having a pure virtual function as a member, the derived class also becomes an abstract class (no instance of an abstract class can be created). Thus, if a base class declares itself an abstract class by having atleast one pure virtual function, then the derived classes are forced to provide suitable implementation for the virtual functions in their respective classes, failing which they also become abstract classes.

One cannot use an abstract class as the type of an explicit conversion, as an argument type, or as the return type for a function. However, a pointer or reference to an abstract class cannot be declared.

Overriding and Hiding

If a base class contains a virtual function and a derived class also contains a function of same signature (same name, same return type and same number, type and order of parameters), then a call of the virtual function for an object of derived class invokes function of the derived class (evenif access is through a pointer or reference to the instance of the base class). The derived class function is said to override the base class function. If function signatures (not only return types) are different, functions are different and virtual mechanism is not invoked. Virtual function definition in derived class cannot have different return type as defined in the base class. Here's an example (see Example 10.7).

EXAMPLE 10.7:

```
class A
{
   public:
      virtual void f1();
      virtual void f2();
      virtual void f3();
      void f4();
```

```
};
class B : public A
{
  public:
     void f1();
     void f2(int); // hides A::f2(), different signature
                   // dynamic binding not possible
     char f3(); // Error: overriding virtual function
                // differs in return type from A::f3
     void f4();
};

void fun()
{
  B b;
  A *pa = &b; // allowed: derived pointer to base pointer
  pa->f1(); // calls B::f1, dynamic binding
  pa->f2(); // calls A::f2, B::f2 has different signature
  pa->f4(); // calls A::f4, static binding
}
```

Virtual Destructor

When destroying dynamically created objects with the *delete* operator, a problem can arise—if *delete* is applied to a base class pointer, the compiler calls the base class destructor, even if the pointer points to an instance of a derived class. The solution is to declare the base class's destructor as virtual, even though they don't share the same name as the base class's destructor. Then if delete is applied to a base class pointer, the appropriate destructor is called, no matter what type of object the pointer is pointing to.

Constructors cannot be virtual. Because, they have the job of bringing an object into existence. It is also the constructor's job to set up the *vptr* and *vtbl*, without which the virtual function mechanism does not work. Since destructors are not inherited, a virtual destructor that is declared pure must have a definition.

Virtual Operators

Operator functions are usually not called directly. They can be explicitly called, though, as

```
Fraction a = b.operator +(c); // same as: Fraction a = b + c;
```

The following table (10.2) shows permissible things like virtualness and ability to have return types as applicable to different operators and functions.

Table 10.2

Operations/ Functions	*Inherited*	*Can be Virtual*	*Can have a Return Type*	*Member or Friend*	*Generated by Default, if not Provided*
constructor	no	no	no	member	yes
destructor	no	yes	no	member	yes
conversion	yes	yes	no (explicitly) yes (implicitly)	member	no
copy constructor	no	yes	no	member	yes
= operator	yes	yes	yes	either	no
( )	yes	yes	yes	member	no
[ ]	yes	yes	yes	member	no
–>	yes	yes	yes	member	no
()	yes	yes	yes	member	no
new operator	yes	no	void *	static member	no
delete operator	yes	no	void	static member	no
other operator	yes	yes	yes	either	no
other member	yes	yes	yes	member	no
friend	no	no	yes	friend	no

Accessibility in Derived Classes

The access rules can be summarized as in Table 10.3.

Table 10.3

Base Class	*Derived Class (public base class)*	*Derived Class (private base class)*	*Derived Class (public base class)*
private	inaccessible	inaccessible	inaccessible
protected	protected	private	protected
public	public	private	protected

If a base class is public, the public members of the base class are also public members of the derived class. If it is private, the public members of the base class become private members of the derived class. They can be accessed by member and friend functions of the derived class, but they are not accessible to users of the derived class. If it is protected, the public members of the base class become protected members of the derived class. They can be accessed by member and friend functions of the derived class, and members and friend functions of the derived class of derived class, but they are not accessible to users of the derived class.

Access to Virtual Functions

Access to virtual functions is determined by the declaration of a virtual function and is not affected by the rules for a function that later overrides it, as for example, refer to Example 10.8.

EXAMPLE 10.8:

```
class A
{
   public:
     virtual void f();
};

class B: public A
{
   void f(); //private by default
};
void f()
{
   B  b;
   A  *pa = &b;
   B  *pb = &b;
   pa->f(); // ok: A::f() is public, B::f() is invoked.
   pb->f(); // Error: B::f() is private
}
```

Access is checked at the point of invocation using the type of the expression used to denote the object for which the member function is called (A * in the example). The access of the member function in the class in which it is defined (B in the example) is, in general, not known.

Private virtual functions provide a way for the implementation of a base class to reply on derived classes without the functions involved being exposed to the general users of the base class. Whether the derived class chooses to expose the function to its users is not a concern for the base class implementer.

Linking C file in C++ program

Previously compiled (compiled by a C compiler not by a C++ compiler) C program files and associated functions can be linked together with C++ program files compiled by a C++ compiler. This is done by a special linkage specification surrounding those C function declarations (in order to prevent being name mangled by the C++ compiler). C++ compilers use name mangling to generate unique names for all functions and operators by mangling with the signature, the class name for which it is member and of course the name or abbreviated name of the function or operator. The linkage specification is given as:

```
#include <iostream.h>
extern "C"
{
   // The linkage specification tells C++ that myCLib
   // functions were compiled with C compiler
   // (not a C++ compiler)
   #include "myCLib.h"
}
```

And then we can use as:

```
int main()
{
   cout << myFunc(); // MyFunc (C-function)(in myCLib.h),
                     / compiled by C compiler
   return 0;
}
```

SUMMARY

The key concepts introduced in this chapter are as follows:

- Abstract Data Types (ADT) help programmers to concentrate on "what" can be done with the data rather than concentrating on the data representation.
- An object should only know about the data it needs to know about. All *data* not required by an object should be *hidden* from it.
- *Inheritance* defines a class for specialization from a generalized existing class through IS-A relationship. *Multiple inheritance* allows declaring a derived class or subclass that inherits properties from more than one base class or superclass.

- The protected members (data or function) are accessible by member functions and friends of the class in which it is declared and by member functions and friends of the derived class or subclasses.
- When an object belonging to the subclass is constructed, the superclass constructor is called prior to the subclass constructor. Destruction goes in a reverse way.
- If two or more derived classes have a common base class (must be indirect, cannot be direct base), one can use a *virtual base class* to ensure that the two classes share a single instance of the base class. Constructor and destructor calling sequences have been discussed for virtual base classes.
- Friendship is granted to a class, a particular member function of a class, a non-member function to grant the access privileges same as that of members of the granting classes.
- In C++, the basic unit of protection is class, not object.
- In C++, dynamic binding is achieved by virtual function, which is a member function in a class such that it is expected to be redefined in the derived classes.
- An abstract class contains at least one *pure virtual function*. A pure virtual function has no definition and cannot be executed. One cannot create objects of an abstract class.
- Derived classes can be accessed. Certain rules are followed for this through private, protected and public inheritance.
- Previously compiled (compiled by a C compiler not by a C++ compiler) C program files and associated functions can be linked together with C++ program files compiled by a C++ compiler.

REVIEW QUESTIONS

1. Can destructors be virtual? What is the purpose of a virtual destructor? Can a constructor be virtual?
2. Can you inherit a friend function or an assignment operator?
3. What is a virtual member function? What is a pure virtual function? When should you define a member function as virtual? How do you override a virtual member function?
4. How does C++ perform static typing while supporting dynamic binding?
5. What is the benefit of inheritance? What does class inheritance mean?

6. What is the difference between an IS-A and HAS-A relationship?
7. Can you achieve reuse in C++ without using inheritance?
8. What is abstract base class? What is a concrete derived class?
9. What does public inheritance mean? Also explain protected and private inheritances.
10. Why cannot a derived class access the private members of its base class?
11. What will be printed by the following program? Explain why.

```
#include <iostream.h>

class Poly
{
  protected:
     int width, height;
  public:
     void setval (int a, int b)
     {width=a; height=b; }
     virtual int area (void) = 0;
     void printarea (void)
     {cout << this->area() << endl;}
};

class Rect: public Poly
{
  public:
     int area (void) { return (width * height); };
};

class Triangle: public Poly
{
  public:
     int area (void)
     {return (width * height / 2); }
};

int main ()
{
  Rect rect;
  Triangle trgl;
  Poly * Pp1 = &rect;
  Poly * Pp2 = &trgl;
  Pp1->setval (4,5);
```

```
    Pp2->setval (4,5);
    Pp1->printarea();
    Pp2->printarea();
    return 0;
}
```

12. Show the class declarations to support the following class hierarchy.

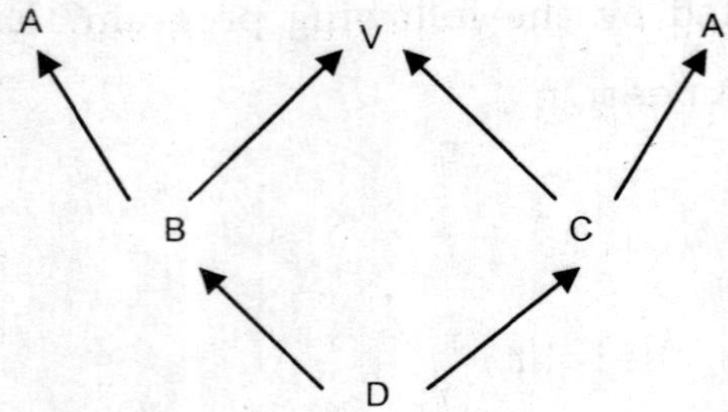

13. Consider the following class declarations:

```
#include <iostream.h>
class A
{ public:
      virtual void f() {cout << "A::f()" << endl;};
      virtual void g() {cout << "A::g()" << endl;};
      virtual void h() {cout << "A::h()" << endl;};
      virtual void k() {cout << "A::k()" << endl;};
};
class B: public virtual A
{ public:
      void g() {cout << "B::g()" << endl;};
};
class C: public virtual A
{ public:
      void f() {cout << "C::f()" << endl;};
};
class D: public B, public C, public virtual A
{ public:
      void h() {cout << "D::h()" << endl;};
};
int main()
{
   D *pd = new D();
   C *pc = pd;
```

```
    pc->f();
    pc->g();
    pc->h();
    pc->k();
    pd->f();
    pd->g();
    pd->h();
    pd->k();
    return 0;
}
```

What is the output of the program?

14. If delete operator is applied to a base class pointer, the base class destructor is called even if the pointer points to an instance of a derived class. What changes should be done so that appropriate destructor is called? Explain with suitable examples.

15. What are the different member access controls? Define with proper examples.

16. How do you define (a) a class as a friend to another class? (b) a non-member function as friend to a class? (c) a member function of a class to be friend of another class?

What are the implications in terms of access control?

17. What is the difference between static binding and dynamic binding? Explain with examples.

18. Does C support static or dynamic binding? What about C++?

19. In designing a class relationship, what decisions lead to have a class as a client or a subclass of another class?

11 Advanced Concepts

I think that any language that aspires to mainstream use must provide a broad base for a variety of techniques—including object-oriented programming (class hierarchies) and generic programming (parameterized types and algorithms). In particular, it must provide good facilities for composing programs out of separate parts (possibly writing in several different languages). I also think that exceptions are necessary for managing the complexity of error handling. A language that lacks such facilities forces its users to laboriously simulate them.

—Bjarne Stroustrup

LEARNING OBJECTIVES

The objective of this chapter is to acquaint you with:

- Concept of template—class and function templates
- Namespace
- Need and mechanism of exception handling
- Advanced cast opeators—static_cast, dynamic_cast, reinterpret_cast and const_cast
- typeid operator

INTRODUCTION

In earlier chapters we have covered basic features of C++ and by now you should be familiar with the concepts of data abstraction and data types, classes, member functions, operator overloading, polymorphism, static vs. dynamic binding and so on. Now, we will take you to some more advanced topics of C++. They will include templates, exception handling and namespace concepts. Many a times, we write similar classes varying by only the data type, structurally looking the same, there we need some kind of blueprint description of the classes where the data type is parameterized. And in some cases, program abnormally terminates, or is forced to do so because of some catastrophic failure, which cannot be recovered. On such cases, some emergency measures need to be taken so as to ensure minimal losses due to abnormal termination of the program. This may include closing an already opened file or database or communication link on abnormal exit of the program. Sounds interesting? Well, let's get going.

TEMPLATE

C++ is a language that supports static type checking. Static type checking helps to spot many errors during compilation, because the programmer has to fix the type of a name used. Any violation of the type model leads to an error message and cancels compilation. So, run-time errors decrease.

Templates are very useful when implementing generic constructs like vectors, stacks, lists, queues which can be used with any arbitrary type. C++ templates provide a way to reuse source code (compile-time reuse) as opposed to inheritance and composition which provide a way to reuse object code (runtime reuse). A template definition uses one or more data types as argument and defines a class or function based on the argument(s) which are data types (not data). When we generate the individual classes or functions from these templates, we simply specify the template name and pass the data type(s) for the particular class or function as argument(s) of the template. Thus, one can use templates to define a family of types or functions. C++ provides two kinds of templates: *class templates* and *function templates*. We use function templates to define generic functions that can be used with arbitrary types. For example, one can write searching and sorting routines which can be used with any arbitrary data type. The Standard Template Library (STL) generic algorithms have been implemented (and provided with standard C++ compilers) as function templates, and the containers have been implemented as class templates.

A template definition contains the ***template*** keyword and one or more datatype argument(s), to declare or define a generic class or a generic function based on argument data type(s) alongwith other data type(s). It takes the following two forms:

```
template <class typename_indetifier> function_or_class_declaration;
template <typename typename_indetifier> function_or_class_declaration;
```

Friendship can be established between a class template and a global function, a member function of another class (or a template class), or even an entire class (or a template class).

Class Template

The relationship between a class template and an individual class is like the relationship between a class and an individual object. An individual class defines how a group of object instances can be constructed from the individual class, while a class template defines how a group of classes can be generated from the template class. Here's a template:

```
template <class T>
class Array
{
  protected:
  int  length;
     T *  arr;
  public:
     Array(int size); // constructor
     virtual ~Array();  // destructor
     T& operator [](int index); // overloaded index operator
   };
```

Table 11.1 shows what the classes Array<int>, Array<char*>, and Array<XYZ> look like:

Table 11.1

*Array***<int>** *integers;*	*Array***<char *>** *charptrs;*	*Array***<XYZ>** *xyzs;*

class Array<**int**>
{
protected:
int length;
int * arr;
public:
Array(int size);
virtual ~Array();
int& operator []
(int index);
};
	class Array<**char ***>
	{
	protected:
	int length;
	char * * arr;
	public:
	Array(int size);
	virtual ~Array();
	char * & operator[]
	(int index);
	};
		class Array<**XYZ**>
		{
		protected:
		int length;
		XYZ * arr;
		public:
		Array(int size);
		virtual ~Array();
		XYZ& operator []
		(int index);
		};

The declarations create the following objects:

- integers of type Array<int>
- charptrs of type Array<char *>
- xyzs of type Array<XYZ>

These three classes have different names. The data types that are contained within the angular braces (<>) are not arguments to the class names, but part of the entire class names. Array<int> and Array<char *> and Array<XYZ> are all class names, however, a class called Array (with no template argument list) is undefined.

Let's now see the generic implementation of the Array<T> and its instantiation with particular data type in greater detail in Program Source Code 11.1.

Program Source Code 11.1
ARRAY.HPP

```
template <class T>
class Array
{
   protected:
      int length;
      T *   arr;
   public:
      Array(int size = 0); // constructor
      virtual ~Array();  // destructor
      T& operator [](int index);  // overloaded
                                  // index operator
};

template <class T>
Array<T> :: Array<T> (int size)
{
   cout << "constructor called" << endl;
   length = size;
   if (size > 0 )
      arr = new T [length];
   else
   {
      length = 0;
      arr = (T*) NULL;
   }
}

template <class T>
Array<T> :: ~Array<T> ()
```

(*contd.*)

Program Source Code 11.1 *(contd.)*

```
{
   cout << "destructor called" << endl;
   if (arr != NULL)
      delete [] arr;
}

template <class T>
T& Array<T> :: operator [] (int index)
{
   static T dummy;
   if ((index >= 0) && (index < length))
      return arr[index];
   else
   {
      cout << "Error: out of range" << endl;
      return dummy;
   }
}
```

TESTARR.CPP

```
#include <iostream.h>
#include "array.hpp"

int main()
{
  int i;
  char *numbers[] = {"zero", "one", "two", "three",
                     "four"};

  // create instance of Array<int> and Array<char *>
  // having 5 elements each
  Array<int> integers(5); // array of 5 integers
  Array<char *> charptrs(5);   // array of 5 character
                               // pointers

  // assign values to the elements in the array objects
  for (i = 0; i < 5; i++)
  {
     integers[i] = i;
     charptrs[i] = numbers[i];
  }
```

(contd.)

Program Source Code 11.1 *(contd.)*

```
    // now let's print values which are stored in the array
    // objects
    cout << "The integers object has: ";
    for (i = 0; i < 5; i++)
    {
       cout << integers[i] << "  ";
    }
       cout << "\n The charptrs object has: ";
    for (i = 0; i < 5; i++)
    {
       cout << charptrs[i] << "  ";
    }
       cout << endl;
    return 0;
}
```

Output 11.1

```
constructor called
constructor called
The integers object has: 0  1  2  3  4
The charptrs object has: zero  one  two  three  four
destructor called
destructor called
```

In this example, we have implemented a generic class called Array<T> where T is the data type argument to be passed at the time instantiation of the class object. And we instantiated two object instances: (i) integers as an instance of class Array<int> and (ii) charptrs as an instance of class Array<char *>. In the main program we have used these two objects to assign values to the elements in the objects using overloaded index ([ ]) operator and print them. We have not implemented the generic Array class again and again for two different parameterized types. Without template support, we would have declared Array<int> class as, say, IntArray class such as the following:

```
class IntArray
{
  protected:
     int length;
     int * arr;
  public:
```

```
    Array(int size = 0); // constructor
    virtual ~Array();  // destructor
    int& operator [](int index); // overloaded index operator
};
```

We would have implemented its constructor, destructor and other functions and overloaded operators. Now, if we would like to use similar class for char * type, what methodogy we would have followed? We would have converted IntArray to CharPtrArray class with "int * arr" replaced by "char * * arr" in data area and "int & operator [] (int index)" member function replaced by "char * & operator [] (int index)" (through copy, paste, find, replace?). But the program grows in size with this duplication of effort. Now, what if we need to make some changes to the array implementation in some function, say the overloaded index ([ ]) operator? Its not a very easy task, since the code has been duplicated in many places. Reinventing source code is not an intelligent approach in an object-oriented environment, which encourages reusability. It seems to make more sense to implement an array that can contain any arbitrary type rather than duplicating code. How does one do that? The answer is to use data type parameterization, more commonly referred to as templates, which has been demonstrated in the previous example. C++ templates allow us to implement a generic Array<T> template that has a data type parameter T. T can be replaced with actual data types, for example, Array<int> or Array<char *>, and C++ will generate the class Array<int> or Array<char *>. Changing the implementation of the Array class becomes relatively simple and isolated in one class only. Once the changes are implemented in the template Array<T>, they are immediately reflected in the classes Array<int>, Array<char *> and the like.

Member Function Inclusion

Implementing template member functions is somewhat different compared to the regular class member functions. The declarations and definitions of the class template member functions should all be in the same header file (in the Program Source Code 11.1 array.hpp). The declarations and definitions need to be in the same header file. At the time of instantiations (in Program Source Code 11.1, as in testarr.cpp file), the compiler should have the declarations as well as definitions of the entire class template or function template.

Some compilers require that the entire template is implemented in a single .H or .HPP file, as it cannot cope with doing template method instantiation when template methods are defined in a separate .C or .CPP file.

Function Template

A function template allows to define a group of functions that look the same, except for the types of one or more of their arguments or objects. One must use all specified data type arguments in a function template in the argument list, or in the class qualifier for the function name. However, unlike class template, there is explicit specification of the data type of a template function argument when the template function is called.

Now, let's see an example of a function template. We have already seen an example on a class template named Array<T>, which represents a generic array class. Now, we will first define a simple generic swap function that interchanges two data. If we write a swap function for interchanging two integers, we would have written as follows:

```
void swap(int& a, int& b)
{
    int tmp;
    tmp = a;
    a = b;
    b = tmp;
}
```

Here, a and b are passed as reference (not value), and they can be changed from within the function body. With the help of a third local variable called ***temp***, we perform the interchange of these two variables a and b. Now, if we do want to write the similar swap function for two short numbers, or two character pointers (***char*** *) or any other data type, what we would have done, we would have copied, pasted, searched and replaced ***int*** to ***short*** or ***char*** *. And a better way of doing this is C++ function template as follows:

```
template <class T>
void swap(T& a, T& b)
{
    T tmp;
    tmp = a;
    a = b;
    b = tmp;
}
```

Here, T stands for a parameterized data type as it were in case of class template and swap becomes a function template.

A template function chooses the name of its function template, and the particular function to resolve a given template function call. It determines the name and the function by the type of the calling arguments. In the preceding example of swap, if variables x and y are of ***int*** type, the call swap(x,y) is effectively a call to swap(int& a, int& b). If variables x and y are of ***float*** type, the call, swap(x,y), is effectively a call to swap(float& a, float& b).

We can now see another relatively bigger example in Program Source Code 11.2 where we write a bubblesort function that sorts given sequence of values in nondecreasing order. The function takes two parameters (i) Array<T> object and (ii) size of the array, i.e. maximum number of elements that can be stored in Array<T> object. A bubblesort algorithms has two subtasks: (i) to find the largest value and (ii) to interchange it with ith value. The second subtask can be done through the swap function to interchange two given values. The first subtask can be solved by assuming the largest is Array[i], checking Array[i] with Array[i+1], Array[i+2], ... and whenever a larger element is found, it is swapped with Array[i] so that after swapping, Array[i] remains as `ith` large value in the list. We have two loops in the function. The first loop index (i) runs from value 0 to size - 2 whereas second loop index (j) runs from value i+1 to size - 1 so that when Array[i] and Array[j] are compared, the larger one remains in Array[i] (swapping is done if necessary) so that eventually Array[i], i = 0....size-1, remains as `ith` large value in the sequence. And, thus, we don't have to write bubblesort function again and again for different data types. We write the function once as a template function and reuse the source code for several data types. Isn't it nice? The code example follows with the sorted sequences given at the end:

```
4 > 3 > 2 > 1 > 0 and "four" > "three" > "two" > "one" > "zero"
```

For integer numbers, 4, 3, 2, the sorted sequence 4 > 3 > 2 > 1 > 0 can be explained easily, but how could you explain "four" > "three" or "three" > "two"? If you think of lexicographic order (as in dictionary), the word three appears after four and two appears after three. So, if we would have used the strcmp function to compare two strings, then the string values "two" > "three" > "four", then how do we get this sequence as sorted?, i.e. "four" > "three" > "two"? Hmmmm.....Are we comparing values of the strings "two, "three", "four"? No.... We are comparing values of character pointers (char *), i.e. these string values are stored in a local array named numbers, as

```
char *numbers[] = {"zero", "one", "two", "three", "four" };
```

When we compare numbers[0] and numbers[1], irrespective of the values of the contents, we are comparing pointer values numbers[0] and numbers[1], and as in contiguous array allocation rules, numbers[4] > numbers[3] > numbers[2] > numbers[1] > numbers[0]. Thus, if we would have stored strings "E", "D", "C", B", "A" in the array in sequence, then according to value of the pointers (not values of array elements), it is interpreted as "A" > "B" > "C" > "D" >

"E", more precisely, numbers[4] > numbers[3] > numbers[2] > numbers[1] > numbers[0], irrespective of the contents. That explains the result of the sorted sequence we get.

Program Source Code 11.2

ARRAY.HPP

```
.....as given in Program Source Code 11.1
```

TESTARR2.CPP

```
#include <iostream.h>
#include "array.hpp"

template <class T>
void swap(T& a, T& b)
{
   T tmp;
   tmp = a;
   a = b;
   b = tmp;
}

template <class T>
void bubblesort(Array<T> &arrayobj, int size)
{
   // sort in nondecreasing order using bubblesort algorithm
   int i, j;
   for (i = 0; i < size - 1; i++ )
   {
      // bubble through the list the (i+1)th largest value
      for (j = i+1; j < size; j++)
      {
         if (arrayobj[i] < arrayobj[j])
            swap(arrayobj[i], arrayobj[j]);
      }
   }
}

int main()
{
   int i;
   char *numbers[] = {"zero", "one", "two", "three",
                     "four"};
```

(contd.)

Program Source Code 11.2

```
// create instance of Array<int> and Array<char *>
// having 5 elements each
Array<int> integers(5); // array of 5 integers
Array<char *> charptrs(5); // array of 5 character
                           // pointers

// assign values to the elements in the array objects
for (i = 0; i < 5; i++)
{
   integers[i] = i;
   charptrs[i] = numbers[i];
}

// now let's print values which are stored in
// the array objects(before sorting)
cout << "The integers object has (before sorting): ";
     << endl;
for (i = 0; i < 5; i++)
{
   cout << integers[i] << "  ";
}
cout << "\n The charptrs object has (before sorting): ";
     << endl;
for (i = 0; i < 5; i++)
{
   cout << charptrs[i] << "  ";
}
cout << endl;

// now sort the two lists
bubblesort(integers, 5);
bubblesort(charptrs, 5);

// now let's print values which are stored in
// the array objects(after sorting)
cout << "The integers object has (after sorting): ";
     << endl;
for (i = 0; i < 5; i++)
{
   cout << integers[i] << "  ";
}
cout << "\n The charptrs object has (after sorting): ";
     << endl;
for (i = 0; i < 5; i++)
```

(*contd.*)

Program Source Code 11.2 *(contd.)*

```
    {
        cout << charptrs[i] << "  ";
    }
    cout << endl;

    return 0;
}
```

Output 11.2

```
constructor called
constructor called
The integers object has (before sorting):
0  1  2  3  4
The charptrs object has (before sorting):
zero  one  two  three  four
The integers object has (after sorting):
4  3  2  1  0
The charptrs object has (after sorting):
four  three  two  one  zero
destructor called
destructor called
```

Now, we can make some changes in the file TESTARR2.CPP in Program Code 11.3 (shown as bold in TESTARR3.CPP). The change in output is shown in bold. Now, we have two overloaded function named **less** that returns TRUE or FALSE depending on if the compared value one (parameter one) is less than value two (parameter two). For integer data comparison, it is same as the < operator, but for char * data comparison, it is not as < operator (where pointer values are compared), it's return value of strcmp function which compares two string values (not pointer values), and now we see changes in output as sorted string sequence as: "zero" > "two" > "three" > "one" > "four" (in order of appearance of words in dictionary).

Program Source Code 11.3
ARRAY.HPP

```
....as given before....
```

TESTARR3.CPP

```
#include <iostream.h>
#include "string.h"
#include "array.hpp"
```

(contd.)

Program Source Code 11.3 *(contd.)*

```
typedef enum Boolean {FALSE, TRUE};
Boolean less(const char * a, const char * b)
{
   return (strcmp(a,b) < 0)? TRUE : FALSE;
}
Boolean less(const int& a, const int& b)
{
   return (a<b)? TRUE : FALSE;
}

template <class T>
void swap(T& a, T& b)
{
...... // as before, no changes
}

template <class T>
void bubblesort(Array<T> &arrayobj, int size)
{
   // sort in nondecreasing order using
   // bubblesort algorithm
   int i, j;
   for (i = 0; i < size - 1; i++)
   {
      // bubble through the list the (i+1)th largest value
      for (j = i+1; j < size; j++)
      {
         if (less( arrayobj[i], arrayobj[j]))
            swap(arrayobj[i], arrayobj[j]);
      }
   }
}

int main()
{
   ...... // as before, no changes
}
```

```
Output 11.3
constructor called
constructor called
The integers object has (before sorting):
0  1  2  3  4
The charptrs object has (before sorting):
zero  one  two  three  four
The integers object has (after sorting):
4  3  2  1  0
The charptrs object has (after sorting):
zero  two  three  one  four
destructor called
destructor called
```

Parameter Values for Templates

In addition to the arguments preceded by ***class*** or ***typename*** keyword that represent a data type, class templates and function templates may include constant values as well. In the earlier example of class template Array<T>, we have taken the size of the array, i.e. number of elements in the constructor argument so as to decide how many elements we need to allocate in the Array<T> template class constructor. We could have taken that number as an argument to the template class as follows. The changes are shown in bold (Program Source Code 11.4). We have used a statically allocated array (predetermined size which is given through the template argument) instead of dynamically allocated array (size determined through argument passing in constructor call).

```
Program Source Code 11.4
ARRAY2.HPP
template <class T, int length>
class Array
{
   protected:
      T arr [length];
   public:
      Array();   // constructor
      virtual ~Array();  // destructor

      T& operator [](int index); // overloaded index
                                 // operator
};
```

(contd.)

Program Source Code 11.4 *(contd.)*

```
template <class T, int length>
Array<T,length> :: Array<T,length> ()
{
}

template <class T, int length>
Array<T,length> :: ~Array<T,length> ()
{
}

template <class T, int length>
T& Array<T,length> :: operator [] (int index)
{
   static T dummy;
   if ((index >= 0) && (index < length))
      return arr[index];
   else
   {
      cout << "Error: out of range" << endl;
      return dummy;
   }
}
```

TESTARR4.CPP

```
#include <iostream.h>
#include "array2.hpp"

int main()
{
   int i;
   char *numbers[] = { "zero", "one", "two", "three",
                       "four" };

   // create instance of Array<int> and Array<char *>
   // having 5 elements each
   Array<int,5> integers; // array of 5 integers
   Array<char *,5> charptrs; // array of 5 character
                             // pointers

   // assign values to the elements in the array objects
   for (i = 0; i < 5; i++)
```

(contd.)

Program Source Code 11.4 *(contd.)*

```
{
   integers[i] = i;
   charptrs[i] = numbers[i];
}
// now let's print values which are stored in the
// array objects
cout << "The integers object has: ";
for (i = 0; i < 5; i++)
{
   cout << integers[i] << " ";
}
cout << "\n The charptrs object has: ";
for (i = 0; i < 5; i++)
{
   cout << charptrs[i] << " ";
}
cout << endl;
return 0;
}
```

Output 11.4

```
The integers object has: 0 1 2 3 4
The charptrs object has: zero one two three four
```

The name of a template class is a compound name that consists of the template class name and the complete (not partial) template argument list that is enclosed in angular braces (< >). Any references to a template class must use this complete compound name. For example:

```
template <class T, int length>
class Array
{
   // ..... data and member functions
};
And, the object instances as:
   Array<int,5> integers; // valid
   Array<int> a; // Error: too few template arguments
   Array b; // Error: use of class template requires
            // template argument list
```

C++ requires this explicit naming convention to ensure that it can generate the appropriate class.

Now, we see another variation of TESTARR4.CPP and ARRAY2.HPP in TESTARR5.CPP and ARRAY3.HPP. This time we write a macro called **CallFunc** that takes two arguments FunctionName to be called as Function and Message to be printed as Message. The macro is defined as follows:

```
#define CallFunc(Function, Message) \
cout << "The integers (" #Message ") ... "; \
integers.Function(); \
cout << "The floats (" #Message ") ... "; \
floats.Function(); \
cout << "The charptrs (" #Message ") ... "; \
charptrs.Function(); \
cout << endl;
```

This calls the named function (passed as macro argument one) for three objects integers, floats and charptrs in sequence and each time before calling the Function, it prints a message like The integers(***)...., The floats(***)... etc. appropriately with the *** replaced by the message string passed (passed as macro argument two). Also, we have made a print() function as a member function of the template class to print its contents and also have made bubblesort() as a member function of the template class and made suitable changes accordingly. The template function ***less*** compares the arguments passed and returns TRUE or FALSE according to that argument one is less than argument two or not. For ***char**** variables, it compares pointer values (not the contents). The program listing follows (Program Source Code 11.5):

Program Source Code 11.5
ARRAY3.HPP

```
typedef enum Boolean {FALSE, TRUE};
template <class T> Boolean less(T a, T b)
{return (a<b)? TRUE : FALSE ;}

template <class T, int length>
class Array
{
  protected:
    T arr [length];
  public:
    Array();     // constructor
    virtual ~Array(); // destructor
    T& operator [](int index); // overloaded index operator
    void print();
    void bubblesort();
```

(*contd.*)

Program Source Code 11.5 *(contd.)*

```
};

template <class T, int length> Array<T,length> ::
Array<T,length> () {}

template <class T, int length> Array<T,length> ::
~Array<T,length> () {}

template <class T, int length>
T& Array<T,length> :: operator [] (int index)
{
   static T dummy;
   if ((index >= 0) && (index < length))
      return arr[index];
   else
   {
      cout << "Error: out of range" << endl;
      return dummy;
   }
}

template <class T, int length>
void Array<T,length> :: print()
{
   int i;
   for ( i = 0; i < length; i++)
      cout <<  arr[i] << "  ";
   cout << endl;
}

template <class T>
void swap(T& a, T& b)
{
   T tmp;
   tmp = a;
   a = b;
   b = tmp;
}

template <class T, int size>
void Array<T,size> :: bubblesort()
```

(contd.)

Program Source Code 11.5 (*contd.*)

```
{
   // sort in nondecreasing order using bubblesort algorithm
   int i, j;
   for (i = 0; i < size - 1; i++ )
   {
      // bubble through the list the (i+1)th largest value
      for (j = i+1; j < size; j++)
      {
         if ( less(this->arr[i], this->arr[j]))
            swap(this->arr[i], this->arr[j]);
      }
   }
}
```

TESTARR5.CPP

```
#include <iostream.h>
#include "string.h"
#include "array3.hpp"

#define CallFunc(Function, Message) \
   cout << "The integers (" #Message ") ... "; \
   integers.Function(); \
   cout << "The floats (" #Message ") ... "; \
   floats.Function(); \
   cout << "The charptrs (" #Message ") ... "; \
   charptrs.Function(); \
   cout << endl;

int main()
{
   int i;
   char *numbers[] = { "zero", "one", "two", "three",
                       "four" };

   // create instance of Array<int>, Array<float>,
   // Array<char *> having 5 elements
   Array<int,5> integers; // array of 5 integers
   Array<float,5> floats; // array of 5 floats
   Array<char *,5> charptrs; // array of 5 character pointers

   // assign values to the elements in the array objects
   for (i = 0; i < 5; i++)
```

(*contd.*)

Program Source Code 11.5 *(contd.)*

```
    {
        integers[i] = i;
        floats[i]= (float) i + 0.5;
        charptrs[i] = numbers[i];
    }

    // now let's print values which are stored in
    // the array objects(before sorting)
    CallFunc(print, before sorting);

    // now sort the two lists
    CallFunc(bubblesort, being sorted);

    // now let's print values which are stored in the array
    // objects(after sorting)
    CallFunc(print, after sorting);

    return 0;
}
```

Output 11.5

```
The integers (before sorting) ... 0  1  2  3  4
The floats (before sorting) ... 0.5  1.5  2.5  3.5  4.5
The charptrs (before sorting) .. zero  one two  three  four
The integers (being sorted) ... The floats (being sorted)
... The charptrs (being sorted) ...
The integers (after sorting) ... 4  3  2  1  0
The floats (after sorting) ... 4.5  3.5  2.5  1.5  0.5
The charptrs (after sorting) ... four  three  two  one  zero
```

It is also possible to set default values to any template parameter, similar to what is done in function parameters. Examples of some such are:

template <class T> // The commonly used parameter:
// one data type parameter.

template <class T, class U> // Two data type parameters.

template <class T, int N> // A data type parameter and
// an integer parameter.

template <class T = char> // One data type paremeter with
// a default value.

template <int Tfunc (int)> // A function with int argument,
// return type int as parameter.

```
template <class T=int, int length=10> class Array { ..... };
```

Then a declaration such as:

```
Array<> anArray;
```

would instantiate (at compile time) a 100 element Array template object named anArray of integer elements; this template class would be of type Array<int, 10>.

If you specify a default template parameter for any formal parameter, the rules are the same as for functions and default parameters. Once a default parameter is declared, all subsequent parameters must have defaults. Default arguments cannot be specified in a declaration or a definition of a specialization.

Template Specialization

A template specialization allows making specific implementations in a template when the pattern is a concrete type. Say, in the previous example, we would like to provide an overloaded function template implementation for less applicable to ***char**** variables. We would like to compare the contents (not just pointer values as stated in the generic template function). To specialize, we add the following template function applicable to ***char**** arguments:

```
template <>
Boolean less<char *>(char *a, char * b)
{
    return (strcmp(a,b) < 0)? TRUE : FALSE;
}
```

The template specialization, as part of the template definition, must begin with the empty template declaration template <>. After the template class or function name which we need to specialize, we must include the type that is being specialized enclosed between angle-brackets <>, e.g. less<char *>. If we specialize a class template, we must also define all the members required to support the specialization (even if the generic implementation is the same, because no member is inherited from the generic template to the specialization). An example follows (Program Source Code 11.6).

Program Source Code 11.6
ARRAY4.HPP

```
#include "array3.hpp"
template <>
Boolean less<char *>(char *a, char * b)
{
   return (strcmp(a,b) < 0)? TRUE : FALSE ;
}
```

TESTARR6.CPP

```
  #include <iostream.h>
#include "string.h"
#include "array4.hpp"

#define CallFunc(Function, Message) \
........ < rest of the program as in TESTARR5.CPP" >
.......
```

Output 11.6

```
The integers (before sorting) ... 0  1  2  3  4
The floats (before sorting) ... 0.5  1.5  2.5  3.5  4.5
The charptrs (before sorting) ... zero  one  two  three  four

The integers (being sorted) ... The floats (being sorted)
... The charptrs (being sorted) ...
The integers (after sorting) ... 4  3  2  1  0
The floats (after sorting) ... 4.5  3.5  2.5  1.5  0.5
The charptrs (after sorting) ... zero  two  three  one  four
```

See the differences in the charptrs (after sorting): It is sorted on the values of the contents (through specialized template function `less<char *>`), not on the pointer values (not like the generic template function `less<T>` implementation).

Some compilers also allow partial template specializations. A partial specialization matches a given actual template argument list if the template arguments of the partial specialization can be deduced from the actual template argument list.

Template Inheritance

Template classes can be inherited similar to normal classes. An example program is given in Program Source Code 11.7. We define a template class Stack<T, Size> inherited from template class Array<T, Size> (as defined in ARRAY3.HPP). A stack is an ordered list in which all insertions and deletions are made at one end. The restrictions on a stack imply that if five integers 0, 1, 2, 3, 4 are inserted to the stack one by one, then 4 occupies the topmost position. It has to be removed first before any other element (following a Last-In-First-Out, i.e. LIFO manner). Instead of rewriting the entire Stack<T, Size> from scratch, we inherit from template class Array<T, Size> through private inheritance so that Stack objects and its derivatives are forced to use the underlying array in LIFO order only (using array, anybody can access any of the contents through publicly accessible overloaded index operator i.e. [ ]). Stack class has two additional data members: (i) maximum stack size which is MaxSize (initialized through template parameter Size) and (ii) stack pointer index sp, which is initialized to –1. Stack class provides two public interfaces: (i) push and (ii) pop. The function push takes an argument and inserts the element in desired position (by incrementing the stack pointer), and fails if the stack is full (stack pointer index matching the maximum permissible value). The pop function fails if the stack is empty (stack pointer = –1). Otherwise, it returns the topmost element in the stack (pointed to by the stack pointer index sp) and decrements stack pointer index sp to indicate the topmost element has been popped.

Program Source Code 11.7

ARRAY3.HPP

```
....as given in Program Source Code 11.6
```

STACK.HPP

```
#include "array3.hpp"

template <class T, int Size>
class Stack: private Array<T,Size>
{
        int sp;
        int MaxSize;
    public:
        Stack(): Array<T,Size>()
        {
            sp = -1;
            MaxSize = Size;
        };
        ~Stack(){};
```

(*contd.*)

Program Source Code 11.7 *(contd.)*

```
    Boolean push(const T&);
    Boolean pop(T &);
    void print();
};

template <class T, int Size>
Boolean Stack<T,Size> :: push(const T & data)
{
  if (sp == Size) // stack full
    return FALSE;
  this->arr[++sp] = data;
  return TRUE;
}

template <class T, int Size>
Boolean Stack<T,Size> :: pop(T & data)
{
  if (sp == -1) // stack empty
    return FALSE;
  data = this->arr[sp–];
  return TRUE;
}

template <class T, int Size>
void Stack<T,Size> :: print()
{
  int i;
  if (sp == -1)
  {
    cout << "Stack Empty" << endl;
    return;
  }
  for (i = 0; i <= sp; i++)
    cout <<  arr[i] << "  ";
  cout << endl;
}
```

TSTSTACK.CPP

```
#include <iostream.h>
#include "string.h"
```

(contd.)

Program Source Code 11.7 *(contd.)*

```
#include "stack.hpp"

int main()
{
   int i;
   int a;
   float b;
   char * c;
   char *numbers[] = { "zero", "one", "two", "three",
                       "four" };

   // create instance of Array<int>, Array<float>,
   // Array<char *> having 5 elements
   Stack<int,5> integers; // array of 5 integers
   Stack<float,5> floats; // array of 5 floats
   Stack<char *,5> charptrs; // array of 5 character
                             // pointers

   // assign values to the elements in the array objects
   for (i = 0; i < 5; i++)
   {
      integers.push(i);
      floats.push((float) i + 0.5);
      charptrs.push(numbers[i]);
   }

   // now let's print values which are stored in the stacks
   // cout << "The contents of integers stack"
   // "(after five pushes): " << endl;
   integers.print();
   cout << "The contents of floats stack"
        << "(after five pushes): " << endl;
   floats.print();
   cout << "The contents of charptrs stack"
        << "(after five pushes): "<< endl;
   charptrs.print();

   integers.pop(a);  integers.pop(a);  integers.pop(a);
   floats.pop(b);    floats.pop(b);
   charptrs.pop(c);
```

(contd.)

Program Source Code 11.7 *(contd.)*

```
    // now let's print values which are stored in the stacks
    cout << "The contents of integers stack"
         << "(after three pops): "<< endl;
    integers.print();
    cout << "The contents of floats stack"
         << "(after two pops): "<< endl;
    floats.print();
    cout << "The contents of charptrs stack
         << "(after one pop): "<< endl;
    charptrs.print();

    return 0;
}
```

Output 11.7

```
The contents of integers stack (after five pushes):
0 1 2 3 4
The contents of floats stack (after five pushes):
0.5 1.5 2.5 3.5 4.5
The contents of charptrs stack (after five pushes):
zero one two three four
The contents of integers stack (after three pops):
0 1
The contents of floats stack (after two pops):
0.5 1.5 2.5
The contents of charptrs stack (after one pop):
zero one two three
```

Namespace

Sometimes, we encounter same names of functions or classes with varied implementations in different context. How can we avoid name clash? Namespace is the answer to this question. A namespace is purely a syntactic notation. A namespace declaration identifies and assigns a name to a region of declarations.

If we enclose one or more declarations in

```
namespace name {declarations}
```

thereby we can "attach" the given name to each name declared in the declarations. Such names are then considered different from the same names defined in other namespaces. A namespace can contain data and function declarations.

Named Namespace

A namespace attaches an additional identifier name to any names declared inside its declarative region. The identifier in a namespace declaration must be unique in the declarative region in which it is used. The identifier is the name of the namespace and is used to reference its members. It becomes then possible to use the same name in separate namespaces without conflict even if the names appear in the same translation unit. As long as they appear in separate namespaces, each name will be unique because of the addition of the namespace identifier.

If a varible x is defined in namespace A, the most direct way to refer to that variable x from outside A is using the scope variable using the namespace like A::x. From inside A, however, no such scope resolution is necessary. Here's one example:

EXAMPLE 11.1:

```
namespace A
{
   int  x;
   void func() // Defining A:: func()
   {
      x = 100; // A::x = 100
   }
}
namespace B
{
   int  x;
   void func() // Defining B:: func()
   {
      x = 200; // B::x = 200
   }
}
   int x;
   void func()
   {
   x = 300; // x under global scope, same as ::x
   A::x = 400;
   B::x = 500;
   A::func();
   B::func();
}
```

Using Named Namespace

We can also make the contents of a namespace available in the current context as follows:

```
using A::x; // mention single name => x refers to
            // A::x within the current scope
using namespace A; // all names from A are available
                   // without further notice
```

However, making same name available more than once can give rise to ambiguity, for example, if we say,

```
int x;
void func()
{
   using namespace A;
   x = 300; // Ambiguous : which x? ::x (global ) or A::x?
}
```

Members of a named namespace can be defined outside the namespace in which they are declared by explicit qualification of the name being defined. However, the entity being defined must already be declared in the namespace. In addition, the definition must appear after the point of declaration in a namespace that encloses the declaration's namespace (See Example 11.2).

EXAMPLE 11.2:

```
namespace A
{
   namespace B
   {
      void func();
   }
}

void A::func() { }      // ok
void B::func2() { }     // error, func2() is not yet a member of B

namespace B
{
   void func2(); // ok, can add declarations to the namespace B
}
```

The standard library puts all its names in a namespace called **std**, to avoid name clashes with user-defined names. Thus, alternate versions of standard library can be used by changing the name in namespace in a single place only.

Namespace Alias

A namespace-alias is an alternative name for a namespace. A namespace-alias-definition declares an alternate name for a namespace. The identifier is a synonym for the qualified-namespace-specifier and becomes a namespace-alias. For example,

```
namespace a_very_long_namespace_name { ... }
namespace SHNAM = a_very_long_namespace_name;
// SHNAM is now a namespace-alias for
// a_very_long_namespace_name.
```

A namespace-name cannot be identical to any other entity in the same declarative region. In addition, a global namespace-name cannot be the same as any other global entity name in a given program.

Unnamed Namespace

An unnamed-namespace-definition behaves as if it were replaced by:

```
namespace unique {namespace-body}
using namespace unique;
```

Each unnamed namespace has an identifier, represented by unique, that differs from all other identifiers in the entire program, as in the following:

EXAMPLE 11.3:

```
namespace { int x; }          // unique::x
void func1(){x++;}           // unique::x++

namespace A
{
   namespace
   {
      int x;       // A::unique::x
      int y;       // A::unique::y
   }
}
```

```
using namespace A;
void func2()
{
   x++;          //error: ambiguous : unique::x or A::unique::x ?
   A::x++;       //error: A::x undefined
   y++;          // A::unique::y++
}
```

Unnamed namespaces are a superior replacement for the static declaration of variables. They allow variables and functions to be visible within an entire translation unit, yet not visible externally. Although entities in an unnamed namespace might have external linkage, they are effectively qualified by a name unique to their translation unit and therefore can never be seen from any other translation unit.

EXCEPTION HANDLING

When a program runs, there could be situations where program fails to continue running because of some unusual circumstances. The situations could be failure to do something, say, to allocate memory, to open file, or to perform something. A good application should have the capability to recover gracefully from unexpected errors. When an error occurs, the application may need to request user intervention, or it may be able to recover without user intervention. In extreme cases, the application may need to be terminated. Generally speaking, a program (basically the main function in C++), or more specifically a particular function, may have three different outcomes when they are done. They may

1. return on normal route on success as well as failure;
2. return on erroneous execution leading to abnormal termination; or
3. return on exceptional conditions leading to some recovery done before normal route of return to the caller or abnormal termination.

The function may return to the caller on successful completion. This is termed as return on normal route. Some functions usually return an outcome code to the caller indicating the particular outcome (from a predefined set of expected outcomes) of the function. The outcome code may indicate success or a particular error code may indicate failure to achieve success because of unavailability or failure of something. Whatever be the return code (indicating success or failure), it is termed as normal return because the outcome is one of the predetermined set of possible outcomes, for example, the function declared in standard header file <string.h> as "char* **strcpy**(char* s, const char* ct)" which copies string ct to s including terminating NULL character.

The return value from **strcpy** function is the destination string s. There is no return value reserved to indicate an error. Thus, in normal execution, when things go normally, it's fine, but if the source or destination character pointers are NULL pointers, then there is no check for errors and at runtime erroneous behaviour will be encountered. Now, let's take another example—the function declared in standard header file <stdio.h> as "FILE* **fopen**(const char* Filename, const char* Mode)" which tries to open file Filename and returns a stream, or NULL on failure. Mode may be (combinations of): "r", "w", "a", "r+", "w+" and "a+". Returning a null pointer value indicates an error. In user-defined functions, we may define set of predetermined return codes including success and failure codes. Imagine, we write a function called CheckValidData() and our intention is to do the following in sequence: (i) allocate an integer pointer that could hold 5 integers, failing which return 1; (ii) open a named file in binary read mode, failing which return 2; (iii) read 5 integers from the opened file, failing which return 3; (iv) check if first integer read is equal to a predetermined value say 999 or not, failing which return 4; (v) return success code 0 indicating that we have valid data in the named file. Thus, we have 5 different set of return codes from the functions (predetermined set):

0 => success, we have valid data in the named file

1 => memory allocation failed to allocate space for 5 integers

2 => memory allocation was successful, but named file opening failed

3 => memory allocation as well as file open were successful, but reading 5 integers from the file failed

4 => memory allocation, file open, reading 5 integers all were successful, but first integer read was wrong indicating wring set of data

Let us study the Example (11.4).

EXAMPLE 11.4:

```
int  CheckValidData()
{
  int *pa, b;
  FILE *pf;
  // allocate space for 5 integers for pointer pa
  pa = new int[5];
  if (pa == NULL) // memory allocation failed
  return 1;
```

```
//tries to open named file in binary read mode
  pf = fopen("xyz.dat", "rb");
if (pf == NULL)
{
  // file open failed, no point of holding memory
  // allocated in pointer pa
  delete [] pa;
  return 2;
 }
  // attempts to read 5 integers
  b = fread(pa, sizeof(int), 5, pf);
 if (b < 5)
 {
  // attempt to read 5 integers failed,
  // no point holding pa and pf
  delete [] pa;
  fclose(pf);
  return 3;
}
else
{
  // we could successfully read 5 integers
  if (pa[0] != 999)
  {
     // first integer read should be 999, if not,
     // we opened a wrong file
      // no point holding pa and pf
     delete [] pa;
     fclose(pf);
     return 4;
    }
  }
  // success at last! we are done, return success code 0
  // and freepa, close pf
  fclose(pf);
  delete [] pa;
  return 0;
}
```

Many programmers followed this type of success or error handling through normal route of return from function. But this sounds very clumsy, isn't it?

Return on erroneous execution occurs when the caller makes some mistake in passing parameters to the calling function (not just syntax error, because that is caught by the compiler) or calls the function in an inappropriate context. This situation causes an error, and it should be detected by an assertion during program development. The **assert** macro (declared in <assert.h>) prints a diagnostic error message when a predefined expression evaluates to FALSE or 0 and calls system call "abort" to terminate program execution. No action is taken if the predefined expression evaluates to TRUE or non-zero value. The diagnostic message includes the failed expression and the name of the source file and line number where the assertion failed. We usually use the assert macro to indicate a fatal error, where program cannot continue any further and we would like to terminate the program execution. For example, in the earlier example, we could have decided that memory allocation failure is a fatal problem, thereafter, program execution should not continue any further. Whereas, other errors like file-opening failure, failure to read desired number of integers, or wrong integer at wrong place all were not that fatal. They are errors indeed, but not that fatal, and program execution may continue just after returning some predetermined error code to the caller so that the caller may take appropriate action. So, memory allocation failure which was considered to be very fatal, could have been written as :

```
// Assertion fails if memory allocation failed
   assert(pa == NULL);
```

instead of

```
if (pa == NULL) // memory allocation failed
        return 1;
```

Return on abnormal execution or exceptional conditions include situations where the exceptional conditions are outside the control of the program, such as low memory or I/O errors. Abnormal situations should be handled by catching and throwing exceptions. Using exceptions is especially appropriate for abnormal execution. Exception handling enables a function that encounters an unusual situation to throw an exception and pass control to a direct or indirect caller of that function. The caller may or may not be able to handle the exception. A handler is a code that intercepts an exception. Regardless of whether or not the caller can handle an exception, it that may rethrow the exception, that so another handler can intercept it.

Traditional error handling often makes the code more complicated and confusing. C++ separates the details of unexpected error from the main work of the program. The resulting code is clearer to read and therefore have fewer burdens to debug.

C++ provides three language constructs to implement exception handling:

1. *try* blocks—denotes an exception block where exceptions can be generated
2. *catch* blocks—"catches" exceptions to handle recovery
3. *throw* expressions—"throws" exceptions

In a function enclosed within *try* block, a *throw* expression can raise any exceptional situation, by throwing an object (the object that caused the exception, or an object that was constructed when the exception occurred) to pass information back to the caller. If a *catch* block is written as the exception handler, the raised exceptions are caught to handle the recovery mechanism. Now, we rewrite the function CheckValidData using try-catch blocks. We enclose our error checks within try block and error handling (closing of file and/or deallocating memory) is done within catch block. When throw is executed, the try block ends and every object created within the try block is destroyed. After that the control goes to the corresponding catch block. Finally, the program continues right after the catch block. In this case, return code (see Example 11.5).

EXAMPLE 11.5:

```
int CheckValidData()
{
   int *pa, b;
   FILE *pf;
   try
   {
      // allocate space for 5 integers for pointer pa
      pa = new int[5];
      if (pa == NULL) // memory allocation failed
         throw 1;

      // tries to open named file in binary read mode
      pf = fopen("xyz.dat", "rb");

      if (pf == NULL) // file open failed
         throw 2;

      // attempts to read 5 integers
      b = fread(pa, sizeof(int), 5, pf);
      if (b < 5) // attempt to read 5 integers failed
         throw 3;
```

```
    else if (pa[0] != 999)
    {
        // first integer != 999 => we opened
        // a wrong file
            throw 4;
    }
        // success at last! we are done,
        // return success code 0 throw 0;
}
catch(int code)
{
    switch (code)
    {
        case 3:
        case 4:
        case 0:
            // break statement purposefully omitted
            fclose(pf); // close file if code != 1 or 2
        case 2:
            // break statement purposefully omitted
            delete [] pa; // deallocate memory if code != 1
        default:
             // case 1, memory allocation failed
*       break;
    }
}
return code;
}
```

The syntax used by *throw* is similar to that of return. The *catch* block must be placed right after the *try* block without including any other code in between. The *catch* block accepts parameter of any valid type (including C++ objects).

Capturing Matching Typed Exception through Overloaded *Catch* Blocks

Catch can be overloaded to accept different types of parameters. In that case the matching *catch* block is executed (the one that matches with the type of the exception sent i.e. the parameter of *throw*). If more than one *catch* blocks is placed immediately following the *try* block, each *catch* block identifies what type of objects it can *catch* obeying the following rules:

1. If the thrown object matches the parameter of the first *catch* expression, control goes to that particular *catch* block.

2. If the thrown object does not match the parameter of the first *catch* block, subsequent *catch* blocks are searched for a matching type.
3. If no match is found, the search is continued in all enclosing *try* blocks, and then in the code that called the current function.
4. If no match is found after all *try* blocks are searched, a call to terminate() is made to terminate the program. An example program follows (Program Source Code 11.8).

Program Source Code 11.8

```
#include <iostream.h>
#include <string.h>

#define MAX_LENGTH 30

class MyException
{
      char Error[MAX_LENGTH];
   public:
      MyException(char * a)
      {
         cout << "MyException constructor called" << endl;
         // maximum of MAX_LENGTH characters are copied
         strncpy(Error, a, MAX_LENGTH - 1);
         Error[MAX_LENGTH-1] = '\0';
      };
      MyException(const MyException & arg)
      {
         cout << "MyException copy constructor called" << endl;
         strcpy(Error, arg.Error);
      };
      ~MyException()
       {cout << "MyException destructor called" << endl;};
       const char *ShowError() const
      {
         return Error;
      }
};

class TestException
```

(contd.)

Program Source Code 11.8 *(Contd.)*

```
{
  public:
    TestException();
    ~TestException();
};

TestException::TestException()
{
   cout << "TestException constructor called" << endl;
}

TestException::~TestException()
{
   cout << "TestException destructor called" << endl;
}

void TestFunc()
{
  TestException e;
  cout << "In TestFunc(). Throwing exception object  MyException"
      << endl;
  throw MyException("TestFunc: Thrown exception");
}

int main()
{
  cout << "Main program started... try block about to start"
      << endl;
  try
  {
  cout << "Inside main function's try block...calling TestFunc()"
      << endl;
  TestFunc(); // control goes from here,
              // because of a throw exception call
  cout  << "Inside main function's try block...raising exception 1"
        << endl;
  throw 1;// raising another exception 1-not called
          // as control doesnot come here
  }
```

(contd.)

Program Source Code 11.8 (*contd.*)

```
  catch(MyException E)
  {
     cout << "Inside first catch handler : caught MyException object"
          << endl;
     cout << E.ShowError() << endl;
  }
  catch(int code)
  {
     cout << "Inside second catch handler:caught exception code: "
          << code << endl;
  }
 cout << "Main program returning.. outside try.catch blocks"
     << endl;
 return 0;
}
```

Output 11.8

```
Main program started... try block about to start
Inside main function's try block...calling TestFunc()
TestException constructor called
In TestFunc(). Throwing exception object MyException
MyException constructor called
MyException copy constructor called
TestException destructor called
Inside first catch handler: caught MyException object
TestFunc: Thrown exception
MyException destructor called
MyException destructor called
Main program returning.. outside try.catch blocks
```

Ellipsis in *Catch* Block

We can also define a *catch* block that captures all the exceptions independently of the type used in the call to *throw*. We use ellipsis (three dots i.e. ...) as the parameter of the *catch* block.

```
try
{
   // code here
}
catch (...)
{
   cout << "Some exception occurred";
}
```

The *catch* block with ellipsis handles all types of exceptions, including memory protection faults, divide-by-zero, and floating-point violations. An *ellipsis catch handler* must be the last handler for its *try* block.

Nested *Try-Catch* Blocks

Try-catch blocks can be nested. If a *throw* occurs in a function called by an inner *try* block, the control is transferred outward through the nested *try* blocks until it finds the first *catch* block whose argument matches the argument of the *throw* expression. For example:

```
try
{
   // some code here
   try
   {
      // some other code here
   }
   catch (int n)
   {
      throw; // rethrow to outer handler
   }
}
catch (...) // catch all
{
   cout << "Some exception occurred";
}
```

Rethrowing an Exception

If a *catch* block cannot handle the particular exception it has caught, it can be rethrown. The *rethrow* expression (throw with no argument), causes the originally thrown object to be rethrown. The exception handler has already caught the exception at the scope in which the *rethrow* expression occurs. Consequently, the exception is *rethrown* to the next dynamically enclosing try block. Therefore, *catch* blocks at the scope in which the *rethrow* expression occurred cannot handle it. Any *catch* blocks following the dynamically enclosing *try* block have an opportunity to *catch* the exception.

Conditional Expression in a *Throw* Expression

A conditional expression can be used in a throw expression as:

throw (a == 4 ? 3 : 4)

This *throws* 4 or 4 depending on a is equal to 4 or not.

Constructors and Destructors in Exception Handling

When an exception is thrown, control is passed to a *catch* block immediately following the *try* block. Destructors are called for all automatic objects constructed since the beginning of the *try* block that has a direct association with that catch block. If an exception is thrown during construction of an object that consists of subobjects or array elements, calls are made to *destructors* for those subobjects or array elements that are successfully constructed before the program *throws* the exception. A *destructor* is usually called for a local static object only if the program has successfully constructed the object.

Run-time Standard Exceptions

Some functions of the standard C++ language library send exceptions that can be captured when included within a *try* block. These exceptions are of a class derived from std::exception class. This class (std::exception) is defined in the C++ standard header file `<exception>` and serves as pattern for the standard hierarchy of exceptions. One can use the classes of standard hierarchy of exceptions to throw already defined exceptions or derive new exception classes from it. The exception *bad_alloc* is thrown by new operator on failure to allocate memory. The exception *bad_cast* is thrown by *dynamic_cast* when fails with a referenced type. The exception *bad_exception* is thrown when an exception doesn't match any catch. The exception *bad_typeid* is thrown by typeid. The exception *ios_base::failure* is thrown by *ios::clear*. The exception hierarchy of predefined classes are given here as Figure 11.1.

ADVANCED CASTING OPERATORS

Cast operators are used to convert from one type to another type. Some conversions are implicit, performed automatically by the compiler without programmer intervention. The standard C++ conversions and user-defined conversions are performed implicitly by the compiler wherever and whenever needed. Standard conversions are used for following type conversions (we had stated this before):

enum->int	short->int	char->int
int->unsigned int	unsigned int->long	long->unsigned long
unsigned long->float	float->double	double->long double

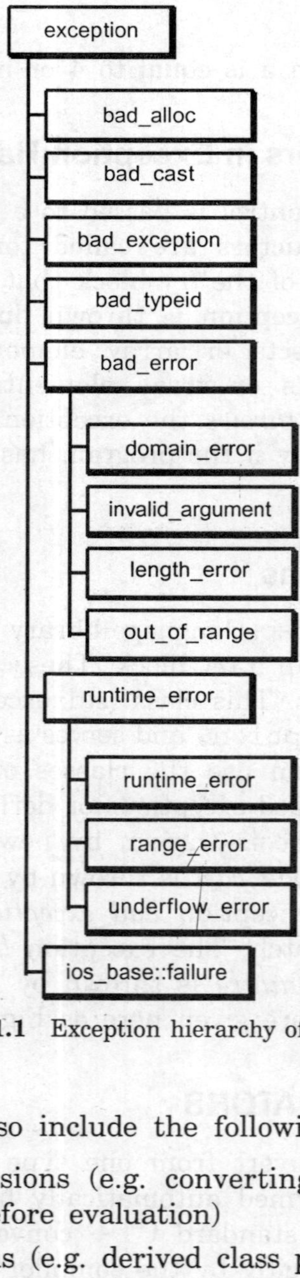

Figure 11.1 Exception hierarchy of predefined classes.

Standard conversions also include the following:

1. arithmetic conversions (e.g. converting operands to the type of the widest operand before evaluation)
2. pointer conversions (e.g. derived class pointer to base class pointer)
3. reference conversions (e.g. derived class reference to base class reference)
4. pointer-to-member conversions (e.g. from pointer to member of a base class to pointer to member of a derived class).

Explicit conversions need to be specified explicitly by the programmer.

A user-defined conversion from a class X to a class Y can be done in two ways:

1. by providing a constructor for class Y that takes an X as an argument: Y(const X& x), or,
2. by providing a class X with a conversion operator: operator Y().

When a type is needed for an expression that cannot be obtained through an implicit conversion, or when more than one standard conversion creates an ambiguous situation, the programmer must explicitly specify the target type of the conversion. For example, for the conversion of class X to class Y, if we provided both (i) Y::Y(const X& x) and (ii) X::operator Y() we have the following conversions:

```
X  x;
Y  y;
Y  y1 = x; // X->Y conversion required. through Y::Y? or X::operator Y()?
```

To resolve this ambiguous situation, we need to explicitly specify the conversion like:

```
Y  y1 = (Y) x; // X::operator Y() is used then Y::operator =(const Y&) is used
```

or

```
Y  y2 = Y(x); // Y::Y(const X&) is used then Y::operator =(const Y&) is used
```

The old C-style casts have the following shortcomings:

1. The syntax is the same for every casting operation, making it impossible for the compiler (or users) to tell the intended purpose of the cast. Is it a cast from a base class pointer to a derived class pointer? Does the cast remove the “constness” of the object? Or, is it a conversion of one type to a completely unrelated type? The truth is, it is impossible to tell from the syntax. As a result, this makes the cast harder to comprehend, not only by humans, but also, by compilers which are unable to detect improper casts.
2. The C-style casts are hard to find. Parentheses with an identifier between them are used all over C++ programs. There is no easy way to search a source file to get a list of all the casts being performed.
3. Old C-style cast allows to cast practically any type to any other type. Improper use of casts can lead to disastrous results. The old C-style casts have created a few holes in the C type system and have also been a source of confusion for both programmers and compilers. Even in

C++, the old C-style casts are retained for backwards compatibility. However, using the new C++ style casting operators will make programs more readable, less error-prone and type-safe, and easier to maintain.

New cast operators have been introduced in C++ language. They are:

- *static_cast*—to convert one type to another type
- *dynamic_cast*—for safe navigation of an inheritance hierarchy
- *reinterpret_cast*—to perform type conversions on un-related types
- *const_cast*—to cast away the "const-ness" or "volatile-ness" of a type

static_cast Operator

The static_cast operator takes the form

```
static_cast<data type> (expression)
```

to convert the given expression to mentioned data type. Such conversions rely solely on static (compile-time) type information.

In general, static_cast can be used to perform arithmetic conversions (e.g. convert an int to an enum) and/or between two classes X and Y within the same class hierarchy to convert

1. a base class pointer X * to a derived class pointer Y *
2. a reference of type X& to another reference of type Y&
3. an object of type X to an object of type Y
4. a pointer-to-member to another pointer-to-member

Such conversions are not always safe and not always implicit type conversions as well. For example, if X is a direct base class of Y, derived class pointer (Y *) to base class pointer (X *) conversion is implicit as well as safe. However, the converse is not implicit and may not be safe, in case base class pointer (X *) does not point to a complete Y class.

```
class X {};
class Y: public X {};
X * px1 = new X;
X * px2 = new Y;
Y * py1 = static_cast<Y *>(px1); // unsafe
Y * py2 = static_cast<Y *>(px2);  // safe
```

The pointer px1 does not point to a complete Y class. Yet, conversion to py1 (pointer to Y type) is allowed because of the static_cast operator. px2 to py2 conversion is safe, as px2 points to a complete Y class. In general, a complete type can be converted to another type so long as some type conversion sequence is provided by the language.

static_cast operator can also be used to perform standard arithmetic conversions, as shown in Program Source Code 11.9.

Program Source Code 11.9

```
#include <iostream.h>

typedef  enum GRADE {E, D, C, B, A};

void PrintGrade(GRADE arg)
{
   switch (arg)
   {
      case A : cout << "Grade A" << endl; break;
      case B : cout << "Grade B" << endl; break;
      case C : cout << "Grade C" << endl; break;
      case D : cout << "Grade D" << endl; break;
      case E : cout << "Grade E" << endl; break;
      default : cout << "Illegal Grade" << endl; break;
   }
}
int main()
{
   int      X = 100, Y = 3;
   GRADE    g = static_cast<GRADE>(Y);
   double   XbyY1 = X/Y;
   double   XbyY2 = static_cast<double> (X)/Y;
   cout << "X / Y = " << XbyY1 << endl;
   cout << "static_cast<double> (X) / Y = " << XbyY2 << endl;
   cout << "static_cast<GRADE>(" << Y <<") => ";
   PrintGrade(g);
   return 0;
}
```

Output 11.9

```
X/Y = 33
static_cast<double> (X)/Y = 33.3333
static_cast<GRADE>(3) => Grade B
```

One interesting side effect of the old C-style casts, was to gain access to a private base class of a derived class. Study the following:

EXAMPLE 11.6:

```
class X
{
      int x;
   public:
      X():x(0){};
      ~X();
      int  GetData() const {return x;}
};

class Y: private X // privately inherited
{
   public:
      Y():X(){};
};

void f()
{
   int i;
   Y * py = new Y;
   X * px1, * px2;

   px1 = (X * ) py; // Warning : Y * to X * is allowed
                    // but is inaccessible (private base)
   px2 = static_cast<X *>(py); // Error: static_cast to private
                               // base class pointer disallowed
   i = py->GetData();   // cannot access public member declared
                        // in class 'X' through Y
   i = px1->GetData(); // oops... access data ..allowed though
                        // side-effect....should we allow?
   i = px2->GetData(); // px2 was not allowed to have
                        // static_cast, thus prevents
                        // data access
}
```

The old C-style casts allows casting from one incomplete type to another! static_cast operator does not allow this. For example:

```
class X; // incomplete
class Y; // incomplete
```

```
void f(X* x)
{
   Y* y = (Y*) x;  // works!
   Y* y2 = static_cast <Y*> x;  // fails!
}
```

dynamic_cast Operator

The dynamic_cast operator takes the form

```
dynamic_cast<data type> (expression)
```

to convert the given expression to mentioned data type. The conversions are meant for pointer or reference type conversions within a class hierarchy. The *dynamic_cast* operator can be used to cast from a derived class pointer to a base class pointer, cast a derived class pointer to another derived (sibling) class pointer, or cast a base class pointer to a derived class pointer. Each of these conversions may also be applied to references. In addition, any pointer may also be cast to a ***void****.

The *dynamic_cast* operator is actually a part of C++'s run-time type information or RTTI sub-system. It has been provided for use with polymorphic classes which have at least one virtual function. *static_cast* operator can be used to perform conversions between non-polymorphic classes. All of the derived to base conversions are performed using the static (compile-time) type information. These conversions may, therefore, be performed on both non-polymorphic and polymorphic types. These conversions will produce the same result if they are converted using a *static_cast* operator.

```
class X {};
class Y: public X {};

void f()
{
   X * px1 = new X;
   Y * py1 = dynamic_cast<Y *>(px1); // Error: 'X' is not a
                                     // polymorphic type
}
```

Another example follows as Program Source Code 11.10. We can use a *dynamic_cast* operator to check that the cast was successful. In case of unsafe conversions (base class pointer to derived class pointer), when not pointing to complete derived object, *dynamic_cast* results in a NULL pointer; *static_cast* does not do so.

Program Source Code 11.10

```
#include <iostream.h>
#include <exception>

class X // polymorphic class
{
   int x;
   public:
      X():x(0){};
      virtual ~X(){};
      virtual void vf1(){};
};
class Y: public X
{
   public:
      Y():X(){};
      ~Y(){};
};

int main()
{
   try
   {
      X * px1 = new X();
      X * px2 = new Y();
      Y * py1, *py2;

      cout << "initially : px1 = " << px1 << " , px2 = " << px2 << endl;
      py1 = dynamic_cast<Y*>(px1);
      py2 = dynamic_cast<Y*>(px2);
      cout << "Result of dynamic_cast :" << endl;
      cout << "py1 = px1 gets " << py1 << " , py2 = px2 gets " << py2;

      py1 = static_cast<Y*>(px1);
      py2 = static_cast<Y*>(px2);
      cout << "\n Result of static_cast : " << endl;
      cout << "py1 = px1 gets " << py1 << " , py2 = px2 gets " << py2;
   }
   catch (std::exception& e)
   {
      cout << "Exception occurred: " << e.what();
   }
   return 0;
}
```

```
Output 11.10
initially: px1 = 0x00420CE0, px2 = 0x00420D10
Result of dynamic_cast:
py1 = px1 gets 0x00000000, py2 = px2 gets 0x00420D10
Result of static_cast:
py1 = px1 gets 0x00420CE0, py2 = px2 gets 0x00420D10
```

conversion of px1 to py1 was unsafe. Thus the dynamic_cast results in a NULL pointer.

reinterpret_cast Operator

The `reinterpret_cast` operator takes the form

```
reinterpret_cast<data type> (expression)
```

to convert the given expression to mentioned data type. This allows conversions between two unrelated types like a pointer of one type to that of another type and casting from pointer to an integer type and vice versa. The operation makes a simple binary copy of the value from one type to the other. The content pointed does not pass any kind of check or transformation between types. The result of the conversion is usually implementation dependent and, therefore, not likely to be portable. One should use this type of cast only when felt absolutely necessary.

An example (11.7) follows

EXAMPLE 11.7:

```
class X {};
class Y{};
X * px = new X;
Y * py = reinterpret_cast<Y*>(px);
```

A reinterpret_cast may also be used to convert a pointer to an ***int*** type. If the ***int*** type is then converted back to the same pointer type, the result will be the same value as the original pointer.

const_cast Operator

The *const_cast* operator takes the form

```
const_cast<data type> (expression)
```

to convert the given expression to mentioned data type. This operator is used to add or remove the "constness" or "volatileness" from a type. Neither of the other three new cast operators can modify the constness of an object. For example;

```
class X {};
const X * px = new X;
X * px2 = const_cast<X*> (px);
```

Let's see another example. Say, we have a function called f, which takes a non-const argument as follows:

```
int f(int &  a);
```

Then, we would like to call function f from another function g:

```
void g (const int& b)
{
    int c1, c2;
    c1 = f(b); // Error: cannot convert parameter b
               // from 'const int' to 'int &'
    c2 = const_cast<int &>(b); // ok, removes the "constness"
}
```

typeid Operator

typeid operator has been introduced recently in C++ language that allows the type of an expression to be determined at run-time. It takes the following form:

```
typeid (expression)
```

The result of a *typeid* expression is a const type_info&. The value is a reference to a type_info object that represents either the *type-id* or the type of the expression, depending on which form of *typeid* is used. The type_info class describes type information generated within the program by the compiler. Objects of this class effectively store a pointer to a name for the type and an encoded value suitable for comparing two types for equality or collating order. Here's an example program as Program Source Code 11.11.

Program Source Code 11.11

```
#include <iostream.h>
#include <typeinfo>

class X
```

(contd.)

Program Source Code 11.11 *(contd.)*

```
{
      int x;
   public:
      X():x(0){};
      ~X(){};
};

class Y: public X
{
   public:
      Y():X(){};
      ~Y(){};
};

int main()
{
   X *pxobj1, *pxobj2;
   X xobj;
   Y yobj;

   pxobj1 = new X;
   pxobj2 = new Y;
   cout << "type of xobj = " << typeid(xobj).name() << endl;
   cout << "type of yobj = " << typeid(yobj).name() << endl;
   cout << "type of pxobj1 = " << typeid(pxobj1).name()
         << endl;
   cout << "type of pxobj2 = " << typeid(pxobj2).name()
         << endl;
   return 0;
}
```

Output 11.11

```
type of xobj = class X
type of yobj = class Y
type of pxobj1 = class X *
type of pxobj2 = class X *
```

Here, the static types (not the dynamic types) are reflected. For example, pxobj2 points to a Y object but its static type is X *, dynamic type is Y *.

SUMMARY

The key concepts introduced in this chapter are as follows:

- C++ templates provide a way to reuse source code (compile-time reuse), as opposed to inheritance and composition which provide a way to reuse object code (runtime reuse). C++ provides two kinds of templates: *class templates* and *function templates.*
- An individual class defines how a group of object instances can be constructed from the individual class, while a class template defines how a group of classes can be generated from the template class.
- The declarations and definitions of the class template member functions should all be in the same header file.
- A template function chooses the name of its function template, and the particular function to resolve a given template function call.
- In addition to the arguments preceded by *class* or *typename* keyword that represent a data type, class templates and function templates may include constant values as well.
- It is also possible to set default values to any template parameter similar to what is done in function parameters.
- A template specialization allows specific implementations in a template when the pattern is of a concrete type.
- Template classes can be inherited similar to normal classes.
- A namespace declaration identifies and assigns a name to a region of declarations. A namespace-alias is an alternative name for a namespace.
- Unnamed namespaces are a superior replacement for the static declaration of variables.
- C++ provides three language constructs to implement exception handling: (i) *Try* blocks—denotes an exception block where exceptions can be generated (ii) *Catch* blocks—"catches" exceptions to handle recovery and (iii) *Throw* expressions—"throws" exceptions.
- *Try-Catch* blocks can be nested. If a throw occurs in a function called by an inner try block, the control is transferred outward through the nested try blocks until it finds the first catch block whose argument matches that of the throw expression.
- If a catch block cannot handle the particular exception it has caught, it can be rethrown.

- New cast operators have been introduced in C++ language, they are: (i) *static_cast*—to convert one type to another type, (ii) *dynamic_cast*—for safe navigation of an inheritance hierarchy, (iii) *reinterpret_cast*—to perform type conversions on un-related types, (iv) *const_cast*—to cast away the "const-ness" or "volatile-ness" of a type.
- typeid operator has been introduced recently in C++ language that allows the type of an expression to be determined at run-time.

REVIEW QUESTIONS

1. What is an exception? When do they occur?
2. How do you provide your own exception handler? Illustrate through examples.
3. Should you pass exception objects by reference or by value?
4. What is the significance of catch(...)?
5. Illustrate usage of nested try block? Is it necessary that number of catch blocks should be equal to the number of try blocks? Can this be more? Can this be less? Justify.
6. What is the difference between a template and a macro?
7. Is it possible to provide a special behavior in one particular instance of a template while not for other instances of the template? Illustrate through suitable examples.
8. Why template class is needed?
9. What is the role of reinterpret_cast operator?
10. What is the difference between static_cast and dynamic_cast operator?
11. Illustrate a use of *typeid* operator.
12. What is the use of unnamed namespace?
13. Why namespaces are required?
14. Create generic functions that return the mean, median and mode of an array of values.

12 The Standard Library in C++

One of the most useful kinds of classes is the container class, that is, a class that holds objects of some (other) type.

—Bjarne Stroustrup

LEARNING OBJECTIVES

The objective of this chapter is to acquaint you with:

- Standard C++ library functions for input and output handling
- Standard Template Library (STL)

INTRODUCTION

In earlier parts, we had introduced Standard C Library Functions. We, however, mentioned that C++ comes with a rich set of library and it's so extensive that it will be difficult to find room to describe them in detail here. However, to acquire knowledge of library functions supported, it is required to consult the library documentation provided by the particular compiler vendor. And once you have acquired the basic language constructs, this will not be difficult to understand the library functions made available by the particular compiler vendor. However, there are some standard libraries available in all the different compiler vendors. These are worth mentioning. In this part, we will list couple of standard library functions available in C++ on top of standard library functions of C.

STANDARD LIBRARY FUNCTIONS

Every part of the library has an associated header file, which makes the prototypes of the classes and functions (declarations only, not definitions) available to the user in the namespace std. The definitions of the classes and functions are in the library files, which need to be linked together with your .obj files to build the final executable file ready to run. For example, if we want to use the standard C++ Input/Output (I/O) library, we must include iostream header file as #include <iostream.h> or #include <iostream> in each of the source file which uses I/O.

Thus, say, our first C++ program is

```
#include <iostream.h>
int main ()
{
    cout << "Hi There"; // Ok
    return 0;
}
```

If we omit the .h extension, we can write the following program and compile:

```
#include <iostream>
int main ()
{
    cout << "Hi There"; // Error: 'cout' is undeclared
    return 0;
}
```

We don't have any clue that cout is cout object defined in std namespace, i.e. std::cout and not any other variable. Thus, we may use:

```
#include <iostream>
using namespace std;
int main ()
{
    cout << "Hi There";
    return 0;
}
```

OR

```
#include <iostream>
int main ()
{
    std::cout << "Hi There";
    return 0;
    }
```

The clean, orthogonal and transparent design of the library shall help to:

1. simplify application design and redesign
2. decrease the lines of code to be written
3. increase the understandability and maintainability
4. provide a basis for standard certifying and quality assurance as in other areas of system architecture, design and implementation.

Input and Output

Input/Output library functions available in native C programming language has served quite well in a vast number of applications. C++ being a superset of C, in fact a better C, it supports all Input/Output functions of native C. In fact, C++ comes with two different sets of I/O libraries: one inherited from C and other as native C++ library. Either of them can be used, but it is strongly recommended that you use the native C++ I/O library. Well, why do we prefer native C++ I/O library to native C I/O library? Mainly for three reasons: (i) improved type safety (ii) improved modularity and reusability, and (iii) capability to extend features from generalized facilities. We will be discussing native C++ I/O library in greater detail now.

The most commonly used function on C I/O library is `printf` for output (or `scanf` for input) which can take variable number and type of arguments. The prototype of the function `printf` is:

```
int printf(const char* format, ...);
```

The first argument is a string literal, with a starting address of a null-terminated character array that describes the format and contents of what to print. Characters other than % prefix are printed as-it-is (escape sequences are special characters like \n for newline, \t for tab etc.). % introduces a format specifier that corresponds to one or more of the succeeding arguments to printf and also says how those arguments are to be formatted in the output to be printed (similar arguments for taking formatted input through `scanf`). The second argument in the `printf` prototype is shown as ellipsis (three dots i.e. ...) which indicates that the compiler will not check the number and types of arguments passed during the call of this function. The format string is checked at runtime for embedded format indications (prefixed by %) of the types of data to be printed. The compiler does not and cannot check the arguments except the first char * pointer. Thus, if the user correctly calls the `printf` function, the correct output is obtained. If not, it may cause memory protection fault or may corrupt the stack to override the function return address, and what not? The example program that uses `scanf` and `printf` correctly is as follows (Program Source Code 12.1):

Program Source Code 12.1 - C style I/O

```
#include <stdio.h>
int main ()
{
    int a, b, c;
    char FormatString[40 + 1]; // including null character
```

(*contd.*)

Program Source Code 12.1 - C style I/O *(contd.)*

```
    printf("Please input two numbers: ");

    // &a, &b passed as pointers to hold the input data
    scanf("%d%d", &a, &b);

    c = a + b;
    printf("Ok... I have added them: %d + %d = %d\n",
           a, b, c);
    printf("\nNow you tell me your format string");
    printf("(max 40 characters)\n");
    printf("I will use that to show input numbers ");
    printf("and their sum\n\n");

    fflush(stdin); // must use before gets call
    gets(FormatString);
    printf(FormatString, a, b, c);
    return 0;
}
```

Output 12.1

```
Please input two numbers: 10 20
Ok... I have added them: 10 + 20 = 30

Now you tell me your format string (max 40 characters)
I will use that to show input numbers and their sum

The sum of two numbers %d and %d is %d
The sum of two numbers 10 and 20 is 30
```

The first part of the program uses `scanf` to input two numbers:

```
scanf("%d%d", &a, &b);
```

&a, &b are the addresses of the variables a and b which are passed as pointers to hold the input data. %d is the format specifier to specify that the input is a decimal number and the number is an integer. The `printf` line that uses format specifier and additional arguments is:

```
printf("Ok... I have added them: %d + %d = %d\n", a, b, c);
```

This shows the contents "Ok... I have added them:........" and %d stands for placeholders for integer number. Other format specifiers were mentioned in the earlier chapter on standard C library functions. This works fine, but, if we pass incorrect number or type of arguments, then the runtime behaviour is unpredictable. For example, if we had called `printf` as:

```
// printf called with less number of arguments
printf("Ok... I have added them: %d + %d = %d\n", a, b);
```

or

```
// printf called with more number of arguments
printf("Ok... I have added them: %d + %d = %d\n", a, b, c, c);
```

The compiler cannot check the mismatch because of the eliipsis (...) in prototype. And, at runtime, depending on the format specifier (first argument which is a null-terminates string), the relevant number and type of additional arguments as specified by the % prefixed specifiers are looked for in the stack (function arguments are pushed to the stack at the time of call of a function). If we don't pass correct number and type of arguments, we get erroneous unpredictable behaviour at runtime. Say, the first part of the program where we use `scanf` to input two numbers:

```
scanf("%d%d", &a, &b);
```

We change this to scanf("%d%d%d", &a, &b); or something like this, then extra data would be popped from stack causing stack corruption leading to program failure.

Also, in the last part of the program, we had taken a format specifier string from the user to use it to print the values of a, b, and c. It's very flexible, if you correctly use it. The function "gets" reads next line from input(stdin) into the string argument given, i.e. FormatString. It replaces terminating newline in input with a null terminator '\0'. However, you could also see one line as

```
fflush(stdin);
```

This clears the contents of the input buffer ensuring that there would be no spurious elements present in the standard input buffer when we read an entire input line through gets. And we could read a clean input line from the input buffer. `fflush` calls need to be used many times when using input/output through standard C I/O functions.

The form that `printf` uses is concise and easy to understand. However, this has three significant disadvantages:

1. It is not type safe, as `printf` relies on unchecked arguments that are handled according to the format string at runtime.
2. `printf` function itself cannot be extended to print contents of user-defined type, say, a new type called FRACTION to print a fraction. In order to do that, we have to invent a function name say, PrintFraction or so, and then within that use `printf` to print portions of the data which match built-in types like ***int***, ***float*** etc. supported by `printf`. This is very inelegant.

3. The decision about what types to print is based on the contents of the format string, which indicates that the type decisions are being made during execution. Had it been in compile time, it would have been faster.

The object-oriented model for I/O is a set of C++ classes that comprise the I/O Stream Class Library. This set of classes implements and manages stream buffers for input and output. Stream buffers can take two forms. They can be arrays of bytes where data is stored between the program and the ultimate consumer for output. Stream buffers can also be between the ultimate producer and the program for input. Stream buffers and manipulators are used to format data. There are two base classes, *ios* and *streambuf*, from which all other classes in the I/O Stream library are derived. The *ios* class and its derivative classes are used to implement formatting of I/O and maintain error state information of stream buffers implemented with the streambuf class. To use the I/O Stream Library, one should include the *iostream.h* header file in the program.

Although input and output are implemented with streams for both C and C++, the C++ I/O Stream Class Library provides the same facilities for input and output as C stdio.h. The I/O Stream Class Library has the following advantages:

1. The extraction (>>) operator and insertion (<<) operator are typesafe. These operators are easier to use than *scanf()* and *printf()*.
2. One can overload the input and output operators to define input and output for own types and classes. This makes input and output across types, including your own, uniform.

The native C++ library uses overloading to deal with all these problems having a high degree of control over formatting with high performance and of course, ease of use. The native C++ I/O library, however, is so large that few people ever use more than a small part of it.

Let's define a few terms which are used with respect to C++ I/O.

Streams

Stream is a sequence of bytes. It is a continuous flow of data elements that are transmitted or intended for transmission in a defined format. It works either as a source from where the data can be obtained or as a destination for the output sent. Source stream that provides data to the program is called *Input Stream*. Destination stream that receives output from program is called *Output Stream*. Two types of input and output streams are supported: text streams and binary streams. Streams may flow into or out of files and strings. Whatever the nature of the source and destination is, C++ tries to offer the same set of commands.

Buffers

It would be rather inefficient to update the destination (usually a file on disc) each time some data is added to the stream. The data is rather written into a buffer, and when the buffer is full (buffer size is predefined and size may be customized), the buffer is flushed (unless premature flush is forced) and the destination gets updated.

State

Each stream has state information indicating whether an error has occured, etc.

Locale

The natural language required by the user has an influence on output—how should a bool value be printed? As true or what? Such preferences are controlled by the locale, which is usually set up appropriately by default.

Text streams. Text streams contain printable characters and, depending on the type of file, control characters. Text streams are organized into lines. Each line ends with a control character, usually a newline. The last record in a text file may or may not end with a control character, depending on what kind of file you are using. Text files recognize the following control characters:

\a	Alarm
\b	Backspace
\f	Form feed
\n	Newline
\r	Carriage return
\t	Horizontal tab character
\v	Vertical tab character

Binary streams. Binary streams contain an ordered sequence of bytes. For binary streams, there is a continuous stream of bytes, and so they ignore any record boundaries. When data is written out to a record-oriented file, it fills one record before it starts filling the next.

Input/output stream. In C, there are three standard files available: stdin as the standard input stream, stdout as the buffered standard output stream, stderr as the unbuffered standard error stream. In C++, comparable input-output streams are predefined as follows:

`cin` an `istream` object from which information can be extracted (through extraction operator >>), by default, connected to the keyboard.

`cout` an `ostream` object, into which information can be inserted (through insertion operator <<), by default, connected to the screen. Insertions are buffered.

`cerr` an `ostream` object, into which information can be inserted (through insertion operator <<), by default, connected to the screen. Insertions are unbuffered.

`clog` an `ostream` object, into which information can be inserted (through insertion operator <<), by default, connected to the screen. Insertions are buffered.

An overview of Input/Output Stream is found in Figure 12.1.

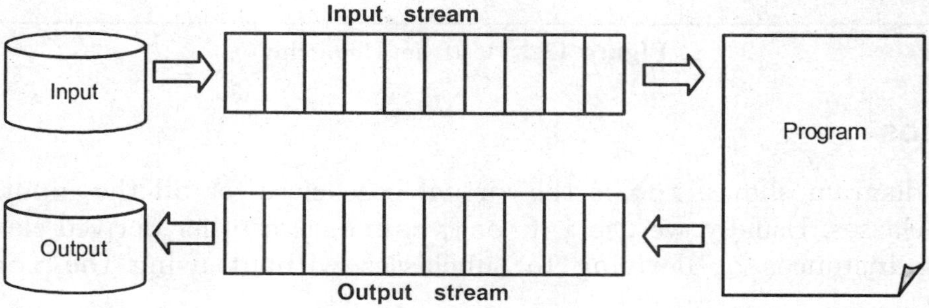

Figure 12.1 I/O Stream.

All predefined streams are tied to `cout`. When we use `cin` and `cerr`, `cout` gets flushed and its contents are sent to the ultimate user. Input to cin comes from `stdin` (unless `cin` is redirected), cout output goes to `stdout` (unless `cout` is redirected) and `cerr` output goes to `stderr` (unit-buffered) (unless `cerr` is redirected).

iostream Class Hierarchy

Header file `iostream.h` declares the basic input-output classes. The `iostream` class hierarchy diagram 12.2 shows some relationships between `iostream` classes.

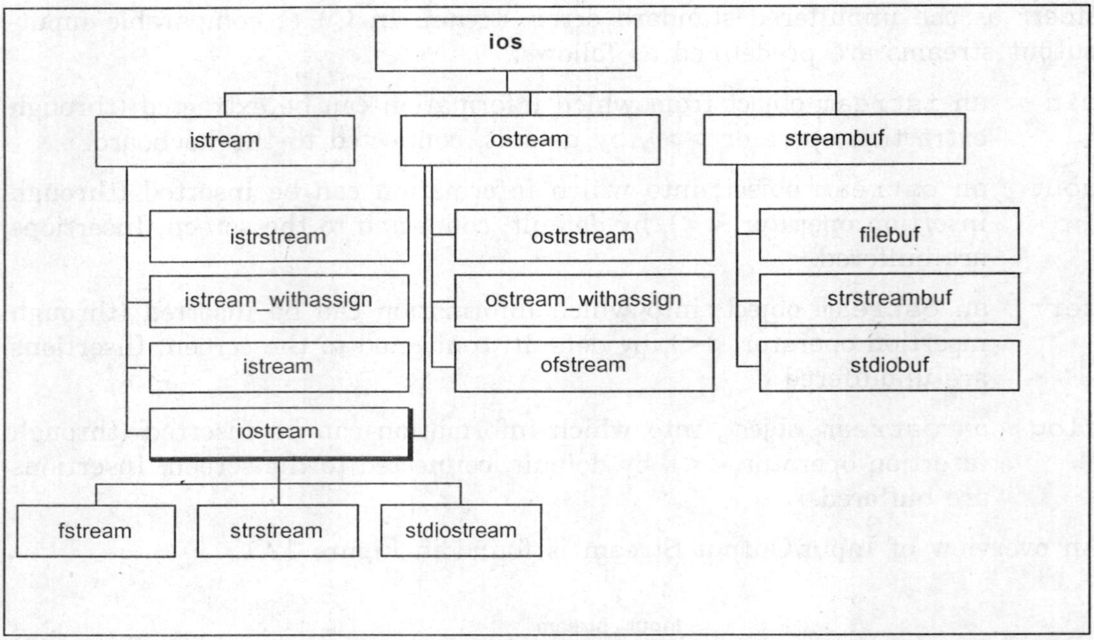

Figure 12.2 Iostream Hierarchy.

Class ios

As the diagram shows, `ios` is the virtual base class for all the input/output stream classes. Usually, we use `istream`, `ostream` or other derived classes for creating instances or deriving to subclasses without using the `ios` class directly.

Class ios declares the following:

1. A pointer to a buffer object that provides temporary storage for input and output data.
2. A field width data.
3. Several state variables whose values govern input-output operations, e.g.

   (a) format state governs how output values will be printed (after formatting) and how input values will be interpreted for mapping to the input variables

   (b) error state indicates whether a previous operation on a stream object has failed; no further operation can be carried out on the object until the error indication is cleared.

4. A number of constants that help us specify the state of a stream object, e.g. we can use the constants `ios::dec`, `ios::oct`, and `ios::hex` to specify whether integer values will be printed in decimal, octal or hexadecimal notation.

C++ associates a set of "manipulators" with the output stream. They change the default format for integer arguments. Manipulators are dec, oct and hex as defined in ios class Program Source Code 12.2.

Program Source Code 12.2

```
#include <iostream>
using namespace std;
int main()
{
   int value = 100;
   cout << "The decimal value is: " << dec << value
        << endl
        << "The octal value is: " << oct << value
        << endl
      . << "The hexadecimal value is: " << hex << value;
   return 0;
}
```

Output 12.2

```
The decimal value is: 100
The octal value is: 144
The hexadecimal value is: 64
```

Format state flags consist of three long parameters namely adjustfield (internal | left | right), basefield (dec | hex | oct), floatfield (fixed | scientific) and fifteen one-bit flags (stored within a long value). The bit values are set different for different bit positions, for example, skipws = 0x0001, left = 0x0002, right = 0x0004, internal = 0x0008, dec = 0x0010, oct = 0x0020, hex = 0x0040, showbase = 0x0080, showpoint = 0x0100, uppercase = 0x0200, showpos = 0x0400, scientific = 0x0800, fixed = 0x1000, unitbuf = 0x2000, stdio = 0x4000. Table 12.1 gives the summary.

Table 12.1

Bitfield	*Flag*	*Description*	*Default*
	ios::skipws	This bit, when set, determines whether to skip leading white space before certain extractions through >> operator.	set
ios::adjustfield (Bit mask for obtaining the conversion base flags)	ios::left	causes a value to be positioned as far to the left as possible (left alignment)	set
	ios::right	causes a value to be positioned as far to the right as possible (right alignment)	reset
	ios::internal	causes a sign or base indication (leading 0, 0x, or 0X) to be left aligned and the rest of the number to be right aligned. Usually, texts are left aligned and numerical values are right aligned.	reset
ios::basefield (Bit mask for obtaining the field padding flags)	ios::dec	when this bit flag is set, integer values are to be inserted or extracted in decimal format.	set
	ios::oct	when this bit flag is set, integer values are to be inserted or extracted in octal format.	reset
	ios::hex	when this bit flag is set, integer values are to be inserted or extracted in hexadecimal format.	reset
	ios::showbase	when this bit flag is set, octal and hexadecimal numbers are printed in usual notation, e.g. octal starts with leading zero and hexadecimal starts with 0x.	reset
	ios::showpos	when this bit flag is set, a positive integer is printed with a plus sign, as in +432.	reset
	ios::uppercase	when this bit flag is set, uppercase letters are used for the E in exponential notation and when printing hexadecimal numbers.	reset
	ios::showpoint	when this bit flag is cleared, trailing zeros to the right of the decimal point are omitted, the decimal point is itself omitted if it is followed only by zeros. When the flag is set, the decimal point and trailing zeros are printed (applies only when both ios::scientific and ios::fixed are cleared, when one of these flags is set, the precision parameter determines how many decimal places will be printed).	reset

(contd.)

Table 12.1 (*contd.*)

Bitfield	*Flag*	*Description*	*Default*
ios::floatfield (Bit mask for obtaining the numeric format)	ios::scientific	when this bit flag is set, a value is printed in scientific notation.	set
	ios::fixed	when this bit flag is set, a fixed point notation is used.	reset
	ios::unibuf	when this bit flag is set, the buffer of an output stream is flushed after each insertion through << operator.	reset
	ios::stdio	when this bit flag is set, it helps preventing certain problems when the standard output and error files are accessed stdio library and the C++ iostream library.	reset

In addition to the above, `ios` class has some member functions as defined in Table 12.2.

Table 12.2

ios Functions	*Task*	*Equivalent Manipulators*
width()	To specify the required field size for displaying an output value.	setw()
precision()	To specify the number of digits to be displayed after decimal for float.	setprecision()
fill()	To specify a character that is used to pad unused portion.	setfill()
setf()	To specify the format flags that can control the form of output display like left-justification right-justification and so on.	setiosflags()
unsetf()	To clear the flags specified by setf( ).	resetioflags()

A program to illustrate these follows (Program Source Code 12.3).

```
Program Source Code 12.3
#include <iostream>
#include <math.h>
using namespace std;
const float PI = 22.0/7.0;
int main()
```

(*contd.*)

Program Source Code 12.3 *(contd.)*

```
{
   cout << "1234567890123456789012345678901234567890"
        << endl;
   cout.precision(3);
   for (float f=0.0;f<2.0*PI;f+=PI/6.0)
   {
      cout.width(8);
      cout<<f;
      cout.width(13);
      cout<< sin(f) << endl;
   }
   cout.precision(10);
   cout<< "sin(2*PI) = " << sin(2.0*PI) << endl << endl;
   return 0;
}
```

Output 12.3

```
1234567890123456789012345678901234567890
       0            0
   0.524          0.5
    1.05        0.866
    1.57            1
     2.1        0.866
    2.62        0.499
    3.14     -0.00126
    3.67       -0.501
    4.19       -0.867
    4.71           -1
    5.24       -0.865
    5.76       -0.498
    6.29      0.00253
sin(2*PI) = 0.0025288396
```

Filling and padding functions can be illustrated as follows (Program Source Code 12.4):

Program Source Code 12.4

```
#include <iostream>
#include <iomanip>
using namespace std;
```

(contd.)

Program Source Code 12.4 *(contd.)*

```
int main()
{
   cout << "1234567890123456789012345678901234567890" << endl;
   cout.fill('*');
   cout.width(10);
   cout<<100<< endl.<< endl;

   cout << "1234567890123456789012345678901234567890" << endl;
   cout.fill('*');
   cout.precision(3);
   cout.setf(ios::internal,ios::adjustfield);
   cout.setf(ios::scientific,ios::floatfield);
   cout.width(15);
   cout<< -12.34567 << endl << endl;

   cout << "1234567890123456789012345678901234567890" << endl;
   cout.setf(ios::showpoint); // display trailing zero
   cout.setf(ios::showpos); //display + sign
   cout.precision(3);
   cout.setf(ios::fixed,ios::floatfield);
   cout.setf(ios::internal,ios::adjustfield);
   cout.width(10);
   cout<<275.5 << endl << endl;

   cout << "1234567890123456789012345678901234567890" << endl;
   cout.fill('.'); // reset filling by space
   cout.setf(ios::showpoint);
   cout << setw(5) << "n";
   cout << setw(15) << "Inverse_of_n";
   cout << setw(15) << setw(15) << "Sum_of_terms" << endl;
   double term, sum = 0;
   for (int n = 1; n< = 10; n++)
   {
      term = 1.0/float(n);
      sum = sum + term;
      cout << setw(5) << n
           << setw(14)  << setprecision(4)
           << setiosflags(ios::scientific) << term
           << setw(13)  << resetiosflags(ios::scientific)
           << sum  << endl;
```

(contd.)

Program Source Code 12.4 *(contd.)*

```
    }
        return 0;
}
```

Output 12.4

```
1234567890123456789012345678901234567890
*******100

1234567890123456789012345678901234567890
-****1.235e+001

1234567890123456789012345678901234567890
+**275.500

1234567890123456789012345678901234567890
....n...Inverse_of_n...Sum_of_terms
+...1+.......1.000+......1.0000
+...2+......0.5000+......1.5000
+...3+......0.3333+......1.8333
+...4+......0.2500+......2.0833
+...5+......0.2000+......2.2833
+...6+......0.1667+......2.4500
+...7+......0.1429+......2.5929
+...8+......0.1250+......2.7179
+...9+......0.1111+......2.8290
+..10+......0.1000+......2.9290
```

The manipulator functions used are described in Table 12.3.

Table 12.3

Manipulators	*What they do?*
setprecision(int d)	Set the floating point precision to d
setfill(int c)	Set the fill character to c
setiosflags(long f)	Set the format flag f
resetiosflags(long f)	Clear the flag specified by f
endl	Insert a new line and flush stream

One can design one's own manipulators as shown in Program Source Code 12.5:

```
ostream & manipulator (ostream & output)
{
   uu.
   uu.code.....
   uu.
}
```

Program Source Code 12.5

```
#include<iostream.h>
#include<iomanip.h>
ostream & currency(ostream & MyOut)
{
   MyOut<<"Rs.";
   return MyOut;
}
ostream & form (ostream & MyOut)
{
   MyOut.setf(ios::showpos);
   MyOut.setf(ios::showpoint);
   MyOut.fill('.');
   MyOut.precision(2);
   MyOut << setiosflags(ios::fixed)<<setw(10);
   return MyOut;
}

int main()
{
   cout << currency << form << 1234.5;
   return 0;
}
```

Output 12.5

```
Rs...+1234.50
```

Other Stream Classes

Class Istream

This class provides facilities for formatted input. It defines extraction operator >> as well as such input functions as get() and getline().

Class Ostream

This class provides facilities for formatted output. It defines insertion operator <<, as well as output function as put() which outputs a single character.

Class Iostream

This class provides facilities for both formatted input and formatted output. The input facilities are inherited from istream class and output facilities are inherited from ostream class. Let's take another example with **get** and **put** functions of input and output stream objects. (Program Source Code 12.6):

Program Source Code 12.6
Alternative One - whitespaces (other than newlines) not skipped

```
#include <iostream>
using namespace std;
int main()
{
   char c;
   cout << "Please input a line of message : ";
   cin.get(c);
   while(c != '\n')
   {
      cout.put(c);
      cin.get(c); // or c = cin.get();
   }
   return 0;
}
```

Output 12.6 - Alternative One

```
Please input a line of message : Hello, do you like C++ I/O?
Hello, do you like C++ I/O?
```

Alternative Two - whitespaces (other than newlines) skipped

```
#include <iostream>
using namespace std;
int main()
{
   char c;
```

(*contd.*)

Output 12.6 - Alternative One *(contd.)*

```
    cout << "Please input a line of message : ";
    cin >> c ;
    while(c != '\n')
    {
      cout << c;
       in >> c ;

    return 0;
}
```

Output 12.6 - Alternative Two

```
Please input a line of message: Hello, do you like C++ I/O?
Hello,doyoulikeC++I/O?
```

getline() and write() functions

`getline` function reads character input into a variable upto a specified size. For example:

```
cin.getline(variable,size);
```

`write( )` function displays an entire line. For example:

```
cout.write(variable,size);
```

If we want to read a complete line upto a specified size, it can be achieved by the following code snippet (Program Source Code 12.7):

Program Source Code 12.7

```
#include <iostream>
#include <string>
using namespace std;
int main( )
{
    const int   SIZE=40;
    char   line[SIZE];
    cout << "Please input a line terminated by '.' : ";

    // third parameter is defaulted to '\n'
     cin.getline(line,SIZE,'.');
     cout.write(line, strlen(line)+1);
    return 0;
 }
```

Output 12.7

```
Please input a line terminated by '.': I am line.
I am line
```

An input stream object needs to be created and associated with a file or string so that the stream knows where to get the input. Other than cin, any other input stream object needs to be explicitly opened using the open command or the constructor. Extra arguments can be provided, but usually just the filename is sufficient (rest of the parameters are defaulted). This is shown in Program Source Code 12.8. We read numbers (till end of file is reached) separated by arbitrary spaces, tabs or newlines (collectively known as whitespaces) from an input file and print them.

Program Source Code 12.8

```
#include <iostream>
#include <fstream>
using namespace std;
int main()
{
    int i;
    ifstream infile;
    // TEST.DAT contains numbers separated through
    // arbitrary number of spaces
    infile.open("TEST.DAT");
    while (infile >> i)
        cout << i << endl;
    infile.close();
    return 0;
}
```

TEST.DAT

```
10 20
30 40
50
```

Output 12.8

```
10
20
30
40
50
```

A file (ifstream or ofstream object) can be opened in the modes listed in Table 12.4.

Table 12.4

Mode	*Means*
ios::app	Append to the end-of-file
ios::ate	Go to the end of file on opening
ios::binary	Binary file
ios::in	Open the file for read only
ios::nocreate	Open fails if the file does not already exist
ios::noreplace	Open fails if the file already exist
ios::out	Open file for writing only
ios::trunc	Delete contents of the file if it exists

The member function open of the ofstream, ifstream and fstream classes include a default mode that varies based on the class selected, such as those found in Table 12.5.

Table 12.5

Class	*Default Mode Parameter*
ofstream	ios::out | ios::trunc
ifstream	ios::in
fstream	ios::out | ios::out

The default value is only applied if the function is called without the parameter. If the function is called with any value in that parameter the default mode is overridden. Since very often the first task that is performed on an object of the ofstream, ifstream and fstream classes is to open a file, the three file stream classes include a constructor that directly calls the open member function and has the same signature. This way, we could also have declared the previous object and conducted the same file open operation in a single statement as follows:

```
ofstream file("example.bin", ios::out | ios::app | ios::binary);
```

Some of the file pointer usages are shown in Table 12.6.

Table 12.6

seekg()	Moves get pointer (i.e. input) to a specified location.
seekp()	Moves put pointer (i.e. output) to a specified location.
tellg()	Gives the current position of get pointer.
tellp()	Gives the current position of put pointer.

Each of the tellg() and tellp() method returns a value of pos_type that is an integer data type representing the current position of the get and put stream pointers respectively. seekg() and seekp() pair of methods serve to change the position of their respective get and put stream pointers. Each is overloaded with two distinct prototypes.

Now to a set of pointer offset calls (see Table 12.7):

Table 12.7

outfile.seekg(0,ios::beg)	Go to start
outfile.seekg(0,ios::cur)	Stay at current position.
outfile.seekg(0,ios::end)	Go to end of file.
outfile.seekg(m,ios::beg)	Move (m+1)th byte in the file.
outfile.seekg(m,ios::cur)	Go foreword m th bytes from current.
outfile.seekg(-m,ios::cur)	Go backward m th bytes from current.

Verification of State Flags

Table 12.8

Method	*Description*
bad()	Returns true if any failure occurs in a read or write operation. For example, attempting to write to a file that was opened for read only or if the disk is full.
fail()	Returns true in the same cases as bad() plus the case when a format error occurs. An example of a format error would be trying to read an integer and an alphanumeric character. The difference between fail() and bad() is subtle when in state of fail() but not bad(), it is assumed.
eof()	Returns true if a file opened for read has reached the physical end of the file.
good()	If the state returned by this method is true, the previous input operation succeeded and next operation will probably succeed. Applying an input operation to a stream that is not in the good() state is a null operation.

An example program (Program Source Code 12.9) follows to show a comparison of C handling of files as well as strings compared to C++ file streams and string streams.

Program Source Code 12.9 - C style I/O

```
#include <stdio.h>
int main()
{
   char   output[30],*result;
   int   data1, data2, data3;
   FILE *   fp;

   // open TEST.DAT file in write mode
   // (destroys previous contents, if any)
   fp =fopen("test.dat","w");

   // read some integer from input, write that integer
   // to the file

   printf("Please input a number: ");
   scanf("%d", &data1);

   printf("Please input another number: ");
   scanf("%d", &data2);

   printf("Now I will add your numbers: ");
   printf("%d and %d\n", data1, data2);
   data3 = data1 + data2;

   printf("And the result of this addition is: ");
   printf("%d\n", data3);
   printf("Now I will store all these numbers ");
   printf("(comma separated)\nin file TEST.DAT\n");

   // writes to the file
   fprintf(fp,"%d,%d,%d", data1, data2, data3);

   printf("Now I will close the file TEST.DAT\n");
   fclose(fp);// closes the file

   printf("Now I will reopen the file TEST.DAT\n");
   fp =fopen("test.dat","r");//reopens the same file

   // retrieve the first line
   if ((result=fgets(output,30,fp))!=NULL)
   {
      printf("value retrieved in first line is ");
      printf("%s \n", output);
```

(contd.)

Program Source Code 12.9 - C style I/O (*contd.*)

```
    }

    fclose(fp);// closes the file
    sscanf(output, "%d%d%d", &data1, &data2, &data3);
    printf("And the retrieved data are: ");
    printf("\n%d\n%d\n%d", data1, data2, data3);

    return(0);
}
```

Output 12.9

```
Please input a number: 40
Please input another number: 50
Now I will add your numbers: 40 and 50
And the result of this addition is: 90
Now I will store all these numbers (comma separate
in file TEST.DAT
Now I will close the file TEST.DAT
Now I will reopen the file TEST.DAT
value retrieved in first line is 40,50,90
And the retrieved data are:
40
50
90
```

Study the C++ counterpart (replacing printf, scanf, sscanf type of functions) given as (Program Source Code 12.10):

Program Source Code 12.10 - C++ style I/O

```
#include <fstream.h>
#include <strstrea.h>

int main()
{
    char output[30], separator;
    int  data1, data2, data3;
    ofstream *outfile;
    ifstream *infile;
    istrstream *instr;
```

(*contd.*)

Program Source Code 12.10 - C++ style I/O *(contd.)*

```
// open TEST.DAT file in write mode
// (destroys previous contents, if any)
outfile = new ofstream("test.dat");

// read some integer from input, write that integer
// to the file

cout << "Please input a number: ";
cin >> data1;

cout << "Please input another number: ";
cin >> data2;

cout << "Now I will add your numbers: " << data1
     << " and " << data2 << endl;

data3 = data1 + data2;

cout << "And the result of this addition is: "
     << data3 << endl;
cout << "Now I will store all these numbers "
    << "(comma separated)" << endl
    << "in file TEST.DAT" << endl;

// writes to the file
*outfile << data1 << "," << data2 << "," << data3;

cout << "Now I will close the file TEST.DAT" << endl;
delete outfile;// closes the file

cout << "Now I will reopen the file TEST.DAT" << endl;

//reopens the same file
infile = new ifstream("test.dat");

// retrieve the first line
infile->get(output,30,'\n');
cout << "value retrieved in first line is "
     << output << endl;

delete infile;// closes the file

instr = new istrstream(output);
*instr >> data1 >> separator >> data2
       >> separator >> data3;

cout  << "And the retrieved data are:" << endl
      << data1 << endl << data2 << endl << data3;
```

(contd.)

Program Source Code 12.10 - C++ style I/O (*contd.*)

```
   delete instr;

   return(0);
}
```

Output 12.10

```
Please input a number: 40
Please input another number: 50
Now I will add your numbers: 40 and 50
And the result of this addition is: 90
Now I will store all these numbers (comma separated)
in file TEST.DAT
Now I will close the file TEST.DAT
Now I will reopen the file TEST.DAT
value retrieved in first line is 40,50,90
And the retrieved data are:
40
50
90
```

Standard Template Library

The Standard Template Library (STL) is a C++ programming library that has been developed by Alexander Stepanov and Meng Lee. It was designed to enable a C++ programmer to do generic programming, and is based on the extensive use of templates, also called *parametrized types*. In the late 70s Alexander Stepanov first observed that some algorithms do not depend on some particular implementation of a data structure but only on a few fundamental semantic properties of the structure.

STL is a component library. These means that it consists of components—clean and formally sound concepts. Such components are containers that are objects, which store objects of an arbitrary type, and algorithms.

The software component space is given as follows in Figure 12.3:

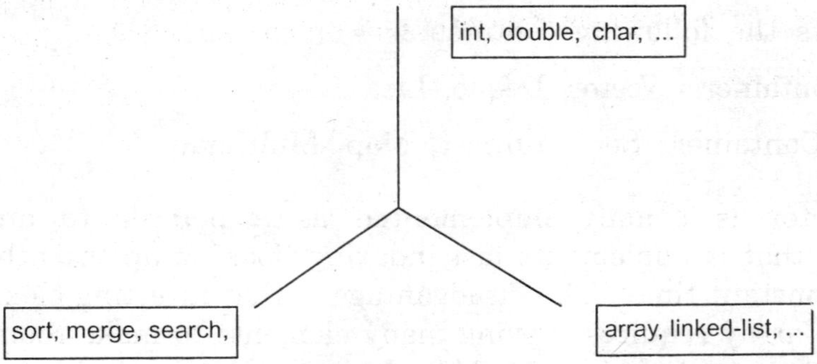

Figure 12.3 Software component space.

STL components are:

— Algorithm
— Container
— Iterator
— Function Object
— Adaptor

Sequence Containers

A sequence is a kind of a container that organizes a finite set of objects, all of the same type, into a strictly linear arrangement as in Figure 12.4. STL provides three basic kinds of Sequence Containers: Vectors, Lists and Deques.

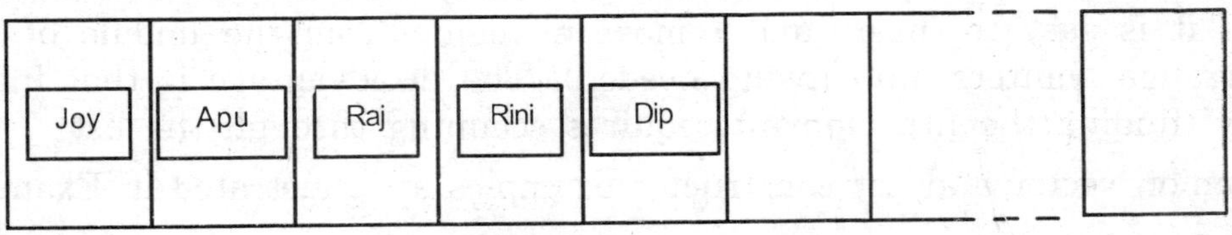

Figure 12.4 Sequence containers.

Associative Containers

Associative containers provide an ability for fast retrieval of data based on keys. Here elements are sorted so fast binary search is possible for data retrieval as shown in Figure 12.5. STL provides four basic kinds of Associative Containers. Set, Map, Multiset and Multimap.

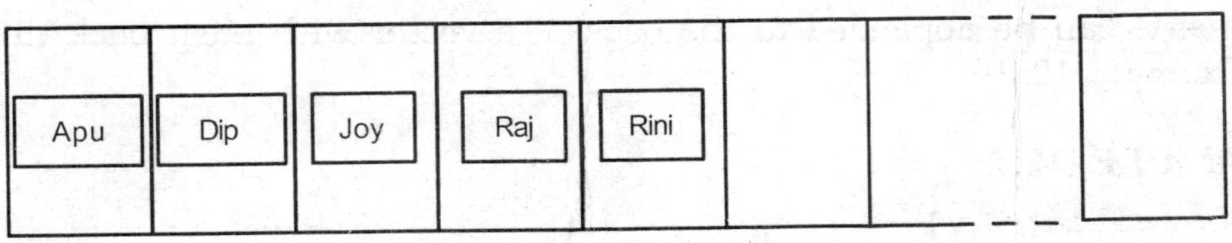

Figure 12.5 Associative containers.

STL supports the following containers:

Sequence Containers: Vector, Deque, List

Associative Containers Set: Multiset, Map, Multimap

Vector. Vector is usually implemented as a pointer to an array. The advantage is that it implements fast indexing (looking up the nth element can be done in constant time). The disadvantage is that inserting elements into the middle of an array requires copying many elements to make room for the new element. Vector can be understood as shown in Figure 12.6:

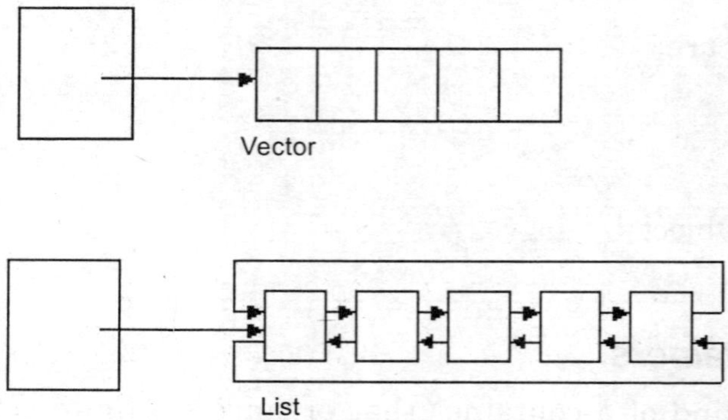

Figure 12.6 Vector.

List. List is usually implemented as doubly linked lists. The advantage is that it is easy to insert and remove elements from the middle of list (just rearrange pointers, no copying needed). The disadvantage is that indexing is slow (finding the nth element requires scanning through the list).

Common vector and list constructor examples are illustrated in Example 12.1:

EXAMPLE 12.1:

```
vector<float> v1; // create an empty vector of floats

// create a vector that initially holds 10 floats,
// each initialised to 5.0
vector<float> v2(10, 5.0);

list<float> l; // create an empty list of floats
```

Elements can be appended to the back of a vector with push_back (illustrated in Example 12.2):

EXAMPLE 12.2:

```
vector<float> v1;
v1.push_back(6.0);
```

```
v1.push_back(7.0);
v1.push_back(8.0);
```

Now v1 contains 3 elements: {6.0, 7.0, 8.0}

Note that the vector is automatically resized so that each new element added with push_back will fit. Isn't that nice?

The first and last elements of vectors and lists can be retrieved with the front() and back() member functions as illustrated in Example 12.3:

EXAMPLE 12.3:

```
vector<float> v1;
v1.push_back(6.01);
v1.push_back(7.01);
v1.push_back(8.01);
v1.push_back(9.01);
float fFront = v1.front();
float fBack = v1.back();
cout << fFront << " " << fBack << endl;
```

This prints: 6.01 9.01

pop_back() removes the last element from the vector. See the following Example 12.4:

EXAMPLE 12.4:

```
vector<float> v1;
v1.push_back(6.01);
v1.push_back(7.01);
v1.push_back(8.01);
v1.push_back(9.01);
v1.pop_back();
cout << v1.front() << " " << v1.back() << endl;
```

This prints: 6.01 8.01

lists support push_front and pop_front (to insert and remove elements at the front of a list), as well as push_back and pop_back (Example 12.5).

EXAMPLE 12.5:

```
list<float> l; // create an empty list of floats
l.push_back(6.01);
l.push_back(7.01);
```

```
l.push_back(8.01);
l.push_front(9.01);
l.pop_back();
cout << l.front() << " " << l.back() << endl;
```

This prints: 9.01 7.01

So a hypothetical, simplified, definition of vector might look like the following:

EXAMPLE 12.6:

```
template <class T> class vector
{
  public:
    vector();
    vector(int n, const T& val);
    void push_back(const T& x);
    void pop_back();
    T& front();
    T& back();
    T& operator[] (int n);
    T& at(int n);
    int size() const;
    bool empty() const;
};
```

A simplified list class would look similar. Here's how it is Example 12.7:

EXAMPLE 12.7:

```
template <class T> class vector
{
  public:
    vector();
    vector(int n, const T& val);
    vector(const vector<T>& x);
    ~vector();
    vector<T>& operator= (const vector<T>& x);
};
```

Vector will have a copy constructor, assignment operator, and destructor. The copy constructor and assignment operator for STL container classes make copies of the entire container. This can be expensive, so if you do not want a copy, you should pass containers by reference like

```
void f(vector<float> &v);
```

rather than by value:

```
void f(vector<float> v); // copies entire vector
```

Even if you never make copies of entire containers, your elements may be copied as they are inserted into the containers (and at other times). So if the elements are classes with pointers, they should implement the correct copy constructor, assignment operator and destructor.

For classes that should not be copied (such as large classes or classes with virtual functions), a container of pointers to objects can be used:

```
vector<Shape*> shapes;
```

Be aware that the container will not delete the pointed-to objects for you:

```
vector<Shape*> shapes;
shapes.push_back(new Circle());
shapes.pop_back(); // problem : memory leak
// Circle was not deleted!
```

Thus, the following code segment is correct:

```
vector<Shape*> shapes;
shapes.push_back(new Circle());
delete shapes.back();
shapes.pop_back();
```

STL allows a container memory management to be customized with user defined allocators (see Example 12.8):

EXAMPLE 12.8:

```
template <class T, class A = allocator<T> > class vector
{
   public:
      typedef typename A::size_type size_type;
      vector();
      vector(size_type n, const T& val);
      vector(const vector<T>& x);
      ~vector();
      vector<T>& operator= (const vector<T>& x);
      void push_back(const T& x);
      void pop_back();
      T& front(); T& back();
      T& operator[] (size_type n);
      T& at(size_type n);
      size_type size() const;
      bool empty() const;
```

EXAMPLE 12.9:

```
template <class T, class A = allocator<T> > class vector
{
  public:
     typedef typename A::size_type size_type;
     vector();
     vector(size_type n, const T& val);
     .....
};
```

For instance, an allocator might be written so that objects are stored in a large, persistent database. In this case, size_type might be larger than a normal int (it might be a 64-bit integer, for instance).

The "= allocator<T>" specifies a default value for vector's allocator, which is used if you do not pass in an explicit allocator of your own. You probably will never have to worry about allocators explicitly; chances are you will only need the default allocator.

However, if you have an old compiler that does not support default template values, you may have to pass in the default allocator explicitly:

```
vector<float, allocator<float> > v1(10, 5.0);
```

Iterator: Iterators are a generalization of pointers that allow a programmer to work with different data structures (containers) in a uniform manner. There are five categories of iterators, as shown in Figure 12.7.

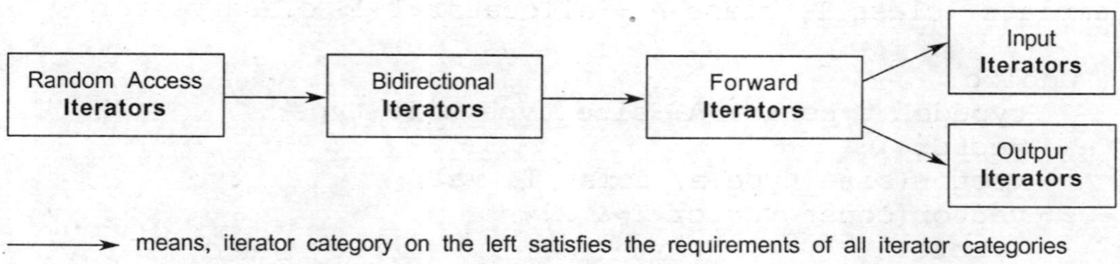

Figure 12.7 Iterators.

Every container class defines one or more iterators that can be used to scan through the elements of the container, as is shown in Examples 12.10 and 12.11:

EXAMPLE 12.10:

```
template <class T, class A = allocator<T> > class list
{
   public:
      typedef typename A::size_type size_type;
      typedef ... iterator;
      typedef ... const_iterator;
      list();
      list(const list<T>& x);
      ~list();
      list<T>& operator= (const list<T>& x);

      void push_back(const T& x);

      void push_front(const T& x);
      void pop_back();
      void pop_front();
      T& front();
      T& back();
      size_type size() const;
      bool empty() const;
};
```

EXAMPLE 12.11:

```
list<float> l;
l.push_back(6.01);
l.push_back(7.01);
l.push_back(8.01);
l.push_back(9.01);

// Use a list iterator to iterate through l:

list<float>::iterator i;
for(i = l.begin(); i != l.end(); ++i)
{
   cout << *i << " ";
}
```

This prints:

```
6.01 7.01 8.01 9.01
```

Most powerful iterator categories that can be used with vector, list and deque are as you can see in Table 12.9:

Table 12.9

Container	*Iterator Category*
vector	random access iterators
list	bidirectional iterators
deque	random access iterators

Algorithms and Function Objects

All the algorithms provided by the library are parametrized by iterator types and are so separated from particular implementations of data structures. Because of that they are called generic algorithms. Function Object is a class that has the function-call operator (operator()) defined.

The algorithms delivered with the library are divided into four groups as shown in Table 12.10.

Table 12.10

Group	*Algorithm Type*
1	mutating sequence operations
2	non-mutating sequence operations
3	sorting and related operations
4	generalized numeric operations

Adaptors

Adaptors are template classes that provide interface mappings. These classes are based on other classes to implement a new functionality. Member functions can be added or hidden or can be combined, to achieve new functionality. Adapters are of three types: Container Adaptors, Iterator Adaptors, Function Adaptors.

SUMMARY

The key concepts introduced in this chapter are as follows:

- The object-oriented model for I/O is a set of C++ classes that comprize the I/O Stream Class Library. Header file iostream.h declares the basic input-output classes.

- In C, there are three standard files available: stdin as the standard input stream, stdout as the buffered standard output stream, and stderr as the unbuffered standard error stream. In C++, comparable input-output streams are predefined objects named cin, cout and cerr.
- The advantages of C++ I/O Stream Class Library over C standard I/O library are: ease of use, typesafeness, and uniformness.
- The Standard Template Library (STL) is a C++ programming library that is designed to enable a C++ programmer to do generic programming, and is based on the extensive use of templates or parametrized types. STL components are algorithm, container, iterator, function object, and adaptor.

REVIEW QUESTIONS

1. What is the role of an insertion operator?
2. What is the role of an extraction operator?
3. What are the different forms of get() function of istream class? Illustrate the uses by citing proper examples.
4. Illustrate the role of string stream objects in C++ compared to string handling functions in native C.
5. Illustrate the method of providing own manipulators?
6. What is the role of I/O manipulators?
7. What will be the output of the following program?

```
#include <iostream>
#include <string>
using namespace std;

int main()
{
    char *str="ABCDEFGH";
    int length=strlen(str);
    for  (int i = 1; i < length; i++)
    {
       cout.write(str,i);
       cout<< '\n';
    }
    return 0;
}
```

8. What is STL? Why should they be used?
9. What do you mean by container classes?

13 Data Structures and Applications in C++

Once you succeed in writing the programs for [these] complicated algorithms, they usually run extremely fast. The computer doesn't need to understand the algorithm, its task is only to run the programs.

—R. Tarjan

LEARNING OBJECTIVES

The objective of this chapter is to acquaint you with:

- Several frequently used fundamental data structures as array and linked list where from other data structures like stack, queue, tree can be made

INTRODUCTION

Before going to a small example case study, we will learn about some fundamental data structures, the knowledge of which is very important in order to design and develop efficient computer programs. Designing and using data structures is an important programming skill. Data structures can be termed as the organized collection of data. Certain rules are followed to access and process the structured data. Thus, some Computer Science pioneers define data structure as:

```
Data Structure = Organized Data + Allowed Operations
```

DATA TYPES

Often, data type is synonymously used as data structure, although they are not the same. A data type usually refers to the kinds of data that variables may hold in a programming language. Most programming languages allow defining typed data of a particular data type and to provide a set of operations that can manipulate these data meaningfully. A data type is defined as:

```
Data Type = Permitted Data Values + Allowed Operations
```

We have already seen how enumerated data types help to define permitted data values. And we also know the ranges of values of data depending on a data type. There are some fundamental data structures which are often used in their own right and can form the basic building block for complex data structures. For example, we have already discussed the concept of array as a basic data structure.

DATA STRUCTURE

Data structure is a representation of the logical relationship among individual elements of data. Since the structure of information will invariably affect the final procedural design, data structure is as important as program structure to the representation of software architecture. Data structure dictates the organization, methods of access, degree of associativity, and processing alternatives for information. The complexity and organization of a data structure is limited only by the ingenuity of the designer. There are a limited number of classic data structures that form the building block for more sophisticated structures. Some classic data structures encountered in the software work are described in this chapter.

Several frequently used fundamental data structures are grouped together as container data structures, for example, the List, the Stack, and the Queue. Containers hold objects of any type and provide standard operations for inserting and removing objects from the container. More interesting data structures are Trees (various kinds), Graphs, and Hash tables.

Classification of Data Structures

We may classify these data structures as *linear* and *non-linear* data structures. However, this is not the only way to classify data structures. In linear data structure (e.g. array), the data items are arranged in a linear sequence whereas, in a non-linear data structure (e.g. tree), the data items are not stored in sequence. Data structures may also be classified as *homogenous* and *non-homogenous* data structures. An 'array' is an example of homogenous data structure in which all elements are of same type. In non-homogenous data structures the elements may not be of the same type. 'Records' are common example of non-homogeneous data structures. The third method of classifying data structures is as *static* or *dynamic* data structures. The size and structure of static structures are fixed at compile time. Dynamic data structures may expand or shrink as and when required during the program execution and their associated memory locations and size change.

There are two design aspects to every data structure:

1. ***The interface part.*** The publicly accessible functions are of this type. Functions like creation and destruction of the object, inserting and removing elements (if it is a container), assigning values etc.

2. ***The implementation part.*** Internal implementation should be independent of the interface. Therefore, the details of the implementation aspect should be hidden out from the users.

C++ has powerful language features to define a data structure by providing separate interface and implementation aspects.

The most common data structure is the list. There are two general types of lists: the array or vector, and the linked list.

Scalar Item

A *scalar item* is the simplest among all data structures. As the name implies, a scalar item represents a single element of information that may be addressed by an identifier, that is, access may be achieved by specifying a single address in storage. The size and format of a scalar item may vary within bounds that are dictated by a programming language. For example, a scalar item may be a logical entity one bit long, an integer or floating point number that is 32 or 64 bits long, or a character string, that is hundreds or thousands of bytes long. An example of simple C++ variable declarations is as follows:

```
int a;   /* a scalar integer number */
float b; /* a scalar floating point number */
```

A scalar item can be understood as follows:

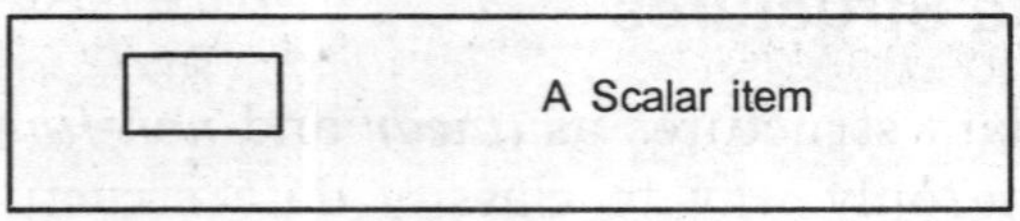

Sequential Vector

When scalar items are organized as a list or contiguous group, a *sequential vector* is formed. Vectors are the most common of all data structures and open doors to variable indexing of information as for example, simple C++ variable declarations such as

```
int a[10];  /* a vector or array of 10 contiguously
                 stored integer numbers */
```

And this can be accessed as in C++ statements like:

```
void f()
{
   int a[10];
   int i;
   for ( i = 0; i < 10; i++)
      a[i] = i;
```

Here, a sequential vector (array) of 10 integer items a is defined. Access to each element of a is indexed in the procedure f so that elements of the data structure are referenced in a definite order. A sequential vector looks somewhat like the following:

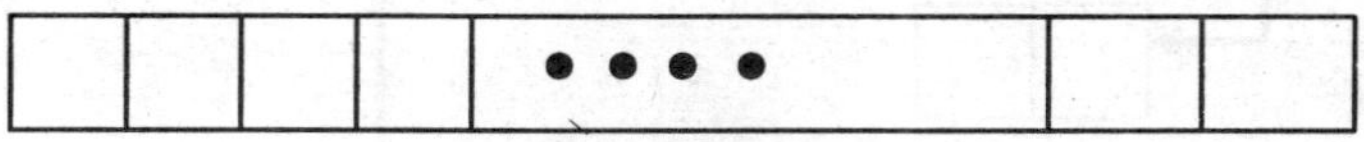

A sequential vector

n-dimensional Space

When the sequential vector is extended to two, three, and ultimately, an arbitrary number of dimensions, an *n-dimensional space* is created. The most commonly used n-dimensional space is the two-dimensional matrix. In most programming languages, an n-dimensional space is called an array. Let us visualize it as in Figure 13.1.

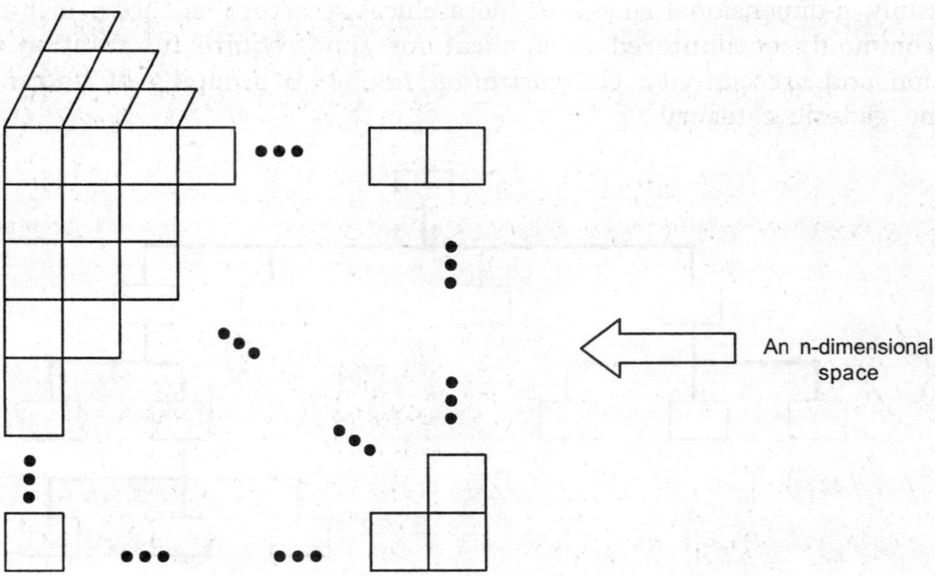

Figure 13.1 Example of an n-dimensional space.

Scalar items, vectors, and n-dimensional spaces may be organized in a variety of formats. A *linked list* is a data structure that organizes non-contiguous scalar items, vectors, or spaces in a manner called nodes, that enables them to be processed as a list. Each node contains the appropriate data organization (e.g. a vector) and one or more pointers that indicate the address of the next node in the list. Nodes may be added at any point in the list by redefining pointers to accommodate the new list (see Figure 13.2).

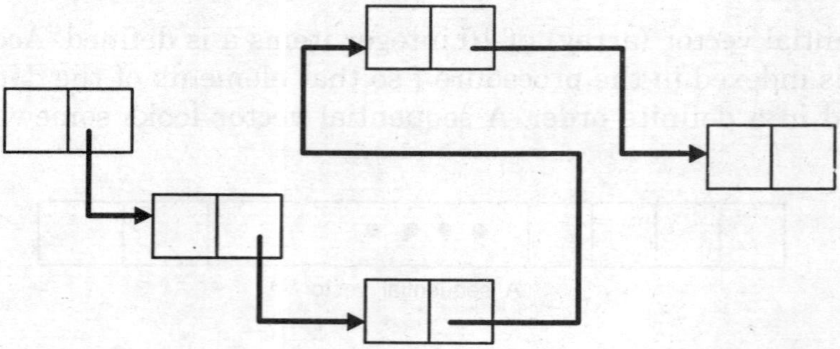

Figure 13.2 A linked list.

Other data structures are incorporated or constructed using these fundamental data structures like scalar items, vector items, n-dimensional space and linked list. For example, a *hierarchical data structure* is implemented using multi-linked lists that contain scalar items, vectors, and possibly, n-dimensional spaces. A hierarchical structure as shown in Figure 13.3 is commonly encountered in applications that require information categorization and associativity. *Categorization* implies a grouping of information by some generic category.

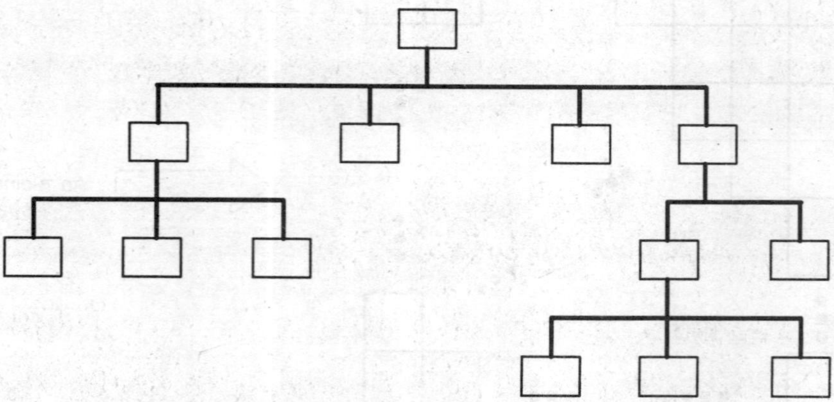

Figure 13.3 A hierarchical structure.

Associativity implies the ability to associate information from different categories, e.g. to find all entries in the PC category that cost less than Rs. 40,000.00 (cost subcategory), run at 833+ MHz (cycle time subcategory), and are made by Indian vendors (vendor subcategory).

Representing Data Structures

Data structures, like program structures, can be represented at different levels of abstraction. For example, a *stack* is a conceptual model of a data structure that can be implemented as a vector or a linked list. Depending on the level of design detail, the internal workings of stack may or may not be specified. The representation of a data structure should be known only to those modules that must make direct use of data contained within the structure. The concept of information hiding and related concept of coupling provide important insight into the quality of a software design.

Another viewpoint is from the input and output data design needs. The input needed for any program is determined by the output desired. The analyst must ask the following questions:

- What information is already in the master file or database?
- What constant data is required that can be entered from some type of control record?
- What information must be supplied by using some type of transaction file?
- What data should be stored and accessed from tables?
- What information can be calculated by the program?

Any time the use of a transaction file is being considered, or the data is to be entered from a terminal, the analyst must check each field to determine whether the data is already in a master file, or might be included in a table. The analyst must be concerned with the program in the most efficient and cost-effective manner as to how and where data is generated. This has a direct impact on a number of other questions. In a cost-accounting system, much of the data is generated when material is put into production. The analyst should attempt to provide a reliable means for entering data directly into the system from the factory. Data collection devices or special terminals can be used to enter some of the data.

For example, in a retail sales system, a type of scanner device—bar code readers—may be used to read price tickets. When charges on sales are made, special readers are available that make it possible to use the data stored on the customer's charge card.

Railways Reservation system presents an input screen simply on entering the train code, travel class and date of travel wherein reservation is asked. The booking officer has to just enter the passenger's details almost in the same way as written in reservation slip.

In large tea gardens of a state spread over several kilometers, handheld terminals in mobile vans are used to enter leaf plucker's code and weight of leaf plucked on a daily basis, moving from one garden to another. Entire data is updated on returning back to computer center. This helps to generate weekly payment reports for the workers and also next days schedule for labour deployment in new gardens. Let's now elaborate some of the fundamental data structures.

Array

A consecutive set of memory locations occupied by homogeneous elements (data) is called an array. The array has a fixed size, and the size is to be specified at the time of declaring an array as in:

```
int iarr[100];   //declares an integer array that can hold
                 //100 integer data contiguously
IntArr ia[100];  //declares an object array that can hold
                 //100 instances of IntArr class contiguously
```

The advantage of the array is that storage required for it is determined and allocated statically (at compile-time). It is convenient to access using an integer index, and also we can easily iterate through an array using a loop index variable. For example:

```
for (int i = 0; i < 100; i++)
{
   iarr[i] = 0;
   ia[i] = 0;  // provided IntArr class has overloaded
               // index operator i.e. [ ] operator
}
```

Through iteration, we step through a list, one data element at a time. We can iterate in forward direction, backward direction or by simply by pointer arithmetic on the memory location where the array is located or using arithmetic on the array index. We can also access any element of the array in constant time, as long as we use a valid (falling within array index range) index value. The index operator for array of built-in data types does not perform bounds checking when accessing an array. However, in the given example we have shown overloading index operator for user-defined classes where we can put necessary bound checks.

The simplest form of an array is a one-dimensional array or vector. For example:

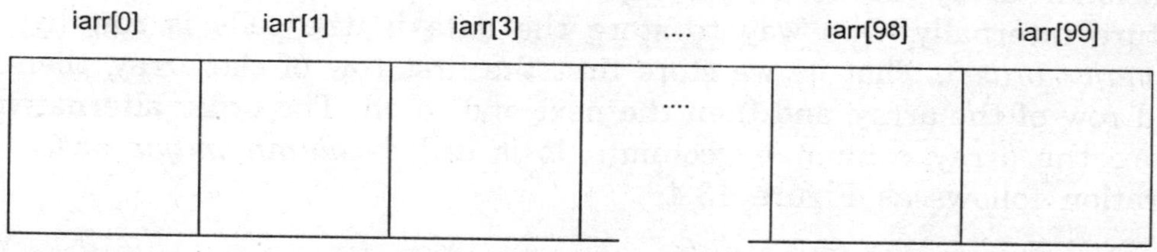

Arrays can be multi-dimensional. Any array defined to have more than one dimension is considered to be multi-dimensional array. It can be 2-dimensional, 3-dimensional, 4-dimensional, or n-dimensional. Two-dimensional arrays, sometimes called matrices, are quite common. We can think of a two-dimensional array as a table of columns and rows: the first dimension in the array referring to the rows, and the second dimension referring to the columns. For example,

```
int   iarr[10][15]; // declares an integer matrix of
                    // 10 rows and 15 columns
```

as follows:

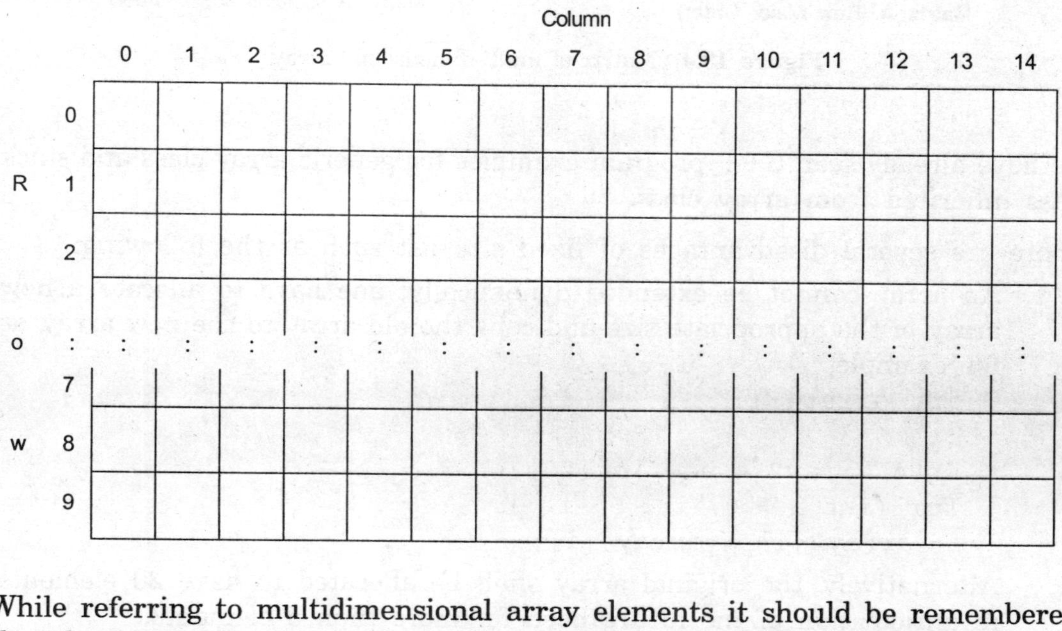

While referring to multidimensional array elements it should be remembered that, by convention, the first subscript of a two-dimensional array refers to a row of the array, while the second subscript refers to a column of the array. Let us now see storage mappings for multi-dimensional arrays. A two-dimensional array is arranged in rows and columns. However, a computer's memory is arranged as a row of memory cells. As such, the rectangular structure of a two-dimensional array needs to be represented as a linear one-dimensional structure internally. One way to store the data in the cells is row by row (*row major order*). That is, we store first the first row of the array, then the second row of the array, and then the next and so on. The order alternative is to store the array column by column. It is called *column major order*. An illustration follows as Figure 13.4:

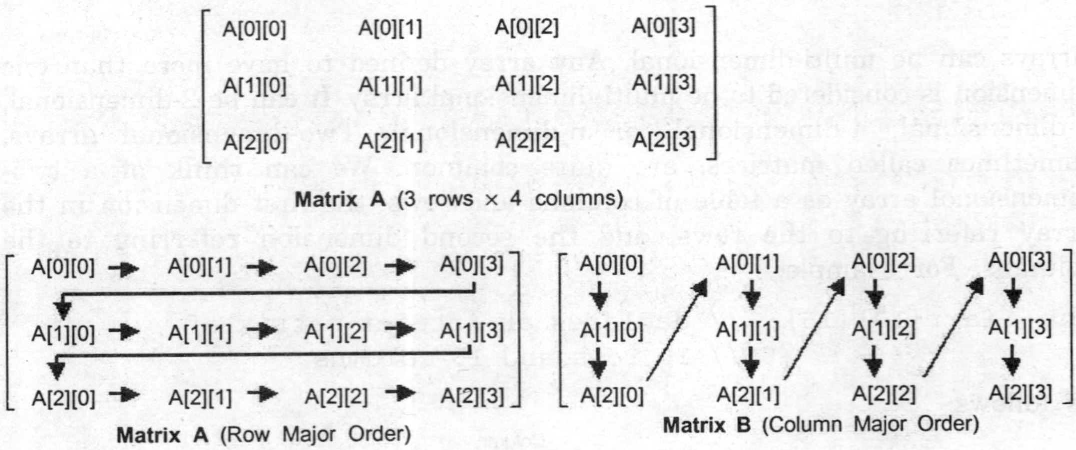

Figure 13.4 Matrix of multi-dimensional array.

We have already seen C++ program examples for generic array class and stack class inherited from array class.

There are several disadvantages of fixed size list such as the following:

1. An array cannot be extended dynamically; one have to allocate a new array of the appropriate size and copy the old array to the new array, as for example,

```
int array[5];
...
int* array2 = new int[20];
for (int i = 0; i < 5; i++)
   array2[i] = array[ i];
```

   Alternatively, the original array shall be allocated to have 20 elements in anticipation of the future need for more than 5 elements.

2. If you want to insert, or remove an element to/from a fixed position in the list, then you must move elements already in the list to make room

for the subsequent elements in the list. Thus, on an average, you probably copy half the elements. In the worst case, inserting into position 1 requires moving of all the elements. Copying elements can result in longer execution times for a program if insert/remove operations are frequent, especially when you consider the cost of copying is huge (like when we copy strings).

Let's now study the definition and examples of Linked List class.

Linked Lists

The linked list is a flexible alternative to the array or vector, with an extra storage usage per list element called a list node, because of the need to keep a pointer to the next node in the list. Each node is dynamically allocated from the heap, so that the node has a unique address. A linked list is formed by having each node contain a "next" pointer that has the address of the next node in the list. The last node in the list has a next pointer with the value NULL, indicating the end of the list. Example programs follows as Program Source Code 13.1 (header file LLIST.HPP) and 13.1a (source file TEST.CPP).

Program Source Code 13.1 (LLIST.HPP)

```
typedef  enum {FALSE, TRUE} BOOLEAN;

typedef enum { SORTEDASCENDING,
               SORTEDDESCENDING,
               UNSORTED} ORDER ;

const int INSERT_AT_END = -1;
const int INSERT_SORT_ASCENDING = -2;
const int INSERT_SORT_DESCENDING = -3;

template <class T>
class NODE
{
     T data;
     NODE *next;

   public:
     NODE(T d);
     virtual ~NODE();
     NODE<T> * insert(NODE<T> * n, int pos);
     NODE<T> * remove(T d);
     NODE * search(T data);
```

(*contd.*)

Program Source Code 13.1 (LLIST.HPP) *(contd.)*

```
    void print(),
    void purge();
};

template <class T>
NODE <T>:: NODE<T>(T d)
{
   this->data = d;
   this->next = NULL;
}

template <class T>
NODE <T>:: ~NODE<T>()
{
   this->purge();
}

template <class T>
NODE<T> * NODE <T>:: search(T d)
{
   if (this->data == d)
      return this;
   else if (this->next == NULL)
      return NULL;
   else
      return this->next->search(d);
}

template <class T>
NODE<T> * NODE <T>:: remove(T d)
{
   NODE *n;
   // return 'this->next' if d matches with current node's
   // data, otherwise, pass to next node returning 'this'.
   if ( this->data == d)
   {
      // return to the caller stating that remove myself
      return this->next;
   }
   else
```

(contd.)

Program Source Code 13.1 (LLIST.HPP) *(contd.)*

```
    {
        if (this->next != NULL)
        {
            n = this->next->remove(d);
            if (n!= this->next)
            {
                // 'this->next' node is to be removed
                delete this->next;
            }
        }
        // return to the caller stating that I am ok
        return this;
    }
}

template <class T>
NODE<T> * NODE <T>:: insert(NODE<T> *n, int pos)
{
    // insert new node (n) at the desired position.
    // pos = INSERT_AT_END => insert at end of the list
    // pos = INSERT_SORT_ASCENDING => insert sorted in
                                      ascending order
    // pos = INSERT_SORT_DESCENDING => insert sorted in
                                      descending order
    // pos >= 0 => insert at desired position,
    // pos 0=> beginning of list
    // return 'this' if n is inserted after 'this' and
    // return n if n is inserted before 'this' object

    NODE<T> *nn;

    switch (pos)
    {
        case INSERT_AT_END:
            if (this->next == NULL)
            {
                // n becomes the last node
                this->next = n;
            }
            else
```

(contd.)

Program Source Code 13.1 (LLIST.HPP) *(contd.)*

```
      {
         // tail of the list is yet to be found
         // ask your next element to handle the insertion
         nn = this->next->insert(n, pos);
         if ( nn != this->next)
            this->next = nn;
      }
      return this;
      break;

   case INSERT_SORT_ASCENDING:
   case INSERT_SORT_DESCENDING:
      if ( ((pos == INSERT_SORT_ASCENDING)
          && ( n->data < this->data ))
         || ((pos == INSERT_SORT_DESCENDING)
          && ( n->data > this->data ))
         )
      {
         // n is to be inserted before 'this'
         n->next = this;
         return n;
      }
      else
      {
         if (this->next == NULL)
         {
            // n becomes the last node
            this->next = n;
         }
         else
         {
            // ask your next element to handle the insertion
            nn = this->next->insert(n, pos);
            if (nn != this->next)
               this->next = nn;
         }
         return this;
      }
      break;
```

(contd.)

Program Source Code 13.1 (LLIST.HPP) *(contd.)*

```
      default:
         // insert at desired position
         if (pos == 0)
         {
            // n is to be inserted before 'this'
            n->next = this;
            return n;
         }
         else
         {
            if (this->next == NULL)
            {
               // n becomes the last node
               this->next = n;
            }
            else
            {
               // ask your next element to handle the insertion
               // pos parameter passed after decrementing
               nn = this->next->insert(n, pos - 1);
               if (nn != this->next)
                  this->next = nn;
            }
            return this;
         }
         break;
   }
}

template <class T>
void NODE <T>:: print()
{
   cout << this->data << "->";
   if (this->next == NULL )
      cout << "NULL";
   else
      this->next->print();
}

template <class T>
```

(contd.)

Program Source Code 13.1 (LLIST.HPP) *(contd.)*

```
void NODE <T>:: purge()
{
   if (this->next != NULL)
   {
      delete this->next;
      this->next = NULL;
   }
}

template <class T>
class LINKEDLIST
{
   NODE<T> *header;

   public:
      LINKEDLIST();
      virtual ~LINKEDLIST();
      void insert(T d, int pos);
      void remove(T d);
      BOOLEAN search(T data);
      void print();
      void purge();
};

template <class T>
LINKEDLIST <T>:: LINKEDLIST<T>()
{
   this->header = NULL;
}

template <class T>
LINKEDLIST <T>:: ~LINKEDLIST<T>()
{
   this->purge();
}

template <class T>
BOOLEAN LINKEDLIST <T>:: search(T d)
```

(contd.)

Program Source Code 13.1 (LLIST.HPP) *(contd.)*

```
{
   if ( (this->header != NULL ) &&
        (this->header->search(d) != NULL)
      )
      return TRUE;
   return FALSE;
}

template <class T>
void LINKEDLIST <T>:: remove(T d)
{
   NODE<T> n;
   if (this->header != NULL)
   {
      n = this->header->remove(d);
      if (n != this->header)
      {
         delete this->header;
         this->header = n;
      }
   }
}

template <class T>
void LINKEDLIST <T>:: insert(T d, int pos)
{
   // insert new NODE made from d at the desired position.
   // pos = INSERT_AT_END => insert at end of the list
   // pos = INSERT_SORT_ASCENDING =>
                    insert sorted in ascending order
   // pos = INSERT_SORT_DESCENDING =>
                    insert sorted in descending order
   // pos >= 0 => insert at desired position,
            = 0 => beginning of list

   NODE <T> *n = new NODE<T>(d);
   NODE <T> * newHeader;
   if (this-> header == NULL)
      this->header = n;
   else
```

(contd.)

Program Source Code 13.1 (LLIST.HPP) *(contd.)*

```
    {
        newHeader = this->header->insert(n, pos);
        if (newHeader != this->header)
            this->header = newHeader;
    }
}

template <class T>
void LINKEDLIST <T>:: print()
{
    cout << endl << "———————————" << endl;
    if (this->header == NULL)
        cout << "Empty Linked List...." << endl;
    else
    {
        this->header->print();
    }
    cout << endl << "———————————" << endl;
}

template <class T>
void LINKEDLIST <T>:: purge()
{
    if (header != NULL)
    {
        delete header;
        header = NULL;
    }
}
```

Program Source Code 13.1a (TEST.CPP)

```
#include <iostream.h>
#include "LList.hpp"

int main()
{
    cout << "Empty LinkedListCreated";
    LINKEDLIST<int> aList;
    aList.print();
```

(contd.)

Program Source Code 13.1a (TEST.CPP) *(contd.)*

```
    cout << "Inserting 3, 5, 2 to be inserted at end ";

    aList.purge();
    aList.insert(3, INSERT_AT_END);
    aList.insert(5, INSERT_AT_END);
    aList.insert(2, INSERT_AT_END);
    aList.print();

    cout  << "Inserting 3, 5, 2 to be inserted in "
          << "sort ascending order ";
    aList.purge();
    aList.insert(3, INSERT_SORT_ASCENDING);
    aList.insert(5, INSERT_SORT_ASCENDING);
    aList.insert(2, INSERT_SORT_ASCENDING);
    aList.print();

    cout  << "Inserting 3, 5, 2 to be inserted in "
          << "sort ascending order ";
    aList.purge();
    aList.insert(3, INSERT_SORT_DESCENDING);
    aList.insert(5, INSERT_SORT_DESCENDING);
    aList.insert(2, INSERT_SORT_DESCENDING);
    aList.print();

    cout  << "Inserting 3, 5, 2 to be inserted "
          << "always at the beginning " << endl
          << "(like stack) ";
    aList.purge();
    aList.insert(3, 0);
    aList.insert(5, 0);
    aList.insert(2, 0);
    aList.print();

    cout  << "Inserting 3, 5, 2 to be inserted at "
          << "position 0, 1, 1 respectively ";
    aList.purge();
    aList.insert(3, 0);
    aList.insert(5, 1);
    aList.insert(2, 1);
    aList.print();

    return 0;
}
```

```
Output 13.1a
Empty LinkedListCreated
_______________
Empty Linked List....

_______________
Inserting 3, 5, 2 to be inserted at end
_______________
3->5->2->NULL
_______________
Inserting 3, 5, 2 to be inserted in sort ascending order
_______________
2->3->5->NULL
_______________
Inserting 3, 5, 2 to be inserted in sort ascending order
_______________
5->3->2->NULL
_______________
Inserting 3, 5, 2 to be inserted always at the beginning
(like stack)
_______________
2->5->3->NULL
_______________
Inserting 3, 5, 2 to be inserted at position 0, 1, 1
respectively
_______________
3->2->5->NULL
_______________
```

There are many more data structures like queue, tree, graph which can be implemented efficiently in C++. We will now move on to a small application case study using C++.

A Small Example Program

In this small example program, we will define four classes—Employee, Manager, Programmer and Secretary. Each has his salary defined as composite figure and name stored in Employee subobject; each class defines its own characteristics. The Program Source Code 13.2 for this is as follows:

Program Source Code 13.2

```
#include <iostream.h>
#include <string.h>

typedef enum {FALSE, TRUE} Boolean;

class Employee
{
      char * name;
      int  salary;
   public:
      Employee(char * nm = NULL, int = 0);
      virtual ~Employee();
      virtual void display();
};

Employee :: Employee(char * nm, int sal)
{
   name = NULL;
   if (nm != NULL)
   {
      name = new char [ strlen(nm) + 1 ];
      strcpy(name, nm);
   }
   salary = sal;
}

Employee :: ~Employee()
{
   if (name != NULL )
      delete [] name;
}

void Employee ::display()
{
   if (name == NULL)
      cout << "No Name available for Employee" << endl;
   else
      cout << "Name of Employee: " << name << endl;
}
```

(contd.)

Program Source Code 13.2 *(contd.)*

```
class Manager : public Employee
{
   public:
      Manager(char *nm, int sal) : Employee(nm, sal) {};
      ~Manager(){};
      void display();
};

void Manager :: display()
{
   Employee :: display();
   cout << "Employee Type : Manager " << endl;
}

class Programmer : public Employee
{
      char *language;
   public:
      Programmer(char *nm, int sal, char * lang);
      ~Programmer(){};
      void display();
};

Programmer :: Programmer(char *nm, int sal, char * lang)
           : Employee(nm, sal)
{
   language = NULL;
   if (lang != NULL)
   {
      language = new char [strlen(lang) + 1];
      strcpy(language, lang);
   }
}

void Programmer :: display()
{
   Employee :: display();
   cout << "Employee Type : Programmer " << endl;
   if ( this->language == NULL )
      cout << "Language Known : None specific " << endl;
```

(contd.)

Program Source Code 13.2 *(contd.)*

```
   else
      cout << "Language Known : " << this->language << endl;

}

class Secretary : public Employee
{
      Boolean steno;
      int TypingSpeed;
   public:
      Secretary(char *nm, int sal, Boolean IsSteno, int typespeed);
      ~Secretary(){};
      void display();
};

Secretary  :: Secretary(char *nm, int sal,
                           Boolean IsSteno, int typespeed)
           : Employee(nm, sal)
{
   steno = IsSteno;
   TypingSpeed = typespeed;
}

void Secretary :: display()
{
   Employee :: display();
   cout << "Employee Type : Secretary " << endl;
   if ( this->steno == FALSE)
      cout << "Cannot perform job of a steno "<< endl;
   else
      cout << "Can perform job of a steno "<< endl;
   cout << "Typing speed is " << TypingSpeed << endl;
}

int main()
{
   int i;
   Employee *e[5];

   e[0] = new Manager("A. Pal", 10000);
```

(contd.)

Program Source Code 13.2 *(contd.)*

```
   e[1] = new Programmer("D. Ghosh", 6000, "C++");
   e[2] = new Programmer("R. Das", 5000, "Java");
   e[3] = new Secretary("S. Ray", 3000, FALSE, 40);
   e[4] = new Secretary("A. Chatterjee", 2500, TRUE, 50);

   for (i = 0; i < 5; i++)
   {
      e[i]->display();
   }

   for (i = 0; i < 5; i++)
      delete e[i];

   return 0;
}
```

Output 13.2

```
Name of Employee: A. Pal
Employee Type: Manager
Name of Employee: D. Ghosh
Employee Type: Programmer
Language Known: C++
Name of Employee: R. Das
Employee Type: Programmer
Language Known: Java
Name of Employee: S. Ray
Employee Type: Secretary
Cannot perform job of a steno
Typing speed is 40
Name of Employee: A. Chatterjee
Employee Type: Secretary
Can perform job of a steno
Typing speed is 50
```

SUMMARY

The key concepts introduced in this chapter are as follows:

- Data structures can be termed as the organized collection of data. Certain rules are followed to access and process the structured data.

- The sizes and structures of static data structures are fixed at compile time. Dynamic data structures may expand or shrink as and when required during the program execution and their associated memory locations and size change.
- Data structures, like program structures, can be represented at different levels of abstraction.
- A consecutive set of memory locations occupied by homogeneous elements (data) is called an *array*.
- The linked list is a flexible alternative to the array or vector, with an extra storage usage per list element, called a list node, because of the need to keep a pointer to the next node in the list.
- There are many more data structures like queue, tree and graph that can be implemented efficiently in C++.

REVIEW QUESTIONS

1. Can you implement a circular Queue class from Array class?
2. Implement a generic Queue class subclassing from generic Array class.
3. Implement a Binary Tree class and provide member functions for counting number of leaves.
4. Modify Linked List program to make it doubly linked list. Can you do this by inheriting from LinkedList class?
5. Modify Linked List class to support overloaded functions for removing a node at a particular position (0=> first position) and return data contained in the removed node.
6. Inherit from modified LinkedList class (as in prob. 4) to implement a Stack class and a Queue class.
7. Can you implement a Binary Search Tree using the Linked List Base class?
8. Implement a generic doubly Linked List class with suitable member functions.

14 Object-Oriented Design and Modelling

The most important single aspect of software development is to be clear about what you are trying to build.

—Bjarne Stroustrup

Each pattern describes a problem which occurs over and over again in our environment, and then describes the core of the solution to that problem in such a way that you can use this solution many times over, without ever doing it the same way twice.

—Christopher Alexander

LEARNING OBJECTIVES

The objective of this chapter is to acquaint you with:

- Software development process from software engineering and quality perspective
- Software architecture concepts
- Best practices of software development
- Phases of software development—inception, elaboration, construction and transition
- OO principles and concepts
- OO modelling from views of Booch, Rumbaugh, Jacobson

INTRODUCTION

The object-oriented paradigm focuses on the behavioural and structural characteristics of entities as complete units. It is concept-centred (holistic) in that, it focuses on all the types of features that constitute any given concept. The paradigm encompasses and supports the four pillars or the first principles as *abstraction*, *encapsulation*, *inheritance*, and *polymorphism*. These pillars are used to facilitate communication, increase productivity and consistency, and enable management of change and complexity with problem-solving efforts.

Abstraction involves formulation of representations by focusing on similarities and differences among a set of entities to extract intrinsic essential characteristics (relevant common features). It also avoids extrinsic incidental characteristics (irrelevant distinguishing features) in order to define a single representation having those characteristics that are relevant to defining every element in the set.

Encapsulation involves the packaging of representations by focusing on hiding of details to facilitate abstraction, where specifications are used to describe what an entity is and what an entity does, and implementations are used to describe how an entity is realized. *Inheritance* involves the relating and reusing of existing representations to define new representations. *Polymorphism* involves the ability of new representations to be defined as variations of existing representations, where new implementations are introduced; but specifications remain the same such that a specification has many implementations.

The idea was originally conceived by three of the most prominent Greek philosophers, Socrates (470-399 BC), Plato (428-348 BC), and Aristotle (384-322 BC) in the *Theory of Forms*. It had evolved since its original conceptualization to become a pivotal force in the evolution of science, technology, and any other domain in which it is applied. In general, problem-solving involves understanding or conceptualizing a problem first, solving the problem next, and finally implementing or realizing the solution. Understanding or conceptualizing a problem involves representing the problem using representational constructs (mental notions or ideas). Solving the problem involves manipulating representational constructs from the problem domain and the solution domain to derive a representation of the desired solution. Realizing a solution involves mapping those representational constructs of the solution unto the solution world, that is, constructing the solution. The use of representational constructs is a very natural process that often occurs subtly, and sometimes unconsciously in problem-solving. Underlying this scheme is the use of a paradigm in determining the possible types of representations utilized in problem-solving efforts. The *object-oriented paradigm* is derived from the convergence of other fundamental paradigms, and is reducible to other paradigms as required by its application via a language or method. The flexibility provided by utilizing this paradigm can be best understood by examining the roots of the paradigm itself within Plato's Theory of Forms.

The first period of Plato's philosophy involved the collaboration of Socrates and Plato to conceive the theory of Forms. The quest for understanding the nature of knowledge began with the premise that something is understood if it can be defined. Socrates proposed that the Socratic method be used as the means for attaining definitions. The Socratic method is a dialectic (converse or discourse) method in which a teacher guides a pupil into recognizing a true conclusion by progressively questioning the pupil, rather than simply indicating that the conclusion is true, until the conclusion is reached by the pupil. This method was demonstrated by Socrates on an individual who is guided to understand the fact behind Pythagorean theorem (within a right triangle, the square of the length of the hypotenuse is equal to the sum of the squares of the lengths of the other two sides). Socrates and Plato concluded that learning involves a pupil's recollection of Ideas (or Forms). The second period of Plato's philosophy involved Plato's formulation of the theory of Forms. Plato theorized that Forms or Ideas are the central elements of knowledge, and to know the Form of a thing is to understand the nature of that thing.

SOFTWARE DEVELOPMENT

The key elements of software development are (i) People, who are the stakeholders, (ii) Project, that depicts specialization of process, (iii) Process, which is a set of organized developed activities, a template for project, (iv) Product, which is the outcome of the development project and (v) Tools, which help in process automation. Factors that affect the effectiveness of *people* are development process, project feasibility, risk management, team structure, project schedule, project understandability and sense of accomplishment.

A software development project comprises of a sequence of changes through a series of iterations. A project follows an organization pattern for people, planning and management. A software system comprises of not only the code, but also requirements, production, installation, operation, tests, sales and so on. Different stakeholders use different aspects of the system. A system has a collection of models. A model is an abstraction of a complete system having a self-contained view. The system is in the eye of beholders (or stakeholders). The multifacetedness of a system is depicted in Figure 14.1. System development is a process of model building. The key is to identify what models to build and what relationship holds between models.

Software development process gives a complete set of activities needed to transform users' requirements into a consistent set of artifacts that represent a software product and, later, to transforms the changes in those requirements into a new, consistent set of artifacts. A process is a template. In other words, a process is a definition of activities, not their execution. Process needs to be instantiated or specialized for individual projects. A software process should cover entire software life cycle. It is essential to modern, complex development. In practice, there is no universally applicable process. The reasons are manifold. Firstly, there are organizational factors comprising of structure, culture, project organization and management, competence and skill levels, prior experience and so on. Secondly, there are domain factors like application domain, which includes mission critical vs word processor, real-time vs batch processing, user community and market competition. Thirdly, there are life cycle factors like time to market, expected life span and planned future releases. Last, but not the least, are the technological factors comprising of programming languages, development tools, databases, middleware, communication and distribution and the like. The bottom line is that the general **process** needs to be specialized.

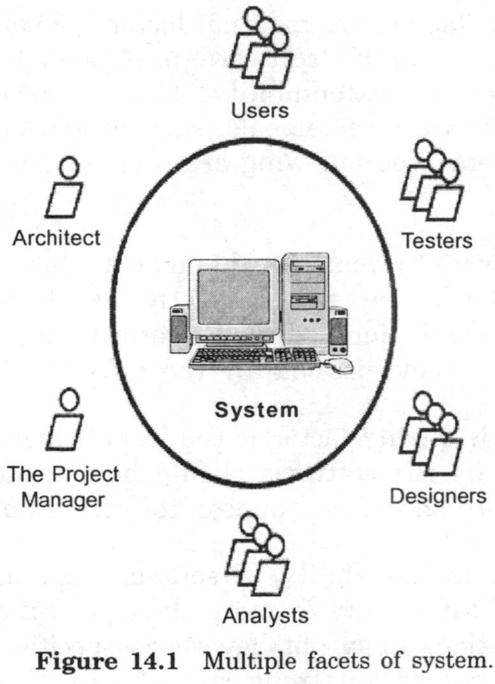

Figure 14.1 Multiple facets of system.

Software development is a complex, risky, expensive and people-intensive venture. Mutual understanding of roles, responsibilities, dependence, communication and coordination among developers and customers is very much essential. A systematic software development process helps in orderly development, improved quality of software, standardized training, repeatability of successful projects and continuous organizational improvement with improved productivity. *Tools* are essential to modern, complex development. They impact and guide process. Formalized development process involves large amount of information and coordination. Automation is essential, for example, software configuration management tools help to manage versions of software being developed to control changes in management. Process drives tools and their development. It specifies the tool functionality and helps to judge feasibility of tools in terms of their support to particular process. In practice, we balance process and tools.

SOFTWARE ENGINEERING PERSPECTIVE

The Desirable Qualities of Software Systems

Producing quality software is the primary goal of any robust software engineering process. The desirable qualities extend to make programs fast, reliable, easy to use, readable, component based or modular, structured and so on. Some of the quality factors are external factors perceivable by the users of the software (who may not be software professionals). These are speed, reliability, ease of use and extendibility. The others are internal factors, perceivable by the software professionals, such as readability, structuredness, modularity etc. In general, the following are some of the desirable qualities of software systems:

1. ***Correctness.*** Software Systems should do what they are meant to do, that is, they should perform the tasks exactly as defined by the system requirements and specifications. Every feature that is desired in the specifications should be made possible by the software.

2. ***Completeness.*** This quality factor is the ideal achievement. Every feature that is made possible by the software should be intended. This means that some unintended feature should not appear to work as a side effect.

3. ***Robustness.*** This is the ability of software systems to work even in abnormal conditions. This quality is more than perfect in the sense that in case of abnormal situations (may not have been specified explicitly in system specifications), system should be strong enough to withstand. Program crash and system hang under abnormal situations is undesirable.

4. ***Reliability.*** This term generally encompasses both correctness and robustness of quality. Software systems should perform as expected by users in terms of the correctness and continue to work, or gracefully terminate (robustness) under abnormalities.

5. ***Extendibility.*** It is the quality factor that makes a software product easy to adapt to changes of specifications or requirements. In principle, software needs to be soft, i.e. flexible enough to cope with changing requirements and adapt to changing technology. Compartmentalization or breaking into multiple

interrelated components and making things simple are two key issues to attain extendibility.

6. ***Maintainability.*** This term is related to extendibility of software systems to make software systems easily maintainable, i.e. it should be easy to make corrections, amendments, and extending features. Long running software systems usually spend more time in maintenance phase than initial development phase when compromises are made in early development phase in terms of design and coding. Reliability is not attained in early development cycle; rather it is usually attained through repeated corrections during the development phase and throughout the lifetime of repeated use of software systems. Software system reliability can be severely hampered by poor maintainability. High maintainability requires flexibility in the design and implementation of software systems. Such flexibility facilitates the kind of incremental development that enhances reliability, usefulness, and user friendliness, as well as the ability to contain costs.

7. ***Reusability.*** This makes a software product being able to be reused as a whole or as a part for other software applications or products. By reusing commonality or patterns, the task of reinventing the same wheel can be avoided. This requires that components of a software system should not be designed to cope with specific problems in specific contexts, but should be designed to provide generic solutions to a class or pattern of problems in different contexts. This makes such general components to be adapted and reused many times. All modern engineering disciplines offer high levels of assurance, predictability and efficiency because new projects are based on a vast, well documented repository of experience, good practice and sound principles. Reusable software components hold the promise of contributing to software development eventually attaining the same status as the established engineering disciplines.

8. ***Compatibility.*** To be able to interact with other software products is a critical factor of a software product. This is possible if we can keep homogeneity in design and have standardized conventions for communicating with other pieces of software available. This requires standardized file format, standardized data structures, standardized protocols, standardized user interfaces and so on.

9. ***Usefulness.*** Software systems should adequately address the needs of their intended users to solve their problems and provide services.

10. ***Timeliness.*** Software systems should be completed on time and on budget.

11. ***User friendliness.*** Software systems should provide user-friendly interfaces tailored to the capabilities, background and psychology of the intended users to facilitate easy use and access to the full extent of the system's capabilities. End users should find the software easy to use, easy to learn the usability of the software, easy to enter data, easy to interpret reports generated, easy to recover from errors due to problems or incorrect usage.

12. ***Efficiency.*** Software systems should make good use of system resources, including processing time, memory, communication with other systems and disk space. Optimal use of space and time is an essential requirement of any good quality software product.

13. ***Portability.*** It is the quality factor that makes easy to transfer software products to various hardware, operating system and other system software environment.

14. ***Verifiability.*** This is the ease of preparing acceptance criteria, particularly test data, procedures to detect failures and ability to trace them to find out bugs during validation and operation phases.

15. ***Integrity.*** This is the ability of software systems to protect their various components (programs, data, documents, system software, hardware environment etc.) against unauthorized access and modification.

Not all of these desirable qualities are attainable, though at the same time, are of equal importance. Often the designer has to employ his own judgement to weigh one against the other, whilst maintaining a reasonable balance. For example, attaining perfect integrity requires lots of protections, barriers, security checks etc. which in turn make system not very easy to use. Optimal efficiency may not be attainable if we like to make our software completely portable across various platforms. This calls for making tradeoffs to prioritize things.

Software Architecture

There are different, but nearly equivalent definitions of software architecture given in the different textbooks. Let me quote three of these from different sources and explain each in turn. As opined by Bass, Clements, and Kazman in "Software Architecture in Practice", Addison-Wesley 1997:

> The software architecture of a program or computing system is the structure or structures of the system, which comprise software components, the externally visible properties of those components, and the relationships among them.

By externally visible properties, we are referring to services offered to others, performance characteristics, exception or fault handling, usage of shared resource and so on. The definition reveals that software architecture must abstract away some information from the system. Otherwise there is no benefit of looking at the architecture, in that case, we simply view the entire system and still provide enough information to be a basis for analyzing, decision making, and thereby reducing risk. Software architecture is a collection of concepts and design decisions.

According to Mehdi Jazayeri, Alexander Ran and Frank van der Linden, in *Software Architecture for Product Families: Principles and Practice*, Addison-Wesley Longman, (2000):

> Software architecture is a set of concepts and design decisions about the structure and texture of software that must be made prior to concurrent engineering to enable effective satisfaction of architecturally significant explicit functional and quality requirements and implicit requirements of the product family, the problem, and the solution domains.

Any software is driven by various functional and quality requirements. Some of the requirements are explicit, some are implicit in terms of platform supported, the functional domains of the problem itself and of course the solution. With the increased size and complexity of software systems, the design problem goes beyond the algorithms and data structures of the computation. Thus, designing and specifying the overall system structure emerges as a new kind of problem. There are various structural issues which include gross organization and global control structure; protocols for communication, synchronization, and data access; assignment of functionality to design elements; physical distribution; composition of design elements; scaling and performance; and selection among design alternatives.

As given by Booch, Rumbaugh, and Jacobson in *The UML Modelling Language User Guide*, Addison-Wesley, 1999:

> An architecture is the set of significant decisions about the organization of a software system, the selection of the structural elements and their interfaces by which the system is composed, together with their behaviour as specified in the collaborations among those elements, the composition of these structural and behavioural elements into progressively larger subsystems, and the architectural style that guides this organization—these elements and their interfaces, their collaborations, and their composition.

The architecture of software-intensive systems is based on the use of multiple, concurrent views. This use of multiple views allows to address separately the concerns of the various stakeholders of the architecture end-user, developers, systems engineers, project managers, etc., and to handle separately the functional and non-functional requirements. The architectural elements and their interfaces, their collaborations, and their compositions as a whole constitute a larger system built from it's smaller subsystems with different views of the stakeholders in mind.

The 4+1 View Model depicted in Figure 14.2, organizes a description of a software architecture using five concurrent views, each of which addresses a specific set of concerns. Architects capture their design decisions in four views and use the fifth view to illustrate and validate them. Kruchten of Rational Corporation proposed 5 (4+1) concurrent views as the following:

1. logical (e.g. class diagrams, E-R, functional decomposition)—describes the design's object model;
2. process (e.g. sequence diagrams, collaboration diagrams, dynamic behaviour)—describes the design's concurrency and synchronization aspects;
3. implementation (classic system layering with import/export relationships, modules and subsystems)—describes the software's static organization in the development environment; and
4. deployment (e.g. deployment diagrams)—desc ibes the mapping of the software onto the hardware and shows the system's distributed aspects.

and the +1 being scenarios (instances of use cases). The scenarios view is redundant but helpful to validate and illustrate the architecture.

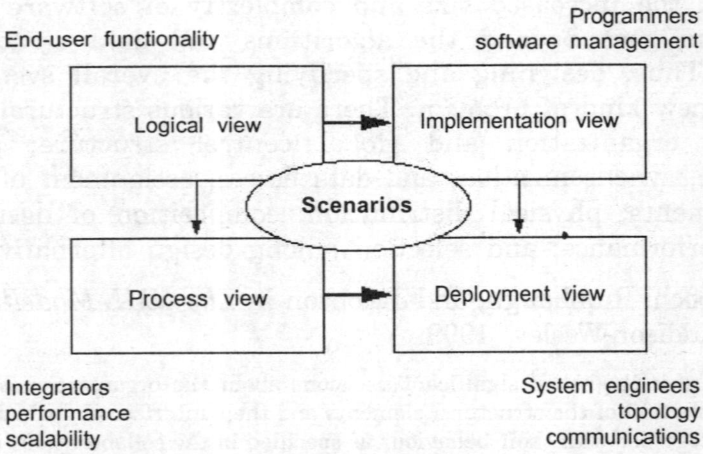

Figure 14.2 4+1 view of architecture.

Software designers can organize the description of their architectural decisions around these four views and then illustrate them with a few selected use of cases or scenarios, which constitute a fifth view. The architecture is partially evolved from these scenarios. The 4+1 View Model allows various stakeholders to find what they need in the software architecture. System engineers can approach it first from the deployment view, then the process view; end users, customers, and data specialists can approach it from the logical view; and project managers and software-configuration staff members can approach it from the implementation view. Software architecture deals with abstraction, decomposition and composition, and style and aesthetics. It also deals with the design and implementation of software's high-level structure. Designers build architectures using several architectural elements in well-chosen forms. These elements satisfy the major functionality and performance requirements of the system as well as other non-functional requirements such as reliability, scalability, portability, and system availability.

Logical View

The logical view primarily supports the functional requirements—the services the system should provide—to its end users. Designers decompose the system into a set of key abstractions, taken mainly from the problem domain. These abstractions are objects or object classes that exploit the principles of abstraction, encapsulation, and inheritance. In addition to aiding functional analysis, decomposition identifies mechanisms and design elements that are common across the system.

Process View

The process view takes into account some non-functional requirements, such as performance and system availability. It addresses concurrency and distribution, system integrity, and fault-tolerance. The process view also specifies which thread of control executes each operation of each class identified in the logical view. Designers describe the process view at several levels of abstraction, each one addressing a different concern. At the highest level, the process view can be seen as a set of independently executing logical networks of communicating programs ("processes") that are distributed across a set of hardware resources, which in turn are connected by a bus or local area network or wide area network. Multiple logical networks may exist simultaneously, sharing the same physical resources. For example, one can use independent logical networks to separate on and off-line operational systems and to represent the coexistence of simulation or test versions of the software. A process is a group of tasks that form an executable unit. Processes represent the level at which the process view can be tactically controlled (started, recovered, reconfigured, shut down, and so on). In addition, processes can be replicated to distribute processing load or improve system availability.

Implementation View

The implementation view focuses on the organization of the actual software modules in the software-development environment. The software is packaged in small chunks—program libraries or subsystems—that can be developed by one or more developers. The subsystems are organized in a hierarchy of layers, each layer providing a narrow and well-defined interface to the layers above it. The implementation view takes into account internal requirements related to ease of development, software management, reuse or commonality, and constraints imposed by the toolset or the programming language. The implementation view supports the allocation of requirements and work to teams, and supports cost evaluation, planning, monitoring of project progress, and reasoning about software reuse, portability, and security. It is the basis for establishing a line of product. The implementation view is represented by module and subsystem diagrams that show the system's export and import relationships.

Deployment View

Deployment view takes into account the system's non-functional requirements such as system availability, reliability (fault-tolerance), performance (throughput), and scalability. The software executes on a network of computers (the processing nodes). Various elements identified in the logical, process, and implementation views—networks, processes, tasks, and objects—must be mapped onto the various nodes. Several different physical configurations will be used, some for development and testing, and others for system deployment at various sites or for different customers. The mapping of the software to the nodes must therefore be highly flexible and have a minimal impact on the source code itself.

Scenarios

This view is redundant with the other ones (hence the "+1"), but it plays two critical roles:

1. It acts as a driver to help designers discover architectural elements during the architecture design.
2. It validates and illustrates the architecture design, both on paper and as the starting point for the tests of an architectural prototype.

Software Process Life Cycle

Every system starts its life the day it is built. Then it is used, maintained and finally it given up to accommodate newer systems. What we mean to say is that every system has a life cycle. There are a number of ways to develop systems. The classical approach is called the Software Development Life Cycle (SDLC). This consists of the stages: Software Requirement Analysis (with Prototyping), Design, Coding, Testing and Maintenance. An effective software process enables an organization to increase its productivity as it is developed for several reasons. By understanding the fundamentals of how software is developed, one can make intelligent decisions regarding tool choice and hiring. It enables to standardize efforts and promote reuse and consistency between project teams. It provides an opportunity to introduce best practices within organizations such as code inspections, configuration management, change control, and architectural modelling to development organization. A software process is needed in order to improve maintenance and support efforts. First, it should define how to manage change and appropriately allocate maintenance changes to future releases of the software, streamlining the change process. Second, it should define how to smoothly transform software into operations and support, and then how the operations and support efforts are actually performed. Without effective operations and support processes the software will quickly become shelfware. Last but not the least, it should help manage the complexity of software efforts. The reality is that software is growing more and more complex, and without an effective way to develop and maintain that software, the chances of succeeding are bleak. A sound software process helps to manage project portfolio. Most organizations may have several software projects, some of which could be currently in development and many more could be in maintenance projects that need to be managed effectively. The nature of the software that are being built is also changing, from simple batch systems of the 1970s that structured techniques geared up towards, to the interactive, international, user-friendly, high-transaction, high-availability online systems that object-oriented and component-based techniques are aimed at.

Systems development refers to all the activities that go into producing an information systems solution to an organizational problem or opportunity. The basic activities that must be performed in any information system development process are:

1. ***Systems analysis.*** System analysis is the analysis of the problem that the organization will try to solve. Systems analysis generally address three important areas:

   a. Thorough investigation and understanding of the requirements the system must satisfy.

   b. An analysis of the existing system.

   c. Resulting in a feasibility study and requirements specification.

The *feasibility study* is used to determine whether the project is feasible. Normally, the feasibility study will investigate and report on several possible options, such as

- Do nothing
- Improve existing system(s)
- Develop or purchase completely new system(s)

Requirements specification is documentation of the system requirements. Perhaps the most important (but also difficult) part of the process is getting the system requirements right. It is no good building a "great" system if it is the answer to wrong question! Good requirements definition involves cooperation between developers and users. Defining user requirements is often more difficult than it appears—there may be disagreements about business processes, ownership disputes, misunderstandings and confusions. Having a good set of requirements enhances the likelihood of getting a successful system.

2. ***Systems design.*** After the systems analysis stage, if the decision is made to proceed with development, systems design begins. Systems design is concerned with how the system will satisfy the what (i.e. the requirements) identified by the systems analysis. Like analysis, design must be a cooperative effort between developers and users.

Designers must consider the following:

- Inputs to the system (what, and from where?)
- Outputs that it will be required to produce
- User interface issues (how should it look and interact with users?)
- Processing and Performance (what are the computations it must perform and how quickly?)
- Database design(what data is needed and how is it structured?)
- Security (access rights, audit trails, recovery methods)
- Documentation (user and technical)
- Conversion (how is the change from the old to the new to be effected most successfully?)
- Training
- Organizational changes (how will relevant jobs and roles be affected?)

The design of the system can be broken into the following:

a. *Logical design*. This lays out the components of the system and their relationship to each other (high level, conceptual).

b. *Physical*. This translates the abstract logical model into specific technical design (low level, detailed).

3. ***Implementation.*** Once the design process is done, the system is actually constructed, that is implemented, in accordance with the design specifications. It is at this stage that programming begins. Not uncommonly, those responsible for analyzing and designing the system also implement it. Programming is the process of translating design specification into program

code. Most systems with varied sizes are designed as a series of semi-independent modules. Each of these modules will generally be worked on by a small team within the project as a whole.

4. ***Testing.*** Before any software product is delivered it must be subjected to rigorous testing. Testing must be based on a test plan, which not only prescribes tests of expected conditions but also extreme cases and incorrect operation or inputs. Some testing is often done during the implementation stage.

In a system of any size and complexity there are different levels of tests:

a. *Unit or program tests.* These are tests of individual program components or modules of the system, often conducted soon after they are built.
b. *System tests.* These are tests of the whole, or large parts of the system to see if the components/modules function together properly.
c. *Acceptance tests.* These are the final tests to see if the system performs to the specification before it is passed on to production.

The project development team often conducts unit and system tests. Acceptance tests are overseen by, and the results must be acceptable to, user representatives and management.

5. ***Maintenance.*** Once the conversion process has taken place the system is said to be in production, and further work on it is called maintenance. Maintenance may be required because certain features or processing prove to be inadequate or incorrect (despite testing), or because new requirements have arisen since the original requirements definition.

6. ***Commissioning/decommissioning.*** There are several possibilities for conversion from the old system to the new. They are listed as follows:

a. *Parallel.* The old and the new are run together until the new is proved safe though expensive.

b. *Direct cut-over.* The old is turned off and the new turned on, on an appointed day. This is somewhat risky.

c. *Pilot.* The new system is used in limited part of the organization until proven. This is safe but slow.

d. *Phased.* The new system is introduced in stages, by function or organizational unit, until it is fully installed.

As an important part of the conversion process, training and documentation must be provided to users and maintainers of the production system. Often, soon after conversion, a post-implementation review is undertaken. This review tries to determine what worked well and what did not, during the entire development process, so that the way things were done might be improved next time.

Software Development Life Cycle Processes include the following steps:

1. ***Project initiation.*** This initiates the project.

2. ***Requirements definition.*** This process is meant to define the customer's requirements completely and unambiguously.

3. ***Project development planning.*** This process is meant to control and monitor the project life cycle. The major elements identified here are the Deliverables, Milestones, Effort Estimation and Resource Allocation.

4. ***Quality planning.*** This process addresses all the quality related aspects of the projects that may include defect tracking, control of non-conforming products and corrective actions.

5. ***Configuration management planning***. This process identifies and organizes software components and related documents, and controls their modification.

6. ***Design documentation.*** This process clearly defines the functionality of each module and clear definition of interfaces across modules to facilitate the process of coding. This process addresses the traceability between the software requirement specifications and the design document itself.

7. ***Coding.*** This process is the translation of the design document to code that has to ultimately meet the customer's requirements as stated earlier.

8. ***Testing and validation.*** This process consists of validation of code against the requirements' specifications. Testing is done independently by executing the software against test plan. The different categories of testing are: Unit, Integration, System Testing.

9. ***Replication, delivery, installation.*** This comprises of deployment of the software built to the client machine, including delivering the software and installing it on client machine.

10. ***Acceptance.*** Acceptance checks whether the delivered software conforms to the agreed acceptance criteria as given by the customer. Once deliverables are created, they need to be verified for appropriateness, correctness, and

relevance. There are certain people or groups who can do this verification. They are customers, domain experts, peer developers, testing groups, and documentation groups.

11. ***Maintenance.*** This process is concerned with the defect fixing and providing software enhancements.

All these can be depicted as a diagram (see Figure 14.3).

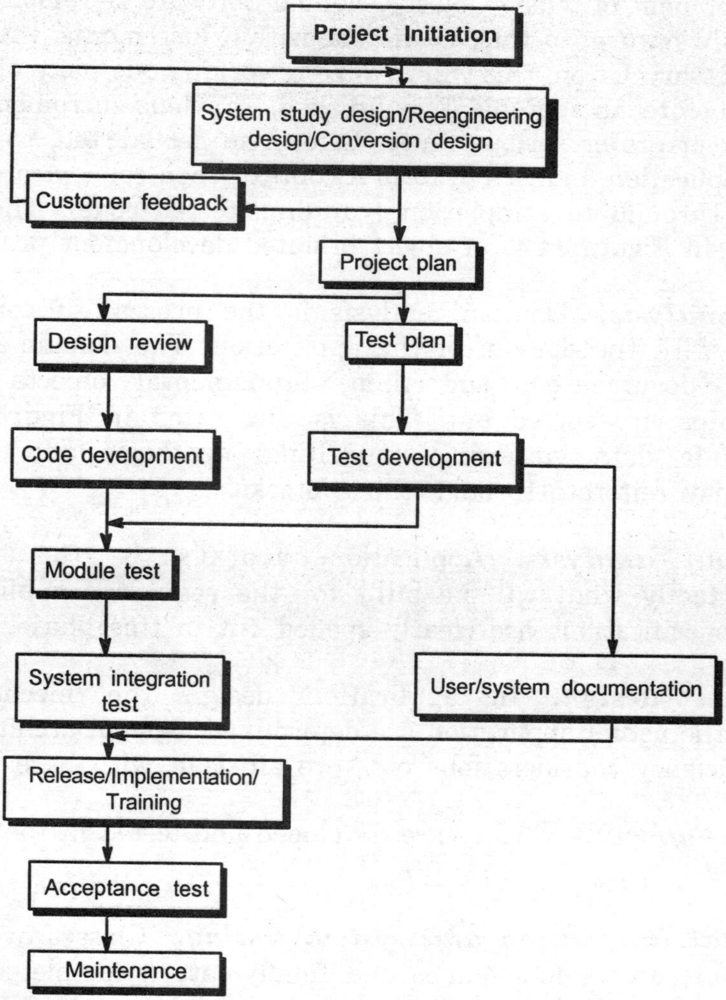

Figure 14.3 Software development process life cycle phases.

The other related processes include document control, customer complaint, purchase, included software, customer supplied item, version control, measurement, training, tools and techniques. Document control process, for example, is intended to ensure that required documents are retrievable in a consistent and timely way.

Object-Oriented Process

Object Orientation has become the predominant paradigm for almost all software development of today. Object Oriented Software Development Process is incremental in nature. In this, we iterate within increments, with prototype support as necessary. Often, this will involve reworking one piece of the system several times before an increment is finished. Previous increments are only revisited to fix errors or serious flaws. Before we get started, we do enough domain and application analysis to form a context, then concentrate on driving an increment through to completion (running, tested code). The five main phases (shown in Figure 14.4) of object oriented development process are:

1. ***Domain analysis.*** Domain analysis is the process of coming to an understanding with the domain of the application. The domain is modelled, clarified, and documented, and then, fundamental objects and their interrelationships are sorted out. This is illustrated in Figure 14.5. The subtasks include data gathering, modelling, synthesis and abstraction. Refinements may reiterate through the subtasks.

2. ***Application analysis.*** Application analysis is the process of determining exactly what will be built for the requested application. The requirements specifications are clearly spelled out in this phase.

3. ***Application design.*** In application design the mechanisms for implementing the actual application are determined. System architecture, data structures, efficiency considerations etc., are all dealt with here.

4. ***Class development.*** Classes are developed and tested in the language of implementation.

5. ***Incremental integration and system testing.*** Classes are integrated into cluster and subsystem modules and finally into a complete application. Integration testing verifies that these modules work correctly, effectively, and meet requirements.

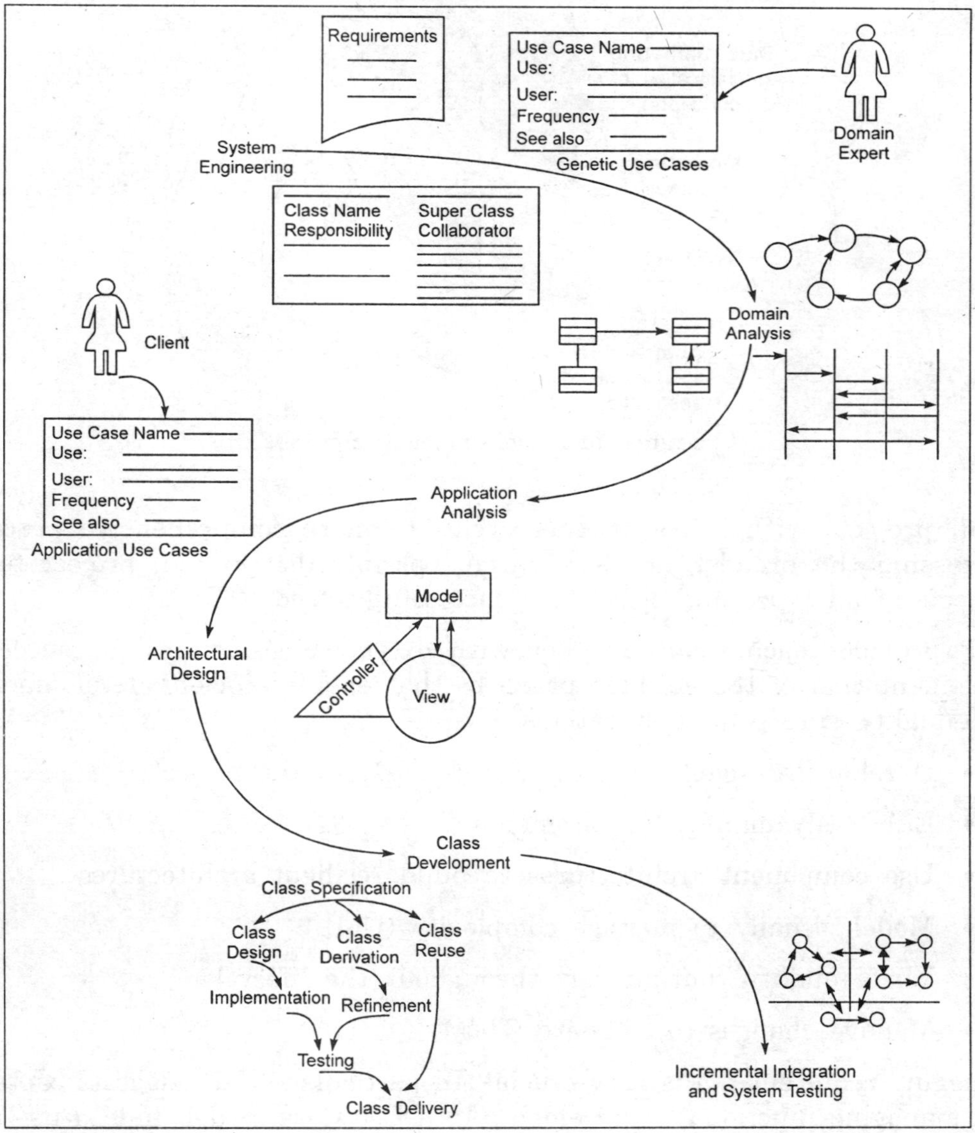

Figure 14.4 Object-oriented application development life cycle.

Best Practices of Software Development

The Rational Corporation's Rational Unified Process (RUP) is a proven software process that captures many of the best practices in modern software development in a form that is suitable for a wide range of projects and organizations. It uses Unified Modelling Language (UML) as the principal notation for the several models that are built and refined during the development processes. RUP vary from lightweight, addressing the needs of

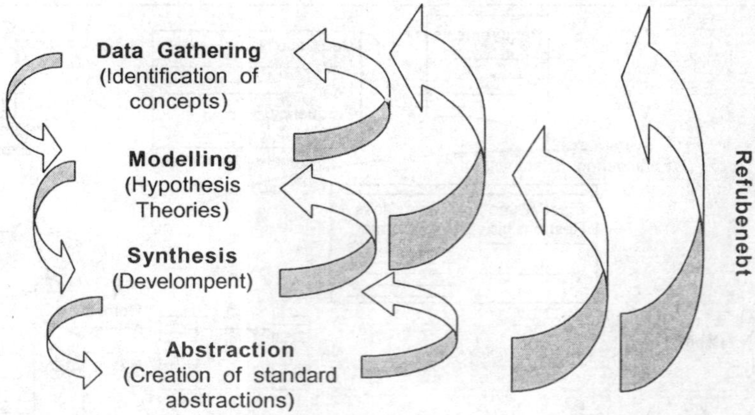

Figure 14.5 Domain analysis process.

small projects with short product cycles to more comprehensive processes addressing the broader needs of large, possibly distributed, project teams. Projects of all types and sizes have successfully used RUP.

RUP provides each team member with extensive guidelines for successful implementation of the six best practices that enable efficient development of high-quality enterprise applications:

- Develop iteratively to mitigate risk early in the project
- Effectively manage requirements
- Use component architectures to build resilient architectures
- Model visually to manage complexity (UML)
- Verify quality continuously throughout the lifecycle
- Manage changes to software (UCM)

Managing requirements is very crucial. In particular, RUP suggests capturing and managing functional requirements in a Use Case model. Indeed use cases are a key concept within the process.

Use of component-based architectures is one of the six best practices. Architecture is used in RUP as a primary artifact for conceptualizing, constructing, managing, and evolving the system under development. The Rational Unified Process emphasizes early development and validation of software architecture as a core concept. It defines two primary artifacts related to architecture, the Software Architecture Description (SAD), which describes the architectural views relevant to the project and the Architectural Prototype. The RUP also defines a worker, called the *Architect*, who is responsible for the architecture. The bulk of the activities related to architectural design are described in the analysis and design workflow, but it spills over to the requirements workflow, the implementation workflow, and the project management workflow.

Many different parties working on computers take interest in its architecture (e.g., the system analyst, the designers, the end user etc.). To allow these parties or stakeholders to communicate, discuss and reason about architecture, we need to have an architectural representation that they understand. Because different stakeholders have different concerns, and because architecture is quite complex, multiple views are required to represent architecture adequately. An architectural view is a simplified description (an abstraction) of a system from a particular perspective or vantage point, covering particular concerns, and omitting entities that are not relevant to this perspective.

Sustained development of quality software which are delivered on time and that meets the budget, requires more than heroic individuals. It also requires cohesive teamwork and a common understanding of development tasks. That's why the implementation of a predictable, repeatable process is crucial to the success. By unifying best practices from many disciplines such as project management, business modelling, requirements management, analysis and design, testing, and change management into one consistent, full life cycle process, the RUP promotes a common vision and culture throughout the development organization (see Figure 14.6). This facilitates team communication, a critical factor in the success of any project, allowing development teams to decrease time to market while increasing the predictability of the software they produce.

To succeed, a software project needs both a good project manager and a good architect. The best management possible and iterative development will not lead to a successful product without a good architecture, and contrarily, a fantastic architecture will fail lamentably if the project is not well managed. It is therefore a matter of balance. Therefore focusing solely on project management will not lead to success. The project manager cannot simply ignore architecture: it takes both architecture expertise and domain expertise to determine the 20 per cent of things that should go into early iterations.

A complex system is more than the sum of its parts—more than a succession of small independent tactical decisions. It must have some unifying, coherent structure to organize those parts systematically, and provide precise rules on how to grow the system without having its complexity explode beyond human understanding. Architecture provides this structure and these rules.

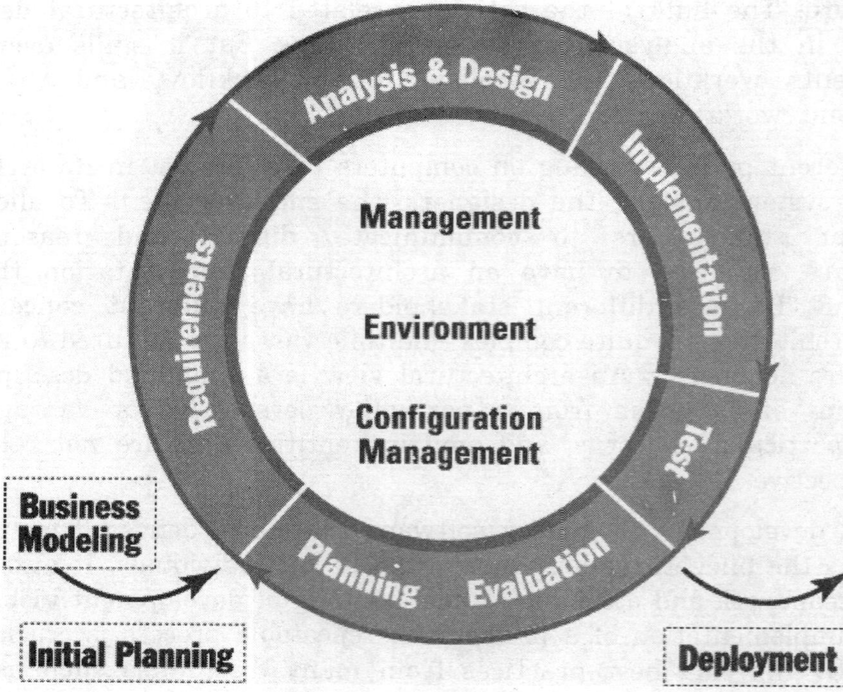

Figure 14.6 Industry proven best partices.

By clearly articulating the major components and the critical interfaces among them, an architecture lets one reason about reuse, both internal reuse (the identification of common parts), and external reuse (the incorporation of ready-made, off-the-shelf components). Architecture can also facilitate reuse on a larger scale—the reuse of the architecture itself in the context of a product line that addresses different functionality in a common domain.

Planning and staffing are organized along the lines of major components, the layers and subsystems.

Phases of Software Development—Inception, Elaboration, Construction, Transition

The four phases of software development can be summarized in the form of a table (Table 14.1) as follows:

Table 14.1

Phase	*Focus On*
Inception	Project scope and business case for the system
Elaboration	Detailed analysis of the problem domain and the definition of an architectural foundation
Construction	Detailed design for the target application as well as the corresponding source code
Transition	Deliver the system to the user community

During Inception, we define the scope of the project—what is included and what is not. This is done by identifying all the actors and Use Cases, and by drafting the most essential use cases (usually approximately 20 per cent of the complete model). A business plan is developed to determine whether resources should be committed to the project.

During Elaboration, we focus on two things—get a good grasp of the requirements (90 per cent complete) and establish an architectural baseline. If we have a good grasp of the requirements and the architecture, we can eliminate a lot of risks and will have a good idea about what amount of work remains to be done. Detailed cost/resource estimations can be made at the end of Elaboration.

During Construction, we build the product in several iterations up to a beta release. During Transition, we transit the product to the end user and focus on end user training, installation, and support.

The amount of time spent in each phase varies. For a complex project with a lot of technical unknowns and unclear requirements. Elaboration may include 3–5 iterations. For a very simple project where requirements are known and the architecture is simple, Elaboration may include only a single iteration.

Let us now study the criteria of these phases.

Inception Phase Criterion: Viability

1. Identify and reduce risks critical to the system's viability
2. Move from a key subset of requirements through use case modelling into a candidate architecture
3. Make initial estimate with broad limits of cost, effort, schedule, and product quality
4. Initiate business case that the product is worth doing (economically) and within broad limits

Elaboration Phase Criterion: Ability to Build System in an Economic Framework

1. Identifying and reducing the risks significantly affecting system construction
2. Specify most of the use cases representing system's functionality
3. Extending candidate architecture to executable baseline proportions
4. Prepare project plan in sufficient details
5. Make estimate with limits narrow enough to justify a business bid
6. Finalizing the business case if the project is worth doing

Construction Phase Criterion: System Capable of Initial Operation in User Environment

1. A series of iterations, leading to periodic builds and increments, so that throughout this phase, viability of the system (hence the project) is always evident in executable form.

Transition Phase Criterion: System Archives Final Operational Capability

1. Modify the product to alleviate problems not identified in earlier phases
2. Correct defects or bugs

Object-Oriented Principles and Concepts Revisited

There are four main object-oriented principles or paradigms, which are important to an overall object-oriented approach—Abstraction, Encapsulation, Modularity and Inheritance. In addition to these concepts, in the following subsections, we revisit the concepts of classes, objects, and class relationships through association, aggregation and composition.

Classes and Objects

Classes are static (compile-time) definition of new type as a collection of data and associated operations (procedures or functions) from which runtime instances called objects can be created. Classes are descriptions of objects with a common implementation. Classes are concerned with the implementation of uniform structural characteristics and behavioural characteristics. Fundamentally, classes are descriptions of objects with common attributes, operation implementations, semantics, associations, and interactions.

Objects are runtime state (instance of a class) of a conceptual framework encapsulating typed data and typed operations that correspond to a real world entity or thing for the purpose of computational modelling. Objects are representational constructs of entities. Objects encapsulate structural characteristics known as *attributes* and behavioural characteristics known as *operations*. Attributes are representational constructs of structural characteristics of entities and determine the possible states of an object. Operations are representational constructs of behavioural characteristics of entities and determine the possible behaviours of an object as invoked in response to receiving a message. Objects have identity and are instances of classes. Fundamentally, objects are abstracted entities that encapsulate state and behaviour.

Modularity

Modularity deals with the physical structuring of the program. As we explained in the beginning about the compilation and linking steps, you must now know that C++, as many other programming languages, allow separate compilation of modules which are then linked together to form the executable code. Normal conventions followed are:

1. Header (.h or .hpp) files are effectively the interfaces of the different modules, and as such contain declarations of classes, structures and preprocessor directives etc.
2. Source (.c or .cpp) files contain the implementation. As such, they contain definitions that match with the corresponding .h or .hpp files, which are to be included by others who would like to use as interfaces.

The extent as to what should constitute a module varies. It may be quite; much depends on the physical constraints. For a small, relatively simple project it may be quite satisfactory to include all classes and objects in one module, whereas in a large project it may be more difficult.

There are two important characteristics of modular design:

1. ***Coupling.*** The manner in which modules interact with each other should be clear and well defined and permit each of the modules to be treated as independently as possible. A change in one module should not necessitate any change in any other module. We say that the modules must be loosely coupled.

2. ***Cohesion.*** The internal elements of a module should be very closely related. If two elements are drastically different from each other then it probably means that the design is flawed and that they should be in different modules. We say that the module should be highly cohesive.

A general rule of thumb is to group logically related classes and objects in the same module, setting up interfaces only to those parts that other modules must see. We have to remember that the goal is two-fold: on the one hand, to simplify documentation under divide and rule principle, and on the other hand, to eliminate unnecessary compilation. The two ideals are cohesion, that is, groups of logically related abstractions, and loose coupling, that is, minimal dependencies between modules.

Once the key abstractions have been identified, it is a relatively simple step to divide physically the implementation into coherent modules. Abstraction, combined with encapsulation, ensures that a given module will include all relevant functions and data. Encapsulation ensures that the modules are unaware of, and hence unaffected by, changes to the implementation details in other modules. This is a major advantage. Regardless of good intentions, in any large system, programmers are often led to make coding decisions, which depend on the internal implementation of another module, perhaps even relying on side effects.

Modularity may of course be affected by other needs: separate processors in a multi-processor system, segment size limits; dynamic calling behaviour in virtual memory systems (consequent on the need for late binding), the building of libraries where reusability is the main objective, and work allocation in large project teams. In any event, it is important to realize that modularity is purely about the physical design: it is the use of classes and objects that form the logical basis of the project.

Abstraction and Encapsulation

Abstraction is the design process that allows us to ignore details. Through encapsulation property, an object can be manipulated through an interface that responds to a limited number of different kinds of message. Internal representation of objects is hidden from the client. In other words, data components of the object cannot be directly accessed. Concentrating on the essential behavioural characteristics of an object which is offering the services allows its users not to base their design on the implementation specifics of the service provider object. In other words, through abstraction we base our design on What? rather than on How?. The essence of the design is to define an object in terms of those published features which are unique to it, or which simply summarize its behavioural characteristics or public member functions in C++(What part). In C++, use of virtual functions and dynamic binding allows the programmer to be abstracted out about the implementation details (How part) of object being operated on. For example, there are many kinds of bank account, but they all hold money of the accountholder. Regardless of the nature of the bank account savings, current, or recurring, and the implementation specifics, the main features, which every bank account has, are to withdraw or deposit money or to query the current account balance. This can be accomplished by the following simplified class declaration:

```
Class BankAccount
{
   public:
      BankAccount();
      virtual ~BankAccount();
      void Deposit (float);
      float Withdraw (float);
      float QueryBalance ();
};
```

The class BankAccount declares an abstraction of a bank account, declaring the public interfaces, which may be performed on classes derived from it namely depositing, withdrawing or determining its current balance. At this design stage, how we do this is ignored. That's why, we do not show any instance data as part of the class and member function bodies. This is abstraction of the class BankAccount.

Encapsulation is also known as information hiding. Data and functions are encapsulated within an object definition to provide a complete abstraction of what part by hiding the how part. It is strongly advised to keep all data in private section and access of instance data members being, through the return of (public) member functions. You already know that C++ provides three levels of access rights: *public* member functions, which effectively implement abstraction, *private* member functions and data, which implement the encapsulation, and *protected* member functions and data, which are somewhere between the two, and are of more concern when considering inheritance. Through *friend* feature, all encapsulation or data hiding is violated and friends can have access to any instance data or member function of the object. Encapsulation ensures that state of an object is not affected other than through public interfaces or friends.

We can now expand the declaration (and for definition, inline functions are used for clarity) of the BankAccount class in Example 14.1:

EXAMPLE 14.1:

```
class BankAccount
{
```

```
    private:
        float currentBalance;
        virtual float MinimumDeposit() = 0;
        virtual float MinimumWithdraw() = 0;
    public:
        BankAccount() {curentBalance = 0;}
        virtual ~BankAccount(){};
        void Desposit(float amt)
        {if ( amt >= MinimumDeposit()) currentBalance += amt;}
        float Withdraw(float amt = 100.0)
        {
            if ((amt >= MinimumWithdraw())&&(currentBalance < amt))
                currentBalance-= amt;
        }
        float QueryBalance(float amt = 100.0) {return currentBalance;}
};
```

We are having encapsulation in BankAccount class. The current account balance information hidden from clients via the private variable currentBalance, and may only be read or altered via the published public interfaces Deposit or Withdraw or QueryBalance.

Association, Aggregation and Composition

Links are representational constructs of entities that relate other entities. Links are instances of associations. Fundamentally, links are abstracted relationships among objects. Associations are descriptions of links with a common implementation. Association represents the ability of one object instance to send a message to another object instance. This is typically implemented with a pointer or reference instance variable, although it might also be implemented as a method argument, or the creation of a local variable. Aggregations are associations that specify a whole part relationship among an aggregate and component parts. Instances cannot have cyclic aggregation relationships (i.e. a part cannot contain its whole). Compositions are aggregations with strong ownership and coincident lifetime constraints among a composite and component parts. The lifetime of the 'part' is controlled by the 'whole'. This control may be direct or transitive, i.e. the 'whole' may take direct responsibility for creating or destroying the 'part' or it may accept an already created part, and later pass it on to some other whole that assumes responsibility for it.

Inheritance

Inheritance is the ability to declare and define new classes as specialization from existing classes. Specialization is defined in terms of added data and/or procedures or methods. There exists an IS-A relation between the specialized class and generalized class. Inheritance allows implementation of one class based on another class, where both internal structure as well as interface is inherited. Generalizations are associations specifying a taxonomic relationship that relate more general representational constructs and more specific representational constructs. The more specific representational constructs are derived from existing more general representational constructs and acquire the characteristics of the more general representational constructs via inheritance. The more specific representational constructs may override characteristics received via inheritance and introduce new characteristics. Because the more specific representational constructs receive the characteristic of the more general representational constructs, instances of the more specific representational constructs may be substituted for instances of the more general representational constructs. Polymorphism enables the same message (operation interface) to invoke the appropriate method (operation implementation) based on the class of the receiver when a more specific instance is substituted for a more general instance.

We can now add some more classes based on BankAccount (see Example 14.2).

EXAMPLE 14.2:

```
class BankAccount
{
  private:
    float currentBalance;
    virtual float MinimumDeposit() = 0;
    virtual float MinimumWithdraw() = 0;
  public:
    BankAccount() {curentBalance = 0;}
    virtual ~BankAccount(){};
    void Desposit(float amt)
    {if ( amt >= MinimumDeposit()) currentBalance += amt;}
    float Withdraw(float amt = 100.0)
  {
    if ((amt >= MinimumWithdraw())&&(currentBalance < amt))
       currentBalance-= amt;
  }
  float QueryBalance(float amt = 100.0)
  {return can be created currentBalance;}
};
```

```
class SavingsBankAccount : public BankAccount
{
     float MinimumDeposit(){return 100.0;};
     float MinimumWithdraw(){return 100.0;};
  public:
     SavingsBankAccount():BankAccount() {}
     ~SavingsBankAccount(){};
};
```

```
class CurrentBankAccount : public BankAccount
{
     float MinimumDeposit(){return 1000.0;};
     float MinimumWithdraw(){return 1000.0;};
  public:
     CurrentBankAccount():BankAccount() {}
     ~CurrentBankAccount(){};
};
```

```
class RecurringBankAccount : public BankAccount
{
     float MonthlyAmtToBeDeposited;
     float MinimumDeposit(){return MonthlyAmtToBeDeposited;};
     float MinimumWithdraw(){return MonthlyAmtToBeDeposited;};
  public:
     RecurringBankAccount(float amt)
        :BankAccount(), MonthlyAmtToBeDeposited(amt) {};
     ~RecurringBankAccount(){};
};
```

OO METHODOLOGY

Need for Modelling

Developing a model for a strong, reliable software system prior to its construction or modification is as essential as having a blueprint for a building. Good models are needed to communicate among project team members and assure architectural soundness. With increased complexity of system, the importance of good modelling techniques increases. There are many additional factors of a project's success, but having a rigorous modelling language standard is essential.

A modelling language must include the following:

1. Model elements—fundamental modelling concepts and semantics.
2. Notation—visual rendering of model elements.
3. Guidelines—idioms of usage within the trade.

In the face of increasingly complex systems, visualization and modelling become essential. The following subsections describe some of the established eminent OO methodologies.

Views of Booch, Jacobson and Rumbaugh Prior to UML

Booch Methodology

The Booch software engineering methodology provides an object-oriented development split in the analysis and design phases. The analysis phase is split into three steps:

1. ***Customer requirement study.*** This generates a high-level description of the system's function and structure from the perspective of customer requirements.
2. ***Domain analysis.*** This is accomplished by defining classes—their attributes, inheritance, and methods. State diagrams for the objects are then established.
3. ***Validation.*** This completes the analysis phase.

The analysis phase iterates between the customer's requirements step, the domain analysis step, and the validation step until consistency is reached. Once the analysis phase is done, the Booch software engineering methodology develops the architecture in the design phase. The design phase is also iterative. A logic design is mapped to a physical design where details of execution threads, processes, performance, location, data types, data structures, visibility, and distribution are established. The process iterates between the logical design, physical design, prototyping and testing.

The Booch software engineering methodology is sequential in the sense that the analysis phase is completed and then the design phase is completed. The methodology is cyclical in the sense that each phase is composed of smaller cyclical steps. There is no explicit priority setting nor a non-monotonic control mechanism. Booch methodology concentrates on the analysis and design phase and does not consider the implementation or the testing phase in much detail.

Rumbaugh's Object Modelling Technique (OMT)

The OMT software engineering methodology deals with object-oriented development in the analysis and design phases. The analysis phase starts with a problem statement, which includes a list of goals and a definitive enumeration of key concepts within a domain. This problem statement is then expanded into three views or models such as the following:

1. ***Object model.*** This represents the artifacts of the system with static, structural, "data" aspects of a system with all its data structures, identifying relations to other objects, attributes and their operations.

2. ***Dynamic model.*** This represents the interaction between these artifacts represented as events, states, and transitions. This is represented as state-transition diagrams to show temporal, behavioural, "control" aspects of a system, sequence of operations in time.

3. ***Functional model.*** This represents the methods of the system from the perspective of data flow. This is represented as data-flow diagrams to show transformational, "function" aspects of a system.

The analysis phase thus generates object-model diagrams, state diagrams, event-flow diagrams, and data-flow diagrams.

In the system design phase, the overall architecture is established. First the system is organized into subsystems, which are then allocated to processes and tasks, taking into account concurrency and collaboration. Then persistent data storage is established along with a strategy to manage shared-global information. Next, boundary situations are examined to help guide trade-off priorities.

The object design phase follows the system design phase. Here the implementation plan is established. Object classes are established along with their algorithms with special attention to the optimization of the path to persistent data. Issues of inheritance, associations, aggregation, and default values are examined.

The OMT software engineering methodology is sequential in the sense that first comes analysis, followed by design. In each phase, a cyclical approach is taken among the smaller steps.

The OMT is very much like the Booch methodology where emphasis is placed on the analysis and design phases for initial product delivery. Both the OMT and Booch do not emphasise implementation, testing, or other life cycle stages.

Jacobson's Object-Oriented Software Engineering

Jacobson's approach is totally use-case driven (i.e. it proceeds from the outside of the system inwards to the objects which implement it) which means that user requirements are given priority. By keeping use cases as the primary unit of system decomposition, we stay user focused.

UML Overview and History

The UML started out as a collaboration among three outstanding object modelling methodologists who are collectively referred to as the Amigos—Grady Booch, Ivar Jacobson, and James Rumbaugh. It is the union of their leading object modelling methodologies: the Booch Method, Jacobson's Object-Oriented Software Engineering (OOSE) and Rumbaugh's Object Modelling Technique (OMT). After its inception in the late 1996, UML quickly gained momentum and became the de-facto standard for object-oriented modelling. Object Management Group (OMG) adopted UML as its standard modelling language and extended the idea with business modelling and other constructs to establish UML as a public international standard.

The primary goals in the design of the UML are as follows:

1. Provide users with a ready-to-use expressive visual modelling language, so that they can develop and exchange meaningful models.
2. Provide extensibility and specialization mechanisms to extend the core concepts.
3. Be independent of particular programming languages and development processes.
4. Provide a formal basis for understanding the modelling language.
5. Encourage the growth of the OO tools market.
6. Support higher-level development concepts such as collaborations, frameworks, patterns and components.
7. Integrate best practices.

OBJECT-ORIENTED DESIGN PATTERNS

Design patterns arose from architecture and anthropology. Years ago, an architect named Christopher Alexander asked himself, Is quality objective? Is beauty truly in the eye of the beholder or would people agree that some things are beautiful and some are not? Now, the particular form of beauty that Alexander was interested in was one of architectural quality: What makes us know when an architectural design is good? For example, if a person were going to design an entrance way for a house, how would he or she know that the design was good? Can we know good design? Is there an objective basis for such a judgement? If there were not some sort of objective basis, we would not be able to make judgements. What is regarded, as good for someone might be bad for someone else. How do we get good quality repeatedly? If we accept that we can even say we have or do not have a good quality design, how do we go about creating them? Alexander asked himself, What is present in a good quality design that is not present in a poor design? and What is present in a poor quality design that is not present in a good quality design? These questions spring from Alexander's belief that if quality in design is objective, then we should be able to quantify what makes designs good and what makes designs bad. Alexander defined a pattern as a solution to a problem in a context. He also said, each pattern describes a problem which occurs over and over again in our environment and then describes the core of the solution to that problem, in such a way that you can use this solution a million times over, without ever doing it the same way twice. Even though Alexander was talking about patterns in buildings and towns, what he says appears to hold true sense about object-oriented design patterns.

Quite often we face the problem of constructing some repetitive pattern over and over again in varieties of diverse applications. In such situations, if we can design a generic common framework of solution to cater such repetitiveness, so that we can either apply the generic solution directly or customize this generic solution to fit the requirements of the specific situations. Design patterns refer to such generic solutions. Design pattern offer proven opportunities for creating flexible and reusable software. They include a reoccurring, language-independent group of classes providing creational, structural or behavioural functionality, and solving a general software design problem. These are usually discovered by experienced people employing good design practices.

Design patterns in programming were first introduced by the Gang of Four (Gamma, Helm, Johnson, Vlissides). Object-oriented design patterns can be defined as descriptions of communicating objects and classes that are customized to solve a general (object-oriented) design problem in a particular context. An object-oriented design pattern describes a recurring generic reusable object-oriented design structure, and not a building block (like linked list) or a domain-specific design. The main focus of the description of the pattern is on situation when it applies, along with its constraints, consequences and trade-offs.

Each design pattern has four essential elements:

1. The pattern name is to identify the pattern with the semantics revealed through the name itself. It works as a handle that we can use to describe

a design problem, its solutions, and consequences in a word or two. Naming a pattern helps us cataloguing design at a higher level of abstraction using our vocabulary of patterns.

2. The problem is to describe the problem and its context and preconditions, i.e. to describe when to apply the pattern. It may include description of specific design problems such as how to represent algorithms as objects. It may describe class or object structures that are symptomatic of an inflexible design.
3. The solution to describe the elements that make up the design, their relationships, responsibilities, and collaborations. This describes a generic pattern of arrangement of the elements (classes and objects) and not a concrete design or implementation. Instead, the pattern provides an abstract description of a design problem and how a general arrangement of elements (classes and objects in our case) solves it.
4. The consequences to address the issues and trade-offs for applying the pattern in terms of software quality measures like flexibility, extensibility, or portability. Consequences are critical for evaluating design alternatives and for understanding the costs and benefits of applying the pattern. The consequences for software often concern space and time trade offs. They may address language and implementation issues as well.

The Gang of Four used a consistent format to describe patterns. They developed a template for describing a design pattern. The template lent a uniform structure to the information and made design patterns easier to learn, compare and use. This template describes a design pattern with

1. Pattern name and classification (all patterns have unique name we identify them with);
2. Intent of the design pattern (the purpose of this pattern);
3. Motivation by which it describes a typical scenario that illustrates the design problem, i.e. the problem the pattern tries to solve;
4. Applicability—when we can apply the design pattern, i.e. the context in which the problem shows up.
5. Structure in other words, a graphical representation of the classes and their collaborations in the pattern. This says how the pattern provides a solution to this problem in the context in which it shows up.
6. Consequences of the design pattern (investigates the forces at play in the pattern to understand the consequences of using the pattern).

7. Implementation of sample code (how this pattern can be implemented; implementations are just complete manifestations of the pattern and should not be construed as the pattern itself).
8. Related patterns.

Design patterns can be classified into two criteria:

1. Purpose, which reflects what a pattern does. Patterns can have creational, structural or behavioural purpose;
   a. Creational patterns concern the process of object creation.
   b. Structural patterns deal with the composition of classes and objects.
   c. Behavioural patterns characterize the ways in which classes and objects interact and distribute responsibility.
2. Scope, which specifies whether the pattern applies primarily to classes or to objects:
   a. Class patterns deal with relationships between classes and their subclasses. These relationships are established through inheritance, so they are static.
   b. Object patterns deal with object relationships, which can be changed at run-time and are more dynamic.

The following table (Table 14.2) shows the classification of design patterns. Note that these are the patterns introduced by the Gang of Four.

Table 14.2

Purpose	*Design Patterns*	*Intent*	*Scope*
Creational (abstract the instantiation process for making a system independent of how its objects are created, composed, and represented)	Abstract factory	Provides an interface for creating families of related or dependent objects without specifying their concrete classes. This exposes the interface not the particular implementation.	Object
	Builder	Separates the creation of an instance of a class from its representation so that the same creation pattern (how a composite object gets created) can be used for creating different representations of the object.	Object

(contd.)

Table 14.2 (*contd.*)

Purpose	*Design Patterns*	*Intent*	*Scope*
	Factory method	Delegates the work of object creation to derived classes of the interface, deals with subclass of object that is instantiated.	Class
	Prototype	Creates new instances of classes by copying its prototype.	Object
	Singleton	Makes sure that at any point of time, there is one and only one instance of a class present and also provides a global pcint of access to the object.	Object
Structural (how classes and objects are composed to form larger structures)	Adapter	Works as interface to an object; used to enable objects with different interfaces to communicate with each other.	Class
	Bridge	Deals with implementation of an object.	Object
	Composite	Composes objects into tree structures to represent part/whole hierarchies. It describes how to break up an object into smaller objects, thereby dealing with structure and composition of an object.	Object
	Decorator	Deals with responsibilities of an object without subclassing.	Object
	Facade	Works for interface to a subsystem.	Object
	Flyweight	Deals with storage costs of objects, i.e. how to support huge numbers of objects at the finest granularities.	Object
	Proxy	Deals with how an object is accessed i.e. its location.	Object
Behavioural (algorithms and the assignment of responsibility)	Chain of responsibility	Represents an object that can fulfil a request.	Object
	Command	Deals with when and how a request is fulfilled.	Object
	Interpreter	Deals with grammar and interpretation of a language.	Class
	Iterator	Deals with how an aggregate's elements are accessed or traversed	Object

(*contd.*)

Table 14.2 (*contd.*)

Purpose	*Design Patterns*	*Intent*	*Scope*
	Mediator	Deals with how and which objects interact with each other.	Object
	Memento	Describes how to encapsulate and save the internal state of an object so that the object can be restored to that state later, i.e. what private information is stored outside an object, and when.	Object
	Observer	Deals with a number of objects that depend on another object; how the dependent objects stay up to date.	Object
	State	Represents states of an object.	Object
	Strategy	Deals with algorithms i.e. how to implement families of algorithms to solve a particular problem.	Object
	Template method	Deals with steps of an algorithm.	Class
	Visitor	Represents an operation to be performed on the elements of an object structure. The visitor lets you define a new operation without changing class(es) of the elements on which it operates.	Object

Solving design problems with design patterns involves the following steps:

1. ***Finding appropriate objects.*** This requires to identify less obvious abstractions and the objects that capture them.
2. ***Determining object granularity.*** This requires identifying the size and number of objects required for an application.
3. ***Specifying object interfaces.*** This requires defining interfaces by identifying their key elements and the kind of data that is sent across an interface.
4. ***Designing for change.*** This requires the ability to adapt and cope with the changing requirements. By making implementation hidden from the client of a class, and dependency is purely on the interface exposed makes it possible.

Design patterns help to create a common design vocabulary for designers that help to communicate, document and explore design decisions. It also aids documentation by applying a common design vocabulary so that detailed description is not needed for the pattern, rather just naming the pattern tells about it. However, do not recast everything as a pattern. Instead, develop strategic domain patterns and reuse existing tactical patterns. Rewards should be institutionalized for developing patterns. Pattern authors should be directly involved with application developers and domain experts. It is necessary to document clearly when patterns apply and do not apply. Expectations should be managed carefully. Mature engineering disciplines have handbooks that describe successful solutions to known problems e.g., automobile designers don't design cars using the laws of physics, and they adopt adequate solutions from the handbook known to work well enough. The extra few per cent of performance available by starting from the scratch typically isn't worth the cost. Patterns can form the basis for the handbook of software engineering. If software is to become an engineering discipline, successful practices must be systematically documented and widely disseminated.

SUMMARY

The key concepts introduced in this chapter are as follows:

- The OO paradigm focuses on the behavioural and structural characteristics of entities as complete units. The paradigm encompasses and supports the four pillars or the first principles as abstraction, encapsulation, inheritance, and polymorphism.
- Problem-solving, in general, involves understanding or conceptualizing a problem first, solving the problem next, and finally implementing or realizing the solution.
- The key elements of software development are people, project, process, product, and tools.
- A systematic software development process helps in orderly development, improved quality of software, standardized training, repeatability of successful projects and continuous organizational improvement with improved productivity. Process drives tool development, tool guides process.
- The desirable qualities of software systems include correctness, completeness, robustness, reliability, extendability, maintainability, reusability, compatibility, usefulness, timeliness, user friendliness, efficiency, portability, verifiability, integrity.
- The architectural elements and their interfaces, their collaborations, and their compositions, as a whole, constitute a larger system built from its smaller subsystems with different views of the stakeholders in mind.

- Software designers can organize the description of their architectural decisions around four views (logical view, process view, implementation view, and deployment view), and then illustrate them with a few selected use cases, or scenarios, which constitute a fifth view.
- The major stages of Software Development Life Cycle include Software Requirement Analysis (with Prototyping), Design, Coding, Testing and Maintenance.
- OO Software Development Process is incremental in nature. In this, we iterate within increments, with prototype support as necessary.
- The six best practices (as suggested by Rational Corporation) enables efficient development of high-quality enterprise applications include: iterative development, effective requirement management, component architecture, visual modelling, continuous quality verification, and change management.
- The four main phases of software development can be broken into inception, elaboration, construction and transition.
- The Booch software engineering methodology provides an object-oriented development split in the analysis and design phases. Rumbaugh's Object Modelling Technique (OMT) deals with object model, dynamic model and functional model viewpoint. Jacobson's Object-Oriented Software Engineering (OOSE) approach is totally use-case driven. UML is the union of these three leading object modelling methodologies.
- Design patterns include a reoccurring, language independent group of classes providing creational, structural or behavioural functionality, and solving a general software design problem.

REVIEW QUESTIONS

1. What is the purpose of Object-Oriented Modelling?
2. What are key elements of a software development? Explain.
3. Software development is a complex, risky, expensive and people-intensive venture. Explain.
4. What are the desirable qualities of software systems?
5. Why software architecture plan is needed?
6. Explain the 4+1 view of software architecture.
7. What do you mean by software development life cycle?

8. Explain the need of domain analysis process in a software project.
9. Explain the object-oriented application development life cycle.
10. What are the best practices of software development?
11. Explain the terms—Inception, Elaboration, Construction and Transition in the context of software development.
12. What is the relationship between abstraction and encapsulation?
13. Explain Booch Methodology in terms of object-oriented modelling.
14. Explain Rumbaugh's OMT in terms of object-oriented modelling.
15. What is the role of design patterns in object-oriented design?

15 Unified Modelling Language

The Unified Modelling Language (UML) is a graphical language for visualizing, specifying, constructing, and documenting the artifacts of a software-intensive system. The UML offers a standard way to write a system's bluprints, including conceptual things such as business processes and system functions as well as concrete things such as programming language statements, database schemas, and reusable software components.

—The OMG (Object Management Group) specification

LEARNING OBJECTIVES

The objective of this chapter is to acquaint you with:

- Basic building blocks of Unified Modelling Language, in short, UML
- Use case and actors
- Structural and behavioural modelling aspects
- Packaging and deployment
- Software development process through UML

INTRODUCTION

Structured programming is an established technique. Object-Oriented (OO) methodologies help to build structured models of the problem domain at hand and to devise well-structured solutions. Moreover, it has been proven that these OO methods lead to more stable architectures and more easily understood than those based solely on function and data flow.

With the proliferation of increased complexity of software, the software production needed some degree of automation with improved quality at a reduced cost in a lesser time. Different techniques such as rapid application development, visual programming, component technology, patterns and frameworks evolved. Businesses also sought techniques to manage the complexity of systems as they increased in scope and scale. The Unified Modelling Language (UML) was designed to respond to these needs.

The UML was released in November 1997 by a consortium of companies led by Rational Software Corporation. In a relatively short period of time in the software engineering community UML has been widely accepted as a dominant OO software analysis/design methodology, since it provides most of the concepts and notations that are essential for documenting OO models. It is an open standard for specifying, constructing, visualizing, and documenting the architecture of a software-intensive system UML is a modelling language using text and graphical notation for documenting specification, analysis, design and implementation of OOSD (Object-Oriented System Development) process. It is a common language that is understandable to all stakeholders and used to define a software system, and to detail the artifacts in the system; it is the language of the blueprint involved in the software project. The Object Management Group (OMG) administers the UML standard. OO paradigm needs to be applied using the principles of UML to analysis, design and implementation of software systems from concept and initiation phases through development and deployment phases.

Architecture (structural as well as behavioural) of a software system need to be defined clearly such that maintenance related to bug fixing and enhancement can be done easily and effectively with the goal to enable desirable quality factors as mentioned earlier. Making a well-designed structure of the entire architecture helps to deal with complexity with increasing size of application. A well-designed structure also aids reusability. Component based architectural design helps to make reusable components, which can be put in a library and different projects can use these already developed components in as they are or after doing necessary customizations. As such, software architecture must be specified, visualized, and documented in a way that meets the needs of the stakeholders associated. A unified accepted notation is thus useful to represent the architecture. UML caters to this need in addition to its modelling capabilities. Modelling is the designing of software applications before actual coding. It is an essential part of large software projects, and helpful to medium and even small projects as well. Modelling can assure that business functionality is complete and correct, end-user needs are met, and program design supports requirements for scalability, robustness, security, extendibility, and other quality aspects, before implementation in code renders changes difficult and expensive to make.

Surveys show that large software projects have a huge probability of failure; in fact, it's more likely that a large software application fails to meet all of its requirements on time and on budget than that it will succeed. Modelling is the only way to visualize the design and check it against requirements before actual coding is started. This aspect is of utmost importance as it provides a tool for practitioners to have a diagrammatic feel of the proposed system. UML is simply a graphic representation of a common semantic model. By combining the most useful elements of OO methods and extending the notation to cover new aspects of system development, UML provides a comprehensive notation for the full life cycle of OO development. It uses a whole range of diagrams appropriate for the various phases of software life-cycle to deal with its static structures and dynamic behaviours. It supports different views of the software's architecture. It can be used with all processes throughout the software development life cycle and across different implementation technologies.

The UML authors promote a development process that is Use Case driven, architecture centric, and iterative and incremental. This process is a unified approach to the methods in a development process called Unified Development Process, but process is not the concern of UML. The important point to note here is that UML is a 'language' for specifying design and not a method or procedure.

In general, UML defines the notation and semantics for the following domains. Though the basic UML has been standardized by OMG, the definitions of the models and views given in this document may be different to some extent in other texts, documentations and schools of thought. Following is a general overview of the domains.

1. ***The user interaction or use case model.*** This describes the boundary and interaction between the system and users. This corresponds in some respects to a requirement's model.

2. ***The dynamic model.*** In this, sequence diagrams are used to display the interaction between users, screens, objects and entities within the system. State charts describe the states or conditions that classes assume over time. Activity graphs describe the workflows the system will implement.

3. ***The logical/static or class model.*** This model describes the classes and objects that will make up the system.

4. ***The physical component model.*** This model describes the software (and sometimes hardware components) that makes up the system.

5. ***The physical deployment model.*** This describes the physical architecture and the deployment of components on that hardware architecture.

The UML also defines extension mechanisms for extending the UML to meet specialized needs (for example Business Process Modelling extensions).

UML Building Blocks

UML provides several basic elements for building models. These basic elements may be grouped into composite elements. Relational elements deal with various kinds of relationships between the model elements. Other elements are there to describe object states and interactions. Annotations are provided for clarifying the meaning. Specifications are saved in files to document responsibilities and capabilities of the model elements. Adornments make symbols mean specific things. In order to cover every possible situation, UML provides notation extending mechanisms. One such mechanism is stereotyping which specializes the general notation to specific application areas. Standard stereotypes and icons are provided, though domain specific stereotypes and icons may be introduced as and when required. Notation extension uses tagged values to add more information. Constraints are used to show restrictions that apply.

Classes are basic model elements. Class names are shown in boldface type. Abstract classes are shown in italic. Objects (class instances) are shown by class elements with underlined names. Class names or object name may be elided (anonymous). Interfaces are indicated by lollipops. No implementation, just operations are provided. Collaborations are indicated by dashed ovals. They realize use cases which are shown as ellipse. Use-case shows a functionality of the system for the external user. Active classes are shown by thick bordered class boxes; they represent independent thread of processing. A component is a combination of one or more classes that forms a physical software. A node is a processor or device (a physical hardware). A composite model element is a package or a subsystem of base or composite elements.

Class relationships are represented by connecting lines, labels and arrows. We show association with solid line between instances, and aggregation with solid line with diamond (empty or full) between whole and part, occasionally directed, labelled, and with multiplicities and role names. Dependency is shown as dashed line, possibly directed and occasionally with a label. Generalization is shown with solid line with hollow arrowhead pointing to the parent. Realization is shown with dashed line with hollow arrowhead, between interfaces and the classes that realize them and between use-cases and collaborations that realize them.

In aggregation, parts may be added or removed; they may survive even after the whole is dead. In containment aggregation (composition) the parts are contained in the whole and die with the container. Dependency refers to relationships between whole classes—type of parameter passed to the calling class or the type of returned value. Association is more loosely coupled than aggregation, and aggregation is more loosely coupled than composition. Generalization is finding the superclass from subclasses, specialization is the opposite. Realization is implementing classes that collaborate to realize the use case. Interfaces are realized by the classes or components that implement them.

State is defined as the snapshot of attribute values taken at some instant. State changes are also referred to as state transitions caused by events and activities. State is shown as rounded rectangle with a name. Attributes of an object change to give transition to another state. Events trigger the transition from one state to another. Links are instances of relationships. Interaction is the message exchange between objects shown as action sequences and links. It is shown as solid line with a solid arrowhead and a label giving the operation name.

Notes are shown as "dog-eared" box i.e. rectangle with top-right corner turned and with textual comment inside. Notes are used to add info for explanation or reminders. Comments are used in notes. Notes may contain stereotypes, e.g., <<requirement>>. Notes may be associated to a diagram element using dashed line.

The basic elements are exhibited in Figure 15.1.

On the basis of these elements, UML defines several models to represent systems:

- The class model
- The state model
- The use case model
- The interaction model
- The implementation model
- The deployment model

These models are graphically represented. Many different perspectives can be constructed for a base model, each showing all or part of the model and are represented by one or more diagrams.

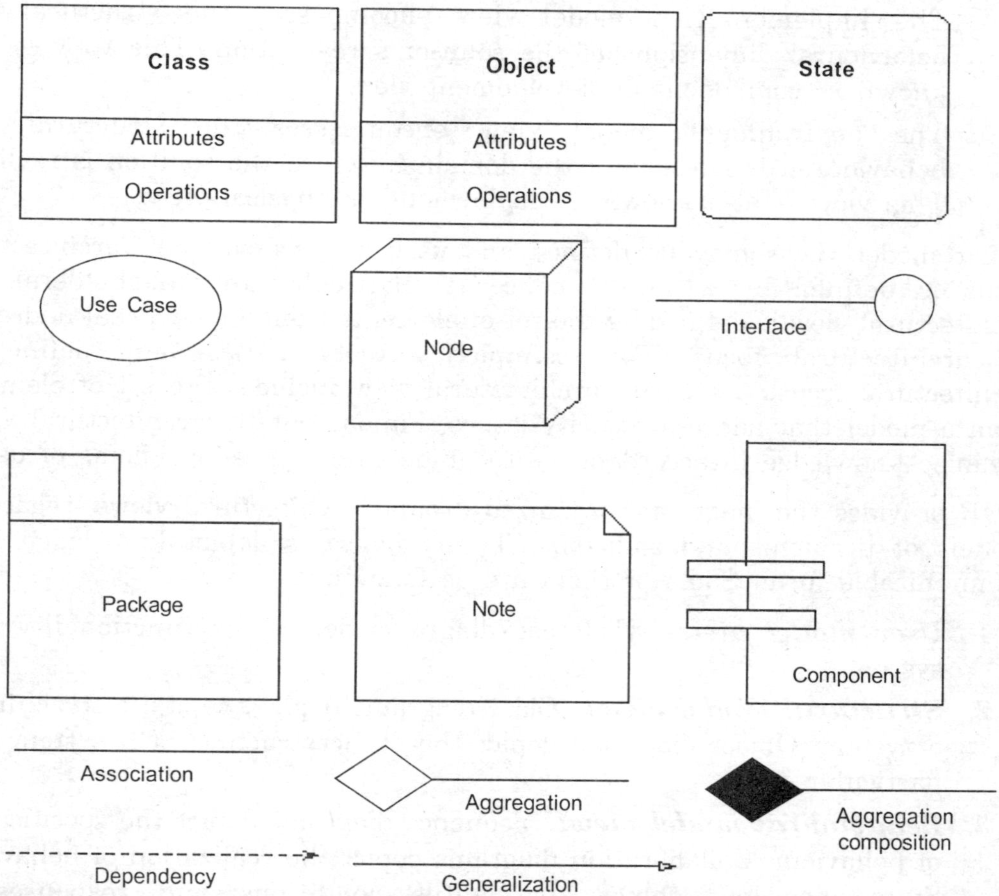

Figure 15.1 Basic UML elements.

UML architectural views organize models and knowledge around specific sets of concerns (architectural focus). The UML provides the following architectural views regarding models of problems and solutions:

1. The user model view encompasses a problem and its solution as understood by the users. This view is also known as the use case or scenario view.
2. The structural model view encompasses the structural dimension of a problem and solution. This view is also known as static or logical view.
3. The behavioural model view encompasses the behavioural dimension of a problem and solution. This view is also known as the dynamic, process, concurrent, or collaborative view.

4. The implementation model view encompasses the structural and behavioural dimensions of the solution's realization. This view is also known as component or development view.
5. The environment model view encompasses the structural and behavioural dimensions of the domain in which the solution is realized. This view is also known as deployment or physical view.

Other model views may be defined and used as necessary. An architectural focus is defined by a set of concerns (particular to stakeholders). An architectural view is defined by the set of elements from a model that addresses an architectural focus. For example, security issues may define an architectural focus. A security architectural view includes the set of elements from a model that address security issues. Fundamentally, architectural views organize knowledge in accordance with guidelines expressing idioms of usage.

UML provides the diagrams, organized around architectural views, regarding models of problems and solutions. These diagrams depict knowledge in a communicable form. Some of them are as follows:

1. ***User model view.*** Use case diagrams depict the functionality of a system.
2. ***Structural model view.*** Class diagrams depict the static structure of a system. Object diagrams depict the static structure of a system at a particular time.
3. ***Behavioural model view.*** Sequence diagrams depict the specification of behaviour. Collaboration diagrams depict the realization of behaviour. State diagrams depict the status conditions and responses of participants involved in behaviour, and activity diagrams depict the activities of participants involved in behaviour.
4. ***Implementation model view.*** Component diagrams depict the organization of solution components.
5. ***Environment model view.*** Deployment diagrams depict the configuration of environment elements and the mapping of solution components onto them.

Other diagrams may be defined and used as necessary. Fundamentally, diagrams depict knowledge (syntax).

Thus, UML defines twelve types of diagrams, divided into three categories:

- Structural diagrams
- Behaviour diagrams
- Model management diagrams

The twelve types of diagrams are as follows:

1. Four diagram types (Structural diagrams) represent static application structure:
    - Class diagram
    - Object diagram
    - Component diagram
    - Deployment diagram
2. Five diagram types (Behaviour diagrams) represent different aspects of dynamic behaviour:
    - Use case diagram
    - Sequence diagram
    - Activity diagram
    - Collaboration diagram
    - Statechart diagram
3. Three diagram types (Model management diagrams) represent ways for organizing and managing application modules:
    - Packages
    - Subsystems
    - Models

Use Case, Actors and Use Case Diagrams

Problem-solving, in general, involves understanding or conceptualizing a problem, solving the problem, and implementing or realizing the solution. Conceptualizing a problem requires representing the problem using representational constructs (mental notions or ideas). Solving the problem requires manipulating representational constructs from the problem domain and the solution domain to derive a representation of the desired solution. Realizing a solution requires mapping those representational constructs of the solution unto the solution world, that is, constructing the solution. This process of problem-solving comes very naturally and often occurs subtly and sometimes unconsciously in problem-solving. Models represent complete abstractions of systems. Models are used to capture semantic knowledge about problems and solutions. Architectural views represent abstractions of models. Architectural views are used to organize knowledge in accordance with guidelines expressing idioms of usage. Diagrams represent graphical projections of sets of model elements used to depict syntactical knowledge about problems and solutions. Within the fundamental UML notation, concepts are depicted as symbols, and relationships and concepts depicted as paths or lines connecting symbols.

Use case modelling from the user model view (also known as the use case or scenario view), which encompasses a problem and solution as understood by those individuals whose problem the solution addresses, involves use case diagrams to depict the functionality of a system. A use case represents a discrete unit of interaction between a user (human or machine) and the system. It is a single unit of meaningful work; for example, login to system, register with system and create order are all use cases. Each use case has a description, which describes the functionality that will be built in the proposed system. A use case may 'include' another use case's functionality or 'extend' another use case with its own behaviour.

Use cases are typically related to 'actors'. An actor is a human or machine entity that interacts with the system to perform a meaningful work. An actor uses a use case to perform some piece of work, which is of value to the business. The set of use cases an actor has access to define their overall role in the system and the scope of their action. An example of a use case diagram is shown in Figure 15.2. Here we show an order booking system.

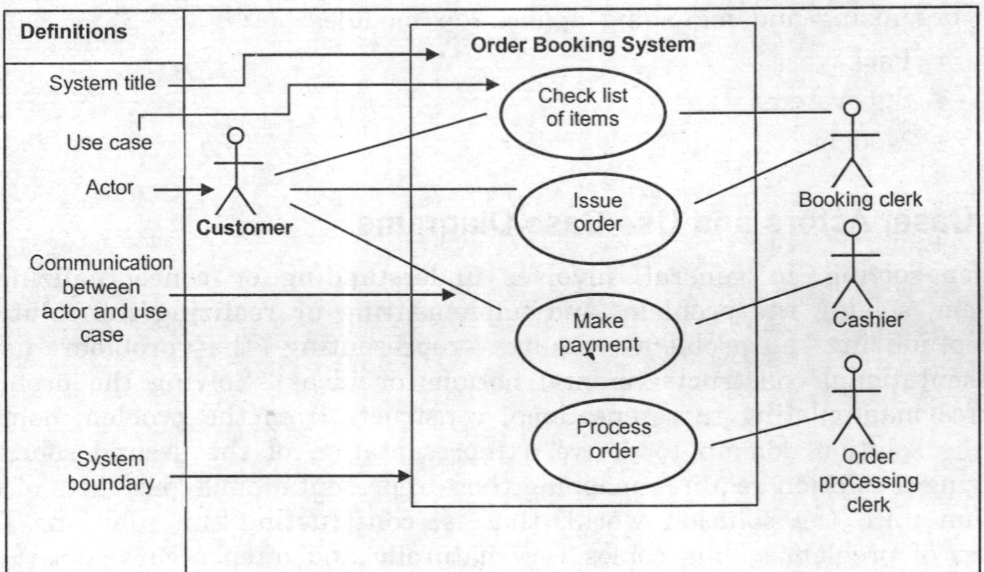

Figure 15.2 A use case diagram.

We identify use cases and actors to define system boundary, outline who and what (actors) will interact with the system and what functionality (use cases) is expected from the system, capture and define in a glossary of common terms that are essential for creating detailed descriptions of the system's functionality. In a use case, a system name is given. For example, in the given Figure 15.2, it is Order Booking System. Actors could be customers, booking clerks cashiers and order processing clerks. Within the system boundary of Order Booking System, use cases through which the actors communicate with the system are checking list of items, issuing orders, making payments and processing orders. All actors do not communicate with every use case. For example, we can see that an order processing clerk actor is only interested in processing order use case, whereas making payment is the concern of the customer as well as the cashier actors. Customer actor is responsible to check list of items, issuing order and making payment but not for processing order. Booking clerk actor helps the customer actor by interacting jointly in same use case namely check list of items and issue order.

Generally, it is assumed that the included use case will be called every time the basic path is run. An example may be to list a set of customer orders to choose from before modifying a selected order. In this case the <list orders> use case may be included every time the <modify order> use case is run.

A use case may include one or more use cases, so it helps to reduce duplication of functionality by factoring out common behaviour into use cases that are re-used many times. One use case may extend the behaviour of another, typically when exceptional circumstances are encountered. For example, if before modifying a particular type of customer order, a user must get approval from some higher authority, then the <get approval> use case may optionally extend the regular <modify order> use case. The notations of use case relationships are shown in the following table (Table 15.1):

Table 15.1

Relationship	*Function*	*Notation*
Association	The communication path between actor and a use case that it participates in	————————
Extend	The insertion of additional behaviour into a base use case that does not know about it	<<extend>> - - - - - - →
Use case generalization	A relationship between a generalized use case and a more specific use case that inherits and adds features to it	————▷
Include	The insertion of additional behaviour into a base use case that explicitly describes the insertion	<<include>> - - - - - - →

An example of a use case relationship follows as Figure 15.3. In this case, use case named 'Provide customer data' and 'Order selected product' includes base use case 'Issue order'. 'Pay by cash' and 'Pay by credit/debit card' are special use cases derived from 'Make payment' use case.

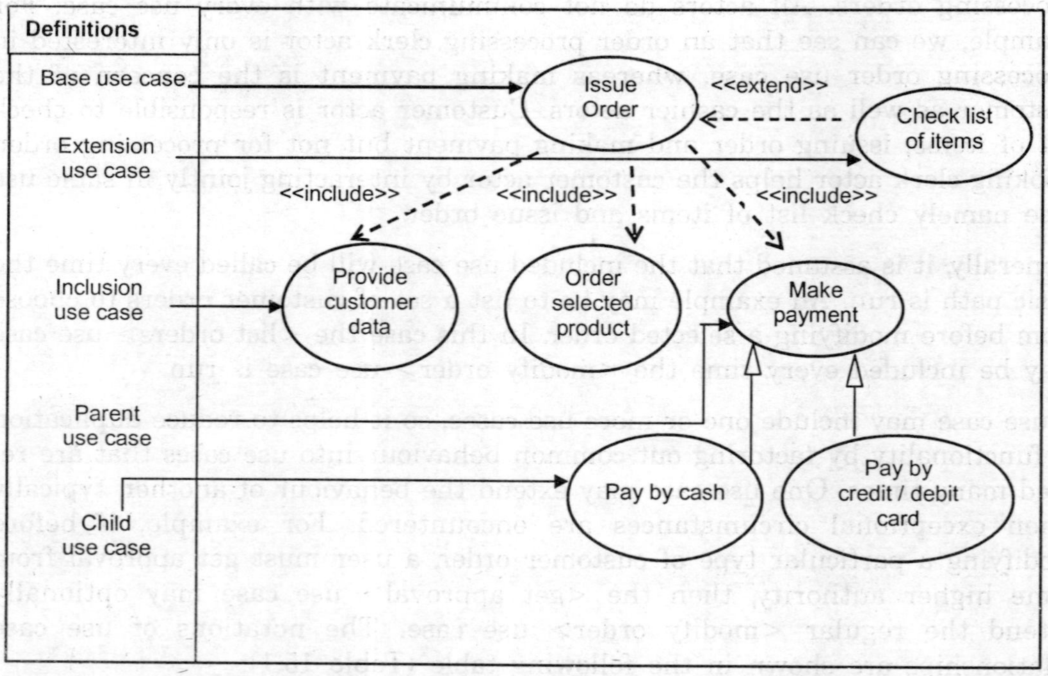

Figure 15.3 An example of a use case relationship.

A use case description generally includes the following:

1. General comments and notes describing the use case.
2. Requirements—Things that the use case must allow the user to do, such as <ability to update order>, <ability to modify order> etc. These are the formal functional requirements that a use case must provide to the end user. They correspond to the functional specifications found in structured methodologies. A requirement is a contract that the use case will perform some action or provide some value to the system.
3. Constraints—Rules about what can and cannot be done. These are the formal rules and limitations that a use case operates under, and includes pre, post, and invariant conditions. Pre-conditions specify what must have already occurred or is in place before the use case may start, e.g. <create order> must precede <modify order>. Post-conditions document what will be true once the use case is complete, e.g. <order is

modified and consistent>. Invariants specify what will be true throughout the time the use case operates, e.g. an order must always have a customer number.

4. Scenarios—Sequential descriptions of the steps taken to carry out the use case; may include multiple scenarios to cater to exceptional circumstances and alternate processing paths. Scenarios are formal descriptions of the flow of events that occur during a use case instance. These are usually described in text and correspond to a textual representation of the sequence diagram.
5. Scenario diagrams are sequence diagrams to depict the workflow, similar to scenarios, but graphically portrayed.
6. Additional attributes such as implementation phase, version number, complexity rating, stereotype and status.

UML provides a graphical means of depicting object interactions over time in sequence diagrams. These typically show a user or actor, and the objects and components they interact with in the execution of a use case. One sequence diagram typically represents a single use case 'scenario' or flow of events.

Sequence diagrams are an excellent way to document usage scenarios and to both capture required objects early in analysis and to verify object usage later in design. Sequence diagrams show the flow of messages from one object to another, and as such correspond to the methods and events supported by a class/object.

The diagram illustrated in Figure 15.4 shows an example of a sequence diagram, with the user or actor on the left initiating a flow of events and messages that correspond to the use case scenario. The messages that pass between objects will become class operations in the final model.

Sequence diagrams are used to display the interaction between users, screens, objects and entities within the system. It provides a sequential map of message passing between objects over time. Frequently these diagrams are placed under use cases in the model to illustrate the use case scenario—how a user will interact with the system and what happens internally to get the work done. Often, the objects are represented using special stereotyped icons, as in Figure 15.4.

The object labelled Login Screen is shown using the user interface icon. The object labelled Authentication Manager is shown using the controller icon. The object labelled users repositary is shown using the entity icon.

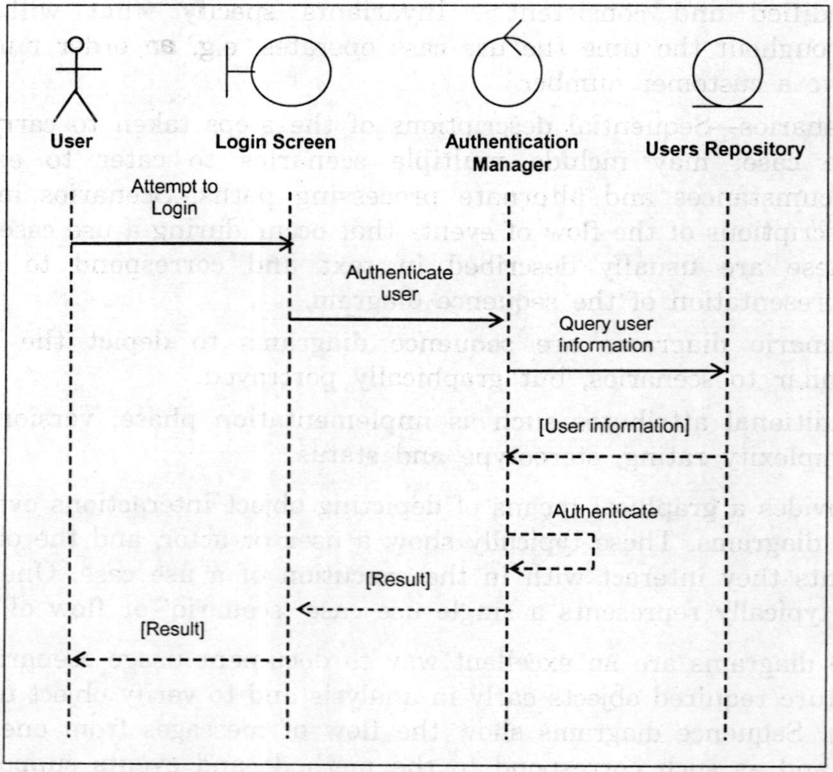

Figure 15.4 Example of a sequence diagram.

Basic steps of use case modelling is finding the actors, finding the use cases, briefly describing each use case, describing the use case model (including glossary) as a whole, describing use cases in detail. Steps do not have to be performed in any particular order.

Structural Modelling

Structural diagram is the static architectural representation of a software project and often a good starting point. It defines the overall object structure of the software system. Structural diagrams represent static application structure, and include the following types:

- Class diagram
- Object diagram
- Component diagram
- Deployment diagram

Class Diagram

This allows to document how the class relates to other classes. This shows a set of classes, interfaces, and collaborations and their relationships. Graphically, a class diagram is a collection of vertices and arcs. Class diagram is used to model the static design view of a system and to model the vocabulary of the system, modelling collaborations or modelling schemas. Class diagram is important for visualizing, specifying, and documenting structural models and for constructing an executable system through forward and reverse engineering.

A class is represented in UML, for example, as follows (Figure 15.5):

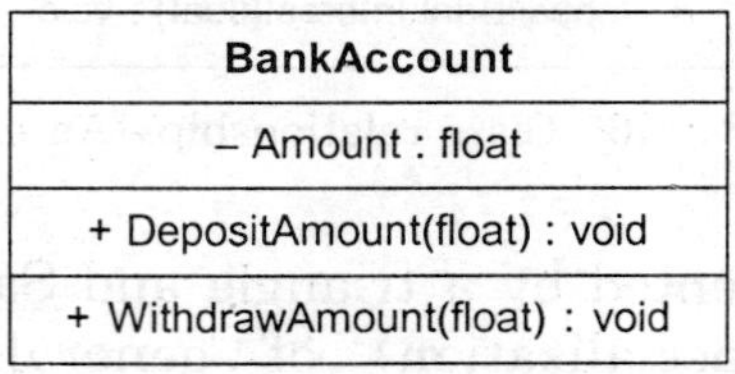

Figure 15.5 A class in UML.

The class named BankAccount represents an account in a Bank. The attribute named amount represents the current available amount of money in the account. The term visibility refers to the ability of an element to reference any other element that is in a different namespace from the referencing element. It is a part of the relationship between an element and the container that holds it. Three types of visibility can be identified. They are:

1. ***Public.*** Any element that can see the container can also see the indicated element (denoted as +).
2. ***Protected.*** Only an element within the container or a descendent of the container can see indicated element, other elements may not reference it or otherwise use it (denoted as #).
3. ***Private.*** Only an element within the container can see the element. Other elements, including elements in descendents of the container, may not reference it or otherwise use it (denoted as –).

DepositAmount and WithdrawAmount are the two available methods responsible for transacting some amount of money to/from respectively the bankaccount. The – and + signs show that DepositAmount and WithdrawAmount methods are publicly accessible and the attribute Amount is privately declared. The void after the colon in the methods show the return types from these methods when called. Class relationships can also be represented through UML class diagrams as in Figure 15.6:

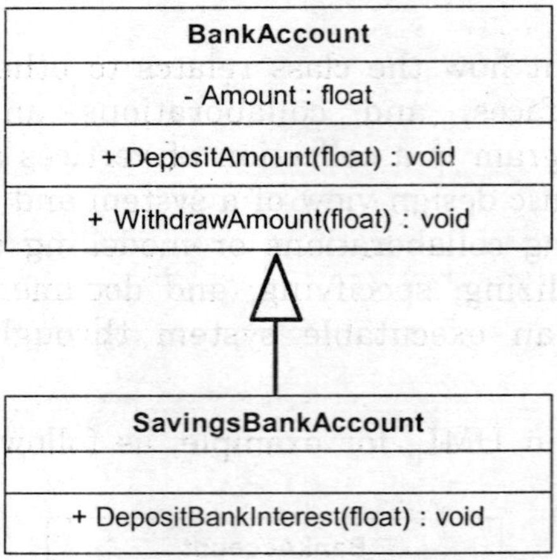

Figure 15.6 Class relationship—An example.

The Inheritance is represented by a triangle and SavingsBankAccount class is declared a subclass (specialization) of generalized BankAccount class, inheriting all of the attributes and operations of the generalized BankAccount Class. The DepositBankInterest is a method added to the class SavingsBankAccount.

Aggregation is represented by a diamond symbol. Let us understand this by means of an example given here as Figure 15.7. A bank may have many bank accounts. The asterisk near the Bank Account represents many and the 1 near the bank represents one. It shows that there is a one to many relationship between bank and accounts, i.e. a bank has many bank accounts whereas a particular account is held by one bank only. CheckingAccount is another specialization from account class.

This diagram shows that the bank has many BankAccounts, some of which are SavingsBankAccounts and some of which are CurrentBankAccounts. UML also includes a notation called stereotypes and they can be found on all diagrams. Stereotypes are displayed as text inside a "<< ... >>" bracket. i.e. <<communicates>>. Stereotypes were invented by the designers of UML as a way to give different UML shapes more specialized roles to describe a diagram component.

An example of a stereotype for operations might be that for all the get or retrieval kind of operations such as getName, getAddress etc., we call <<accessors>>. <<accessors>> means specialized operation for retrieval. Stereotypes are very helpful, because we don't have to keep finding new shapes for things that already cover the general case for something we have described. Classes can have stereotypes such as <<persistent>>, <<interface>>, <<Business>>, <<core functionality>> etc. to show the designated meaning.

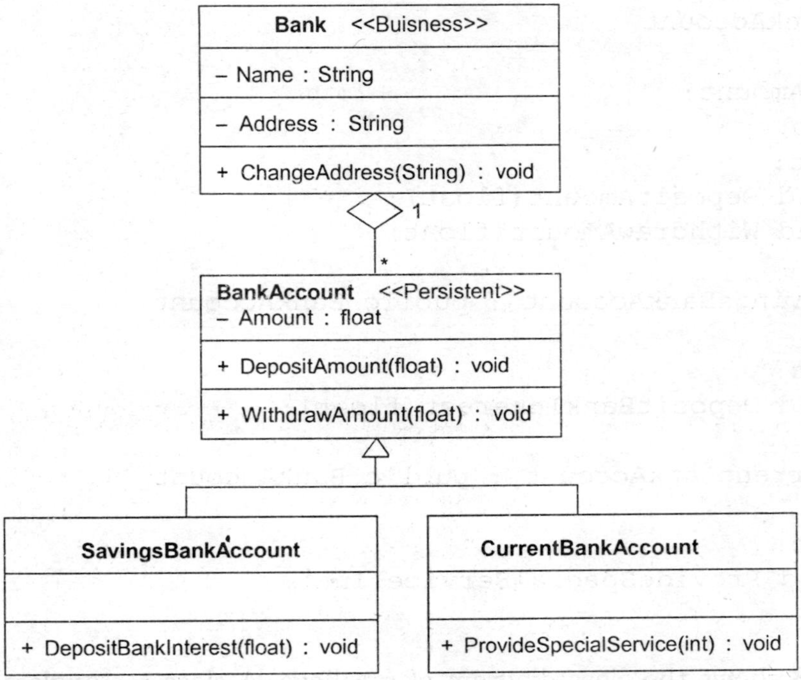

Figure 15.7 Class relationship—Inheritance and aggregation.

For example, <<persistent>> objects means the values stored in the attributes will be stored persistently, i.e. remember its values on next initiations. <<Business>> objects designate that these objects are special purpose object (as singleton object may be) responsible for the prime business functionality. Stereotypes are quite flexible and give the designer a very broad way of describing UML notation types. They also help the UML designers to extend the UML notation without making it overly more complex.

An equivalent C++ code skeleton is provided as Example 15.1.

Example 15.1:

```
class BankAccount;
class Bank
{
   BankAccount *ba;
   String Name;
   String Address;
   public:
      void ChangeAddress(String);
```

```
class BankAccount
{
   floatAmount;
   Bank b;
   public:
      void DepositAmount(float);
      void WithdrawAmount(float);
};
class SavingsBankAccount : public BankAccount
{
   public:
      void DepositBankInterest(float);
};
class CurrentBankAccount : public BankAccount
{
   public:
      void ProvideSpecialService(int);
};
```

Figure 15.8 shows the class diagram of a college. A class rectangle shows class name (e.g. College), its attributes (e.g. name, address) and operations applicable (e.g. addStudent, removeStudent etc.). This also shows inter-class relationships like aggregation, association, and composition.

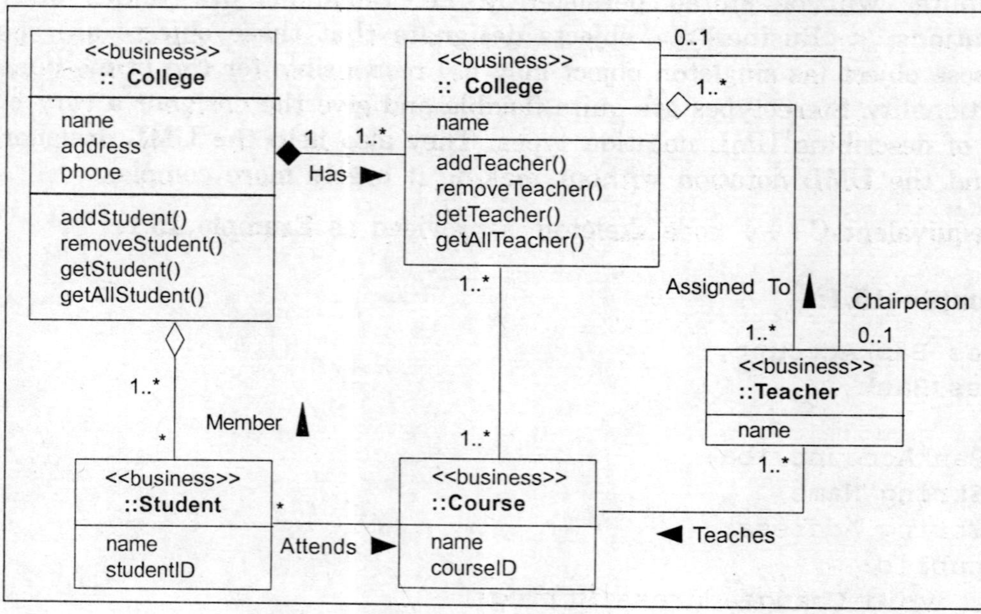

Figure 15.8 Class diagram of a college.

An association is a structural relationship that describes a set of links, a link being a connection among objects. An aggregation shows models the "whole/part" relationship, in which one class represents a larger thing (the "whole") which consists of smaller things (the "parts"). Composition is a form of aggregation with strong ownership and coincident lifetime as part of the whole. In the figure, School composes of departments, department has number of instructors out of whom one is designated as Chairperson etc. A department is associated with a number of courses. Notations like 1(exactly one), 1..*(one or more), 0..1(zero or one) etc. show multiplicity, which states how many objects, may be connected across an instance of an association.

Another example of class diagram is shown in Figure 15.9, with different parts of it properly labelled. It shows class view of a performance show reservation system. A customer is associated with many reservations. A reservation can be a group reservation or individual reservation (specialization). In either case, a ticket is issued. Corresponding multiplicities are shown, however with a constraint that individual or group reservation is mutually exclusive. One Ticket books one seat in the performance. This has been shown by a qualifier. One performance is associated with one show. Corresponding multiplicity and labels are also shown.

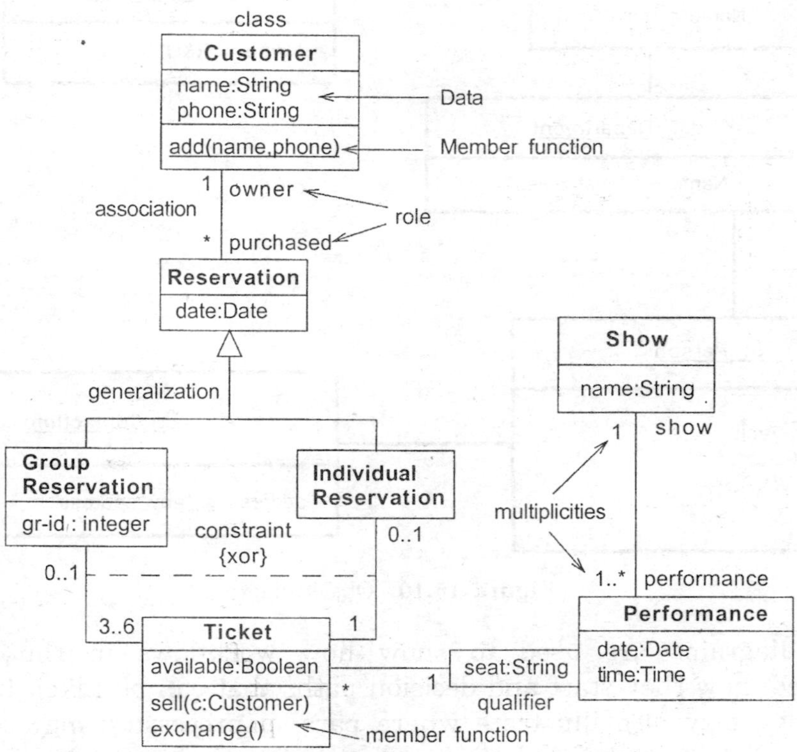

Figure 15.9 Class view of a performance show reservation system.

Object Diagram

An object diagram is a snapshot of the objects in a system at a point in time. Since it shows instances rather than classes, an object diagram is often called an *instance diagram*. It is used to show an example configuration of objects. This is very useful when the possible connections between objects are complicated. You can tell that the elements above are instances because the names are underlined. Each name takes the form instance name: class name. Both parts of the name are optional, so "BankAccount" and ":Bank" are legal names.

An object diagram is a special kind of diagram and shares the same common properties as all other diagrams, that is, a name and the graphical contents that are a projection into a model as follows, in Figure 15.10.

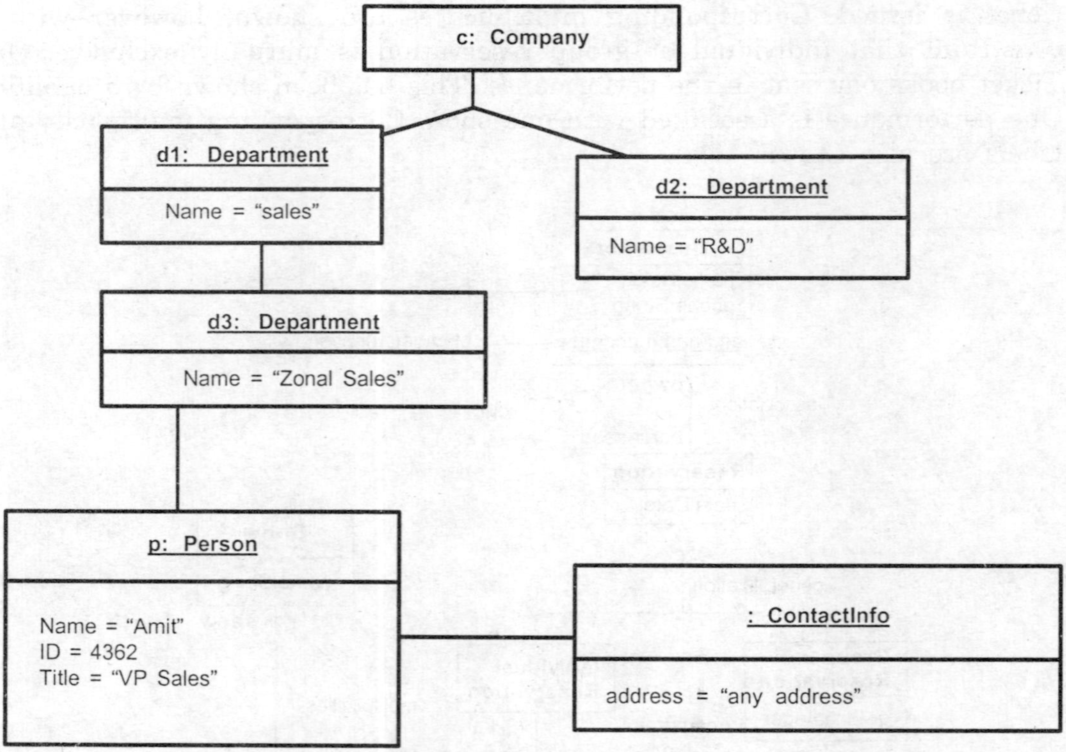

Figure 15.10 Object diagram.

Activity diagrams are used to show how workflows in the system are constructed, how they start and decision paths that can be taken from start to finish. They may also illustrate where parallel processing may occur in the execution of some activities. An example of activity diagram is shown in

Figure 15.11. State charts are used to detail the transitions or changes of state an object can go through in the system. They show how an object moves from one state to another and the rules that govern that change. State charts typically have a start and end condition.

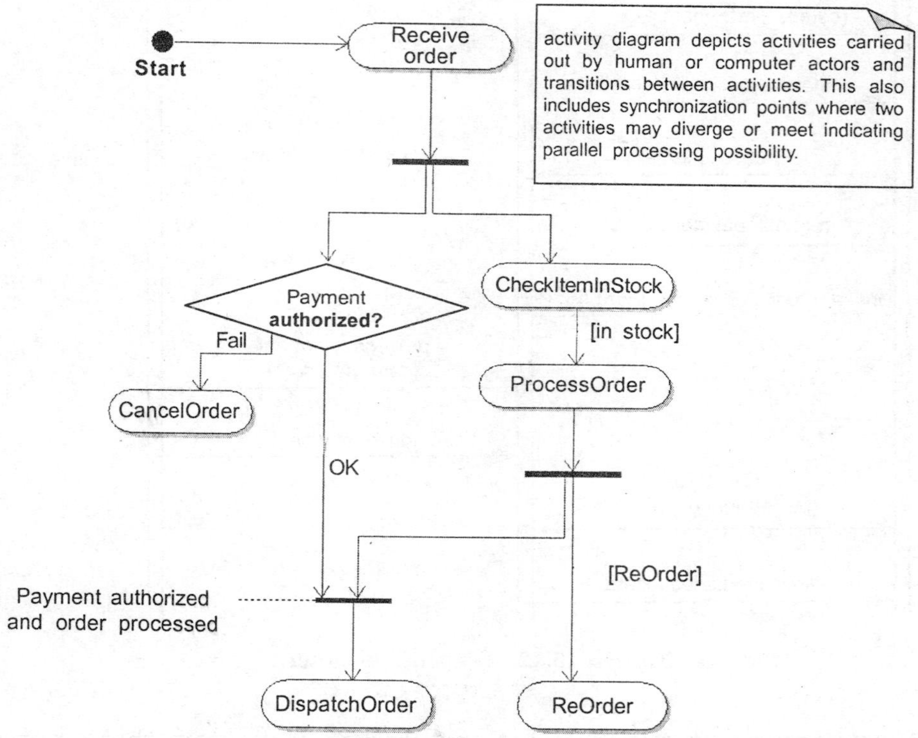

Figure 15.11 Example of an activity diagram.

Various types of diagrams are:

1. ***Interaction diagram.*** This applies to several types of diagrams that emphasize object interactions. An Interaction diagram shows an interaction, consisting of a set of objects and their relationships including the messages that may be dispatched between them. Sequence diagram shows message sequence arranged in time sequence. They can be used to show a scenario—an individual history of a transaction. One use is to show the behaviour of a use case. Collaboration diagram models and links are meaningful within an interaction. One use is to show the implementation of an operation. Collaboration diagram shows parameters and local variables of the operation. It emphasizes relationship among roles, and time sequence is implicit. Sequence diagram emphasizes time sequence and relationship among roles implicit.

2. ***Sequence diagram.*** This is an Interaction diagram that emphasizes the time ordering of messages. An example is shown in Figure 15.12.

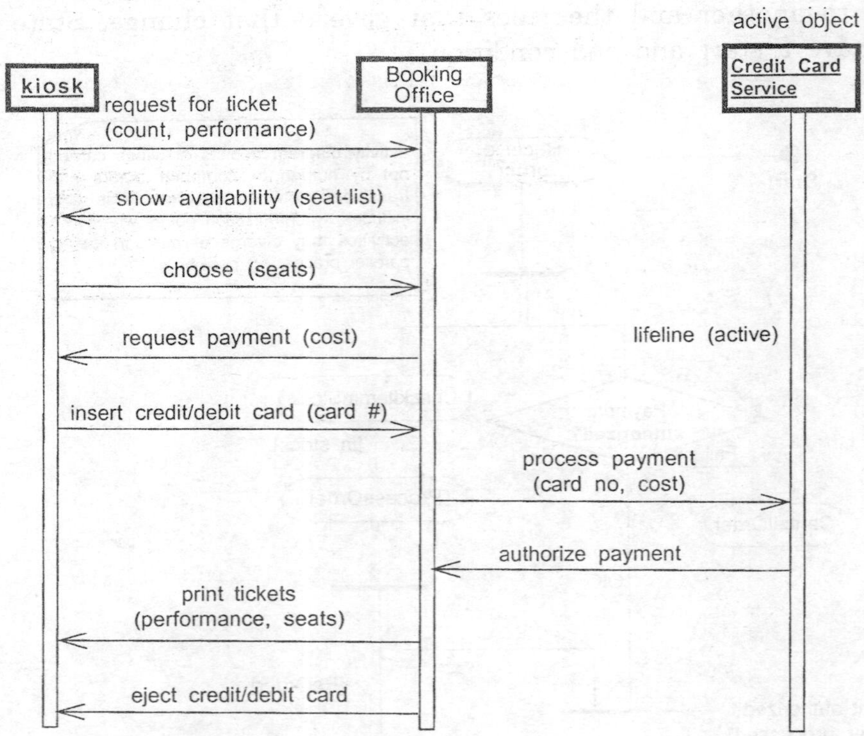

Figure 15.12 Sequence diagram.

3. ***Collaboration diagram.*** This is an Interaction diagram that emphasizes the structural organization of the objects that send and receive messages. An example is shown in Figure 15.13.

4. ***State transition diagram.*** This shows a state machine, consisting of states, transitions, events and activities and addresses the dynamic view of the system. This is used to model the behaviour of an interface, class or collaboration, and emphasises the event ordered behaviour of the object.

5. ***Activity diagram.*** This is a special kind of State transition diagram that shows the flow from one activity to another.

A variant of a state machine showing the computational activities is provided in Figure 15.14. An activity state represents an activity, a workflow step or execution of an operation. Models real-world workflow of an organization or software activities. This is helpful in understanding high-level execution behaviour without involving internal details of message passing.

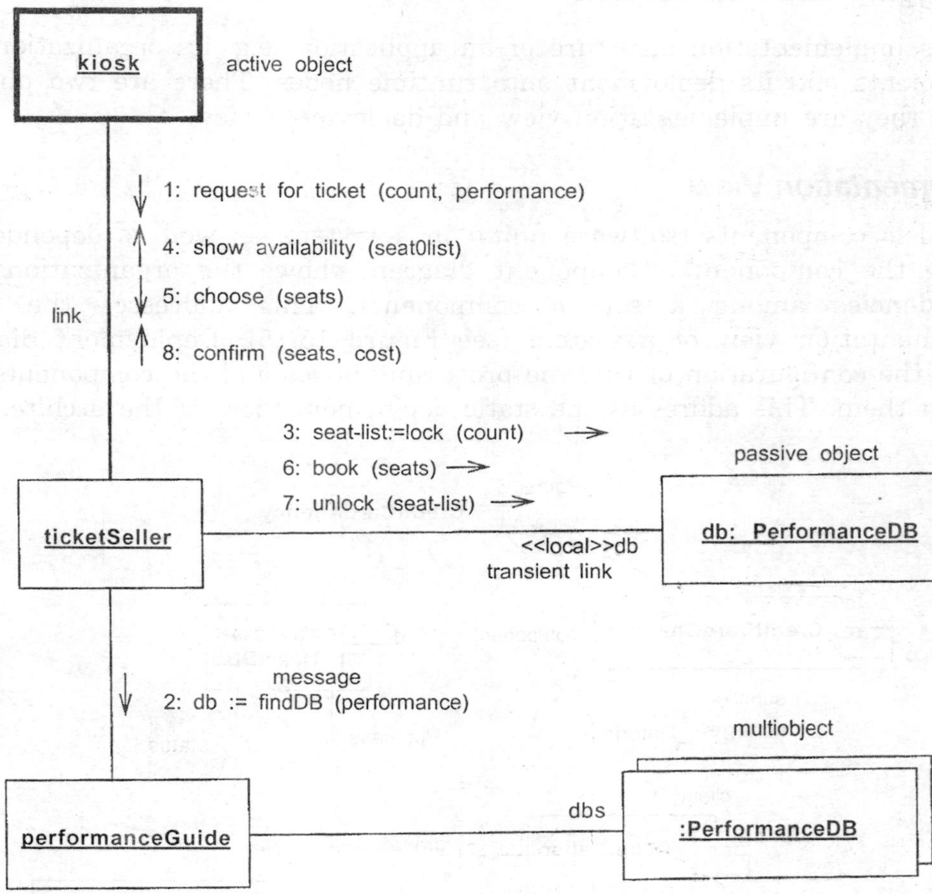

Figure 15.13 Collaboration diagram.

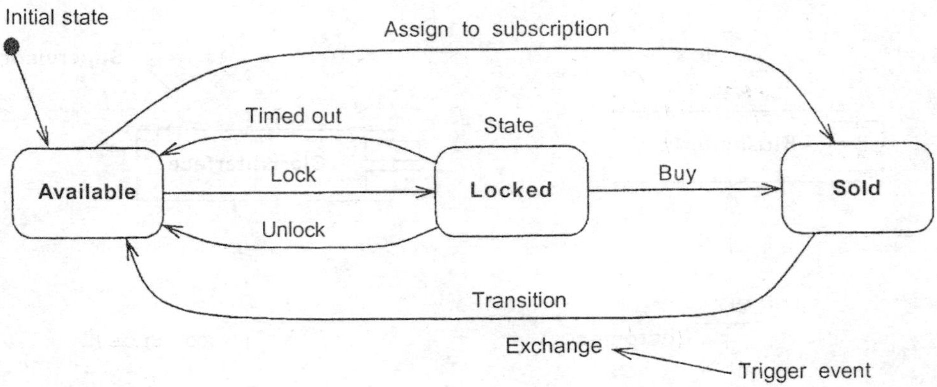

Figure 15.14 State machine view.

Packaging and Deployment

Models implementation structure of an application, e.g. its organization into components and its deployment onto runtime nodes. There are two physical views, they are implementation view and deployment view.

Implementation View

It models components (software units) in a system, as well as dependencies among the components. Component diagram shows the organizations and dependencies among a set of components. This addresses the static implementation view of a system (see Figure 15.15). Deployment diagram shows the configuration of runtime processing nodes and the components that live on them. This addresses the static deployment view of the architecture.

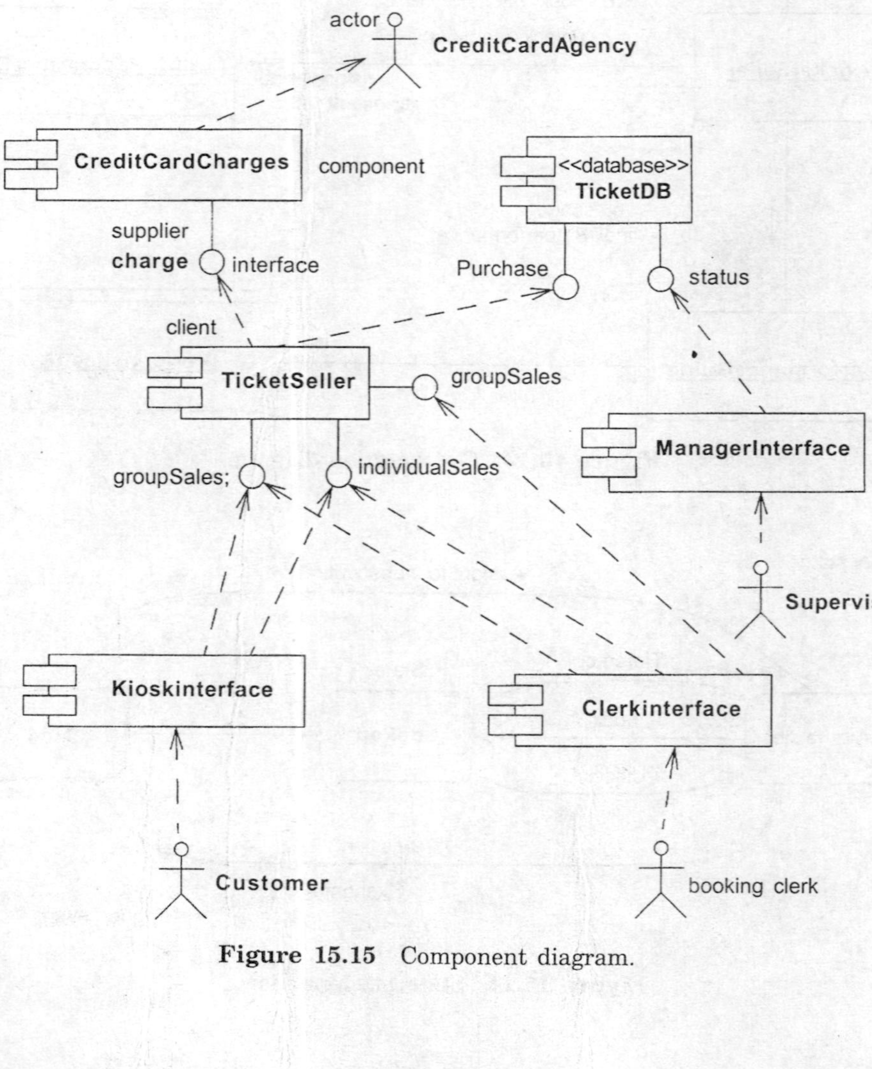

Figure 15.15 Component diagram.

Deployment View

It represents the arrangement of runtime component instances on node instances. A deployment diagram shows the physical relationships among software and hardware components. It is a good place to show that components and objects are routed and move around a distributed system. Each node on a deployment diagram represents some kind of computational unit, in most cases, a piece of hardware (may be a simple sensor, PC, mainframe etc.). Connections among nodes show the communication paths over which the system interacts. Component diagrams may well be combined with deployment diagrams. In this case, the Node can be seen as a physical domain in which a particular component can be found. It has two parts.

1. ***Descriptor level view.*** This shows kinds of nodes in the system and kinds of components they hold (see Figure 15.16).

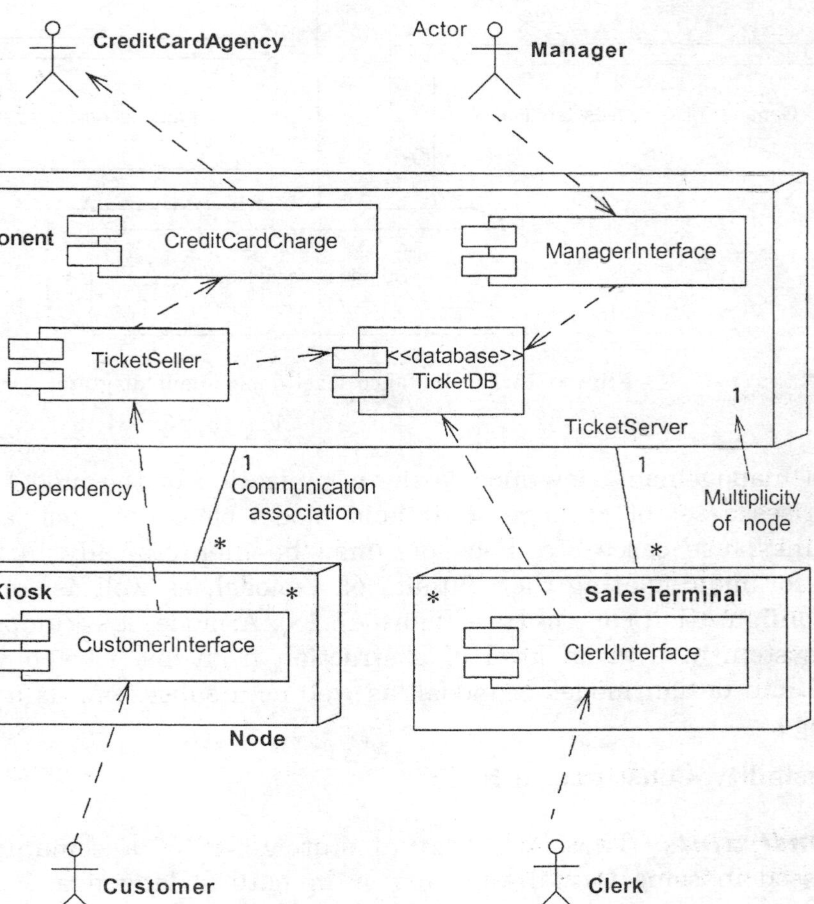

Figure 15.16 Descriptor level deployment diagram.

2. ***Instance level view.*** This view shows individual nodes and their links in a particular version of the system (see Figure 15.17).

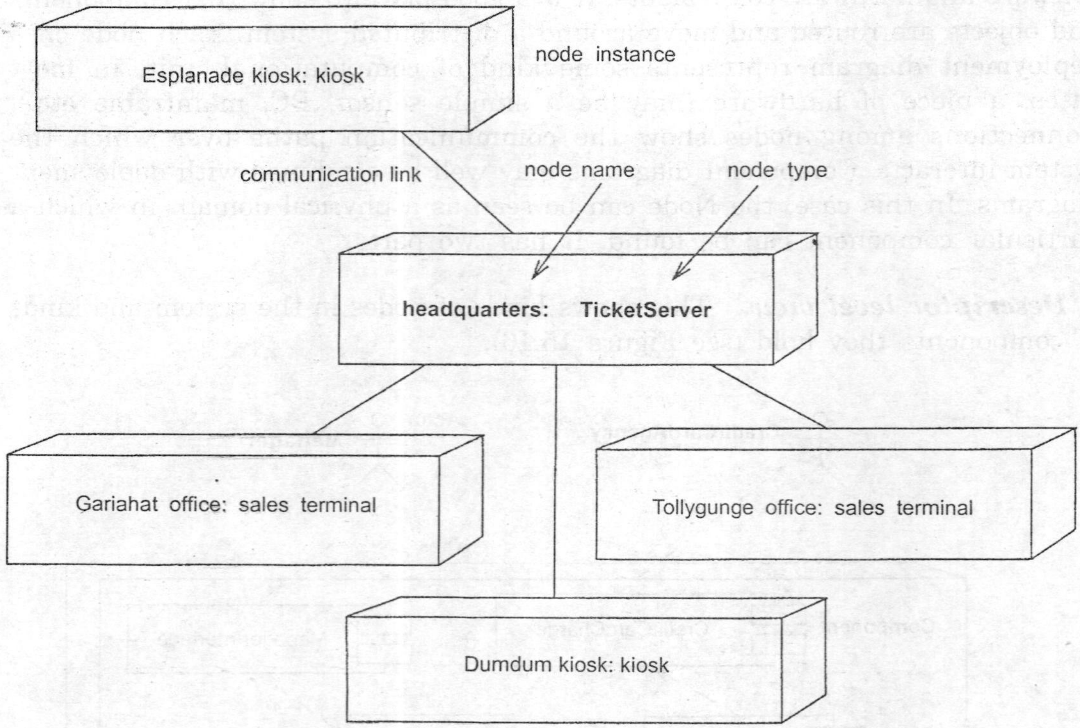

Figure 15.17 Instance level deployment diagram.

Model management view models the organization of the model itself. A model comprises a set of packages that hold model elements, such as classes, state machines, use cases etc. Packages may be hierarchically formed. They are units for manipulating the contents of a model, as well as for access control and configuration control (see Figure 15.18). A model is a complete description of a system at a given level of abstraction from one viewpoint, e.g. analysis model and design model. A model, as well as a subsystem, is a special kind of package.

Extensibility Constructs include:

1. ***Constraints.*** These are textual statements of a semantic relationship expressed in some formal language or in natural language.

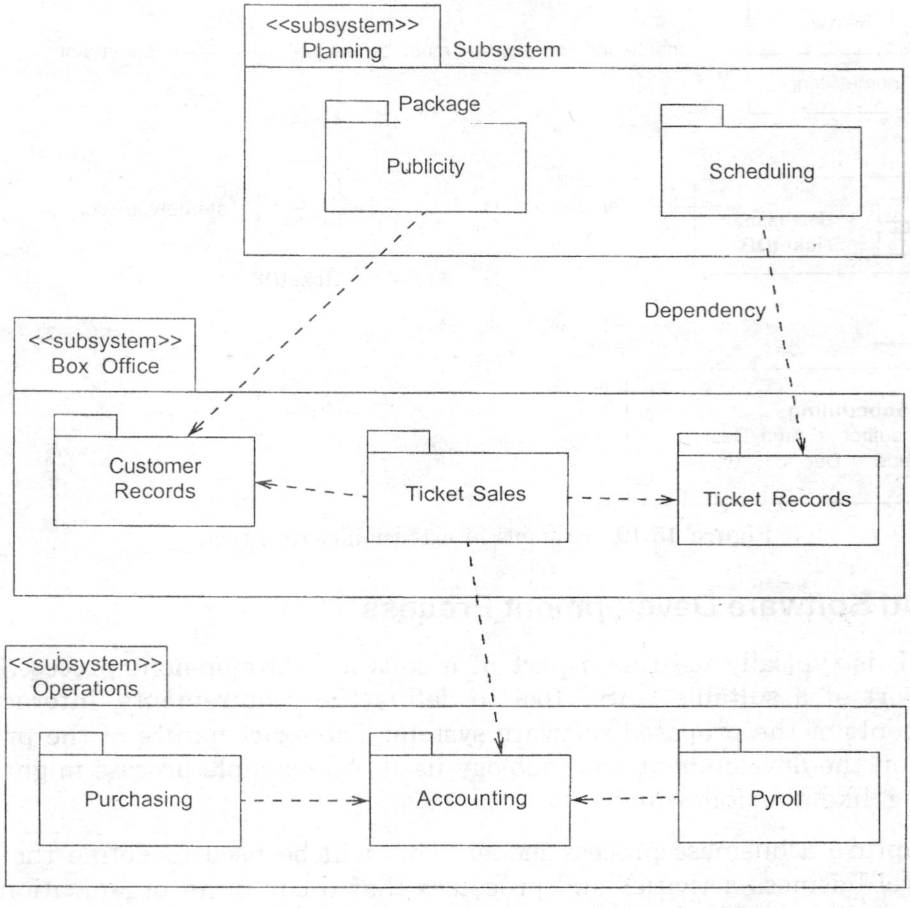

Figure 15.18 Packages (showing subsystem relationships).

2. ***Stereotype.*** This is a new kind of model element designed/utilized by the modeller and based on an existing kind of model element.

3. ***Tagged value.*** This is a named piece of information attached to any model element. Let us summarize these in a diagram (see Figure 15.19).

Using these diagrams with a high level of abstraction, complex systems can be modelled through a small set of nearly independent diagrams. UML provides two aspects for constructs.

1. ***Semantics.*** The UML metamodel defines the abstract syntax and semantics of object modelling concepts.

2. ***Notations.*** UML defines graphical notations for the visual representation of its model elements.

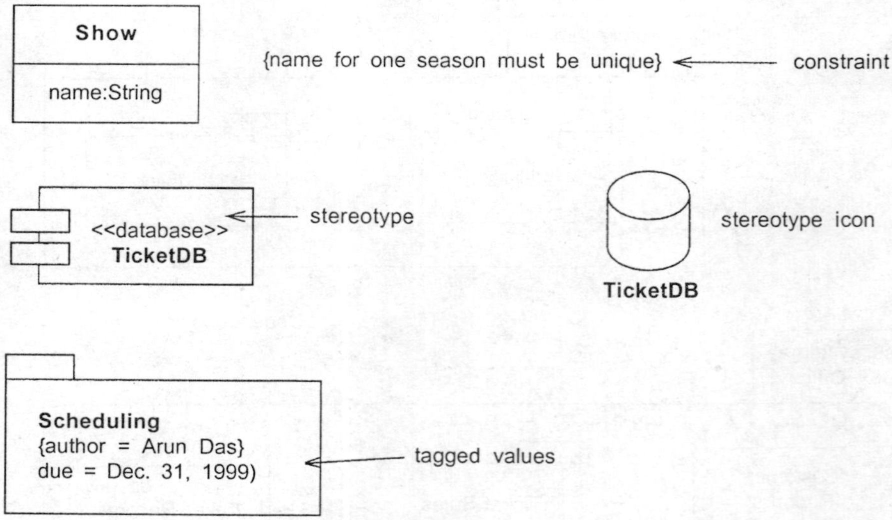

Figure 15.19 Example of extensibility constructs.

UML and Software Development Process

The UML is typically used as a part of a software development process, with the support of a suitable CASE tool to define the requirements, interactions and elements of the proposed software system. The exact nature of the process depends on the development methodology used. An example process might look something like the following:

1. Capture a business process model. This will be used to define the high level business activities and processes that occur in an organization and to provide a foundation for the use case model. The business process model will typically capture more than a software system will implement (i.e. it includes manual and other processes).
2. Map a use case model to the business process model to define exactly what functionality you are intending to provide from the business user perspective. As each use case is added, create a traceable link from the appropriate business processes to the use case (i.e. a realization connection). This mapping clearly states what functionality the new system will provide to meet the business requirements outlined in the process model. It also ensures no use cases exist without a purpose.
3. Refine the use cases—include requirements, constraints, complexity rating, notes and scenarios. These informations unambiguously describe what the use case does, how it is executed, and the constraints on its execution. Make sure the use case still meets the business process requirements. Include the definition of system tests for each use case to define the acceptance criteria for each use case. Also include some user

acceptance test scripts to define how the user will test this functionality and what the acceptance criteria are.

4. From the inputs and outputs of the business process model and the details of the use cases, begin to construct a domain model (high level business objects), sequence diagrams, collaboration diagrams and user interface models. These describe the 'things' in the new system, the way those things interact and the interface a user will use to execute use case scenarios.
5. From the domain model, the user interface model and the scenario diagrams create the class model. This is a precise specification of the objects in the system, their data or attributes and their behaviour or operations. Domain objects may be abstracted into class hierarchies using inheritance. Scenario diagram messages will typically map to class operations. If an existing framework or design pattern is to be used, it may be possible to import existing model elements for use in the new system. For each class define unit tests and integration tests to thoroughly test (i) that the class functions as specified internally and that, (ii) the class interacts with other related classes and components as expected.
6. As the class model develops, it may be broken into discrete packages and components. A component represents a deployable chunk of software that collects the behaviour and data of one or more classes and exposes a strict interface to other consumers of its services. So, from the class model, a component model is built to define the logical packaging of classes. For each component define integration tests to confirm that the component's interface meets the specification given in it in relation to other software elements.
7. Concurrent with the work you have already done, additional requirements should have been captured and documented. For example, Non functional requirements, Performance requirements, Security requirements, responsibilities, release plans etc. Collect these within the model and keep up to date as the model matures.
8. The deployment model defines the physical architecture of the system. This work can be begun early to capture the physical deployment characteristics—what hardware, operating systems, network capabilities, interfaces and support software will make up the new system, where it will be deployed and what parameters apply to disaster recovery, reliability, back-ups and support. As the model develops, the physical architecture will be updated to reflect the actual system being proposed.
9. Build the system; take discrete pieces of the model and assign them to one or more developers. In a use case driven build this will mean

assigning a use case to the development team, having them build the screens, business objects, database tables, and related components necessary to execute that use case. As each use case is built, it should be accompanied by a completed unit, integration and system tests. A component driven build may see discrete software components assigned to development teams for construction.

10. Track defects that emerge in the testing phases against the related model elements, e.g. system test defects against use cases, unit test defects against classes and etc. Track any changes against the related model elements to manage 'scope creep'.
11. Update and refine the model as work proceeds, always assessing the impact of changes and model refinements on later work. Use an iterative approach to work through the design in discrete chunks, always assessing the current build, the forward requirements and any discoveries that come to light during development.
12. Deliver the complete and tested software into a test then production environment. If a phased delivery is being undertaken, then this migration of built software from test to production may occur several times over the life of the project.

The process is given as an example of how the UML may be used to support a software development project.

The UML is non-proprietary and open to all. It addresses the needs of user, scientific and business communities, as established by experience with the underlying methods on which it is based. Many methodologists, organizations, and tool vendors have committed to use it. Since the UML builds upon similar semantics and notation from Booch, OMT, OOSE, and other leading methods and has incorporated input from the UML partners and feedback from the general public, widespread adoption of the UML should be straightforward.

There are two aspects of "unified" that the UML achieves:

1. It effectively ends many of the differences, often inconsequential, between the modelling languages of previous methods.
2. It unifies the perspectives among many different kinds of systems (business versus software), development phases (requirements analysis, design and implementation), and internal concepts.

Although the UML defines a precise language, it is not a barrier to future improvements in modelling concepts. The UML can be extended without redefining the UML core. The UML, in its current form, has been established to be the basis for many tools, including those for visual modelling, simulation and development environments. As interesting tool integrations are developed, implementation standards based on the UML will become increasingly available.

While UML defines coherent constructs and interchangeable semantics, it does not intentionally provide the explicit format to exchange the model information. The ability to exchange models is quite important, because the network environment, especially the Internet, is growing exponentially and it is likely that a development team resides in separate places. Application interconnectivity is required so that the model information can be exchanged between various tools such as CASE (Computer Aided Software Engineering) tools, diagram editors, reverse engineering tools and design metrics tools. As such, the application-neutral format is necessitated to expand the ability to encode, exchange and reuse the model information. In the years to come, we can expect continued steady growth of UML with substantive improvements in modelling tools and methods, with increased software productivity and quality.

SUMMARY

The key concepts introduced in this chapter are as follows:

- The Unified Modelling Language (UML) is an open standard for specifying, constructing, visualizing, and documenting the architecture of a software-intensive system.
- The UML is typically used as a part of a software development process, with the support of a suitable CASE tool, to define the requirements, the interactions and the elements of the proposed software system.
- UML defines several models to represent systems including class model, state model, use-case model, interaction model, implementation model, and deployment model.
- UML provides several architectural views regarding models of problems and solutions including user model view, structural model view, behavioural model view, implementation model view, and environment model view.
- UML defines twelve types of diagrams divided into three categories including structural diagrams (class, object, component and deployment), behaviour diagrams (use case, sequence, activity, collaboration and statechart) and model management diagrams (packages, subsystems, models).
- A use case represents a discrete unit of interaction between a user (human or machine) and the system. An actor is a human or machine entity that interacts with the system to perform meaningful work. An actor uses a use case to perform some piece of work, which is of value to the business.

- Sequence diagrams show the flow of messages from one object to another, and as such correspond to the methods and events supported by a class/object.
- Class diagram shows a set of classes, interfaces, and collaborations and their relationships. An object diagram is a snapshot of the objects in a system at a point in time.
- Activity diagrams are used to show how workflows in the system are constructed, how they start and decision paths that can be taken from start to finish.

REVIEW QUESTIONS

1. What is UML?
2. What are the different diagrams used in UML?
3. Making a well-designed structure of the entire architecture helps to deal with complexity with increasing size of application. Explain.
4. What are the basic building blocks of UML?
5. What are the role of actors and use cases? Explain with suitable examples.
6. Draw a use case diagram for Railway Reservation System.
7. What does a use case description usually include?
8. Which diagrams are needed for structural modelling? Explain with examples.
9. What is the difference between class diagram and object diagram.
10. Provide a suitable C++ header file and skeleton implementation for a mini banking system with SavingsAccount and CheckingAccount facility. State all your assumptions.
11. What is the role of behavioural modelling? Illustrate with suitable examples.
12. What is the role of a sequence diagram? Illustrate with suitable example.
13. Illustrate usage of collaboration diagram.
14. Explain the relationships between Component Diagram and Deployment Diagram with suitable examples.
15. What are extensibility constructs?
16. What role does UML play in a software development process?

Problems
(for Laboratory Workouts)

Assume suitable function prototypes for the functions/operators mentioned.

1. Write a program to convert
   (a) a given temperature from Celsius to Fahrenheit or vice versa. The input temperature scale will be indicated by the user.
   (b) a binary number (real as well as integer) to the equivalent decimal number.
   (c) a decimal number to the equivalent decimal number. (try for both real as well as integer numbers like 123 and 123.45). (*Hint:* Take input from user how much precision he/she wants.)
2. Design and implement a function to convert a binary number to the equivalent octal number.
3. In the Binary Coded Decimal (BCD) scheme each digit is represented by a 4 bit binary code. Write a program that accepts a decimal number as input and converts it to the equivalent BCD number.
4. Write a program to check whether
   (a) a given number is palindrome or not, e.g. 1221, 131 are palindromes.
   (b) a given character string is palindrome or not, e.g. "abba", "madam", "liril", "malayalam" "WAS IT A CAR OR CAT I SAW", "pull up if i pull up", "A MAN, A PLAN, A CANAL, PANAMA" are palindromes. (*Hint:* Ignore spaces, commas etc. delimeters and case sensitivity.)
5. Write a recursive program to find the factorial of an integer. Write an iterative variant of the same program.
6. Write a program to delete duplicate elements in a vector. (*Hint:* You need to shift the contents of the vector up when you delete a row and the size of the vector reduces too.) Design and implement appropriate classes and member functions.

7. Write a program to delete duplicate elements from
   (a) a single linked list. Design and implement appropriate classes and member functions.
   (b) a doubly linked list. Design and implement appropriate classes and member functions.
8. Write the smallest C++ program that can be compiled and executed.
9. Write a program that displays "Learning C++" on the screen.
10. Write a program to find
    (a) GCD (greatest common divisor) of two numbers.
    (b) if an integer is odd, even, prime or a perfect factorial.
    (c) if an integer is odd or even without using if statement.
    (d) LCM (least common multiplier) of two integers.
    (e) LCM (least common multiplier) and GCD of two integers.
11. Write a program to enter a string of characters of any length, and print the various number of words possible. (The words formed may or may not have any meaning.)
12. Implement a *String* class that can be used like other primitive data types such as integer or character. (*Hint:* You should overload the assignment operator and relational operators. You can feel free to add other relevant operations in your String class.)
13. In your *String* class as above, write a function
    (a) *String::CharDelete*, that accepts a character *c* and returns the string with all occurrences of *c* removed. Can you do this with '-' operator overloaded?
    (b) *String::frequency* that determines the frequency of occurrence of each of the distinct characters in the string.
    (c) *String::Delete*, that accepts two integers, *start* and *length* and computes a new string that is equivalent to the original string, except that *length* characters beginning at *start* have been removed. Can you do this with '–' operator overloaded?
    (d) concatenating two strings using overloaded + operator.
14. Write a function to
    (a) make an in-place replacement of a substring *w* of a string by the string *x*. Note that *w* may not be of the same size as *x*.
    (b) insert a substring into a string.
    (c) find the position of the first occurrence of a substring in a main string. If the substring is not in the main string then the function should return –1.

15. Implement a Complex number class that can be used like other numerical data types of C++. (*Hint:* You should overload at least assignment operator, mathematical operators and input and output stream operators.)
16. Implement a class *Quadratic* that represents second degree polynomials, i.e. polynomials of type $ax^2 + bx + c$. The class will require three data members corresponding to *a, b, c*. Implement the following operations:
    (a) A constructor (including a default constructor which creates the 0 polynomial).
    (b) Overload the addition operator to add two polynomials of degree 2.
    (c) Overload << and >> operators to print and read polynomials. You should decide the input and output format of the Polynomials.
    (d) A function to compute the value of a polynomial for a given value of x.
    (e) A function to compute the two solutions of the equation $ax^2 + bx + c = 0$.
    (*Hint:* You should use the class Complex mentioned in the previous question.)
17. Design and implement a function to sort a collection of n ($n>=1$) numbers into non decreasing order by Selection sort method. Then use this function in a program that sorts the company names and corresponding share prices (you may take closing values of the previous day as available in the newspaper) of a Stock Exchange in increasing order of share prices. (*Hint:* The basic idea of Selection sort can be expressed here as follows:– From those numbers that are currently unsorted, find the smallest and place it next in the sorted list.)
18. Design and implement a class *Array* which is like the one-dimensional C++ array (i.e. the index set is a set of consecutive integers starting at 0) that
    (a) performs range checking.
    (b) allows one array to be assigned to another array through the use of the assignment operator (e.g. arr1 = arr2).
    (c) supports a function that returns the size of the array.
    (d) allows the reading or printing of arrays through the use of *cout* and *cin*.
19. Design and implement a *SquareMatrix* class. There should be a copy constructor, a null constructor (i.e. which creates a null matrix where

all elements are zero) and destructor. Also implement following operations appropriately:

(a) Addition of two matrices

(b) Subtraction of two matrices

(c) Multiplication of a matrix by a scalar

(d) Multiplication of two matrices

(e) Transposition of a matrix. (*Hint:* The matrix A^T of order n by m obtained by interchanging rows and columns in a matrix A of order m by n is called the transpose of A.)

20. Write a function to check whether a given matrix is **Magic Square** or not. (*Hint:* A magic square is an n by n matrix of the integers 1 to n^2 such that the sum of every row, column and diagonal is same.)

21. An m by n matrix has a **Saddle point**, if some entry a[i] [j] is the smallest value in row i and the largest value in column j. Write a function to find the location and value of a saddle point if one exists.

22. Write a function to verify whether a given square matrix is

    (a) **Scalar matrix** (*Hint:* A square matrix in which each element of the main diagonal equals a scalar c (say) and all other elements are zero, is called a *scalar matrix*.)

    (b) **Idempotent** (*Hint:* A square matrix A is called idempotent if $A^2 = A$ i.e. A.A = A)

23. Write a function/program to find whether two given square matrices
    Commute (i.e. AB = BA)
    Anticommute (i.e. AB = –BA)
    None of the above (i.e. AB != BA).

    You can use another function for multiplication of two matrices.

24. Write a function to check if a given square matrix is **Symmetric** or **Skew-symmetric** or none. (*Hint:* A square matrix $A = (a_{ij})_{n \times n}$ is called symmetric if *Transpose of* A = A; i.e. if $a_{ij} = a_{ji}$ for all pairs of subscripts i and j. On the other hand, A is called skew-symmetric if *Transpose of* $A = -A$, i.e. if $a_{ij} = -a_{ji}$ for all i and j.

25. Write a function to generate a set of pseudo-random numbers.

26. The problem of Dutch national flag involves starting out with a row of n buckets, i.e. bucket[*1..n*], each bucket containing a single pebble that is either red, white or blue. You have to arrange the pebbles so that all reds occur before all whites, which in turn occur before all blue pebbles. Design and implement a function in C++ to solve the Dutch national flag problem.

27. Write a function to generate first n terms of the sequence

    1 2 4 8 16 32 ...

    without using multiplication.

28. Write a function to compute the sum of the first n terms ($n >= 1$) of the series

    $$s = 1 - 3 + 5 - 7 + 9 - .....$$

29. Write a program to print the following pattern using loops. Try with all different kind of loops supported.

********	*	1	1
*******	***	121	121
******	*****	12321	12321
*****	*******	1234321	1234321
****	*****	12321	123454321
***	***	121	12345654321
**	*	1	1234567654321
*			

30. Write a function to compute
    (a) $1/ n\,!$.
    (b) $x^n / n\,!$ for a given x and a given n.

31. Write a function to determine whether a number is a factorial number.

32. Design and implement a function which, given some integer n, finds the largest number present as a factor in n (e.g. 18 is the largest factor of 36).

33. Write a function to simulate multiplication by addition. Two integers (may be zero, positive, or negative) should be passed for calling the function as input parameters.

34. Using C++ compute the sum of the first n terms of the series $0! + 1! + 2! + 3! + 4! + ... + n!$. ($n >= 0$ and $0! = 1$).

35. The exponential growth constant e is characterized by the expression

    $$e = 1/ 0! + 1/ 1! + 1/ 2! + 1/ 3! + 1/ 4! ....$$

    Write a program to compute e to n terms. n will be specified by the user.

36. The first few number of the Lucas sequence is given below.

    1 3 4 7 11 18 29 ....

    Write a program to generate first n elements of the Lucas sequence. n will be specified by the user.

37. Design and implement a function that accepts a positive integer and reverses the order of its digits, i.e. if 125 is input then 521 will be returned by the function.
38. Write a function that
    (a) counts the number of digits in an integer.
    (b) sums the digits in an integer. The integer may be positive, negative or zero.
39. Write a function in C++ to convert a decimal integer to its corresponding octal representation.
40. Write a program
    (a) to produce a list of all exact integer divisors of a given positive integer.
    (b) to find the smallest positive integer that has n or more divisors. The number n will be input by the user.
41. A perfect number is one whose divisors add up to the number. Write a program to list all perfect numbers between 1 and 1000.
42. Write a program to generate the nth member of the Fibonacci sequence. n will be input by the user. (*Hint:* The first few terms of the Fibonacci sequence are 0 1 1 2 3 5 8 13 .)
43. Implement a FRACTION class that can store numerator and denominator with the following member functions/operators
    (a) constructor with default argument taken as numerator = 0, denominator = 1
    (b) copy constructor
    (c) destructor
    (d) operator =, +, *, +=, ==, >, ++(pre), ++(post)
    (e) cast operator to int and float
44. Implement an INTARRAY class that can store integer array of different size (size of the array will be provided as argument to constructor) with the following member functions/operators
    (a) constructor with default argument taken as array size = 0
    (b) copy constructor
    (c) destructor
    (d) operator =, ==, [ ]

45. Implement a STACK class subclassing from INTARRAY class so that only the following functions are exposed as public interface ([ ] operator shouldn't be exposed)
    (a) push
    (b) pop
    (c) top
    (d) constructor, copy constructor, destructor
46. Reimplement
    (a) INTARRAY class as given earlier using template so that array can be for integer, float etc.
    (b) STACK class as given earlier using template so that stack can be for integer, float etc.
47. Using template, implement one generic QuickSort and one generic BubbleSort routine which can sort an array of any type of data.
48. Write the definition of a class template for implementing a list of objects of various types. Consider that the list is to be implemented as a linked list using pointers where each node contains data of different types and a pointer to the next element. That is, each node is also a template class. A list object contains a pointer to the first node. Your implementation must support the following:
    (a) Initializing an empty list object with no node.
    (b) Adding a node at the end of the list given the data of the node as an argument to the "add" function.
    (c) Deletion of the first element of the list and returning that data content of that element.
49. A program is given as follows:

```
#include <stdio.h>
class INT
{  int i;
public:
   INT(int a): i(a) {};
   ~INT(){};
};
int main()
{  int x = 3;
   INT y = x;
   y++ = ++y;
   x = y;
   return 0;
}
```

What extra functions/operators are required in the INT class to make the main program work? Provide suitable implementation for the added functions/operators.

50. (a) A knight starts moving from any square of a chessboard and covers the entire chessboard (without repeating any square) and reaches its starting point. Find the various numbers of ways possible.

    (b) The same knight starts moving from a corner square and reaches its opposite corner along the diagonal. Find the various numbers of ways possible.

51. n queens are placed in a $n \times n$ square chessboard such that none of the queens attack each other. Make a program in which the user inputs k and prints the number of ways this arrangement is possible.

52. Enter two dates in (dd,mm,yy) format and find the number of days in between them. (*Hint:* Define and implement suitable Date class and use that to solve the problem.)

53. Enter a year and print the calendar for that year. (*Hint:* Define and implement suitable Year class and use that to solve the problem.)

54. Make a calculator which calculates arithmetic expressions. For example, the input will be given as 4 * 2 + 3 * 6, and the output will be computed as 26.

55. Implement the Tower of Hanoi problem.

56. Find the value of a nth order determinant using recursion.

57. Multiply two matrices (*Hint:* For matrix multiplication to be possible, they should be of the form $a[m \times n] \times b[n \times p] = c[m \times p]$.)

58. Write a program to reverse a given string using pointer.

59. Write a program that has a class called POINT which stores co-ordinates in (x, y) form. Define constructor, destructor, and overloaded '–' operator to calculate distance between two points.

60. Write a program in C++ to implement queue data structure using linked list. It may support the following operations:

    (a) Delete a node from queue

    (b) Insert a node at the front of queue

    (c) Find out the length of a queue

QUESTIONS

1. Indicate whether the following statements are TRUE or FALSE.
   (a) Lifetime of an object created by *new* is restricted to the scope in which it is created.
   (b) A default argument cannot be redefined later with different value, but can be redefined with same value.
   (c) An overloaded operator cannot have default arguments.
   (d) A *friend* declaration has to appear in the declaration of the class of which it is a friend.
   (e) A class can have *virtual* constructors.
2. Fill up the blanks using most appropriate word/phrase.
   (a) A class having at least one pure virtual function is called ________ class.
   (b) A ________ object may be initialized, but its value may not be changed thereafter.
   (c) How many of the following function(s)/operator(s) a class can have?
      (i) constructor
      (ii) = operator
      (iii) destructor
   (d) In a C++ struct, all members are ________ by default, whereas in a C++ class, all members are ________ by default.
   (e) A local variable can be returned from a function by ________.
3. Choose the best possible answer.
   (a) Derived class is related to base class through ________ relationship.
      (i) IS-A (ii) HAS-A (iii) abstract (iv) no
   (b) By default, members of a class are
      (i) private (ii) protected (iii) public (iv) virtual
   (c) Default arguments are used in a call where arguments are missing.
      (i) beginning (ii) trailing
      (iii) all (iv) none of the
   (d) A friend of a class can access data and function members appearing only in section(s).
      (i) private (ii) private and protected
      (iii) all of the (iv) none of the

(e) A ________ defines a conversion from one class to another without modifying the declaration for other class.

(i) constructor (ii) cast operator
(iii) copy constructor (iv) = operator

(f) Dynamic binding can be achieved by ________ function.

(i) static (ii) virtual
(iii) destructor (iv) abstract

(g) A constructor's name is same as ________.

(i) class name (ii) file name
(iii) object name (iv) none of the above

(h) Overloading extraction operator (>>) can be done by making the operator declared as ________.

(i) member (ii) static (iii) virtual (iv) friend

(i) In a copy constructor, the argument can be passed by ________.

(i) value (ii) reference
(iii) value or reference (iv) none of the above

(j) New is a/an

(i) function (ii) operator
(iii) macro (iv) preprocessor directive

(k) A destructor cannot be ________.

(i) virtual (ii) non-static member
(iii) static member (iv) protected

4. What does the statement #include do?
5. What is the difference between a // comment and a /* ... */ comment?
6. Can C++ comments be nested?
7. Why *main( )* is different from any other function written in C++?
8. Why it is better to use the keyword *'const'* for defining a constant rather than the *'#define'* ?
9. State whether a negative number is evaluated to true or false in a logical expression in C++.
10. What is a C++ expression? Explain with some examples.
11. What is a function? State several advantages of use of functions.
12. What is the difference between passing a parameter by value and passing by reference? Does C allow passing by reference? If not, can you simulate

passing by reference behaviour in C? Does C++ allow passing by reference? Illustrate with example. Can you simulate the passing by value feature using passing by reference?

13. What happens when a pointer is passed as a function argument? Illustrate usage through suitable examples when a pointer is passed as value and when pointer is passed as reference.
14. What is the difference between array of pointers and pointer to arrays? How do they differ in their syntax? Illustrate through suitable examples.
15. How is a multidimensional array defined in terms of a pointer to a collection of contiguous arrays of lower dimensionality?
16. What is the difference between static and dynamic memory allocation?
17. What is the difference between compile-time error and run-time error? What is exception handling?
18. What do you understand by an *lvalue* and an *rvalue* in C++. Explain with an example.
19. Write a code segment to demonstrate the application of the *conditional operator* (? :). Why it is different from any other operator in C++?
20. What are the differences between
    (a) function prototype and the function definition?
    (b) a declaration and a definition?
    (c) a structure and a class in C++?
21. Explain function overloading and polymorphism in C++ with suitable examples.
22. Explain the following terms with suitable examples: *encapsulation, abstraction, class, object, constructor, default constructor, copy constructor, destructor, method, data member, private, protected, public, friend, template, namespace, exception handling, try-catch block, dynamic memory allocation, reallocation and deallocation in C++, operator overloading, function overloading, static and dynamic binding, abstract class, virtual function, pure virtual function, virtual function table, linking C program in C++, virtual base class, loops, parameter passing in C as well in C++, cast operators, type conversions through constructor, virtual destructor, static member, overloading the subscript operator.*
23. Illustrate the differences of malloc function and new operator? Which one is preferred in C++ and why?
24. Explain the use of the *break* statement and the *continue* statement with two suitable examples.

25. Explain the difference between following three statements:

```
const int *pA;
int * const pB;
const int * const pC;
```

26. What is the relation among a const object, a const member function of the object class and a pointer to the const object in a C++ program?
27. What is a stray or dangling pointer?
28. What is the *this* pointer?
29. What is a reference? How it is different from a pointer? Illustrate situations when reference is preferred to pointers, and any situation when pointer is preferred to reference.
30. What is a constant reference? When it should be used?
31. What is a default parameter? Can an overloaded function have a default parameter?
32. What is the difference between overloading a function and overriding a function in a C++ program?
33. What is virtual inheritance?
34. What is a pure virtual function? How it is related to data abstractions in C++?
35. What are the characteristics of a static data member and a static function member of a class? Write a program to demonstrate the use of these members.
36. What is containment? Explain with an example.
37. What are the different storage class specifiers? Explain their difference with respect to default value, scope and lifetime.
38. A class hierarchy is declared as follows:
    (a) class A {public : int g(); protected : int x;};
    (b) class P {protected : int f(); char c;};
    (c) class Q : public A, public virtual P {public : int f(); char c;};
    (d) class R : public A, public virtual P {};
    (e) class S : public Q, public R {void h();};

    (i) Draw a directed acyclic graphical (DAG) representation of the class hierarchy.

(ii) S:: h() is implemented as follows:

```
void S::h()
{
 x++;
 f();
 g();
 c = 'i';
}
```

Comment on the usage of the statements in S::h().

39. A class STRING is declared as follows:

```
class STRING
{
 public:
    STRING(const char * = (char *) NULL;);
    ~STRING();
    STRING(const STRING &);
    STRING & operator = (const STRING &);
};
```

And a function f() is defined in four different ways.

(a) STRING f()

```
  {
    STRING s("abc");
    return s;
  }
```

(b) STRING f()

```
  {
    STRING *ps = new STRING("abc");
    return *ps;
  }
```

(c) STRING & f()

```
  {
    STRING s("abc");
    return s;
  }
```

(d) STRING & f()

```
  {
    STRING *ps = new STRING("abc");
    return *ps;
  }
```

Comment on the implementation of f() in the above four ways. Explain whether each approach has some problem or not.

40. C++ supports protection per class, not per object. Explain with suitable examples.

41. What will be the output of the following programs?

(a)
```
#include  <iostream.h>
int main()
{
    int j(3);
    int i = j+= 2;
    cout << i;
    return 0;
}
```

(b)
```
#include  <iostream.h>
int main()
{
    int j(3);
    int &i = *&j;
    j = 4;
    cout << i;
    return 0;
}
```

(c)
```
#include  <iostream.h>
int main()
{
    int j(3);
    int *i = &j;
    int *&k = i;
    *(k--) = 4;
    cout << j;
    return 0;
}
```

(d)
```
#include  <iostream.h>
int main()
{
    int j(3);
    int *i = &j;
    int k = *i**i;
    cout << k;
    return 0;
}
```

(e)
```
#include  <iostream.h>
#define a 2;
int main()
{
  int j(3);
  int i = a+j++;
  cout << i;
  return 0;
}
```

(f)
```
#include  <iostream.h>
int main()
{
  int j(3);
  int i = j+++j;
  cout << i;
  return 0;
}
```

(g)
```
#include  <iostream.h>
int main()
{
  int j(3);
  int i = ++j + ++j;
  cout << i;
  return 0;
}
```

(h)
```
#include  <iostream.h>
int main()
{
  int i(3);
  if (i = 2)
     cout << i;
  cout <<i;
  return 0;
}
```

(i)
```
#include  <iostream.h>
int i = 3;
int main()
{
  for (int j = 0;  j < 1;  j++)
```

```
    {
        int i;
        for (i = 0; i < 4; i++)
      cout <<i;
      }
      cout << i;
      return 0;
    }
```

(j)
```
#include  <iostream.h>
    char i = 251;
    int main()
    {
      for (i++; i++; i++)
         cout << (int) i << endl;
      return 0;
    }
```

(k)
```
#include  <stdio.h>
    int g = 5;
    void f(int a, int *& b)
    {
      a = g;
      *b = g + 1;
      b = &g;
      *b = g + 2;
    }
    int main()
    {
      int i = 10;
      int &j = i;
      int *pi = &i;

      f(i, pi);

      printf( "%d, %d, %d, %d, %d\n", g, i, j, *pi, *pi**pi);
      return 0;
    }
```

42. OOP has two important philosophies: *data hiding* and *data abstraction*. Explain with suitable examples.
43. What is the role of a copy constructor? Explain with a suitable example.

44. What is the difference between C++ struct and C++ class? Is there any difference between C++ struct and C struct?
45. Can you chain member function calls? For example, if aObj is an object instance, can you call like aObj.func1().func2()? If it is possible, what is the inner semantics? Illustrate through proper example.
46. "One must define the static member outside of the class declaration". Do you agree? Explain with proper example. How does a static class member initialization differ from (a) static data initialization within a function definition and (b) static data initialization within a file outside any function or class declaration or definition?
47. What is the order of destructor calling sequence in terms of superclass object, component objects, local member objects, class static member objects? Is it fixed sequence as defined by the compiler or can you change it?
48. What is the order of constructor calling sequence in terms of superclass object, component objects, local member objects, class static member objects? Is it fixed sequence as defined by the compiler or can you change it?
49. Do you need special handling for array of objects destruction compared to single object destruction? Is there any difference for automatically created objects and manually created objects in case of array of objects destruction? Illustrate through proper examples.
50. Can delete operator be called for local objects created automatically? For example, an object is created as "SomeClass aObj;" Can you call "delete &aObj"? Justify your answer.
51. In a destructor call, which things need to be explicitly destroyed and which things are implicitly destroyed? Explain.
52. Can exception be thrown while within a destructor call? Justify your answer.
53. Is there any problem if you self-assign an object, like say, "$x = x$"? What precautions you can take while overloading an assignment operator to prevent self-assignment like this?
54. Can you write the statement "delete this" from within a member function? What implications do this statement has? Can you issue this statement from within a destructor?
55. Is there any way to check automatically that the call to new operator is returning a NULL instead of manually checking whether the returned pointer is equal to NULL?

56. How do you dynamically allocate/deallocate an array of objects? Illustrate with proper examples. Do you find any difference from allocation/deallocation of a single object?
57. How do you manage to allocate/deallocate two-dimensional array? Illustrate with suitable example.
58. "C arrays are bad, there is no array boundary check". Do you agree? What can be done in C++ to make it better? Illustrate with proper examples.
59. Draw a UML class diagram and object diagram for looping statements in C-programming language.
60. A directory file system contains information about files in a directory, including both ordinary files as well as other directory systems. Prepare a UML class diagram which models directory files and ordinary files. Can you define actors and some suitable use cases?
61. Design an employee class hierarchy for university type system. Show all types (single and multiple) inheritances, important methods in each class, public and private subclasses. Design constructors in each class and explain its purposes.
62. The university wants to computerize its admission process. The system should contain data of all students, their results, issue admission letter, allocate various study centres etc. Make a brief object oriented analysis and design of the stated problem, present through suitable UML diagrams and notations.
63. Design an AUTOMOBILE base class. Define all its possible methods and data structures. Through inheritance mechanisms, create one class namely CAR. Implement its data structure and important methods. Observe the following while designing classes:
    (a) Clearly indicate public and private classes
    (b) Design constructors in each class and explain its purpose
64. Given the program:
    ```
    #include <iostream.h>
    int main()
    {
      cout << "Hello" << endl;
    }
    ```
    Modify it to produce the output as follows:
    ```
    Initialize
    Hello
    Cleanup
    ```
    Do not change main() in any way.

65. Define a class for storing, evaluating and printing simple arithmetic expressions consisting of integer constants and the operators +, –, * and /. The public interface should look like this:

```
class expr {
  // ...
public:
              expr(char *);
              int eval();
              void print();
              };
```

The string argument for the constructor

expr::expr() is the expression. The function expr::eval() returns the value of the expression, and expr::print() a representation of the expression on the cout. A program might look like this:

```
expr x("123/4 + 123*4 - 3");
cout << "x = " << x.eval() << endl;
x.print();
```

Define class expr twice: once using a linked list of nodes as the representation and once using a character string as the representation.

66. Design a linked list base class. Define all its possible methods and data structure. Through inheritance mechanism, create one class namely Binary Search Tree. Implement its data structure and important methods. Observe the following while designing classes:
    (a) Clearly indicate public and private class.
    (b) Use pointers to implement classes.
    (c) Design constructors in each class and explain its purpose.
    (d) Identify data structure and methods which can be inherited.
    (e) Implementation should be in C++.
67. Design an EMPLOYEE base class. Define all its possible methods and data structures. Through inheritance mechanism, create one class namely MANAGER. Implement its data structure and important methods. Assume that you are making this design for the purpose of making a salary statement. Observe the following while designing classes:
    (a) Clearly indicate public and private classes
    (b) Design constructors in each class and explain its purpose
    (c) Identify data structure and methods which can be inherited
    (d) Implementation should be in C++.
68. Design a template class to find a key value in a list of elements.

Glossary

Don't ask what it means, but rather how it is used.
—L. Wittgenstein

A kind of (AKO)
= *is-kind-of*

Abstract class
A class having at least one pure virtual function. Abstract classes cannot have any object instances; references and pointers to abstract class can be used. Abstract classes can be used as a base class for other classes.

Abstract data type (ADT)
A definition of a set of objects having data and operations that can be performed on that data.

Abstract type
A type to supply common behaviour to a broad set of subtypes.

Abstraction
A representation of abstract data types to expose the interface, not the implementation, data is hidden inside the type, operations are exposed.

Access control
The way a programming language may limit access to *class methods*.

Access specifier
C++ keywords—private, protected or public, that defines member access type allowed.

Accessor function
Accessor functions that return meaningful abstractions about the object's state.

Active object
An *object* that monitors events & takes autonomous action (=*demon, agent, trigger*).

Activity diagram
Used to show how workflows in the system are constructed, how they start and decision paths that can be taken from start to finish.

Actor
A human or machine entity that interacts with the system to perform meaningful work.

Ad hoc polymorphism
= operator overloading

Ada
An *object-based* language with Pascal-like syntax developed for US Dept of Defence.

Agent
(1) An *object* that can both operate on other objects and be operated upon (2) *Active object.*

Aggregate object
= *composite object*

Aggregation
The process of building *objects* by combining other *objects* (= *composition, assembly, is-part-of, is-made-up-of, consists-of*). Aggregations are associations that specify a whole-part relationship among an aggregate and component parts. Instances cannot have cyclic aggregation relationships (i.e. a part cannot contain its whole).

Alexander
Christopher Alexander, an architect whose work on building patterns underpins the discipline of software *patterns.*

Ancestor
A *class* higher up the *inheritance* hierarchy than another *class.*

Anthropomorphic design
Design methodology that imputes life to *objects* in order to uncover the relationships between them (often synonymous with *responsibility driven design).*

Application framework
Subsystem of cooperating classes that can be reused for a particular task or application domain.

Applicator
A *method* that applies one of its *arguments* to its other *arguments.*

Argument
= *parameter,* a value that is passed to a *method.*

Assembly
= *Composition*

Association
The relationship between two *objects* in which one *object* uses another. Associations are descriptions of links with a common implementation. Association represents the ability of one object instance to send a message to another object instance.

Attribute
A property of an *object.*

Base class
(1) The most generalized *class* in an *inheritance hierarchy,* (2) a *superclass* in C++.

Behaviour
How an *object* acts/reacts.

Behaviour driven design
= *responsibility driven design*

Behaviour sharing
Where a number of *objects* have the same interface by means of *polymorphism* or *overloading.*

Binding
The mechanism by which variables are attached to their values and *objects* to their *classes/methods.*

Booch design method
An OO design method developed by Grady Booch.

Business model
A simulation of a business and the events it responds to.

C++
An object oriented superset of the language C developed by Bjarne Stroustrup.

Candidate class
Potential *class* identified in the initial stages of an OO analysis (later defined as a class or discarded).

Cardinality
Definition of the number of *instances* involved in relationships between two or more *classes.*

Catalysis
OO design methodology developed by Desmond D'Souza and Alan Wills.

CBD
Component Based Development.

Child
= *subclass*

Class
(1) Group of *objects* with same structure and *behaviour*, (2) template for creating new *objects* of the same type.

Class based
= *class oriented*

Class diagram
Diagram to show *classes* and their relationships (e.g. in the Booch methodology).

Class hierarchy
Inheritance relationships between *classes* in a system.

Class library
A collection of generic *classes* that can be tailored for an application.

Class method
A method used by a *class* (as opposed to an *instance*) e.g. to enable the *class* to create new *instances* of itself = *static method.*

Class operation
= *class method*

Class oriented language
Programming language where *objects* belong to a *class,* but not all *classes* have *superclasses.*

Class specification
Template for a *class* describing its variables, *methods* and *relationships.*

Class structure
= *class hierarchy*

Class variable
A variable common to all *instances* of a *class* used to represent the state of the *class.*

Classic Ada
An OO version of the language *Ada.*

Class-Responsibility-Collaborator
An approach to OO design e.g. method of *Wirfs-Brock* et al.
= CRC

Client
An *object* that uses another *object.*

CLOS
Common Lisp Object System—an object oriented version of the language Lisp.

CLU
Programming language based on *abstraction* and *abstract data types.*

Clustering
Storing of *objects* together (on disk) for efficient accessing.

Coad-Yourdon
OOA and *OOD* methodology.

Collaboration
Request from a *client* to a *server.*

Collaboration graph/diagram
An interaction diagram that emphasize the structural organization of the objects that send and receive messages.

Collaborator
= *helper*

Component
An *object* which can easily be plugged together with a variety of other objects.

Component object
An *object* which is part of a composite *object.*

Composite object
Object made up of other *objects* (e.g. a car is made up of wheels, engine etc.).

Composition
Compositions are aggregations with strong ownership and coincident lifetime constraints among a composite and component parts. The lifetime of the 'part' is controlled by the 'whole'. This control may be direct or transitive. i.e. the 'whole' may take direct responsibility for creating or destroying the 'part' or it may accept an already created part, and later pass it on to some other whole that assumes responsibility for it.

Concrete class
A *class* that has at least one *instance.*

Consists-of
Aggregration relationship between *composite class* and its *component objects.*

Constructor
C++ *code to* initialize *a newly created object.*

Consumer
= *client*

Container class
Class with the function of containing elements (e.g. an array or a bag).

CRC
OO design methodology based on *Class-Responsibility-Collaborator.*

CRC cards
Simple aid to designing using CRC method.

CRH
Class-Responsibility-Helper (=*CRC*).

Data abstraction
In OOP, the process of reducing an object to its essence so that only the necessary elements are represented.

Data hiding
Protecting data from users of a *class.*

Data members
Variables within an *object.*

Data model
The entities, their operations and consistency rules.

Deferred class
= *abstract class*

Deferred method
Abstract class method implemented by *subclasses.*

Delegation
(1) Creation of an *object* to supervise other *objects* in the accomplishment of a *responsibility.*
(2) An *agent* receiving a message and passing on to another object.
(3) (Rarely) *inheritance.*

Demon
= *active object*

Depends-on
objects in one *subsystem* needing to use *objects* in another.

Derivation
= *inheritance*

Derived classes
= *subclass*

Descendent
= *subclass*

Destructor
A function that frees the state of an object and/or destroys an object (so as to free computer memory).

Dynamic binding
Binding at execution time.

Early binding
= *static binding*

Eiffel
OOP language developed by Bertrend Meyer.

Encapsulation
Bundling of *behaviour* and *data* within a *class/object.*

Enrichment
= *inheritance* where new *methods* are added.

Enterprise model
= *Business model*

Event driven
Program based on responding to user actions.

Extension
The collection of *instances.*

Extreme programming
A programming technique sometimes used in **OOP** which emphasises rapid, incremetal development.

Field
= *instance variable*

Formal parameter
An argument of a method assigned by a client when a message is sent.

Framework
Class library for a particular type of application.

Friend
An *object* with privileged access to the all (including private and protected) members of another object (in C++).

Friend function
C++ functions permitted to access *private members* of a class.

Gang of Four
E. Gamma, R. Helm, R. Johnson and J.Vlissides, the authors of "Design Patterns: elements of reusable software", the first book to introduce the use of *design patterns* for software.

Garbage collection
Memory management to remove/reclaim the space used by inactive *objects,* data etc.

Generalization
Making a *class* applicable to more circumstances than before, i.e. creating a *superclass.*

Generic class
= *parameterized class, templates.*

Generic function
(1) *Method* whose *behaviour* depends on the types of the arguments it receives.
(2) *Message passing* mechanism in *CLOS.*

Generic package
Ada package that includes *generic parameters.*

Genericity
Ability to paramaterize *classes.*

Gen-spec-structure
= *inheritance*

GoF
see *Gang of Four.*

GOOD
The General Object Oriented software Development methodology.

Has-a
= *consists-of*

Header file
Module interface used in *C++*.

Heir
= *subclass*

Hierarchy
Usually refers to *inheritance hierarchy* (but may also refer to *aggregation).*

Hierarchy graphs
Diagrams to illustrate the *inheritance hierarchy*.

HOOD
The Hierarchical OO Design Methodology.

Hybrid object oriented languages
'Traditional' procedural programming languages with OO capabilities (like C++).

Identity
That which distinguishes an *object* from all other *objects.*

Immutable
Not changeable e.g. a variable that cannot be assigned to another value after initialization.

Information hiding
When an *object* conceals design decisions concerning itself from another *object.*

Inheritance graph
Inheritance hierarchy for multiple inheritance.

Inheritance hierarchy
(1) A description (often diagramatically) of the *inheritance* connections between all *classes* in a system, (2) a shorthand way of referring to the *inheritance* relationships within a system.

Initialization
Act of giving the data of an *object* value(s) at its creation or soon after.

Instance
see *instantiation*

Instance connection
= *association*

Instance method
The code which implements a *message* sent to an *instance* of a *class.*

Instance variable
(1) A variable which stores a reference to an *object*, (2) a piece of data about, and belonging to, an *object.*

Instantiation
Process whereby an *object (instance)* is created from a *class.*

Interaction diagram
Diagram showing the execution of a *scenario* or *use case.*

Interface
= *protocol*

Is-a/is-kind-of
Inheritance relationship between *instance* and *class*, or a *class* and its *superclass*.

Is-a-Part-of
Aggregation relationship between a *component object* and its *composite object*.

Iterator
A method that allows all parts of a container *object* to be visited.

Java
Object-oriented programming language, named after a brand of coffee, originally created in *Smalltalk* and having a C++ like syntax.

Key abstraction
Part of the vocabulary of the problem domain.

Late binding
= *dynamic binding*

Life-cycle service
Operation to manage creation, deletion, equivalence, copying etc. for *objects*.

Link
= *association*

LOOPS
An OO extension of Lisp.

L-value
An expression that represents a data object that can be both examined and altered.

Main method
The *method* which is the first be executed in a C or C++ program.

Manipulator
A value in an expression that causes side-effects.

Member
The *instance variables* and *methods* of an object (used in C++).

Member function (= Membership function)
Operation defined within an *object's class* body with access to both the *public & private members* of the *class* concerned (used in C++).

Message
A request to an *object* to perform one of its *methods*.

Message passing
The process of requesting an *object* to fulfil one of its *methods*.

Meta class
A *class* with instances that are classes (unlike an *abstract class*, which has no *instances*, but has *subclasses*).

Meta type
A type with instances that are types.

Method
The code for an operation carried out by a class.

Module
A group of related *classes* together (in *C++* or *CLOS;* similar to packages in *Ada*).

Monomorphism
(1) opposite of *polymorphism*—a *message* has only one interpretation in a system, (2) whereby a variable declaration may only denote *objects* of the same *class*.

MOOD
Multiple-View Object Oriented Design Methodology.

MOSES
Methodology for Object-oriented Software Engineering of Systems—developed by Henderson-Sellers & Edwards.

MPD
Model-Pane-Dispatcher is an *application design framework* used in *Smalltalk/V* applications.

Multiple inheritance
when a *class* can *inherit* from two or more *superclasses*.

Mutability
The level of changeability of data within an *object*.

MVC
Model-View-Controller is an *application design framework*.

NextStep
An object-oriented operating system developed by NeXT.

O2
An OO database.

Object
Something (actual or conceptual) that can have things done to it—it has state, *behaviour* and *identity.* Usually an *instance* of a class.

Object based
Having some but not all object-oriented principles—usually *inheritance* and *polymorphism* are missing (e.g. the programming language *Ada*).

Object centred design
= *responsibility driven design*

Object centred view
From the perspective of an individual *object*.

Object community view
Looking at interactions between individual *objects*.

Object diagram
In UML, the static structure of a system at a particular moment in time.

Object identity
= *identity*

Object method
= *instance method*

Object model
(1) the software engineering paradigm of *object orientation,* (2) diagram used in *OMT* to show the *objects* within a system, their relationships, attributes & *methods*.

Object orientation
The software engineering paradigm of *abstraction, encapsulation,* modularity, *inheritance,* concurrency & *persistence*.

Object repository
Library of code for *objects*.

Object structure
= *aggregation* structure of a *composite object*.

Object type
An entity with operations encapsulating data structure. A *class* is an implementation of an *object* type.

Objectory
OO analysis and design methodology (developed by Jacobson).

ObjectStore
An OO database.

Objectworks
OO environment based on C++ or *Smalltalk-80*.

OML
Open Modelling Language – a generic notation for OO analysis and design.

OMT
Object-oriented Modelling Technique for analysis & design (developed by Rumbaugh et al.).

Ontos/db
OO database derived from *VBase*.

OOA
(1) Object-Oriented Analysis, (2) the analysis methodology developed by Coad-Yourdon.

OOD
(1) Object-Oriented Design, (2) the design methodology developed by Coad-Yourdon.

OODBMS
An Object-Oriented DataBase Management System.

OODLE
The Object-Oriented Design LanguagE —a set of diagrams used in OOSA.

OOM
OO Methods.

OOP
Object-Oriented Programming.

OOPL
Object-Oriented Programming Language.

OOPS
British Computer Society Object Oriented Programming and Systems Group.

OOPSLA
Object-Oriented Programming Systems, Languages and Applications, an annual object oriented conference held in the USA.

OOSA
Object-Oriented Systems Analysis—a design methodology developed by Shlaer/Mellor.

OOSD
Object-Oriented Structured Design Methodology—a design methodology developed by Wasserman et al.

OOSE
Object-Oriented Software Engineering.

OOT
Object-Oriented Technology.

OPEN Process
An object-oriented analysis and design methodology developed by Brian Henderson-Sellers, Ian Graham and others.

Operation
An action that an *object* performs on another. In an object oriented context often taken to mean a *method* that an *object* can perform.

Operator overloading
When an operator symbol (or *message*) is permitted to have more than one meaning in a system.
= *ad hoc polymorphism*

OQL
Object Query Language.

Overloaded function name
A function name with more than one meaning, either number, or order or type of parameters vary.

Overloading
= *operator overloading*

Overriding
The ability of a *class* to redefine a *method inherited* from its *superclass*

Package
(1) a program unit in *Ada* consisting of a set of declarations (similar to modules in C++), (2) a group of related *classes* in *Java*, (3) a group of *classes* developed as a unit.

Parameter
= *argument*

Parameterized type/class
Whereby a *class* (typically a *container class*) must be instantiated (its parameters filled in) before *objects* can be created.

Parent
= *superclass*

Part
= *component*

Passive object
An *object* that only changes state when acted on.

Pattern
A template for relationships between *objects*.

Persistence
Ability of an *object* to exist over time.

Persistent object
An *object* which demonstrates *persistence*.

Polymorphism
Whereby a *message* is responded to differently by different *objects*—can be restricted to objects which have a shared *superclass* and are doing "the same method used in a different way"; however, it sometimes includes any form of operator overloading.

Private base class
Whereby all *base class* members are *private* to the *derived classes,* and are not available to users of *objects* of the *derived class* (in C++).

Private member
Data/*method* accessible only by *methods* within its class (not even by subclasses) and friends in C++.

Private method
Method required by an *object* but inaccessible by other *objects*.

Private parts
Parts that cannot be used objects, except subclasses/instances.

Private responsibility
= *private method*

Private service
= *private method*

Protected member
Like *private member,* except that the data/*method* is accessible by subclasses and friends in C++.

Protocol
The *public methods* of an *object*.

Public interface
= *public methods*

Public member
Data/*method* accessible throughout a program(in C++).

Public methods
Methods accessible by other *objects*.

Public services
= *public methods*

RAD
Rapid Application Development.

Relationship
Any connection between two *objects* or *classes* such as *inheritance, association* or *aggregation*.

Request
= *message*

Responsibility
The purpose and place of an *object*—the knowledge it has and actions it can perform.

Responsibility driven design (RDD)
Design method such as that of Wirfs-Brock et al. based on *classes* and their *responsibilities*.

Re-use
Adaptation of existing code for another application.

Role
The *responsibilities* that an *object* can carry out.

Rumbaugh
Person behind OMT design methodology.

Scenario
Sequential descriptions of the steps taken to carry out the use case.

Sequence diagram
Typically show a user or actor, and the objects and components they interact with in the execution of a use case. One sequence diagram typically represents a single Use Case 'scenario' or flow of events.

Shlaer-Mellor
OOSA

Signature
The list of arguments of a *method* or *function*.

Simple inheritance
= *single inheritance*

Simula
Class-based programming language.

Single inheritance
By which a *subclass inherits* directly from one and only one *superclass* (but may *inherit* from *superclasses* of that *superclass*).

Smalltalk
The first pure object oriented language and its environment—the most significant development in the history of computer science: discuss.

Smalltalk/V
A commercial version of *Smalltalk* for PC's.

Smalltalk-80
First commercial development of *Smalltalk*.

SOMA
Semantic Object Modelling Approach-an object oriented analyisis and design methodology developed by Graham.

Specialization
Through inheritance, extra properties including data members as well as methods are added in addition to inherited properties.

State
One of the conditions in which an *object* can exist.

State space
All possible states of an *object*.

State diagram
Depict the status conditions and responses of participants involved in behaviour.

Static binding
Binding at compilation time.

Static method
= *class method*

Strong typing
When all expressions must be type consistent.

Subclass
A *class* that *inherits* from one (or more) other *classes*.

Subsystem
A cohesive collection of *classes*.

Superclass
A *class* from which others *inherit*.

Syntropy
Object oriented design methodology developed by Cook & Daniels.

Taligent
An IBM/Apple collaboration to produce an object oriented architecture and operating system.

Thread
Operating system supported mechanism by which memory address space can be shared, light weight process, threads run in same address space.

Transient object
An *object* whose existence is limited to the life time of the process that created it.

Trellis/Owl
A combined object oriented programming and data manipulation language.

Trigger
= *active object*

Type/typing
Definition of values/operations that can be performed on an *object*.

UML
Unified Modelling Language—a notation for object oriented analysis and design adopted by the *OMG* as an industrial standard.

Unified Software Development Process
Object oriented analysis and design process developed by Grady Booch, Ivar Jacobson and James Rumbaugh for Rational.

Use case
A Use Case represents a discrete unit of interaction between a user (human or machine) and the system. A Use Case is a single unit of meaningful work.

Vbase
Early object oriented database.

Versant
An object oriented database system.

Virtual function
A virtual function is a member function in a class such that it is expected to be redefined in the derived classes.

Visibility
Ability of an *object* to see (and thus use) another.

Weak typing
Whereby expressions need not be type consistent.

Whole part structure
= *aggregation*

Wirfs-Brock
A CRC-based, *responsibility-driven* object oriented design methodology.

XP
= *Extreme Programming*

Bibliography

Ambler, Scott, W., "Completing the Unified Process with Process Patterns", *Ambysoft white paper,* AmbySoft Inc., 2000.

Booch, Grady, James Rumbaugh, and Ivar Jacobson, *The Unified Modeling Language User Guide,* The Addison-Wesley Publishing Company, 1998.

Eckel, Bruce, *Thinking in C++: Introduction to Standard C++,* Prentice Hall Inc., 2000.

Ellis, Margaret, A. and Bjarne Stroustrup, *The Annotated C++ Reference Manual,* The Addison-Wesley Publishing Company, 1990.

Fowler, Martin and Kendall Scott, *UML Distilled: A Brief Guide to the Standard Object Modeling Language,* The Addison-Wesley Publishing Company, 1999.

Horowitz, E. and S. Sahani, *Fundamentals of Data Structures,* Galgotia Publications, 1999.

Jacobson, Ivar, Grady Booch, and James Rumbaugh, *Unified Software Development Process,* The Addison-Wesley Publishing Company, 1999.

Jacobson, Ivar, Magnus Christerson, Patrik Jonsson, and Gunnar Övergaard, *Object-Oriented Software Engineering—A Use Case Driven Approach,* The Addison-Wesley Publishing Company, 1992.

Kernighan, Brian, W. and Dennis Ritchie, *C Programming Language,* Prentice Hall Inc., 1988.

Kruchten, Philippe, "From Waterfall to Iterative Lifecycle—A tough transition for project managers", *Rational Software White Paper TP-173 5/00,* Rational Software Corporation, USA, 2000.

——— "The 4+1 View Model of Architecture", *IEEE Software,* 12(6), November 1995, pp. 42-50, IEEE, USA.

Meyer, Bertrend, *Object-Oriented Software Construction,* Prentice Hall International (UK), 1988.

Mullar Pierre-Alain, *Instant UML,* Wrox Press Inc., 1997.

Pressman, R.S., *Software Engineering—A practitioner's approach,* McGraw-Hill Int. Ed., McGraw-Hill, 2001.

Rational Software Corporation, USA "Rational Unified Process: Best Practices for Software Development Teams", *Rational Software White Paper TP026B,* Rev 11/01, 1998.

Richter, Charles, F., *Designing Flexible Object-Oriented Systems with UML,* Macmillan Technical Publishing, 1999.

Rumbaugh, James, Ivar Jacobson, and Grady Booch, *The Unified Modeling Language Reference Manual,* The Addison-Wesley Publishing Company, 1998.

Rumbaugh, James, Michael Blaha, William Premerlani, Frederick Eddy, and William Lorensen, *Object-Oriented Modeling and Design,* Prentice Hall of India Private Limited, 1997.

Stroustrup, Bjarne, *The C++ Programming Language,* The Addison-Wesley Publishing Company, 2000.

Index